ИЗДАТЕЛИ

CELIBACY IN THE EARLY CHURCH

STEFAN HEID

Celibacy in the
Early Church

*The Beginnings of a
Discipline of Obligatory Continence
for Clerics in East and West*

Translated by Michael J. Miller

IGNATIUS PRESS   SAN FRANCISCO

Original German edition:
Zölibat in der frühen Kirche:
Die Anfänge einer Enthaltsamkeitspflicht
für Kleriker in Ost und West
© 1997 Ferdinand Schöningh GmbH, Paderborn

Cover art: *Romanized Christ as the Good Shepherd*
Third century fresco
Catacomb of Priscilla, Rome, Italy
Erich Lessing/Art Resource, New York

Cover design by Roxanne Mei Lum

© 2000 Ignatius Press, San Francisco
ISBN 0-89870-800-1
Library of Congress control number 00-100232
Printed in the United States of America ∞

Contents

Preface

Celibacy polarizes, whatever position one may take on the matter. Discussions about it as a rule involve arguing with history. The subject of the present work is not celibacy today. The question posed is rather: What was the attitude of ordained men in the early Church toward sexuality? Was the life-style of the clerics of the early Christian era a matter of taste? Or was there already something like obligatory celibacy? During her first centuries, as the Church was being consolidated as an institution, she also laid down the line that would be followed until today in clerical questions. Therein lie the explosives. And one can already make the statement: Without the early Church there would be no celibacy today. The Church of the first centuries contributed more to celibacy than is often thought. But when exactly was the switch thrown and the track determined? And whose efforts were decisive here? What arguments and motives played a role in the development?

Much research has already been done on this topic, and one might imagine that there is nothing more to be gained. The author thought so, too, when he became involved with preparing a lecture on the foundations of celibacy in the early Church. The investigation brought to light some surprising findings, which brought home the fact that the whole subject needed rethinking. Many discussions and various suggestions have expedited this process. Thus the present book is amicably dedicated first of all to my confreres in the priestly and diaconal ministry. I wish to express my thanks to Ferdinand Schöningh Verlag for their outstanding supervision of this publishing project, to the Media Services Department of the German Bishops Conference for subsidizing the printing costs, and to Frau Silvia Cichon, a theology student in Cologne, for preparing the bibliography and proofreading the manuscript.

Neuss, October 1996
Stefan Heid

I. The Labyrinthine Paths of the Inquiry

There is no disputing the fact that already during the first centuries of the Church there were clergymen, including married men as well as unmarried, who after receiving holy orders renounced all sexual intercourse. To what extent was this a question of a purely personal decision made by individuals? Is it possible that for clerics there was something like an obligation to live in continence? Furthermore, how should we evaluate the fact that married clerics, too, observed continence? Can historical roots of the present discipline of celibacy be found in the early Church?

1. Celibacy Is an Inadequate Notion

At least in one respect the balance sheet is unambiguous: the early Church knew of no obligation for deacons, priests, and bishops to be in the unmarried state. So in this sense there was in the early Church no celibacy (from the Latin *caelebs* = unmarried). Some deduce from this that obligatory celibacy was a late invention of the papal Church. The prohibition against marriage is often connected with the Second Lateran Council in the year 1139. In the Church at her beginnings, in any case, no cleric was required to be unmarried, and this remained so well into the Middle Ages. That, indeed, is unassailable. During the first centuries the celibate clergyman was not exactly the exception, but neither was he the rule.

Since the nineteenth century this indisputable fact has sparked a number of popular and academic controversies. For many people it is a sign that action is needed, in many places giving rise to the wish that obligatory celibacy in the Roman Catholic Church would be abolished. Their program is expressed in the urgent title of a book from the pen of a concerned party: *Priests Are Allowed to Marry.*[1] Of course, historical

---

[1] H.-J. Vogels, *Priester dürfen heiraten: Biblische geschichtliche und rechtliche Gründegegen den Pflichtzölibat* (Bonn, 1992).

research into the discipline of celibacy is by no means complete. In recent years, certainly, voices have been raised that call into question the accuracy of what has developed as a consensus about the clerical discipline of the early Church. The picture we have of the cleric's way of life has changed to such a degree that one must now approach celibacy differently.

The broad outline of the last fifty years of celibacy scholarship shows that something has occurred that not infrequently causes misunderstandings in historical research: a one-sided formulation of the question has produced one-sided answers. Scholars took the present discipline of celibacy in the Roman Catholic Church as their point of departure and searched for a pattern of clerics in the unmarried state in the first centuries. This, however, they did not find—at any rate, not for all clerics. The question that they should have asked is whether the early Church perhaps knew a different discipline of continence. This was the approach of the older German scholarship in the nineteenth century. But that was thought to have been refuted scientifically, and so these contributions were consigned to oblivion.[2]

Actually, if this deficit has not become evident already, it ought to when one looks at the Church's legislation. That is to say, according to canon law an exclusively unmarried clergy, as we know it today, existed at all only after the Council of Trent (1521–1545). Even the above-mentioned Second Lateran Council, which is repeatedly cited as the beginning of the history of celibacy, did not intend to exclude married men from holy orders; it merely declared marriages contracted after the reception of orders to be invalid (canon 7). Nevertheless ecclesiastical legislation from as early as the fourth century was intensely concerned with rulings that restricted the sexual freedom of clergymen. Is all of that only a tantalizing prelude to celibacy, which then finally represents a complete break with the original tradition of the early Church? Did the bark of Peter tack for one-and-a-half millennia, zig-zagging its way through laws that were somehow haphazard? Or was perhaps something established at the beginning that was more comprehensive than what we understand today as celibacy? In fact more recent scholarship points in this direction.

The exclusive discipline of celibacy, understood in the strict sense

---

[2] Cf. C. Cochini, *The Apostolic Origins of Priestly Celibacy*, trans. Nelly Marans (San Francisco, 1990), 32–38.

of the word as an unmarried clergy, applies to the time after Trent. In the time before the Council of Trent the unmarried state played instead a secondary role. It was clear somehow that there were always unmarried clerics, too. There was no need to dwell on that any further. More interesting was the life-style of the married clerics. They were required, it appears, in principle to renounce all sexual activity after their ordination. So not only the unmarried clergymen were affected by such a discipline of clerical continence; the married clerics and their wives were, too. Only someone who is not married can live in the unmarried state. Anyone, though, can live in sexual continence, even a married man. This is the decisive approach to early Christian clerical discipline.

The present study attempts to demonstrate that there was in fact in the early Church an obligation of all higher clerics to practice complete sexual continence. If this proves to be correct, then one would have to view the present celibacy requirement as being in a historical continuity with the original discipline of clerical continence: without the general requirement of continence in the early Church, there would be today no obligation that Latin-rite priests be unmarried. Western celibacy would be, accordingly, the vestigial form of an originally more comprehensive practice of continence. In order to give a terminological expression to this, one could accordingly distinguish between a celibacy *of continence* in the early Church (of married, widowed, and virginal higher clerics) and a later *unmarried* celibacy (of widowed and virginal higher clerics).[3]

2. In the Beginning There Was a Legend

The thesis that a celibacy of continence existed in the early Church meets with opposition even today. The blame for this belongs, in no small measure, to a legend that many take to be true, although its legendary character has since been proven. Therefore, at the very outset of our discussion, we ought to say a final farewell to it. We are referring to the famous, touching story of the Egyptian monk-bishop Paphnutius. Ceremoniously he addressed his colleagues in the episcopacy gathered

---

[3] Cochini, ibid., speaks on p. 63 of a "celibate-continence law".

at the Council of Nicaea in the year 325 with a distinct message on
the subject of a discipline of obligatory clerical continence:

> Now, in those days, Paphnutius was bishop of Upper Thebes, and he was
> such a friend of God that he was able to perform miracles. During the
> times of persecution, he had one of his eyes plucked out. The emperor
> had such a great devotion to this man that he often had him brought to
> the palace; so great was the reverence Constantine felt for this man, that
> the emperor would kiss Paphnutius' empty eye-socket.
>
> I will now relate what was decided thanks to his advice for the ad-
> vantage of the Church and the honor of the clergy. It had seemed good
> to the bishops [of the Council of Nicaea] to introduce a new law in
> the Church: consecrated men—I mean bishops, priests, and deacons—
> should not sleep any more with the wives they had married while they
> were laymen. As the matter was under discussion, Paphnutius stood up in
> the middle of the episcopal assembly and, with a strong voice, protested
> that such a heavy yoke should not be imposed on consecrated men. The
> conjugal bed is honorable, and marriage has no stain, he said. One should
> fear lest, through an excess of severity, the bishops might bring harm to
> the Church. Not all are strong enough to live asceticism in total dispas-
> sion, and the chastity of the spouses would not be safeguarded with so
> many opportunities. It was by the name of chastity that Paphnutius did
> not hesitate to call a life in common with a legitimate wife. It is quite
> enough [he said] to require of these clerics that they not remarry [after
> ordination], in accordance with the ancient tradition of the Church; but
> let us not separate them from the wives whom, monogamous as they are,
> they once married when they were laymen.
>
> Thus spoke Paphnutius, though he himself had nothing to do with
> marriage and, in fact, no experience with women. From childhood on,
> he had been raised in a monastery, and he was praised as a man of very
> great chastity if there ever was one. The college unanimously rallied to
> his proposal. They therefore remained silent on the issue and left it to the
> judgment of those who were ready to abstain from conjugal intercourse
> with their wives.[4]

---

[4] Socrates, *Historia ecclesiastica*, 1, 11; PG 67, 101b–4b. [Translation as found in Cochini,
Origins, 195–96.] Παφνούτιος γὰρ μιᾶς τῶν πόλεων τῆς ἄνω Θηβαΐδος ἐπίσκοπος ἦν· οὕτως
δὲ ἦν ἀνὴρ θεοφιλής, ὡς καὶ σημεῖα θαυμαστὰ γίνεσθαι ὑπ' αὐτοῦ. Οὗτος ἐν καιρῷ τοῦ δι-
ωγμοῦ τὸν ὀφθαλμὸν ἐξεκόπη· σφόδρα δὲ ὁ βασιλεὺς ἐτίμα τὸν ἄνδρα καὶ συνεχῶς ἐπὶ τὰ
βασίλεια μετεπέμπετο καὶ τὸν ἐξορωρυγμένον ὀφθαλμὸν κατεφίλει. Τοσαύτη προσῆν τῷ βασιλεῖ
Κωνσταντίνῳ εὐλάβεια. Ἕν μὲν οὖν τοῦτο περὶ Παφνουτίου εἰρήσθω· ὃ δὲ πρὸς λυσιτέλειαν
τῆς ἐκκλησίας καὶ κόσμον τῶν ἱερωμένων διὰ τῆς αὐτοῦ συμβουλῆς τότε γέγονεν, διηγήσομαι.
Ἐδόκει τοῖς ἐπισκόποις νόμον νεαρὸν εἰς τὴν ἐκκλησίαν εἰσφέρειν, ὥστε τοὺς ἱερωμένους, λέγω
δὲ ἐπισκόπους καὶ πρεσβυτέρους καὶ διακόνους καὶ ὑποδιακόνους, μὴ συγκαθεύδειν ταῖς γα-

A situation full of pathos and charm. Paphnutius certainly has all sympathies on his side. The virtuous monk from Egypt steps into the circle of a hundred self-assured bishops from all over the world. These bishops, proponents of a strict clerical discipline who then, however, show discernment, want to impose perfect continence upon married clerics from the day of their ordination. Who can endure that? And so this suggestion is warded off as a result of a brave man's word. Paphnutius has done great service to the cause of opposing obligatory continence. Several arguments convinced his brethren:

1. perfect continence within marriage would be too rigorous a demand;
2. the conjugal bed is honorable and marriage is unstained (cf. Heb 13:4);
3. conduct within a marriage should prevent lechery (cf. 1 Cor 7:2);
4. perfect marital continence would be an innovation—the older tradition witnesses only to the prohibition of [subsequent] marriage.

The arguments are intriguing. At first sight the text seems reliable; after all it is handed down by a Church historian by the name of Socrates (d. after 439). If he is to be trusted, then obligatory clerical continence is unthinkable at least until the middle of the fourth century; neither the unmarried state nor sexual abstinence within marriage was required. In that city in Asia Minor called Nicaea, a considerable part of the Eastern hierarchy was represented at the time. Consequently, according to the will of these bishops, it was from then on the rule everywhere: whoever, being a deacon, a presbyter, or a bishop, lived as a celibate or continently with his wife did so on his own and had to cope with it as well as he could.

μεταῖς, ἃς ἔτι λαϊκοὶ ὄντες ἠγάγοντο. Καὶ ἐπεὶ περὶ τούτου βουλεύεσθαι προὔκειτο, διαναστὰς ἐν μέσῳ τοῦ συλλόγου τῶν ἐπισκόπων ὁ Παφνούτιος ἐβόα μακρά, μὴ βαρὺν ζυγὸν ἐπιτιθέναι τοῖς ἱερωμένοις ἀνδράσιν, τίμιον εἶναι (τὸν γάμον αὐτῶν) καὶ τὴν κοίτην ἀμίαντον λέγων, μὴ τῇ ὑπερβολῇ τῆς ἀκριβείας μᾶλλον τὴν ἐκκλησίαν προσβλάψωσιν· οὐ γὰρ πάντας δύνασθαι φέρειν τῆς ἀπαθείας τὴν ἄσκησιν οὐδὲ ἴσως φυλαχθήσεσθαι τὴν σωφροσύνην τῆς ἑκάστου γαμετῆς (σωφροσύνην δὲ ἐκάλει [καὶ] τῆς νομίμου γυναικὸς τὴν συνέλευσιν), ἀρκεῖσθαί τε τὸν φθάσαντα κλήρου τυχεῖν μηκέτι ἐπὶ γάμον ἔρχεσθαι κατὰ τὴν τῆς ἐκκλησίας ἀρχαίαν παράδοσιν, μὴ μὴν ἀποζεύγνυσθαι ταύτης, ἣν ἅπαξ ἤδη πρότερον λαϊκὸς ὢν ἠγάγετο. Καὶ ταῦτ' ἔλεγεν ἄπειρος ὢν γάμου καὶ ἁπλῶς εἰπεῖν γυναικός· ἐκ παιδὸς γὰρ ἐν ἀσκητηρίῳ ἐτέθραπτο καὶ ἐπὶ σωφροσύνῃ εἰ καί τις ἄλλος περιβόητος ἦν. Πείθεται σύμπας ὁ τῶν ἱερωμένων σύλλογος τοῖς Παφνουτίου λόγοις. Διὸ καὶ τὴν περὶ τούτου ζήτησιν ἀπεσίγησαν, τῇ γνώμῃ τῶν βουλομένων ἀπέχεσθαι τῆς ὁμιλίας τῶν γαμετῶν καταλείψαντες.

In the wake of Socrates, researchers thought that modern celibacy scholarship no longer had to deal with the time before Constantine. Celibacy, including obligatory continence for married clerics, could have been accepted at all only after the Council of Nicaea, and then only in the West, while the more humane East shut itself off from this development permanently. Only a half century after Nicaea, toward the end of the fourth century, the words of Paphnutius would be forgotten by Popes Damasus and Siricius. Since that time, at least in the Latin-Roman Church, married higher clerics and their wives have been expected to live in perfect continence.

We must realize to what extent the Paphnutius legend has influenced modern historical research. After all, Nicaea was not just any event, but the first ecumenical council, endowed with the highest authority. Of course, Friedhelm Winkelmann, a Byzantine specialist in East Berlin, definitively unmasked the story about Paphnutius in 1968 as a fifth-century legend glorifying Paphnutius.[5] Probably there was a man by that name, but whether he was a bishop is extremely doubtful, and he did not participate in the Council of Nicaea. The entire text, therefore, is of no use for the study of the clerical discipline of the first four centuries. To be sure, this finding is still far from being general knowledge.[6]

---

[5] Paphnutius. Accepted by G. Denzler, *Das Papsttum und der Amtszölibat*, vol. 1: *Die Zeit bis zur Reformation*, PuP 5, 1 (Stuttgart, 1973), 9ff.; idem, *Die Geschichte des Zölibats* (Freiburg, 1993), 30f., 122; E. Schillebeeckx, *Christliche Identität und kirchliches Amt: Plädoyer für den Menschen in der Kirche* (Düsseldorf, 1985), 289; R. Gryson, "Dix ans de recherches sur les origines du célibat ecclésiastique: Réflexion sur les publications des années 1970–1979", RTL 11 (1980): 164f. (Not yet the argument of idem, *Les Origines du célibat ecclésiastique du premier au septième siècle*, RSSR.H 2 [Gembloux, 1970], 87–93); C.-G. Pitsakis, "Clergé marié et célibat dans la législation du Concile in Trullo: Le Point de vue oriental", in G. Nedungatt and M. Featherstone, eds., *The Council in Trullo Revisited*, Kanonika 6 (Rome, 1995), 263–306, at 272f., 293; H. J. Sieben, *Vom Apostelkonzil zum Ersten Vatikanum: Studien zur Geschichte der Konzilsidee* (Paderborn, 1996), 18f.; A. M. Stickler, *The Case for Clerical Celibacy: Its Historical Development and Theological Foundations*, trans. Brian Ferme (San Francisco, 1995), 17, 62–64; R. Cholij, *Clerical Celibacy in East and West*, 2d ed. (Herefordshire, 1990), 85–92; Cochini, *Origins*, 195–200. Cf. H. C. Brennecke, "Nicäa", in TRE 24 (1994), 429–41 at 432; J. Gribomont, "Pafnuzio", in DP 2 (1983), 2567.

[6] It is particularly annoying when newer lexicons and reference works uncritically maintain a scholarly position that has long been outdated, e.g., J. Eber, "Zölibat", in *Evangelisches Lexikon für Theologie und Gemeinde*, vol. 3 (1994), 2217f.; J. Rist, "Paphnutios", in LMA 6 (1993), 1663; J. S. Hohmann, *Der Zölibat: Geschichte und Gegenwart eines umstrittenen Gesetzes* (Frankfurt, 1993), 21f.; R. Lorenz, *Die Kirche in ihrer Geschichte*, 1, C, 2: *Das vierte Jahrhundert (der Osten)* (Göttingen, 1992), C 216; A. Kazhdan and A. Papadakis, "Celibacy", in *The*

3. New Insights Blaze a Trail

Once Winkelmann proved the legendary character of the Paphnutius story, one of the most important pieces of evidence for the late introduction of obligatory continence became untenable. Now the entire subject had to be reconsidered based on new assumptions. Mention should be made in the first place of the studies by the Jesuit Christian Cochini (1981)[7] and the Ukrainian Catholic priest Roman Cholij (1989).[8] They represent the interpretation that there has always been an obligation for higher clerics to abstain from sexual relations. This, of course, was the duty not only of unmarried clergymen but also of those who were married. The latter, accordingly, from the day of their ordination on, had to live their married lives in continence and renounce all sexual relations with their wives. We do hear of this even in the Paphnutius legend, although it objects to such a discipline.

The French- and English-language contributions of Cochini and Cholij met with wide approval in the academic world internationally, which was reflected in two dozen or more reviews. In Germany, however, they were scarcely noticed; indeed, Cholij's work appeared for the first time in 1987 in the *Annuarium Historiae Conciliorum,* a journal printed in Paderborn, before it was published as a monograph, but only Cochini's work was reviewed.[9] The two books in question had practically no effect on the existing consensus. The history of celibacy continues to be written about here [in Germany] exclusively as the

---

Oxford Dictionary of Byzantium, vol. 1 (1991), 395f.; K. Baus and E. Ewig, *Die Reichskirche nach Konstantin dem Großen: Von Nikaia bis Chalkedon,* HKG 2, 1 (Freiburg, 1973), 288. In numerous articles, also, erroneous statements are repeated, e.g., in S. N. Troianos, "Zölibat und Kirchenvermögen in der früh- und mittelbyzantinischen kanonischen Gesetzgebung", in D. Simon, ed., *Eherecht und Familiengut in Antike und Mittelalter* (Muniuch, 1992), 135; R. Hotz, "Soll jeder Priester Mönch sein? Zur ostkirchlichen Tradition des verheirateten Priesters und des Zölibats", *Diakonia* 16 (1985): 404–11 at 407.

[7] *Origines apostoliques du célibat sacerdotal* (Paris, 1981). Quotations are from the English translation cited above.

[8] *Clerical Celibacy in East and West,* cited above.

[9] R. Cholij, "Married Clergy and Ecclesiastical Continence in Light of the Council in Trullo (691)", AHC 19 (1987): 71–230, 241–99. None of the five or so reviews of Cholij and only one of the around twenty reviews of Cochini appeared in a German periodical: GuL 55 (1982): 237 (by J. Sudbrack). Denzler, *Die Geschichte,* names Cochini, Cholij, and Stickler in the bibliography without taking note of their subject matter. "Silent mention" of Cochini is also found in Schillebeeckx, *Identität.* Vogels, *Priester,* 45, rejects Cholij flat out.

history of unmarried clergy. To my knowledge, only two other voices in the German-speaking world can be heard that have confronted Cochini's thesis: Heinz Kruse (1985), a Jesuit living in Tokyo, and the Austrian curia official Alfons M. Cardinal Stickler (1993).[10]

Fear of touching the subject is not very helpful. An aversion to an early obligatory continence often results from a spurious blend of historical research and dogmatic appraisal. It is necessary to make distinctions here, above all with regard to the concept of apostolicity. Cochini programmatically entitles his book: *Origines apostoliques du célibat sacerdotal* (*The Apostolic Origins of Priestly Celibacy*). Here the thesis is presented that celibacy, in the sense of a discipline of obligatory continence, goes back to the time of the apostles and their successors. For a long while extreme caution prevailed in theological scholarship concerning the time of the apostles; it was believed to be lost far away in the obscurity of history or of ecclesiastical mythology.[11] With respect to celibacy, Cochini is confident that he can assert the apostolic origin of a clerical continence practiced throughout the Church during that period. Apostolicity here means primarily a chronological reference to New Testament times, not a dogmatic determination that this discipline was unchangeable. One can discuss candidly such a historic apostolicity of continence celibacy without necessarily arousing an immediate suspicion that one has prejudged the dogmatic question.

4. As Yet No Definitive Line

In the discussion about clerical discipline in the early Church, there are at present two opposing interpretations, which are based largely upon the same source texts but arrive at completely different conclusions. The history of ecclesiastical celibacy is conventionally depicted as a development from clerical freedom to obligatory celibacy. A prominent proponent of this view is Roger Gryson. His opinion is as follows:[12]

---

[10] H. Kruse, "Eheverzicht im Neuen Testament und in der Frühkirche", FKTh 1 (1985): 113 (published in Augsburg); Stickler, *Celibacy* originally published in Abensberg.

[11] A certain turning point is marked by the studies of H.-J. Schulz, *Die apostolische Herkunft der Evangelien*, 2d ed. (Freiburg, 1995); J. A.T. Robinson, *Redating the New Testament* (London: SCM Press, 1976).

[12] Gryson, *Origines*, following the argument of J. P. Audet, *Mariage et célibat dans le service pastorale de l'Église: Histoire et orientations* (Paris, 1967). Similarly A. Franzen, *Zölibat und*

In the first three centuries most clerics were married and freely exercised their sexual prerogatives in marriage. Possibly here and there some practiced voluntary continence. As time went on, a movement inimical to marriage and the body, and fed by murky, pagan streams, entered into the life of the Church wherein, from the second century, charismatic virginity and later monasticism were highly rated and increasingly set the tone. Starting in the third century, this development was accompanied by an increasing sacralization of ecclesiastical office, so that foreign notions of cultic or ritual purity made their way into the Christian understanding of worship. Finally in the fourth century, with the Spanish Synod of Elvira (around 306 or even as late as 380), this asceticism and sacralization began a partnership with clerical discipline. And so it came about that in the Latin and the Greek Church both clerics and laypeople abstained from marital intercourse on days when the Eucharistic Liturgy was celebrated. Whereas the East (Asia Minor, Syria, Palestine, and Egypt) retained the practice of infrequent Divine Liturgies, and hence the married clerics could engage in marital intercourse with certain restrictions, the West (North Africa, Spain, Gaul, and Italy) introduced the daily celebration of the Eucharist toward the end of the fourth century. This led logically then to complete continence for the clergy. Thereby the way was simultaneously left open for the gradual displacement of the married clerics by unmarried colleagues.[13]

Behind this *opinio communis* concerning a gradual intrusion of obligatory continence into the discipline for clerics, there is some sort of idea that in the beginning the clergy "naturally" made use of their marriage rights without specific regulations; the "unnatural" continence became widespread only gradually through the influence of ideas that were hostile to the body. It is considered improbable that an entire professional class would live more or less continently. At the same time this thesis is not infrequently associated with a particular image of the Church. If an ecclesiastical discipline of continence begins with an assembly of

---

Priesterehe in der Auseinandersetzung der Reformationszeit und der katholischen Reform des 16. Jahr., KLK, 29, 2d ed. (Münster, 1970) 9–12; Denzler, *Papsttum*, 5–7. Cited by Cochini, *Origins*, 38–40.

[13] Thus, for example, B. Kötting, *Der Zölibat in der Alten Kirche*, Schriften der Gesellschaft zur Förderung der Westfälischen Wilhelms = Universität zu Münster, 61 (Münster, 1970), 26, and, with some modification, R. Kottje, "Das Aufkommen der täglichen Eucharistie feier in der Westkirche und die Zölibatsforderung", ZKG 82 (1971): 228.

bishops, the one in Elvira, then this necessarily creates the impression that it was only gradually imposed from above against the vehement resistance from below. Into this picture, then, are fit the writings of the popes on celibacy, which will have to be discussed thoroughly farther on. So according to this view, Roman severity, under the influence of anticorporeal trends, suppressed the "original" humane practice, as it is still maintained in the Eastern Church.[14] Thus the law that enjoined perfect marital continence upon the higher clerics of the Latin Church first saw the light of day toward the end of the fourth century in Rome.[15]

This prevailing doctrine is called into question by the studies of Cochini and Cholij. Both scholars in essence dispute an evolution of celibacy, as though a discipline of continence had been only a late development, which was then made increasingly more rigorous.[16] On the contrary, they affirm that the discipline of a complete and lasting continence for all higher clerics was widely observed from the very beginning under the influence of the genuinely Christian idea of total dedication to God and to his service. That continence discipline was, therefore, quite comprehensive. It was a secondary question, then, whether the cleric was married or not at the time of his ordination. In the first case he was no longer allowed to engage in marital intercourse with his wife and, hence, could not have any more children. The virginal or widowed higher cleric was not allowed to contract marriage.[17]

A historian handles facts like a natural scientist: he has no interest in theories that can explain only half the story when better ones are available. The present work intends, therefore, to test the soundness of the newer thesis. Indispensable to this is Cochini's book as well as the one by Gryson. The two works can be compared to each other point by point. A new rereading of all the relevant source texts leads

---

[14] Cf. Cochini, *Origins*, 40–42.

[15] Gryson, *Origines*, 127, 197; Schillebeeckx, *Identität*, 290; Denzler, *Die Geschichte*, 27; P. Brown, *Die Keuschheit der Engel: Sexuelle Entsagung, Askese und Körperlichkeit am Anfang des Christentums* (Munich and Vienna, 1991); English: *The Body and Society: Men, Women and Sexual Renunciation in Early Christianity* (New York, Columbia University Press, 1988). (Pages are cited from the German edition, unless otherwise noted.) 365f.

[16] Cochini, *Origins*, 249.

[17] Affected by a continence discipline in the early Church were only the so-called higher clerics, i.e., deacons, priests, and bishops (those in major orders). Our discussions concern them only, even though occasional mention must be made of the lower clerics (the minor orders include the subdiaconate and other lesser degrees).

in fact to a corroboration and a deepening of Cochini's interpretation in many respects. Another discussion of all the texts might seem to be an unnecessary repetition. Nevertheless it cannot be avoided, and it is often justified as well by the new findings that result.[18]

In and of itself it would be methodologically advisable to go from the situation in the fourth or fifth century, about which there is for the most part historical certainty, back to apostolic, New Testament times.[19] The reader would find it more difficult, of course, to get an impression of the course of history. Moreover the thesis of a continence celibacy in the early Church has already been sufficiently established by the investigations cited. Therefore we need not begin at square one. Hence we can justify our procedure of tracing the historical development step by step, beginning with the New Testament and ending with the Second Council of Trullo in the year 691, the so-called Quinisextum.

---

[18] The advance in scholarship made by the present work vis-à-vis Cochini does not lie in its overall conclusions, which confirm the thesis of an apostolic continence celibacy. In many instances, though, the individual interpretations of particular source texts are elaborated or corrected. Furthermore, the historical social background of clerical continence in the early Church is discussed in greater detail. Cochini's excellent study remains indispensable inasmuch as it treats exhaustively the texts as far as the seventh century, including the Nestorian Church and other special cases.

[19] Cf. Cochini, *Origins*, 16f.

II. The Continence of the
Ministers in New Testament Times

What was it like at the very beginning, at the time of Jesus himself? What role did celibacy and continence play? The first hour of Christendom brings up many problems. It is the nature of things that much here will have to remain hypothetical. The statements on this subject are too scarce and in some cases also too late for us to be able to make heady assertions. Hence the following remarks are necessarily relative and should be taken as such.

1. Jesus and Those Who Accompanied Him on His Journeys

Jesus' life-style was the expression of his mission. He certainly perceived it as being normative as well.[1] He left his family circle and relatives behind in order to live as a wanderer, consciously renouncing a permanent residence. He lived as an unmarried man, and that was conspicuous, symbolic behavior—by no means a mere biographical detail. It is worth noting that his unmarried state is assumed everywhere in the traditions about Jesus, but nowhere is it explicitly mentioned.[2] This demonstrates how certain life decisions when put into practice are so self-evident that they are no longer discussed as problematic. That seems to be the case also for the life-style of the apostles—which means here the inner circle of disciples, to which we must now turn our attention.

Eunuchs for the kingdom of heaven. Shocking, puzzling, and yet of breathtaking power, the famous saying of Jesus about eunuchs stands at the beginning of any further reflection on the prehistory of clerical continence. As the Gospel of Matthew (A.D. 90) hands it down to us:

---

[1] Cf. H. D. Betz, *Nachfolge und Nachahmung Jesu Christi im Neuen Testament*, BHTh 37 (Tübingen, 1967). Betz, though, does not address the issue of sexual continence.

[2] K. Niederwimmer, *Askese und Mysterium: Über Ehe, Ehescheidung und Eheverzicht in den Anfängen des christl. Glaubens*, FRLANT 113 (Göttingen, 1975), 40.

[Jesus said,] "And I say to you: whoever divorces his wife, except for unchastity, and marries another, commits adultery; and he who marries a divorced woman, commits adultery."

The disciples said to him, "If such is the case of a man with his wife, it is not expedient to marry." But he said to them, "Not all men can receive this precept, but only those to whom it is given. For there are eunuchs who have been so from birth, and there are eunuchs who have been made eunuchs by men, and there are eunuchs who have made themselves eunuchs for the sake of the kingdom of heaven. He who is able to receive this, let him receive it." (Mt 19:9-12)

Many exegetes refuse to admit Jesus' saying about eunuchs, attributing it to those circles of Palestinian Jewish Christians that were Encratite and so disdained the body.[3] According to that theory, it would be the product of a later Christian sect. That would have the advantage of exonerating Jesus of the charge that he was opposed to marriage. But it is too easy a solution. More convincing is the suggestion of the New Testament scholar Josef Blinzler, who manages to put us right in the middle of a lively scene between Jesus and his critics. He claims that on that occasion Jesus had been reviled and called a eunuch. A hard and insupportable reproach. Jesus responded in his typical manner by seizing the opportunity: he took up the insulting word in order to give it a new meaning.[4]

Often the eunuch-logion is related only to the question of celibacy in the strict sense, as though "eunuch" here meant only the unmarried man. This interpretation, though, involves a narrowing of the sense that is not justified on the basis of the text itself. For Jesus was concerned with a possible unsuitability for marriage, and that can certainly occur in the case of married men also. Only in this way does the eunuch-saying fit into the life situation of Jesus and of the people who followed him, some of whom were married. Their situation is described in another passage:

Then Peter said in reply, "Behold, we have left everything and followed you. What then shall we have?" Jesus said to them, "Truly, I say to you, in the new world, when the Son of man shall sit on his glorious throne, you who have followed me will also sit on twelve thrones, judging the twelve tribes of Israel. And every one who has left houses or brothers or

---

[3] Ibid., 57f.
[4] J. Gnilka, *Jesus von Nazaret: Botschaft und Geschichte*, HThK.S 3 (Freiburg, 1990), 178f.

sisters or father or mother or children or lands, for my name's sake, will receive a hundredfold, and inherit eternal life." (Mt 19:27–29)

Those in the immediate circle of Jesus' followers lived without their wives or else in the unmarried state.[5] Jesus gathered about himself numerous disciples who accompanied him on his journeys.[6] Among them were those who were unmarried when they encountered him and who as his followers no longer intended to marry. Others, Peter for instance, gave up their family life and had now entered fully into the company of Jesus.[7] They had left not only their wives (Lk 18:29; cf. 14:26),[8] but also their extended family: house, brothers, sisters, father, mother, children, lands.[9] Then too, they were able to follow after Jesus precisely because their wives and children would be cared for, even without them, by the extended family unit. Therefore they were not abandoning a nuclear family to an uncertain fate. Society then took full responsibility for future generations, however radical the circumstances may have been.[10]

Therefore that personal remark about eunuchs has to be applied to the unmarried disciples, to those who had left married life behind, and to Jesus himself. With such comments many critics took aim at the lifestyle of Jesus' circle. They imputed to them a lack of potency, plain and simple. The catchword "eunuch" not only reflects the fact that Jesus and his circle lived without marriage but also makes a-sexuality the point of the whole subject: Eunuchs are incapable of procreating.

---

[5] E. Schillebeeckx, *Der Amtszölibat: Eine kritische Besinnung* (Düsseldorf, 1967), 17f.

[6] G. Theißen, *Soziologie der Jesusbewegung: Ein Beitrag zur Entstehungsgeschichte des Urchristentums* [Sociology of the Jesus-movement: A contribution to the history of Christianity's origins] (Munich, 1977), 14–21.

[7] J. Blinzler, " 'Zur Ehe unfähig . . .' Auslegung von Mt 19,12" [Incapable of marriage: An interpretation of Mt 19:12], in *Gesammelte Aufsätze*, vol. 1, *Aus der Welt und Umwelt des Neuen Testaments* (Stuttgart, 1969), 20–40, esp. 30.

[8] This addition of the wife in Luke is a clarification of Matthew 19:29, which is completely justified as to both meaning and matter: Whoever leaves house and children automatically leaves his wife, too. Cf. H. Kruse, "Eheverzicht in Neuen Testament und in der Frühkirche", FKTh 1 (1985): 110.

[9] Cf. Mt 8:14: the house of Peter and his mother-in-law. Peter's house is possibly mentioned at Mark 2:1 also; cf. Gnilka, *Jesus*, 179; P. Brown, *Die Keuschheit der Engel: Sexuelle Entsagung, Askese und Körperlichkeit am Anfang des Christentums* (Munich and Vienna, 1991), 55–58.

[10] Thus, when Jesus called that man to follow him without first going to bury his father (Mt 8:21f.), the dead father did not simply remain unburied; there was, of course, the rest of the family who would carry out this pious duty.

Jesus took up the remark and then said: There are various kinds of inability to procreate. Some *can* not, other *must* not, and still others do not *want* to beget children. He and his disciples were eunuchs of the latter sort, and that was equally true for the disciples who were living separated from their wives and for those who were unmarried: they did not *want* to procreate (any more). The disciples of Jesus thus formed a permanent association, for which sexual intercourse was generally taboo. And if Jesus affirmed spiritual castration for himself and his disciples, then this was also an expression of his will that this decision be lasting and final,[11] that is, of course, for both the unmarried and for those separated from their wives. In any case, it cannot be argued, either with respect to the subject matter or from the eunuch comparison, that a temporary state of castration lies within the scope of this logion.

Jesus was certainly not making propaganda for continence here; he simply acknowledged that he and his circle lived continently. And yet we can assume that this did not fail to have its effect and did draw admiring imitators. Here we are in all likelihood at the beginning of what would constitute the later celibacy discipline of clerics: married as well as unmarried men live in continence for the sake of the kingdom of heaven, that is, they do not beget children.[12]

2. The Apostles in Their Own Missionary Travels

The disciples, when they followed Jesus, lived as unmarried men or else without their wives, because they had decided to accompany him on his journeys. Now, after the death of their Master, the prospect arose, especially in the immediate shock of their disappointment, of returning to their hearth and home and, in the case of those who had wives, resuming their married life. That was entirely possible, since their families did not simply break up when they followed Jesus but continued to exist within the extended family unit. Perhaps then they went back home. Only when they went for a certain time on a mis-

---

[11] J. P. Audet, *Mariage et célibat dans le service pastorale de l'Église: Histoire et orientations* (Paris, 1967), 57f.; Schillebeeckx, *Amtszölibat*, 18. Kruse, "Eheverzicht", 103f. correctly suspects a vow of continence.

[12] Cf. Audet, *Mariage*, 69.

sionary journey would they later live separated from their wives. Otherwise, though, they continued their conjugal life.[13]

The disciples of Jesus persevere in their continent way of life. All that is not to be precluded, but it is not very probable, either.[14] On the contrary, it can be assumed that the disciples in the course of time had been instructed by Jesus in the spiritual and missionary meaning of their continent way of life and consciously identified themselves with it also, precisely because of the attacks from their opponents' side. Reflecting on this step in the light of the Resurrection and pondering the teaching of Jesus, the disciples understood better that it is a matter of a spiritual choice: to leave everything so as to gain the pearl of great price and the treasure in the field (Mt 13:44–46). It was a life decision that one does not simply take back again. One who is a eunuch remains so to the end of his life. Jesus' Resurrection, indeed, overturned everything again and brought back to life what the disciples had learned and experienced with their Master. The Gospel hands down the eunuch-logion only because it was so characteristic and claimed validity for the future, too, as a lasting legacy. The continent and unmarried way of life continued to be a challenge. In this practice Jesus himself and his manner of dealing with things remained tangible (Lk 14:26). It was simply part of the "ambiance" of the early Church that the illustrious men who had been chosen by Jesus himself retained their apostolic life-style.

The eunuch-logion found adherents and imitators in the early Church community. The following sequence of pericopes seems to bring this home as well. Possibly the eunuch-logion led very soon in many circles to a fundamental rejection of procreation. This could explain why the Evangelist immediately adds the pericope about blessing the children (Mt 19:13–15). Matthew is thus deliberately representing a Catholic *via media*, which would be accepted also in the centuries to come. We will find it again in the writings of the early theologian Clement of Alexandria. He maintains the ideal of the apostolic way of life, which entails strict continence within marriage, while warding off any antipathy to marriage or childbearing (see below, pp. 65–66).

Let us assume that not wanting to have (any more) children was a permanent ideal. Then the apostles, of all people, would scarcely have gone back home to the extended families they had started or resumed

---

[13] Ibid., 82–85.
[14] Theißen, *Soziologie*, 16f.

the marriages they had definitively broken off. This is not invalidated by Jesus' prohibition of divorce (Mt 19:6) or by the saying of Paul that a man should not send away his wife (1 Cor 7:11). A formal termination of marriage with a letter of divorce did not take place; on the contrary, the wife would have consented to this separation.[15] After Easter, as will be explained, the apostles set out again on their journeys. Therefore a continuation of marriage must have appeared difficult.

For them, marriage was not the sort of binary relationship that we imagine today on the basis of modern living conditions; such an anachronism has led to many misinterpretations of the marital situation of the apostles. In those days the entire household was always implicated, the *oikos*.[16] The apostles could not simply transplant this from Galilee to Jerusalem, for instance. It would have been just as impractical for them to remove their wives and children from the extended family and take them along, since they then would have been socially uprooted and insecure. The apostolic way of life with its numerous journeys could not be combined with the care of an *oikos*. Based on his own experience, therefore, Paul formulates his vote in favor of celibacy (1 Cor 7:32f.). Apostolic availability in building up the Church and a continent way of life, as known from the years with Jesus, belonged together. It would be rather inconsistent if the apostles were in fact to attend to their apostolic service without maintaining the established apostolic way of life, as it found expression in the saying about eunuchs.[17]

The right of the apostles to have a woman with them. After Easter the itinerant life of the apostles did not cease. The missionary journeys of

---

[15] Kruse, "Eheverzicht", 110.

[16] For the outstanding significance of Οἶκος for the Jewish people of the Old Testament, see F. Laub, "Sozialgeschichtlicher Hintergrund und ekklesiologische Relevanz der neutestamentlich-frühchristlichen Haus- und Gemeinde-Tafelparänese: Ein Beitrag zur Soziologie des Frühchristentums", MThZ 37 (1986): 259.

[17] As for the subsequent fate of the wives and children of the apostles, Kruse, "Eheverzicht", 110–12, proposes an interesting thought that prescinds from the social institution of the extended family. He claims to find a reflection of their subsequent fate in the account about the widows of the early Christian community (Acts 6:1). According to his argument, the wives of the apostles together with their children made up a good part of the original Christian community in Jerusalem. This communal sort of life (Acts 2:44f.) was supposed to prevent them, after their husbands went away, from living alone—which was unthinkable for women in antiquity—or from having to remarry. The relatively large number of these "widows" caused a considerable problem in providing for them, a duty that the deacons then assumed.

Paul testify to this. He traveled untiringly in the Mediterranean region in order to spread the faith. No woman was with him. His colleagues, the other apostles, traveled around, too. But what was the situation with their wives? Did the married apostles really practice continence, as they had done when they walked with Jesus? Only one remark in Paul's letters somewhat lifts the veil from this question. It is so short and, as it were, accidental that it does not allow us to judge with certainty. At any rate, women or wives in the company of the apostles are mentioned. Paul speaks in the First Letter to the Corinthians, hence around the year 55, about the right of the apostles to bring women along with them:

> For you [Corinthians] are the seal of my apostleship in the Lord. This is my defense to those who would examine me. Do we not have the right to our food and drink? *Do we not have the right to take about with us a woman, a sister* [i.e., a Christian woman; cf. 1 Cor 7:15], *as do the other apostles, and the brethren of the Lord, and Cephas?* Or is it only Barnabas and I who have no right to refrain from working for a living? (1 Cor 9:2–6)[18]

The original Greek text at the critical place has been handed down in two versions. According to one reading, Paul is speaking about the right to bring with him *a sister as a woman/wife*; according to the other reading, he speaks in general of having *women* with him. We leave open the decision as to which is the original text and take all possibilities into account in our further discussion.

In reading the text one wonders why Paul reacts with such irritation. Paul had enemies, and they were saying, "You are not a real apostle, because in your high-handed manner you don't let yourself be supported by the community, and you don't have a woman/wife with you either, as the other apostles do." Thus Paul aroused suspicion. Astonishing, after all! Having a woman in one's company seems to have been the mark of a genuine apostle. The text leaves completely open the question of whether it is referring to the wives of the apostles. In the context of the letter Paul simply wants to remind his readers of the right of the apostles to be supported by the community, regardless of whether or not he avails himself of this right. He has the right to eat and drink

---

[18] Ἡ γὰρ σφραγίς μου τῆς ἀποστολῆς ὑμεῖς ἐστε ἐν κυρίῳ. Ἡ ἐμὴ ἀπολογία τοῖς ἐμὲ ἀνακρίνουσίν ἐστιν αὕτη. Μὴ οὐκ ἔχομεν ἐξουσίαν φαγεῖν καὶ πεῖν; μὴ οὐκ ἔχομεν ἐξουσίαν ἀδελφὴν γυναῖκα περιάγειν ὡς καὶ οἱ λοιποὶ ἀπόστολοι καὶ οἱ ἀδελφοὶ τοῦ κυρίου καὶ Κηφᾶς; ἢ μόνος ἐγὼ καὶ Βαρναβᾶς οὐκ ἔχομεν ἐξουσίαν μὴ ἐργάζεσθαι.

at the community's expense. He has the right, at the community's expense, to have "women" (or else "a baptized woman") in his company, and he has the right to give up his trade and be dependent upon the community. It follows from this that the apostles traveled around, like Paul, and in doing so were accompanied by women. Paul is comparing his way of life, which was characterized by unabated missionary work, with the activity of the other apostles. And only because his colleagues were performing their apostolic duties could they have any claim to the support of the faithful for the women in their company as well.

Probably the women mentioned in this passage were not "wives". For, at least in Peter's case, it would have been very strange if all the world could see how he had gone back on his former declaration, "Behold, we have left everything and followed you" (Mt 19:27). [19] It is a sufficient and acceptable interpretation to say that the involvement of these women in the work of the apostles was limited to auxiliary services. At least that is how the aforementioned Clement of Alexandria viewed it. Of course that does not exclude the possibility that Paul is speaking here about the wives of the apostles. [20] But neither is it clear that we can assume the wives were in the company of the apostles. For they had not been left alone by their husbands back in Galilee or some other place, so that after Easter they would again have to be taken into their care. Besides, according to the one reading they were "baptized women". It may have happened that some wives did not seek baptism on account of their ties with the extended family, which involved religious duties as well; in such instances accompanying the apostles would have been out of the question. Therefore, if the emphasis is on the baptism of the accompanying women, it is obviously because the subject here is not wives, but women in general. In order to avoid all misunderstanding, Paul emphasizes that these women were baptized, hence capable of continence and completely above suspicion. Thus, Paul describes the apostles as having a "baptized woman" with them as a helper in the apostolate, without entering into an intimate relationship with her. In a similar manner even Jesus has women with him, who supported him and his disciples (Lk 8:1-3).

But let us suppose for the moment that the apostles did bring their wives along. That by no means implies that they had conjugal rela-

---

[19] Kruse, "Eheverzicht", 98f.
[20] Clement of Alexandria, *Stromata* 3, 6, 52, 5-53, 3 (GCS Clem. Alex. 2⁴, 220, 15-24).

tions with them. There is no evidence of that. It would be just as unfounded simply to presuppose that the apostles, those who were still single, would have had the right to marry. Paul, at least, speaks only of the right to have women (wives) in one's company at the community's expense. It is a only a question of who pays the bills. No further statement is intended in this passage. And if the apostles ever did take their wives out of the *oikos* back home and bring them along, then it would hardly have been so as to found a new family in Jerusalem or somewhere else.

One might wonder why, in the cited passage from Paul, only wives are mentioned and not the children that the apostles and brothers of the Lord may have had. The community probably had to provide for their support, too; for a father who gives up his job cannot feed either his wife or his children. The addition of children at least would have lent greater emphasis to Paul's argument: Even the children have to be supported by the community. Thus we can conclude from the fact that children are not mentioned that there were no children in the company of the apostles and that the apostles therefore did not have marital intercourse.

The apostles become examples of continence. Christianity spread in the early years through the efforts of the apostles and of numerous traveling missionaries, both in public appearances and also in synagogues and houses. One can assume, based on the previous reflections, that the lifestyle of these missionaries was continent. And naturally it would happen that the missionaries would be considered models in just that point of discipline. The apostolic example inspired people. They wanted to vie with these heroes of the faith. No wonder Paul presents his celibacy as exemplary and, all told, recommends continence (1 Cor 7). We then find this widely confirmed in the apocryphal acts of the apostles. Those were Christian novels from the second century, whose popularity spread rapidly. Their heroes were the apostles John, Paul, Peter, Andrew, and Thomas. And their message was more or less: continence, which is unabashedly propagated as the absolute Christian ideal.

If one reads this literature, which is embellished with exaggerations and extravagances, it quickly becomes clear what one has to make of it. It is a historically inauthentic and in general distorted view of the life of the apostles. But people knew that already back then. The early Church for this reason included none of these stories about the apostles (except for the book of Acts) in her canon of sacred writings; they were considered unreliable and were not read aloud during the Divine Liturgy. The apocryphal writings do show, however, that people in the second century were convinced that the apostles had lived continently. Sexual continence was at that time popular among many Christians, and they were strengthened in their resolutions by the apostolic way of life.

If Tertullian of Carthage around 217, during his Montanist period, adopted the view that all the apostles except Peter had been unmarried and had women with them as helpers,[21] then this is really not so different from the statement of the Catholic Clement that the apostles actually had been married but then lived continently with their wives. Therefore even the astonishing pronouncement of Clement that Paul himself had been married is completely inconsequential. For he too had no sexual intercourse with his wife. It is evident therefore: in the Church at large as well as in those Catholic circles in which the apocryphal acts of the apostles made the rounds, the apostolic ideal of continence was unquestioned.

3. Paul's Challenge: "Touch No Woman"

When, in connection with an early history of clerical continence, the conversation comes round to Paul, then the notorious seventh chapter of his First Letter to the Corinthians is sure to be the subject as well.[22] In this excerpt, which is terribly offensive to contemporary ears, he clearly casts a vote in favor of the unmarried state. He does not speak explicitly about the sexual asceticism of the apostles, and not at all about the continence of any deacons, priests, or bishops. And yet this is a text that, on account of its authority, was supposed to have a considerable influence on the clerical way of life, as the pastoral letters already give us to understand. A formal exegesis of the text cannot be performed here. Ultimately the interpretation of this chapter will always be disputed. In essence the passage paves the way for a forthright, unbiased appreciation of celibacy, which can fit together seamlessly with a discipline of continence practiced by Jesus and the apostles:

---

[21] Tertullian, *De Monogamia* 8, 4; 6 (CCL 2, 1239, 21f.; 1240, 36–39).

[22] Fundamental for this topic is L. Legrand, "Saint Paul et le célibat", in J. Coppens, ed., *Sacerdoce et célibat: Études historiques et théologiques* (Louvain: Gembloux, 1971), and W. Schrage, *Ethik des Neuen Testaments*, GNT 4 (Göttingen, 1982), 217–20.

Now concerning the matters about which you wrote [I reply as follows].
It is well for a man not to touch a woman. But because of the temptation
to immorality, each man should have his own wife and each woman her
own husband. The husband should give to his wife her conjugal rights,
and likewise the wife to her husband. For the wife does not rule over
her own body, but the husband does; likewise, the husband does not rule
over his own body, but the wife does. Do not refuse one another except
perhaps by agreement for a season, that you may devote yourselves to
prayer; but then come together again, lest Satan tempt you through lack
of self-control. I say this by way of concession, not of command. I wish
that all were as I myself am. But each has his own special gift from God,
one of one kind and one of another.

To the unmarried and the widows I say that it is well for them to
remain single as I do. But if they cannot exercise self-control, they should
marry. For it is better to marry than to be aflame with passion.

To the married I give charge, not I but the Lord, that the wife should
not separate from her husband (but if she does, let her remain single or
else be reconciled to her husband)—and that the husband should not
divorce his wife.

To the rest I say, not the Lord, that if any brother has a wife who is an
unbeliever, and she consents to live with him, he should not divorce her.
If any woman has a husband who is an unbeliever, and he consents to
live with her, she should not divorce him. For the unbelieving husband
is consecrated through his wife, and the unbelieving wife is consecrated
through her husband. Otherwise, your children would be unclean, but
as it is they are holy. But if the unbelieving partner desires to separate,
let it be so; in such a case the brother or sister is not bound. For God has
called us to peace. Wife, how do you know whether you will save your
husband? Husband, how do you know whether you will save your wife?

Only, let every one lead the life which the Lord has assigned to him,
and in which God has called him. This is my rule in all the churches.
Was any one at the time of his call already circumcised? Let him not seek
to remove the marks of circumcision. Was any one at the time of his call
uncircumcised? Let him not seek circumcision. For neither circumcision
counts for anything nor uncircumcision, but keeping the commandments
of God. Every one should remain in the state in which he was called.
Were you a slave when called? Never mind. But if you can gain your
freedom, avail yourself of the opportunity. For he who was called in the
Lord as a slave is a freedman of the Lord. Likewise he who was free when
called is a slave of Christ. You were bought with a price; do not become
slaves of men. So, brethren, in whatever state each was called, there let
him remain with God.

Now concerning the unmarried, I have no command of the Lord, but I give my opinion as one who by the Lord's mercy is trustworthy. I think that in view of the impending distress it is well for a person to remain as he is. Are you bound to a wife? Do not seek to be free. Are you free from a wife? Do not seek marriage. But if you marry, you do not sin, and if a girl marries she does not sin. Yet those who marry will have worldly troubles, and I would spare you that. I mean, brethren, the appointed time has grown very short; from now on, let those who have wives live as though they had none, and those who mourn as though they were not mourning, and those who rejoice as though they were not rejoicing, and those who buy as though they had no goods, and those who deal with the world as though they had no dealings with it. For the form of this world is passing away.

I want you to be free from anxieties. The unmarried man is anxious about the affairs of the Lord, how to please the Lord; but the married man is anxious about worldly affairs, how to please his wife, and his interests are divided. And the unmarried woman or girl is anxious about the affairs of the Lord, how to be holy in body and spirit; but the married woman is anxious about worldly affairs, how to please her husband. I say this for your own benefit, not to lay any restraint upon you, but to promote good order and to secure your undivided devotion to the Lord.

If any one thinks that he is not behaving properly toward his betrothed, if his passions are strong, and it has to be, let him do as he wishes: let them marry—it is no sin. But whoever is firmly established in his heart, being under no necessity but having his desire under control, and has determined this in his heart to keep her as his betrothed, he will do well. So that he who marries his betrothed does well; and he who refrains from marriage will do better.

A wife is bound to her husband as long as he lives. If the husband dies, she is free to be married to whom she wishes, only in the Lord. But in my judgment she is happier if she remains as she is. And I think that I have the Spirit of God. (1 Cor 7:1–40)

The first sentence does not sound very flattering. "It is well for a man not to touch a woman." In order to acquit Paul as much as possible from any tendencies inimical to the body, many exegetes say that he does not speak here at all for himself but quotes a formulation of the Corinthians. That is very nice of them but perhaps also too expedient. We can safely assume that we have here in this passage Paul's own opinion. Let us try to reconstruct the situation in which he spoke. That is critical, for on it depends how his message is to be interpreted.

Paul founded the Christian community in the Greek city of Corinth.

At the time when he was writing the letter, however, he was no longer there. He had on hand a written message[23] that had been sent to him about the conditions in Corinth. It also dealt with Christian marriage and continence, whereby marriage did not come off very well. Behind the message there was certainly no ascetical splinter group within the community, nor some outside group that had infiltrated and had caused problems with its Encratite propaganda.[24] On the contrary, one must suppose that the community in Corinth itself was experiencing a charismatic spiritual awakening that manifested itself in a pronounced bias in favor of continence.[25] That must have been one of the subjects discussed in the lost message from the Corinthians.

Paul, however, had been informed by another party as well. Against this background the official description, so to speak, of the community organization and of how it had conducted itself in his absence necessarily struck him as arrogant (1 Cor 4:19; 5:2), self-important (1 Cor 5:6), and whitewashed when confronted with the deplorable state of affairs that had reached his ears (1 Cor 5:1; 6:15). There were all sorts of lewd conduct in the community. In his letter Paul names them by name so as to bring the Corinthians down to earth at last (1 Cor 5f.). After all, they had been hyper-enthusiastic about a Christian ideal of continence, modeled on his, which they were simply not capable of putting into practice (1 Cor 7).

The community displayed here, as also in other matters, a certain overzealousness. This can be explained as the result of an overly emotional and unthinking attachment to the preaching of Paul. The Corinthians took many statements of the apostle too literally. In a sermon he set a headline, "do not associate with immoral men" (1 Cor 5:9), and immediately they wanted to apply this across the board. And they seemed to latch on to another statement in an exaggerated manner: "not to touch a woman" (1 Cor 7:1). They proudly informed Paul that marriage and marital relations had to be viewed as questionable.

---

[23] 1 Cor 7:1 does not speak of an "inquiry" (as the German Church Unity Translation would have it). The Corinthians boast, rather, of how magnificently their community has been developing during the absence of Paul. And now it has already attained even the ideal of continence, after the great example of Paul.

[24] Niederwimmer, *Askese*, 81.

[25] N. Baumert, *Ehelosigkeit und Ehe im Herrn: Eine Neuinterpretation von 1 Kor 7*, FzB 47 (Würzburg, 1984), 20.

Paul stands by his statement here, too, not taking it back in any way, but effectively qualifying it.

The formula set at the beginning: "It is well for a man not to touch a woman", is intended to give advice not only to men but also to women (cf. 1 Cor 7:2ff.). The basic thesis, "have no sexual intercourse", has its validity as a principle. It indicates a fundamental option that can then be applied to three groups of persons who are concerned: those who are continent in marriage, the unmarried, and the widowed.

In the first place Paul turns to those who are already married; hence he is speaking about continence within marriage (1 Cor 7:1–7).[26] As such marriage is the obvious choice precisely for those who cannot live continently. It normally includes conjugal relations. Anyone who wishes to live continently should for that reason not marry. Paul is willing to grant, in any case, that a Christian married couple could practice continence temporarily, probably for a few months at most. Therefore, when he made the remark in Corinth about "not touching women", he intended by that only to express his personal preference for celibacy (1 Cor 7:25). It was incorrect to apply that then to married people, as though it would be good for them, too, to forgo sexual intercourse. Paul has to set the record straight: He was speaking only about the unmarried, that is, those who are *perfectly* continent, when he said that it is well for a man not to touch a woman at all in the first place. Only outside of marriage is sexual intercourse (as fornication) to be rejected on principle (1 Cor 7:2).[27]

It is important for the later pastoral letters that Paul here intends to say: "When I speak about marriage between baptized persons, which guards you against immorality, then I ask you, please, not to misinterpret my meaning, as though I were *commanding* baptized people to marry. Naturally there can be no question of that. It is a *concession* that I am making for you—indeed, on account of your weakness."[28] Paul is propagating celibacy (1 Cor 7:1), and yet he can prescribe immediately after: "because of the temptation to immorality, each man should have his own wife" (1 Cor 7:2). Of course one has to add: That is true provided that he touches a woman at all. It is similar, therefore, to

---

[26] R. Schnackenburg, *Die sittliche Botschaft des Neuen Testaments*, vol. 1, *Von Jesus zur Urkirche*, HThK.S 1 (Freiburg, 1986), 206ff.

[27] Paul does not speak of "the *temptation to* immorality" (RSV).

[28] Niederwimmer, *Askese*, 95.

the passages in the pastoral letters, where the bishop *"must* be . . . the husband of one wife" (1 Tim 3:2). Here, too, it should be added: on the condition that he is married. No obligation to marry is formulated in either passage.

As for the unmarried and the widowed, only one point needs to be mentioned here, which is important for what follows. Paul would like the unmarried and the widowers to remain as they are after their conversion. If someone cannot live continently, however, he certainly may marry also as a Christian. Actually Paul sees a necessity of marrying only on the basis of sexual needs. The remarriage of a widow or a widower is for him always an indication that the person in question is not capable of refraining from further sexual activity. That is certainly a narrow view. Love, or the duty of caring for children from a first marriage, for instance, do not come into consideration for Paul. Marriage is for him something quite provisional that, strictly speaking, one does not take upon oneself.

We can summarize, therefore, and this will be valid then for the entire seventh chapter of the First Letter to the Corinthians: Paul recognizes only one alternative—either marriage and within it sexual intercourse, or else celibacy (or widowhood, if that is the case). He neatly distinguishes marriage and celibacy and gives to both their due, even if there is a clear preference for celibacy: before a Christian enters marriage, he should first find out whether he can live as a celibate. There is the superiority of renouncing marriage, and there is the concession of marriage.[29] Paul's concern, in any case, is not to incriminate sexuality as such, which would require marriage to be an absolutely spiritual relationship,[30] as the Encratites wanted. The alternative facing the individual is not "Yes or no to sex (within and outside of marriage)?" but rather "Yes or no to marriage?"

What is so good about celibacy? What, then, were the motives that prompted Paul to make his speech in defense of celibacy? Two aspects of the question strike one at first glance: the strongest motive was freedom for the sake of Christ. And this freedom had to be concrete. Marriage as such was an institutionalized dependence. Sexuality was

---

[29] Ibid., 90.

[30] 1 Cor 7:36–38 does not allow for a spiritual marriage, either; A. Oepke, "Ehe I (Institution)", in RAC 4 (1959), 659; Schnackenburg, *Botschaft*, 208. On the other hand, Niederwimmer, *Askese*, 117–20, claims that Paul is speaking here of *syneisaktoi.*

only one of the many concomitant factors. Paul, though, was praising independence: total dedication of self, body and soul, to Christ,[31] and in this context marriage represented attachment to the things of this world. All the cares of a human being should be directed toward Christ, not toward another person and the worldly affairs connected with that (1 Cor 7:26–35).

This involved the entire realm of social commitments that one entered into through marriage and which could not be limited to the spouse alone or to procreative acts. Paul is careful not to narrow his advice, "touch no woman!", to the sexual domain. He does not wish to be misunderstood in that way, because that would introduce problems into many quite different departments of life, which are then listed in the seventh chapter. Therefore it is out of the question that Paul was a proponent of some "principle of sexual asceticism".[32] One finds in his writings no sexual pessimism.[33] Present here is not a "christological foundation for sexual asceticism",[34] but rather a christological foundation for celibacy.

Again and again the Pauline view of marriage and celibacy is seen as following from an apocalyptic expectation of the last day (cf. Jer 16:1–4) and from an associated Platonic disdain for the world. It is said that Paul wanted to flee from the world, which would soon be at an end, and from its concerns, so as to be free for the pure spiritual world: "to have as though one did not possess" (cf. 1 Cor 7:29–31). Parallel texts from popular Greek philosophy, in which the Neoplatonic ideal of *ataraxia* (freedom from passion) is very common, seem to support such an intended flight from the world. Paul seems to be pursuing an ascetical ideal of inner freedom: a vision of the eternal things, which is incompatible with the worries of marital interests and duties. But such comparisons ultimately remain mere speculation; one could draw them with respect to Jesus, and they would be just as unproductive.[35]

No doubt Paul lived in expectation—the time was short, the form of this world was passing away (1 Cor 7:29–31)—but that is a far cry from disdain for the world. As long as the end had not yet come, life

---

[31] Niederwimmer, *Askese*, 116.
[32] Contrary to ibid., 84.
[33] Contrary to ibid., 97.
[34] Contrary to ibid., 113.
[35] Compare Gnilka, *Jesus*, 177.

was still to be lived. Of course, from then on new priorities had to be determined. And that did not mean living now amid the pale appearances of imperishable goods and Ideas, but rather pleasing Christ in everything. If one is looking for echoes of the popular philosophy of the day, one ought rather to point out that the itinerant philosophers did not necessarily understand *ataraxia* to be a Buddhist ideal but rather the freedom to undertake a religious mission, the placing of oneself at the service of the Deity, which precluded a concern about wife and children.[36]

Thus Paul is striking a philosophical note in order to present his actual concern in a convincing way. He adopts fragments of popular philosophical thought but orders them in a completely new way to his christocentric world view. The opposite of "anxiety about worldly affairs" is not precisely anxiety about spiritual values but "being anxious about the affairs of the Lord". That means, therefore, "pleasing the Lord", directing one's entire activity toward the Christian apostolate. That includes renouncing the intention of pleasing a wife. This "pleasing a wife (or a husband)" had little to do with the modern romantic notion of marriage; it meant, rather, the entire service rendered in a marriage, ultimately it meant care for the larger social unit, the οἶκος, care for the well-being of the spouse, the children, relatives, slaves, and domestics. Such demands would necessarily have stood in the way of an intensive apostolate of the sort that Paul is pursuing.

4. The Key Is Found in the Pastoral Letters

Thus far we have tried to obtain a picture of the life-style of Jesus and of his band of apostles. Paul stepped into the spotlight, not to mention the twilight, as a staunch advocate of celibacy. All that was important but still only preliminary. For there has been no mention so far of ecclesiastical officials, neither in the sayings of Jesus nor in the writings of Paul. It is quite likely that Jesus and the apostles were either unmarried or else lived without their wives (or with their wives but continently). But was that true then also for the next generation of leaders, for those who headed and governed the early Church communities? The task

---

[36] Epictetus, *Dissertationis ab Arriano digestae* 3, 22, 23–76; H. Dörrie, *Der Platonismus in der Antike*, vol. 1, *Die geschichtlichen Wurzeln des Platonismus* (Stuttgart and Bad Cannstatt, 1987), 238–45, 513–20.

therefore still remains of finding in the New Testament passages that would provide a basis for obligatory clerical continence. As a matter of fact one trail leads to the pastoral letters. What we learn about clerical discipline from the First Letter to Timothy and the Letter to Titus is important not only for the New Testament period. On the contrary, here we hit upon the fundamental and perennial reference point for the discussion of clerical continence in the following centuries.

a. The Minister Should Be "The Husband of One Wife"

Most exegetes do not attribute the pastoral letters to Paul himself but more likely to a writer from the missionary field of Asia Minor (today Turkey) in which he worked. The general opinion is that they were composed, at the earliest, a generation after his stay there. Three passages demand our full attention. At first glance they have nothing at all to do with a discipline of celibacy; indeed, they even seem to speak explicitly against the idea of obligatory continence. That is to say, they deal with the wives and children of bishops, priests, and deacons.[37] Already in the early Church, consequently, many thought that the pastoral letters required those who held office to be married and to beget children. This interpretation is held by modern exegetes as well.

Whether that gets at the real meaning of the texts, though, may be doubted. A deeper analysis ought to make this clear. "Paul" gives directions in the aforementioned letters to his missionary assistants Timothy and Titus about what sorts of candidates they should select to hold office in their mission territories. The prerequisites for the aspirants are listed in a catalogue:[38]

[1] If any one aspires to the office of bishop, he desires a noble task.[39]
[2] Now a bishop must be above reproach, the husband of one wife, temperate, sensible, dignified, hospitable, an apt teacher, [3] no drunkard, not violent but gentle, not quarrelsome, and no lover of money. [4] He must manage his own household well, keeping his children submissive and

---

[37] For problem of the terminology for ecclesiastical offices in the pastoral letters, see G. Schöllgen, "Hausgemeinden οἶκος-Ekklesiologie und monarchischer Episkopat", JAC 31 (1988): 84f.

[38] Parts of the following discussion are developed more fully in S. Heid, "Grundlagen des Zölibats in der frühen Kirche", in K. M. Becker and J. Eberle, eds., Der Zölibat des Priesters, Sinn und Sendung, 9 (St. Ottilien, 1995), 51–68.

[39] Καλὸς ἔργος, see The Shepherd of Hermes 38, 8.

respectful in every way; [5] for if a man does not know how to manage his own household, how can he care for God's church? [6] He must not be a recent convert, or he may be puffed up with conceit and fall into the condemnation of the devil; [7] moreover he must be well thought of by outsiders, or he may fall into reproach and the snare of the devil. (1 Tim 3:1–7)[40]

This passage deals with bishops. Similar formulas are found relative to priests and deacons (Tit 1:5–9; 1 Tim 3:8–12).[41] Alongside the many requirements for holders of office, the essential question for us concerns the proviso that bishops, priests, and deacons should be "the husband of one wife", that is, should only have one wife. What is meant by that?

Impediments to orders are being listed. Most exegetical commentaries represent the view that the catalogue of requirements for clerics just cited consists of rather vague prescriptions with respect to an exemplary way of life for officeholders. They say that this is only a matter of loosely formulated recommendations and not at all a question of the demands of Church law.[42] But the whole thing is not so non-binding

---

[40] Εἴ τις ἐπισκοπῆς ὀρέγεται, καλοῦ ἔργου ἐπιθυμεῖ. Δεῖ οὖν τὸν ἐπίσκοπον ἀνεπίλημπτον εἶναι, μιᾶς γυναικὸς ἄνδρα, νηφάλιον σώφρονα κόσμιον φιλόξενον διδακτικόν, μὴ πάροινον μὴ πλήκτην, ἀλλὰ ἐπιεικῆ ἄμαχον ἀφιλάργυρον, τοῦ ἰδίου οἴκου καλῶς προϊστάμενον, τέκνα ἔχοντα ἐν ὑποταγῇ· μετὰ πάσης σεμνότητος (εἰ δέ τις τοῦ ἰδίου οἴκου προστῆναι οὐκ οἶδεν, πῶς ἐκκλησίας θεοῦ ἐπιμελήσεται;), μὴ νεόφυτον, ἵνα μὴ τυφωθεὶς εἰς κρίμα ἐμπέσῃ τοῦ διαβόλου. Δεῖ δὲ καὶ μαρτυρίαν καλὴν ἔχειν ἀπὸ τῶν ἔξωθεν, ἵνα μὴ εἰς ὀνειδισμὸν ἐμπέσῃ καὶ παγίδα τοῦ διαβόλου.

[41] Tit 1:5–9 (emphasis added): "This is why I left you in Crete, that you might amend what was defective, and appoint elders in every town as I directed you, if any man is blameless, *the husband of one wife*, and his children are believers and not open to the charge of being profligate or insubordinate. For a bishop, as God's steward, must be blameless; he must not be arrogant or quick-tempered or a drunkard or violent or greedy for gain, but hospitable, a lover of goodness, master of himself, upright, holy, and self-controlled; he must hold firm to the sure word as taught, so that he may be able to give instruction in sound doctrine and also to confute those who contradict it."

1 Tim 3:8–12 (emphasis added): "Deacons likewise must be serious, not double-tongued, not addicted to much wine, not greedy for gain; they must hold the mystery of the faith with a clear conscience. And let them also be tested first; then if they prove themselves blameless let them serve as deacons. The women likewise must be serious, no slanderers, but temperate, faithful in all things. Let deacons be *the husband of one wife*, and let them manage their children and their households well."

[42] Pertinent but opposing this view is H. Schlier, "Die Ordnung der Kirche nach den Pastoralbriefen", in K. Kertelge, ed., *Das kirchliche Amt im Neuen Testament*, WdF 189 (Darmstadt, 1977), 475–500 at 480f. Cf. A. Harnack, *Entstehung und Entwicklung der Kirchenverfassung und des Kirchenrechts in den zwei ersten Jahrhunderten* (Darmstadt, 1980), 49–51. This

as that. In any case it does not stop at exhortations to virtue (sobriety, prudence, and so on). At least in part these are concrete criteria, verifiable in practice, which are not intended for Christians in general but are tailored to the clerical ministry.

The formula: deacons, priests, and bishops should be "the husband of one wife" (μᾶς γυναικὸς ἀνήρ / unius uxoris vir) is used identically in three places (1 Tim 3:2, 12; Tit 1:6). It is evident, chiefly from the ceremonious, even bureaucratic sound of the formula that behind it stands a precise, concrete legal demand.[43] Hence it is erroneous to see in "unius uxoris vir" a general Christian maxim along the lines of "clergymen should live a decent married life and love their wives."[44] That would have been formulated differently; furthermore, such a saying would have been trivial. It can also be excluded on the basis of 1 Timothy 5:9, where it is stated that widowed women can be placed on the Church's roll only if they are at least sixty years old and have been "the wife of one husband". This refers to a clear legal norm, namely, a prohibition against second marriages (also called "successive polygamy").[45] Even in pagan and Jewish inscriptions the word μόνανδρος (or univira) means the exclusive fidelity of a wife to her first and only husband, continuing in some cases beyond his death (that is, no remarriage).[46] In any case, the Letter to Timothy does not have in view a prohibition of simultaneous polyandry for widows enrolled by

---

continues a development that can be recognized already in 1 Corinthians 7; cf. Niederwimmer, *Askese*, 83.

[43] Cf. H.-W. Bartsch, *Die Anfänge urchristlicher Rechtsbildungen: Studien zu den Pastoralbriefen*, ThF 34 (Hamburg-Bergstedt, 1965), 92; K. Mörsdorf, "Zölibat", in LThK, 2d ed., vol. 10 (1965), 1395–1400 at 1396.

[44] Against P. Trummer, "Einehe nach den Pastoralbriefen: Zum Verständnis der Termini μᾶς γυναικὸς ἀνήρ und ἑνὸς ἀνδρὸς γυνή", *Biblica* 51 (1970): 471–84; E. Schillebeeckx, *Christliche Identität und kirchliches Amt: Plädoyer für den Menschen in der Kirche* (Düsseldorf, 1985), 289; L. Oberlinner, *Die Pastoralbriefe*, HThK 11, 2, 1 (Freiburg, 1994), 120f.; H. J. Vogt, "Bemerkungen zur frühen Amts- und Gemeindestruktur", ThQ 175 (1995): 192–98 at 193.

[45] I. de la Potterie, " 'Mari d'une seule femme'; Le Sens théologique d'une formule Paulinienne", in L. de Lorenzi, ed., *Paul de Tarse, Apôtre du notre temps*, SMBen.P 1 (Rome, 1979), 637; M. Meinertz, *Die Pastoralbriefe des heiligen Paulus*, 4th ed. Die heilige Schrift des Neuen Testaments, vol. 8 (Bonn, 1931), 42f. at 64, with convincing arguments.

[46] Μόνανδρος and *univira* in inscriptions (for examples, see B. Kötting, "Digamus", in RAC 3 [1957], 1019) by no means refer only to the praise of marital fidelity (which is the opinion of Audet, *Mariage*, 93–96, Schillebeeckx, *Amtszölibat*, 16 et al.), but also to a refusal to remarry (B. Kötting, *Die Beurteilung der zweiten Ehe im heidnischen und christlichen Altertum* [diss., Bonn, 1942], 76–99). Strictly speaking, it is a matter of the wife's exclusive fidelity to

the Church; it would be quite senseless to require of a widow that she must never have practiced polygamy.[47]

The interpretation of the phrase ἑνὸς ἀνδρὸς γυνή in the sense of a unique marriage can scarcely be avoided. For in the context of the question about widows, the Letter to Timothy is concerned precisely with remarriage. In principle widows are indeed allowed to remarry, but that then becomes an impediment to their being included on the Church's roll of widows (1 Tim 5:11, 14). Accordingly, the Church's widows are to have been married only once. We should undertake an analogous interpretation for the "husband of one wife" of the bishops, priests, and deacons. This can hardly be intended to impede the ordination of men who have practiced polygamy or adultery.[48] Polygamy may indeed have been rather widespread in the society of that day. But that was completely unacceptable for Christians. In the early Christian era a multiple marriage was never discussed; a second marriage, on the other hand, most likely was. Polygamous men a priori were never even considered as potential clerics because of the strict moral demands of the Christians. It can be said therefore that the pastoral letters intend to exclude legally from holding office in the Church any man who has been married successively two or more times. A cleric must have been married only once (precept of monogamy / prohibition of digamy).

Now, though, it is of crucial significance that we clarify to whom the catalogues of requirements in the pastoral letters were directed. Of course, deacons, priests, and bishops were affected by them, but they were not the individuals being addressed. The catalogues were meant, rather, for the recipients of the pastoral letters in their entirety, for the apostolic assistants Timothy and Titus. They were being told how they should select candidates for clerical ministry. That has one crucial consequence: by "deacons, priests, and bishops" were meant, not ordained ministers (not yet in any case), but rather candidates for ordination.[49] It follows too that the catalogues of requirements were

---

her first and only husband. For prohibitions against remarriage in the case of candidates to the pagan priesthood, see Kötting, "Digamus", 1018f.

[47] G. Bickell, "Cölibat eine apostolische Anordnung", ZKTh 2 (1878): 28.

[48] Thus G. Denzler, *Das Papsttum und der Amtszölibat*, vol. 1, *Die Zeit bis zur Reformation*, PuP 5, 1 (Stuttgart, 1973), 4. Audet, *Mariage*, 93, rejects this view.

[49] Criteria for examining candidates for orders are mentioned also by Hippolytus, *Traditio apostolica* 2 (FC 1, 214, 13–16); John Chrysostom, *De sacerdotio*, 2, 5 (SC 272, 122, 55–124, 76); Gregory of Nyssa, *Hom. 7 in Cant.* 4:3 (FC 16, 2, 434, 3–7); Ambrose, *Epistulae* 63,

not an instruction in the duties of ministers addressed to those who were already serving. On the contrary, the catalogues were the basis for a canonically binding examination of candidates for orders (1 Tim 3:10). Such an examination was taken quite seriously in the Church from the very beginning.[50] It could happen all too easily that unsuitable men would be ordained and then do great damage in the Christian communities.

Thus, according to the pastoral letters, candidates, while they were still laymen,[51] had to fulfill certain conditions. The catalogues, however, did not list positive criteria of suitability. No candidate was required to demonstrate all that he could do and how outstanding he was. The decision rested with Timothy and Titus. And they were only interested in factors that would make candidates unsuitable for clerical ministry. Thus the initial presumption was that the candidates—who had probably been recommended by members of the community— were suitable. They intervened only when there was public knowledge of something that weighed against their ordination.

Thus the catalogues of requirements constituted criteria for excluding candidates from orders; they listed impediments to orders (irregularities). Not every male layman who fulfilled all the requirements was necessarily suitable for ministry. Yet a man who failed to fulfill even one of the requirements stated in the catalogue had to be turned away. Therefore a man who was not completely "above reproach" (1 Tim 3:2; Tit 1:6) could not be admitted. Candidates were not required to show proof that they were married, had children, and so on. Nevertheless—and now comes a crucial impediment to orders—if they had been married at least a second time, they could not be ordained. Candidates for orders could be at most the husband of one wife; that means that they were not allowed to have a second or a third wife. And so it was with all the conditions that proved to be canonically significant criteria: notorious drunkenness, violence, and so on, excluded a man from orders.

59–63 (CSEL 82, 3, 265, 588–268, 651); Siricius, *Epistulae* 10, 8 (PL 13, 1187AB). Similarly, the criteria in 1 Tim 5:3–16 apply to the time before widows were enrolled by the Church.

[50] C. Richert, *Die Anfänge der Irregularitäten bis zum ersten Allgemeinen Konzil von Nicäa,* StrThS 4, 3 (Freiburg, 1901), 7–13.

[51] We may suppose that candidates for the priesthood and the episcopacy were laymen also. There is no indication of a *cursus honorum*.

With this we have arrived at an important conclusion: married men were not the only possible candidates for holy orders. The pastoral letters do not express the requirement that clerics be married. At first glance it may seem so. The reason for that, however, is that monogamy is mentioned at the beginning of the criteria for excluding a candidate from the episcopacy and the priesthood (1 Tim 3:2; Tit 1:6). This might cause one to think that the passages concern married clerics exclusively and that every further requirement pertains to them alone. But we are dealing with a questionnaire, whereby the aspirant is to be examined with respect to each requirement separately. The pastoral letters collect and catalogue rather unsystematically all the irregularities that could be at issue for all possible aspirants. Among the candidates, then, there could very well have been, besides married men, virgins and widowers also. The criteria for exclusion were just as applicable to them; for instance, if they were drunkards or newly baptized, then they should not be ordained. To be sure, what is today the rare exception was customary in the early Church: married deacons, priests, and bishops. But it would be erroneous to assume that originally all holders of ecclesiastical office were married and only later did an unmarried clergy exist as well. On the contrary, the pastoral letters confirm what is substantiated by other sources, that the clergy were always recruited from two groups: married and unmarried men.

In principle, then, all adult males could be considered as candidates for holy orders. Furthermore age made practically no difference in one's eligibility. The mention of middle-aged men who had stood the test (that is, of married life—men referred to today as *viri probati*) has led in this regard to misinterpretations. For it does not say that the married candidate had to have children at all, much less older children. But if a candidate did have children and was said to have made a bad reputation for himself in this respect, then he could not be ordained. Young candidates were considered just the same as older ones. As a rule the older candidates would have been the married ones, while the unmarried candidates could have been younger. Even Timothy himself appears to have been still at a youthful age (1 Tim 4:12; 2 Tim 2:22).

Monogamy for the sake of continence. The conditions of the catalogue, therefore, were meant to be taken seriously; we are dealing with canonical criteria for excluding unsuitable candidates from holy orders. Let us return now to the decisive statement about monogamy. A candidate who has already been married a second time or more should not be ordained. This very likely constituted a major criterion in the selection of candidates.[52] Ignace de la Potterie has adduced spiritual reasons for this based on a kind of ecclesiological symbolism: By his monogamy the minister must represent the exclusive spousal relationship between Christ and his Church. Of course, this thesis can hardly be proved, even though it has the advantage of a connection with the Pauline tradition (2 Cor 11:2). To find the reason for the monogamy criterion, however, we must take another tack, which brings us back to our subject: clerical continence.

Generally speaking, a second marriage was not forbidden to Christians (1 Tim 5:14). Why, then, was there such a categorical prohibition in the case of candidates for orders, behind which there was obviously concealed a particular duty associated with a state in life, a condition both for acceptance into the clergy and also for inclusion on the Church's roll of widows?[53] Why should Timothy and Titus reject candidates for orders who had already been married a second time? One might think that this was to obviate eventual claims for care and support originating in earlier marriages. But that would not have been along the same lines as the other conditions, which looked to the personal capabilities of the candidates. Or should ministers have been married only once before ordination, whereas after ordination they were completely free to enter into a second or a third marriage? But that would have been completely arbitrary.

The real meaning of the "unius uxoris vir" and of the condemnation of remarriage expressed therein probably lies elsewhere. To this purpose one must refer to the seventh chapter of the First Letter to the Corinthians. In doing so we have recourse to a text that demonstrably stands in a tradition closely connected to the pastoral letters[54] and hence is best suited for clarifying difficult passages in the pastoral letters. Let us put into perspective then what Paul is saying about marriage. He values it as a cure for sexual appetite, as a *remedium concupiscentiae* (1 Cor 7:2). That is to say: persons who are looking for sexual fulfillment must do so within marriage, since marriage is the only le-

---

[52] Cf. Trummer, "Einehe", 476f.

[53] Potterie, "Mari", 636f. "Normal" widows may remarry (1 Tim 5:11), but for the "real" widows on the Church's roll this is categorically forbidden (1 Tim 5:9); cf. Oberlinner, *Pastoralbriefe*, 120f.; erroneously interpreted by Trummer, "Einehe", 480.

[54] According to J. Roloff, *Der erste Brief an Timotheus*, EKK 15 (Zurich and Neukirchen-Vluyn, 1988), 39f., 1 Timothy is dependent mainly on Romans and 1 Corinthians.

gitimate place for sexual activity. Once someone is widowed, in Paul's opinion, he normally does not enter into another marriage. For in the course of his married life his sexual needs have been put to rest. If he does enter another marriage, though, then the only reason Paul can see for that is that he still cannot live continently (οὐκ ἐγκρατεύονται) (1 Cor 7:8f., 39f.). Therefore he must want to keep having children (cf. 1 Tim 5:14).

For the moment let us disregard the fact that naturally there can be other reasons entirely for entering a second marriage, for instance, the care of children, and so on. Paul does not see that; he focuses stubbornly on the question of continence. Already in pagan antiquity remarriage bore the stigma of incontinence.[55] One may share this view or not: what is essential is that the First Letter to Timothy accepts this Pauline judgment about remarriage. This is evident in the case of the widows: frequently younger widows marry again because they cannot live continently. Those widows who want to take a vow of widowhood, therefore, must be over sixty years old and married only once. That is to say, they should already be tested with respect to continence, so that they will not be having any more ideas about marriage (1 Tim 5:9–12).[56] Hence, marrying a second time is, for the pastoral letters also, tantamount to being unable to live continently. Indeed, Paul recommends forgoing remarriage for everyone, but he does not impose such a rule, precisely because not everyone can live continently.

Though such a one-sided view of remarriage may well be problematic, the only thing that really matters for our subject is the conclusion that we can draw from it concerning the clerical discipline of the pastoral letters. They likewise presuppose that a candidate for orders who is living in a second marriage cannot live continently. He has, so to speak, not passed the continence test during his time as a widower.[57] A notorious inability to be continent, then, excludes the married candi-

---

[55] Kötting, *Beurteilung*, 128; idem, " 'Univira' in Inschriften", in W. den Boer et al., eds., *Romanitas et Christianitas: Festschrift J. H. Waszink* (Amsterdam and London, 1973), 195–206.

[56] R. Cholij, *Clerical Celibacy in East and West* (Herefordshire, 1989), 19f.

[57] This important connection had already been recognized in various studies: Richert, *Anfänge*, 66–72; H. Deen, *Le Célibat des prêtres dans les premiers siècles de l'église* (Paris, 1969), 32–34; A. M. Stickler, "Tratti salienti nella storia del celibato", SacDo 60 (1970): 585–620 at 588f. (cf. idem, *The Case for Clerical Celibacy: Its Historical Development and Theological Foundations* (San Francisco, 1995), 91). E. Vacandard, "Célibat ecclésiastique", in DThC 2, 2 (1932), 2070 rejects this view. My essay "*Grundlagen*" was written before I had come across these contributions.

date from orders. Yet one cannot just stop there, as though this lack of continence would merely be an unseemly flaw in a minister; as though a second marriage in those days would simply have been considered inappropriate. On the contrary, there is at bottom more to it. Obviously it was expected that married ministers would practice sexual continence.

The relation of the "unius uxoris vir" to continence is in fact essential, as is demonstrated by the above-mentioned position of the Letter to Timothy with regard to the "unius viri uxor" of widows (1 Tim 5:9–12). This also invalidates the objection that the "unius uxoris vir", understood as prohibiting second marriages, is not within the framework of the other criteria for suitability, inasmuch as a remarriage is thought to be a purely private matter having no relation to the demands of pastoral work.[58] In reality a purely formal prohibition of second marriages would scarcely be intelligible. But the proposed interpretation is able to demonstrate that behind the prohibition stands a concrete perspective as to the life-style that is professionally appropriate for married ministers.

But how are we to envisage that concretely? Was continence expected of the married candidates starting on the day of their ordination or only when their wives had died? The latter case would follow from the prohibition against remarriage after the death of the spouse. That can hardly be what is meant, because that would fail to explain why the minister is explicitly permitted only one wife. It would not make much sense, either, to expect before ordination a capability to live continently that would only become pertinent ten or possibly twenty years later, at the death of the wife. Therefore we can assume that the pastoral letters expect perfect continence from the candidates starting on the day of their ordination. Finally, behind the "unius uxoris vir" stands the thought: If someone as a widower believed himself unable to resist sexual desire and therefore remarried, how would he ever be able to practice together with his wife this *total* abstinence, which a widower without a spouse must also practice?

This was, therefore, not simply a matter of periodic continence, for instance at times appointed for the Divine Liturgy. Paul does in fact know of this (1 Cor 7:5). But it was precisely a concession to married people who could not live continently. The pastoral letters presuppose

---

[58] Audet, *Mariage*, 93.

that ministers were to meet more stringent requirements than were usual for the laity, in that a second marriage was allowed for the latter (1 Cor 7:8f.) but not for the former. This question of impediments to orders was concerned above all with canonically definable characteristics. Periodic continence, though, was not a tangible criterion for disciplinary law. On the other hand, it was assumed *bona fide* that a minister lived continently without exception as long as he begot no children. Only when such a public event occurred was disciplinary action seen as necessary.

Now it might still be objected: Why do the pastoral letters not declare explicitly, as is later on the case at the Spanish Synod of Elvira, "A married cleric must live continently" or "A married cleric must not beget any more children"? The answer has already been given: We are dealing here with criteria for excluding men from orders. Therefore it can only be a question of indications already present before ordination that the married candidate would not be able to live continently after ordination. A candidate in a first marriage did not have to live continently while still a layman. He could be admitted to holy orders, even if he had begotten children, because it was assumed *prima facie* that he was capable of continence.[59]

After ordination a cleric is not allowed to marry again. Having reached this point in our argument, we can now begin to draw conclusions with regard to a general precept of continence for ministers after their ordination. For if continence was required of the married aspirant after ordination, that would also apply to the widowed and virginal candidates. The fact that it is not explicitly stated: "A virginal or widowed minister must live continently" can again be explained by noting that the catalogues for evaluating the suitability of candidates consisted of criteria for excluding men from orders. But single or virginal candidates obviously lived continently (unless the contrary was proved).

After ordination a widowed minister was no longer permitted to marry. For if a second or a third marriage excluded one from orders, then it could not be allowed after ordination. To that extent there was a prohibition against second marriages. On the basis of the previous

---

[59] Before ordination a decent and in this sense chaste way of life is in general demanded: σώφρων (1 Tim 3:2; Tit 1:8, in the sense of sexual self-control, see U. Luck, "σώφρων", in ThWNT 7 [1964], 1094–1102), ὅσιος (καὶ) ἐγκρατής (Tit 1:8, cf. 1 Cor 7:9; *The Shepherd of Hermas* 32, 3. Epiphanius, *Panarion lxxx haeresium* 59, 4, 1 [GCS Epiph. 2², 367, 9f.] relates ἐγκρατής [Tit 1:8] to 1 Tim 3:2).

considerations, one has to assume a prohibition of marriage from the day of ordination for someone ordained while a virgin as well. For if marital relations were not permitted [to men in orders], then that was all the more reason to prohibit candidates for orders from marrying, since they would never be able to consummate their marriage.[60] Furthermore, since 1 Corinthians 7:8f. is behind the second-marriage criterion, it is likely that the entire text was made binding upon those who held office. And that passage speaks not only of widows but also in the same sentence of the unmarried: they must not marry.

Thus the pastoral letters presuppose a discipline that demanded continence of every minister from the day of his ordination. Since the widows officially enrolled by the Church made a promise not to remarry when they were admitted (1 Tim 5:16),[61] we cannot rule out the possibility that such an oath of continence was also the practice upon admission to the clerical state. This conjecture is all the more probable when it is considered that the continence of a married minister necessarily involved the wife also and that she of course would have had to declare her consent.

Now it has been said that "unius uxoris vir" cannot signify a preference for continence within marriage and the renunciation of remarriage because the pastoral letters defend marriage (1 Tim 4:3f.)[62] in their clash with Gnosticism and its disdain for the body. Nevertheless, the pastoral letters purely and simply warn against radical asceticism. It is true that they view marriage positively as being completely integrated into the pastoral service of the Church.[63] That, however, by no means precludes continence on the part of candidates for orders who, indeed, are already older and have experienced marriage. Paul opposes Gnostic tendencies chiefly in the seventh chapter of the First Letter to the Corinthians[64] and thus sees his conciliatory judgment of sexuality as an adequate answer to a certain Encratism. A general affirmation

---

[60] Cf. Cholij, *Celibacy*, 36f. on the Council of Elvira, canon 33.

[61] Trummer, "Einehe", 480 n. 1; Oberlinner, *Pastoralbriefe*, 120f. Cf. Tertullian, *De Monogamia*, 13, 1 (CCL 2, 1248, 2–10).

[62] Trummer, "Einehe", 477–79; J. Rohde, *Urchristliche und frühkatholische Ämter: Eine Untersuchung zur frühchristl. Amtsentwicklung im Neuen Testament und bei den apostolischen Vätern*, ThA 33 (Berlin, 1976), 92.

[63] Audet, *Mariage*, 90f.

[64] W. Schrage, *Der erste Brief an die Korinther*, EKK 7, 2 (Dusseldorf and Neukirchen-Vluyn, 1995), 54f.

of marriage in the pastoral letters and the requirement that ministers conduct their marriages continently are by no means mutually exclusive and are completely in keeping with an anti-Gnostic reception of Pauline thought. This is precisely the middle way followed by Clement of Alexandria, too, in the third book of his *Stromata* (see below, pp. 65–66).

There is much, therefore, in favor of the view that the pastoral letters are the first evidence we have for that same discipline of continence that we then find unequivocally in the fourth century. In fact the pastoral letters are best understood against the background of a discipline whereby bishops, priests, and deacons, whether married or unmarried, are forbidden to contract any (further) marriage and are required henceforth to practice continence; otherwise the condition about one marriage only would be hanging in the air and would make no sense at all. With classical brevity Pope Siricius reduced it to a formula: the "unius uxoris vir" of the pastoral letters is intended "propter continentiam futuram", that is, "for the sake of future continence" (see below pp. 242–43). Moreover, if the pastoral letters are in fact to be dated before the year 68 on the basis of the fragments from cave 7 at Qumran, and not around the year 100 as has been assumed until now,[65] then the thesis of an apostolic origin for continence celibacy gains in importance.

b. The Profile of the Married Minister

According to what has been said thus far, the pastoral letters knew of a special clerical discipline. For such an early period that is utterly astonishing. Very early on it was a matter of great concern for the Church, at least in Asia Minor, to select her leaders according to specific criteria and, in doing so, to leave nothing to chance. The essential point was the ability to practice continence. On this subject the pastoral letters refer to the seventh chapter of the First Letter to the Corinthians. Here lies the basis for the legitimacy of clerical continence. But have the pastoral letters gone to the right address in the first place? Paul is not speaking of ministers at all! Is it not a mistake to look for support to Paul, the skeptic about marriage?

---

[65] C. P. Thiede, *Die älteste Evangelien-Handschrift? Ein Qumran-Fragment wird entschlüsselt,* 4th ed. (Wuppertal, 1994), 58–61; J. A. T. Robinson, *Redating the New Testament* (London: SCM Press, 1976), 76–94.

In fact there are several contrasts between Paul and the pastoral letters, although both stand in the same line of tradition. First: Paul clearly recommends celibacy in his Letter to the Corinthians, while the pastoral letters know of married ministers. Second: the categorical prohibition of remarriage for ministers is contradicted by Paul, who merely *advises against* a second marriage (1 Cor 7:8f., 39f.). And third: Paul takes a very skeptical attitude toward complete sexual abstinence within marriage (1 Cor 7:1–7).[66] Nevertheless we must not assume that the pastoral letters wish to interpret Paul in a way contrary to his own intentions. Indeed, they place themselves explicitly under his authority and owe their direct relationship with Paul to the actual disciples of Paul, perhaps even to the living traditions of the community founded by Paul.[67] The pastoral letters and the letters to the Corinthians, therefore, cannot simply be played off against each other, especially since the authentic Timothy and Titus carried out important missions for Paul in Corinth (1 Cor 4:17, 16:10f.; 2 Cor 8:6, 23). How then can these two lines of argument be brought together?

Paul is addressing all Christians in his letters to the Corinthians; the pastoral letters are written to ministers only. That alone explains why there can be discrepancies between the two, yet without contradictions. If Paul wrote only in general terms to the Corinthians without any intention of outlining an ethics for the clerical state, then we can draw the following conclusions: Precisely because he is speaking only in general terms to the community in Corinth, he neglects the special rules for particular professions. He does not deny that they exist, though, since there may have been such rules for the apostles at the very least. Paul's discourses on marriage and sexuality have just as much validity for ministers as for lay persons, whereas the pastoral letters deal exclusively with the marriage of clerics. Thus we can start with the assumption that in the pastoral letters we find the authentic clerical discipline of the early Church, even if the connections with the concrete circumstances of the individual Pauline communities can no longer be elucidated.

Let us take for example marital continence. Paul allows it only during the appointed times of prayer, which surely include, besides Sun-

---

[66] H.-J. Vogels, *Priester dürfen heiraten: Biblische, geschichtliche und rechtliche Gründe gegen den Pflichtzölibat* (Bonn, 1992), 42.

[67] N. Brox, *Die Pastoralbriefe*, 4th ed., RNT 7, 2 (Leipzig, 1975), 68.

days, fast days as well (1 Cor 7:5). Here he is addressing the rank and file married people, who were not governed by any particular religious duty. They should not undertake more ascetic practices than they can bear. But then the final clause: "I say this by way of concession, not of command. I wish that all were as I myself am [that is, continent/unmarried]" (1 Cor 7:6f.), must have been understood also as a challenge to loftier accomplishments. Along the same lines we find the remark, "[F]rom now on, let those who have wives live as though they had none" (1 Cor 7:29). The pastoral letters, now, try to do justice both to the urgent wish of Paul and also to his leniency, in that they require unconditional continence only of ministers. But then there would have to be some guarantee—and because of Paul's pastoral responsibility this was a matter of great importance to him —that the married people really were capable of living continently. Therefore only a man who has beforehand declared himself ready to live continently is to be ordained. There must be no known factor that would cause one to doubt his ability to do so.

Although Paul makes propaganda for celibacy, there were still married ministers. This is probably because the Church was establishing herself and was gradually becoming indigenous. The celibate missionary apostle diminished in importance, and in his place married bishops, priests, and deacons assumed positions of responsibility. Naturally, then, one has to wonder how that can be reconciled: Paul would like celibacy so as to avoid worries about the οἶκος, and the pastoral letters advertise exactly the opposite, namely, the bishop, the priest, and the deacon as master of the house in the fullest sense, as a tried and true head of a household.[68] Even John Chrysostom, the great fourth-century expert on and admirer of Paul, sensed this contradiction.[69]

The οἶκος of antiquity designated a comprehensive social structure, a self-sufficient association held together by ties of property, business, and personal relationship. It constituted nothing short of the infrastructure of the developing Church,[70] and this was so already in Paul's day. The local churches were recruited from the converted οἶκοι (house-

---

[68] Cf. H.-J. Klauck, *Hausgemeinde und Hauskirche im frühen Christentum* (Stuttgart, 1981), 66–68.

[69] John Chrysostom, *Hom.* 10, 1 in 1 Tim. 3:1–4 (PG 62, 548f.). See below, p. 174 [Chrysostom].

[70] M. Gielen, *Tradition und Theologie neutestamentlicher Haustafelethik: Ein Beitrag zur Frage einer christl. Auseinandersetzung mit gesellschaftl. Normen*, BBB 75 (Frankfurt, 1990), 68–103.

holds). These οἶκοι had their validity, even for Paul. With his discourse in the seventh chapter of the First Letter to the Corinthians he does not mean to destroy or replace them. Even those who decided to be celibate remained within the framework of the οἶκος; indeed, it supported and cared for them in their way of life. The οἶκος, therefore, made living as a celibate possible in the first place.

To that extent the οἶκος-ecclesiology of the pastoral letters was not a break with the Pauline tradition. Now many οἶκοι (households) joined to form a local church. At the head of it stood the bishop.[71] And here, in a certain way, Paul's ideal of supraregional apostolic life was combined with the leadership position of the local church. For the bishop was not supposed to lead the church as the master of his own house but rather as the head of God's house. The duties of the bishop extended far beyond his own household. Good management of his own house only furnished a prerequisite for leading the greater house of God. Care for one's own had now in fact to take second place to care for the household of the Church.

Therefore it was by no means misguided to expect of a bishop that he, without giving up his station in life, nevertheless for the sake of his new ministry would set aside the care of his own οἶκος and leave the responsibility to the lady of the house (domina) or to the steward, in order to devote himself entirely to the interests of the local church. That being the case, it was certainly not unthinkable for a woman to be in charge now of managing the household; from the New Testament we know of houses evidently headed by women.[72] For the bishop, priest, and deacon, setting aside the care of one's own οἶκος manifested itself then in another essential way: in the decision not to beget any more children. And indeed, this alone gave the wife, too, the necessary freedom of action to carry out her more extensive duties of supervision in the οἶκος.

---

[71] Laub, "Hintergrund", 262–68; Schöllgen, "Hausgemeinden", 77–80; Gielen, Tradition, 86–94.

[72] Laub, "Hintergrund", 256, n. 39 (1 Cor 1:11; Acts 16:14f.); G. Scharffenorth and K. Thraede, "Freunde in Christus werden . . .": Die Beziehung von Mann und Frau als Frage an Theologie und Kirche (Gelnhausen, 1977), 98f. See also Ignatius, Epistula ad Smyrnenses 13, 2; Polycarp, Epistula ad Philippos 8, 2; and K. Thraede, "Frau", in RAC 8 (1972), 197–269 at 230. Probably the martyr Perpetua, too, was the head of her household; Brown, Keuschheit, 88f. See also the widows, Brown, Keuschheit, 165.

5. Summary

Jesus lived what he proclaimed. That is precisely what made his teaching convincing and trustworthy. That is also what makes his celibacy so interesting. Jesus and his associates led a life of ceaseless journeying on the roads of Palestine. Jesus lived as a celibate and never thought of marrying, for which he was rebuked as a eunuch (Mt 19:12). His disciples, too, had to be prepared for such insults. Many of them, for example Peter, were married. But even for these there was no question of continuing their former married way of life. They left their wives back home. There they were cared for by the extended family, so that their husbands could follow Jesus unreservedly.

Thus every member of the inner circle of Jesus' disciples had to practice complete sexual self-denial "for the sake of the kingdom", and that meant not only the virginal disciples, but also those who were married or widowed. During the time of the journeys and the proclamation of the kingdom of God there was no question about this. But even the crisis of Good Friday and Easter would have changed nothing essential in this option: once a eunuch, always a eunuch. There were new missionary tasks that justified an alternative life-style even after Easter.

Many apostles, to be sure, availed themselves of the possibility of taking with them, as assistants in their travels, women supported by the local churches (1 Cor 9:5). Jesus himself was accompanied by women who served him and his disciples (Lk 8:1-3). There is really no evidence for, and much against, the hypothesis that the apostles had sexual relations with the aforementioned women in their company, assuming they were their wives, and that they continued to have children. So the apostles were quite able to live up to the teaching of Jesus about the eunuchs for the sake of the kingdom of heaven, even if they had their wives in their company, but in that case they had to practice continence within marriage. To be an apostle meant to remain celibate, to leave behind house and home, or to live continently together with one's wife, if she continued to be nearby. This can be termed apostolic continence celibacy. In this there was no break between the periods before and after Easter and also no difference between the Twelve and Paul.

It is not very likely that apostolic continence celibacy was discontinued with the death of the apostles. The transition of leadership from the apostles to the bishops, priests, and deacons allowed the apostolic way of life (*vita apostolica*) to continue in existence as well. The pastoral letters give evidence of such a changing of the guard: apostolic continence celibacy became the continence of the ecclesiastical office-holders. At least in Asia Minor this process was completed during the period between A.D. 50 and 100. There were celibate, widowed, and married ministers. But the married candidates had to live in perfect continence with their wives from the day of ordination on. Moreover, they could not marry again.

All this would appear at least to follow from the requirement in the pastoral letters that aspirants to the diaconate, the priesthood, and the episcopacy must, if married, be living in a first marriage (1 Tim 3:2, 12; Tit 1:6). For a candidate who had already contracted marriage a second time was, according to the Pauline interpretation, incapable of living continently (1 Cor 7:8f.). It is clear that married men in a second marriage were excluded from orders because perfect continence was generally demanded of a minister. This continence requirement applied to the married candidate for orders just as it did to the virginal or widowed candidate. A prevailing plurality of states in life (single, widowed, or married) was accompanied at the same time by a uniformity of life-style (complete sexual continence).

With a high degree of probability, then, the thesis recently advocated by Christian Cochini is correct: Already in the time of the apostles, or at the very least since the late New Testament period, a kind of obligation existed (and not merely an option) for ministers to practice lasting sexual continence—in short, a kind of celibacy law. Mere good intentions could not have provided the foundation for an institution, nor would they account for the unanimity that can be observed in the following centuries.[73] The prevailing opinion—that the New Testament is devoid of any evidence for a discipline of celibacy and even argues against it—can therefore scarcely withstand in-depth and meticulous scrutiny.[74]

---

[73] Kruse, "Eheverzicht", 113.

[74] Cf. L. Scheffczyk, "Der Zölibat als Formkraft priesterlicher Existenz", in T. Maas-Ewerd, ed., *Kleriker: Im Dienste Gottes für die Menschen: Festschrift zum 75jährigen Bestehen des Klerusverbandes und des Klerusblattes in Bayern und der Pfalz 1920–1995* (Munich, 1995), 61–72 at 61 n. 1.

III. Clerical Continence from
the Second Century until 220

An obligation for ecclesiastical officeholders to practice continence appears for the first time in the pastoral letters, albeit attested to only indirectly by the prohibition of digamy found therein. All in all we have only scant information about Christian life in these early times. That remains the case for the following period as well. The second century is, so to speak, the *saeculum obscurum* [dark age] of clerical discipline, "dark" in the sense of a history hidden in the obscurity of the past. This is particularly regrettable. For during this period was completed the transition from the dispersal of the apostles on their missionary journeys to the time of an inculturation of the new faith in the entire Mediterranean region and even beyond.

1. The *Saeculum Obscurum* of Clerical Continence

The second century comprises the time between the pastoral letters and Clement of Alexandria and Tertullian of Carthage. A decisive phase of ecclesiastical self-discovery and organization fell within this period, during which clerical ministry took on a central role.

a. Clerical Ministry Undergoes a Uniform Development

We have reason to assume the existence of a continence discipline for ministers in the second century as well. General considerations lead us to this conclusion. Between the pastoral letters and the next applicable pieces of information lie a hundred years. This was the time of the apostolic fathers and the early Christian apologists. These writers, indeed, made no useful references to such a discipline. In any case, however, ecclesiastical ministry was bound up with a legal structure and could not be fashioned arbitrarily. Although the second century marks a very early period of the Church's history, it was still not true that everyone did as he pleased. The pastoral letters already have given evidence of an advanced stage in a process of regularizing the Church's structure.[1] In other words: there was a Church law, which was connected precisely with the practical formation of the clerical ministry. This development is fully defined in the writings of the apologists. Hence there is nothing that in principle would contradict the existence of a supraregional, largely uniform discipline of continence.

Moreover the early Christians by no means saw marriage as such a *non plus ultra* [an ultimate good] that the idea of refraining from marriage might not even have occurred to them. On the contrary: the apologists give very clear indications of how highly continence was prized as an ideal during that period.[2] Christians then concentrated purposefully on sexual restraint, even in marriage; above it all the mountaintop of total abstinence looms large.[3]

Therefore one must not overvalue the silence of the apologists about clerical continence. Indeed, they say very little at all about clerical ministry, although by their time it was already fully developed. That is simply due to the fact that the large majority of their writings are no longer in existence today. One example will make clear how careful one must be in drawing conclusions about this period. Most of the writings of the apologist Justin Martyr (d. 165) have been lost. But "by chance" he expresses in detail his views about the Christian worship service in his *Apology*, which has been preserved. Here he speaks about the Eucharist as a sacrifice and about the Real Presence of the Lord's Body. Had the *Apology* been lost as well, then talking about the Eucharist as a sacrifice and the Real Presence of Christ would be considered today a theological development from a much later time.

Similarly it would be rash to maintain that at the time of the apologists there "could not yet have been" an obligation for ministers to practice continence. We must at the very least take such a discipline into account, chiefly on the basis of the following reflection. The expansion of the early Church from Jerusalem into the whole world is

---

[1] H. von Campenhausen, *Kirchliches Amt und geistliche Vollmacht in den ersten drei Jahrhunderten*, 2d ed., BHTh 14 (Tübingen, 1963), 116–29.

[2] Justin Martyr, I *Apologia* 15, 1–8; 14, 2; Aristides, *Apologia* 15, 4–6; Athenagoras, *Supplicatio pro Christianis* 33; Minucius Felix, *Octavius* 31, 5. H. Kruse, "Eheverzicht im Neuen Testament und in der Frühkirche", FKTh 1 (1985): 113f.

[3] P. Brown, *Die Keuschheit der Engel: Sexuelle Entsagung, Askese und Körperlichkeit am Anfang des Christentums* (Munich, Vienna, 1991), 75; A. von Harnack, *Die Mission und Ausbreitung des Christentums in den ersten drei Jahrhunderten*, 4th ed. (Leipzig, 1924), 233 n. 1.

often pictured as a completely uncoordinated business. Different conditions found in various localities supposedly led in each case to different decisions as to how the Church should be organized. Local churches with quite varied structures are said to have resulted, each with a distinctive liturgy and discipline, if not even doctrine.

There is some truth and some error to this view. Precisely with respect to ecclesiastical ministry, however, one cannot speak of an arbitrary plurality and variety. One might be able to say that the official functions as we know them today: bishop—priest—deacon, were not present everywhere from the earliest beginnings. But it is still surprising that the threefold structure of ecclesiastical ministry had gained acceptance as early as the second century throughout the universal Church, without encountering any resistance worth mentioning.[4] Because our source materials are scarce we can no longer trace the particulars of this sweeping development. But in any case it was possible to view the threefold structure of ecclesiastical ministry, whether correctly or not, as being authenticated in the New Testament writings, primarily in the pastoral letters: they speak of bishops, priests, and deacons. It is safe to suppose that the pastoral letters, by their wide circulation,[5] contributed in no small measure to the uniform development of the threefold ministry in the entire Church.

The uniform development of ecclesiastical ministry in the second century actually comes as no surprise. It was connected with the early Church's strong awareness of her unity. The intention was not to be just some religious association, but rather to be the one Church of the apostles. This consciousness guided an ever-increasing unification of the Christian way of life in the transition from the postapostolic period to the so-called "early Catholic" era. "The basic presupposition of the process on which all were in principle agreed was the idea that since

---

[4] H. Chadwick, *The Early Church* (Grand Rapids, Mich.: Wm. B. Eerdmans, 1967; Penguin ed. 1968), 51; T. Kramm, "Amt", in RAC.S 1 (1986), 350–401 at 391f.

[5] That the distribution of the pastoral letters can be proved unmistakably only in the late second century is not evidence to the contrary; this is because such proofs involving New Testament writings are notoriously difficult for second-century literature in general, and the strict citation of apostolic writings becomes customary only with the establishment of a New Testament canon. The pastoral letters are included in the canon for the sole reason that they had long been circulated throughout the entire Church.

the Church is one, its beliefs and practices has to be unified."[6] It was precisely the ecclesiastical ministry that should be uniform.

At the same time, necessarily, a distinctive and unified clerical discipline also developed. For a ministry does not develop in the abstract but rather in a concrete form suited to the service rendered—particularly since the offices mentioned in the pastoral letters were bound up with a very detailed list of requirements. Let us assume, then, that the pastoral letters really expected continence of all ministers, whether married or not. This discipline, consequently, had to be replicated almost automatically throughout the entire Church. In antiquity a particular profession or position was always associated with a particular way of life as well, which one had to accept without any questions. We must imagine that it was similar with ecclesiastical ministry already in the early Church. It was one of the most highly qualified professions of that era, as was likewise the case for the pagan priests. Its official character was founded in large measure precisely on the strict norms governing the minister's way of life. And among those in all likelihood was the obligation to practice complete sexual continence.

b. The Early Influence of Movements Hostile to the Body

One cannot treat the subject of clerical continence without considering carefully the thesis that it was the product of early tendencies hostile to the body. Though scholars may assign various dates for the emergence of a discipline of continence for the clergy, they still quite often posit a connection with a phenomenon that is termed Encratism, a collective name for movements hostile to the body and to marriage, which have made their presence known since the second century in different regions with varying degrees of intensity. One product of such movements is said to be the continence discipline for clerics.[7] This theory is correct only to the extent that the clerical discipline is found in the context of late antiquity, which had a great esteem for sexual asceticism, and is related to the widely held belief of the Church that continence had a higher value than marriage. Beyond that, however, a

---

[6] Chadwick, *The Early Church*, 51.

[7] K. Müller, "Die Forderung der Ehelosigkeit für alle Getauften in der alten Kirche", in *Aus der akademischen Arbeit: Vorträge und Aufsätze* (Tübingen, 1930), 63–79 at 79.

direct influence of Encratite views on the clergy's way of life cannot be proved.

There were, to be sure, radically ascetical movements in the Church from the very beginning, but not in every place. Encratism was found as a substantial force only in Asia Minor and Syria. There is from the second and third centuries a copious literature on this subject exhibiting a strong ascetical tendency.[8] The apocryphal acts of the apostles propagate the ideal of continence and virginity, though that is not sufficient reason to classify them collectively as being heretical. We are certainly not dealing with strictly secular literature, but neither are these the Church's didactic writings.[9] Clerics do not appear in the apocryphal works; what prevails instead is an asceticism of women and laypeople.[10]

Now of course the pastoral letters originated in Asia Minor. Does that mean that the clerical continence presupposed by the letters necessarily has to be traced back to the influence of Encratite movements? This can be ruled out, for the pastoral letters testify to a process of discerning what was truly Catholic, whereby heretical distortions were declared to be beyond the pale. Particularly in Asia Minor a consciousness of having the true faith was especially pronounced due to the confrontation with numerous innovations. The two orthodox theologians Justin and Irenaeus testify to this.[11] And it is precisely the pastoral letters that defend marriage against those who disdain the body (1 Tim 4:3).[12] Thus clerical continence, insofar as it may be traced back to the pastoral letters, cannot justifiably be viewed as the product of Encratism. Ecclesiastical ministry underwent its distinctive practical de-

---

[8] B. Lohse, *Askese und Mönchtum in der Antike und in der Alten Kirche*, RKAM 1 (Munich and Vienna, 1969), 148–59; K. Niederwimmer, *Askese und Mysterium: Über Ehe, Ehescheidung und Eheverzicht in den Anfängen des christl. Glaubens*, FRLANT 113 (Göttingen, 1975), 180–86.

[9] Cf. H. Chadwick, "Enkrateia", in RAC 5 (1962), 354f.

[10] Cf. Brown, *Keuschheit*, 169–74.

[11] It is generally assumed that Justin, who was born in Palestine, studied in Ephesus.

[12] Here it is particularly difficult to establish a relation between clerical continence and Encratite tendencies, inasmuch as the pastoral letters are supposed to relate the affirmation of marriage and an optimism about creation with the eucharistic (μετὰ εὐχαριστίας 1 Tim 4:3f.) form of worship, which is at the same time sacerdotal (1 Tim 4:4f.). K. Berger, *Theologie geschichte des Urchristentums: Theologie des Neuen Testaments* (Tübingen and Basel, 1994), 528; to the contrary, L. Oberlinner, *Die Pastoralbriefe*, HThK 11, 2, 1 (Freiburg, 1994), 184. Cf. Clement of Alexandria, *Stromata* 3, 12, 85, 1 (GCS Clem. Alex. 2⁴, 235, 7–15). For Justin, too, the Eucharist is a thanksgiving for the creation of the world (*Dialogus* 41, 1; 1 *Apologia* 13, 2).

velopment precisely in that process of theological clarification which was already driving back the ascetical enthusiasts.

Rome, the center of the orthodox movement of the second century, clearly rejected Encratite demands. On the other hand, evidence from the region of Syria for the first centuries indicates that perfect continence was required of all Christians there and that admission to baptism was made dependent upon such a discipline. That led consequently to the dissolution of existing marriages. Marcion, who was excommunicated in the year 144 in Rome, withheld baptism from married catechumens until such time as they had given up sexual intercourse.[13] The schismatic church that he set into motion would gain a foothold particularly in Syria. Tatian, Justin's pupil in Rome, would be excommunicated only three decades after Marcion on account of his ethical principles.[14] Probably under the influence of Marcion's Encratite views, he demanded that married people renounce sexual relations. It is no coincidence that in the year 172 he went East to the region of Syria, while he was considered heretical in the West.[15]

Encratite movements strengthened the Church by challenging her to develop a prudent and balanced judgment of the body. Thanks to this very conflict with such tendencies, which can already be noted in the pastoral letters, the early Church attained a deeper insight into the coherence of her ethical principles. What was already ascetical practice now needed to be defined more clearly over against erroneous developments. The West was more sober and realistic than the East; only what was possible was demanded, and extremism found no favor. Hence neither can it be said either that the West introduced a discipline of continence for clerics in order to keep pace with the lofty ascetical ideal of the East. The severe asceticism of the Syrians was no example for the West. On the contrary, the influence went in precisely the opposite direction: ever since the fourth century the discipline of

---

[13] Tertullian, *Adversus Marcionem* 1, 29, 1 (CCL 1, 472, 20–473, 22): "Non tingitur apud illum caro, nisi uirgo, nisi uidua, nisi caeleps, nisi diuortio baptisma mercata, quasi non etiam spadonibus ex nuptiis nata." Ibid., 4, 34, 5 (636, 13–17): "Aut si omnino [non] negas permitti diuortium a Christo, quomodo tu nuptias dirimis, nec coniungens marem et feminam nec alibi coniunctos ad sacramentum baptismatis et eucharistiae admittens, nisi inter se coniurauerint aduersus fructum nuptiarum, ut aduersus ipsum creatorem?"

[14] Chadwick, "Enkrateia", 353.

[15] Irenaeus, *Adversus haereses* 1, 28, 1 (SC 264, 354, 8–356, 17). A. Vööbus, *Celibacy: A Requirement for Admission to Baptism in the Early Syrian Church* (Stockholm, 1951), 16–20.

the Syrian Church with regard to continence has adapted itself to the Western practice.[16]

Theology in the West recognized that Platonism, wrongly understood, leads to a dualism that is hostile to the body. Both were found again among the Gnostic heretics and both were rejected. The exaggerated ascetical currents had no lasting influence precisely in the Greek- and Latin-speaking Church. For no sooner had the Encratite movement reached a certain magnitude than Clement appeared in Alexandria, and at about the same time Tertullian in North Africa and Justin in Rome, and they pointed out the dualistic origins of such currents. It is remarkable, now, that anti-philosophical theologians in particular were especially prone to radical asceticism. Marcion and Tatian were outspoken opponents of philosophy. Conversely it was precisely those theologians who were well-versed in the Platonic philosophy of their time, chiefly Clement and Justin, who were able to resist a Gnostic-dualistic disdain for the body. In their writings they analyzed the fatal consequences that an unchristian Platonism had for Christian ethics. Thus the theological antidote was found, and in fact only the Syrian region, which was largely untouched by the findings of these theologians, remained receptive to Encratite views.

2. Further Indications of a Discipline of Clerical Continence

The *saeculum obscurum* ended with two authors from whose pens copious writings have been preserved, among them some statements about clerical continence: Clement of Alexandria and Tertullian of Carthage. Both worked around the end of the second and the beginning of the third century in North Africa, the Greek Clement in Egypt, and the Latin Tertullian in what is today Tunisia. Here we are dealing with a representative of each region: the Greek-speaking East and the Latin-speaking West. This allows us to make inferences about the practice of the universal Church.

---

[16] Ibid., 37–44.

a. Clement of Alexandria Praises Marriage and Continence

Clement (d. before 215) was himself probably unmarried;[17] he had a well-rounded education and worked as a priest[18] and a teacher in what was then the Egyptian metropolitan province of Alexandria. Without him we would not know very much about this early period in a land that was important for the Church of that day. Clement became known as the great moralist of early Christian literature. He expressed in detail his opinions on ethical questions and in particular about the value of marriage and continence.[19] In all this he had a clear concept of what was Catholic and what could no longer be deemed Catholic. His travels to distant places opened his eyes to the difference. In that way he became acquainted with the ecclesiastical situation in Southern Italy, Syria, and Palestine before he made a name for himself as a teacher in Alexandria.[20] He denied that the Christian orientation of the Gnostics was truly Catholic. The controversy with them was his mission in life. In many instances Gnostic Christians manifested a flagrant hostility toward marriage and sexuality. We can certainly suppose that there was a perceptible influence of Syrian-Palestinian Encratism on the Christians in Alexandria, against which Clement managed to bar the door.[21]

These circumstances suggest an approach to interpreting several texts that ought to be examined with respect to the discipline of clerical continence. Clement set forth his views about marriage and virginity in a peculiar work entitled "On Continence [ἐγκράτεια]", which, however, has not been preserved.[22] Surely we would have been able to read there something about the ecclesiastical minister's way of life as well. As it is, we have to refer to a few scattered remarks in his extant writings. It is sufficient to know that Clement decided against the Gnostic disdain for the body in favor of a thoroughly positive perspective on marriage and sexuality, as he emphasized again and again, especially in the third

---

[17] *Stromata* 3, 7, 59, 4 (GCS Clem. Alex. 2⁴, 223, 17–21).

[18] Eusebius, *Historia ecclesiastica* 6, 11, 6 (GCS Eus. 2, 2, 542, 24–27); O. Bardenhewer, *Geschichte der altkirchlichen Literatur*, vol. 2, 2d ed. (Freiburg, 1914), 41.

[19] For a complete presentation, see J. P. Broudéhoux, *Mariage et famille chez Clément d'Alexandrie*, ThH 11 (Paris, 1970).

[20] *Stromata* 1, 1, 11, 1f. (GCS Clem. Alex. 2⁴, 8, 16–9, 3).

[21] Brown, *Keuschheit*, 138f.

[22] Bardenhewer, *Geschichte*, 2:80f.

book of his *Stromata*. Because of this, some have even speculated that such a positive attitude toward marriage and the body could not be consistent with a discipline of continence: as though someone opposing the Gnostic-Encratite hostility toward the body and defending the goodness, even the sanctity of marriage and of sexual relations could only reject a general discipline of continence for clerics.

But did Clement really reject sexual abstinence? Was the goodness of marriage, for him, tantamount to the right to engage in unrestricted sex? We must not allow modern notions of self-fulfillment and sexuality to obscure our view of societal conditions in late antiquity. For Clement, who was in agreement with the medical knowledge and the philosophical ethics of his day, continence within marriage had great importance.[23] To his way of thinking, the perfect Christians, (the "true Gnostics") were those who were married but, after they had performed the service of raising children, by mutual consent no longer engaged in sexual intercourse and lived together henceforth as brother and sister.[24] Clement, like Tertullian, saw no difficulty in Paul's advice that married couples should not refuse one another permanently, but only for a certain time (1 Cor 7:5). It was only while raising a family that couples should not refuse one another for any length of time but rather should beget children. Afterward, though, according to these two Church Fathers, Paul had nothing against complete and permanent continence, provided only that the marriage was not dissolved.[25]

Thus Clement supported a way of life that, according to our interpretation of the pastoral letters, was typical for clerics: after the years of starting a family and raising children came a retreat from sexual life, that is, complete continence. There are in fact clear indications that

---

[23] E. Pagels, *Adam, Eva und die Schlange: Die Theologie der Sünde* (Reinbek, 1991), 73–90.

[24] *Stromata* 6, 12, 100, 3 (GCS Clem. Alex. 2⁴, 482, 7–12); cf. ibid., 3, 3, 24, 1 (206, 20–22); Methodius, *Convivium decem virginum* 9, 4, 251f. (GCS Method. 119, 17–26). Clement's understanding corresponds to the Sentences of Sextus, cf. H. Chadwick, ed., *The Sentences of Sextus: A Contribution to the History of Early Christian Ethics* (Cambridge, 1959), 99.

[25] *Stromata* 3, 18, 107, 5–108, 1 (GCS Clem. Alex. 2⁴, 246, 5–13): >Καὶ μὴ ἀποστερεῖτε<, φησίν, >ἀλλήλους, εἰ μὴ ἐκ συμφώνου πρὸς καιρόν,< διὰ τῆς >ἀποστερεῖτε< λέξεως τὸ ὀφείλημα τοῦ γάμου, τὴν παιδοποιίαν, ἐμφαίνων, ὅπερ ἐν τοῖς ἔμπροσθεν ἐδήλωσεν εἰπών, >τῇ γυναικὶ ὁ ἀνὴρ τὴν ὀφειλὴν ἀποδιδότω, ὁμοίως δὲ καὶ ἡ γυνὴ τῷ ἀνδρί,< μεθ' ἥν ἔκτισιν κατὰ τὴν οἰκουρίαν καὶ τὴν ἐν Χριστῷ πίστιν βοηθός, καὶ ἔτι σαφέστερον εἰπών· >τοῖς γεγαμηκόσι παραγγέλλω, οὐκ ἐγώ, ἀλλ' ὁ κύριος, γυναῖκα ἀπὸ ἀνδρὸς μὴ χωρισθῆναι (ἐὰν δὲ καὶ χωρισθῇ, μενέτω ἄγαμος ἢ τῷ ἀνδρὶ καταλλαγήτω) καὶ ἄνδρα γυναῖκα μὴ ἀφιέναι. Tertullian, *Exhortatione castitatis* 10, 2 (CCL 2, 1029, 13–1030, 18).

Clement also presupposed such a life-style for clerics after the reception of holy orders. First of all, the so-called true Christian Gnostics that Clement spoke of presumably included the clerics, too. Indeed, Clement saw the apostles as perfect Christians, particularly with respect to their continence within marriage.[26] The perfect, those who were true (not heretical) Gnostics, were for him "holy priests of God".[27] Another argument was added: The "Gnostic", that is, the perfect Christian, prayed not at only certain times but always;[28] yet continence was necessary for prayer (1 Cor 7:5).[29] Therefore one must assume that, in Clement's opinion as well, married priests had to live with their wives in perfect continence.

The marriages of the apostles. Clement says still more about the apostles, and this is particularly instructive with regard to clerics also. All of the apostles, including even Paul, are said to have been married and, most of them, to have had children as well.[30] Already in the early Church this statement was considered remarkable:[31] apostles with wives and children! How then could there have been a discipline of obligatory continence for priests? At first glance one might actually conclude that Clement could not have known of any sort of clerical continence. Of course things are not that simple. We have just spoken about the continence of the apostles. It is likely that Peter and Philip, for example, at some time begot children. But Clement is thinking here of the time of their apostolate. For he immediately adds that the apostles had no marital relations with their wives, so as to devote themselves exclusively to the proclamation of the Word, in keeping with their ministry (οἰκονομία). Their wives accompanied them from then on as "helpers".[32]

---

[26] *Stromata* 6, 8, 68, 2 (GCS Clem. Alex. 2⁴, 466, 5–9); 7, 11, 63, 3–64, 2 (GCS Clem. Alex. 3², 46, 1–9); 7, 12, 70, 6 (51, 1–5).

[27] Ibid., 7, 7, 36, 2 (GCS Clem. Alex. 3², 28, 8).

[28] Ibid., 7, 7, 40, 3 (GCS Clem. Alex. 3², 30, 28–33).

[29] Ibid., 3, 12, 79, 1 (GCS Clem. Alex. 2⁴, 231, 16–21); 3, 18, 107, 5 (264, 5–9).

[30] Ibid., 3, 6, 52, 5–53, 3 (GCS Clem. Alex. 2⁴, 220, 15–24).

[31] Eusebius, *Historia ecclesiastica* 3, 30, 1f. (GCS Eus. 2, 1, 262, 7–23).

[32] *Stromata* 3, 6, 53, 1–3 (GCS Clem. Alex. 2⁴, 220, 16–24): Καὶ ὅ γε Παῦλος οὐκ ὀκνεῖ ἔν τινι ἐπιστολῇ τὴν αὑτοῦ προσαγορεύειν σύζυγον, ἣν οὐ περιεκόμιζεν διὰ τὸ τῆς ὑπηρεσίας εὐσταλές. Λέγει οὖν ἔν τινι ἐπιστολῇ· >οὐκ ἔχομεν ἐξουσίαν ἀδελφὴν γυναῖκα περιάγειν, ὡς καὶ οἱ λοιποὶ ἀπόστολοι;< ἀλλ᾽ οὗτοι μὲν οἰκείως τῇ διακονίᾳ, ἀπερισπάστως τῷ κηρύγματι προσανέχοντες, οὐχ ὡς γαμετάς, ἀλλ᾽ ὡς ἀδελφὰς περιῆγον τὰς γυναῖκας συνδιακόνους ἐσομένας πρὸς τὰς οἰκουροὺς γυναῖκας, δι᾽ ὧν καὶ εἰς τὴν γυναικωνῖτιν ἀδιαβλήτως παρεισεδύετο

That is noteworthy. Clement, who more than practically any other
Father of the Church held marriage in high esteem, was at the same
time firmly convinced that the married apostles permanently practiced
continence and that not one of them married (again) after assuming
his office.³³ Why did he emphasize that? It would not in any way have
impaired his theology if the apostles had begotten children even after their calling. Moreover, the observation would necessarily weaken
his position in his battle against the Gnostic Encratites. For now they
could cite the apostles in favor of their rigorous views. A continent
way of life led by the apostles, furthermore, cannot be directly proved
from the New Testament (not even from 1 Cor 9:5). How, then, did
Clement come to believe that the apostles had lived continently?

Actually only one answer remains: Continence for married clerics
and their wives was a discipline observed in those days at least in Alexandria, a practice Clement viewed as being authorized by the apostles.
This is revealed by a remark about the wives of deacons: The wives of
the apostles, says Clement, took on a role similar to that of the wives of
deacons.³⁴ With that Clement is referring to the deacons' wives mentioned in the First Letter to Timothy (1 Tim 3:11). That makes sense
only if the wives of the married deacons lived continently together
with their husbands. If Clement were not alluding here to the contemporary practice of universal continence for clerics, the reference to
deacons' wives would be unintelligible. We must assume, therefore,
that in Egypt deacons and, in general, priests and bishops also lived
with their wives in perfect continence.

The model for the ministry. Yet another passage points in this direction. Clement is the only one of the Church Fathers who transmits

---

ἡ τοῦ κυρίου διδασκαλία. As to Peter, see *ibid.*, 7, 11, 63, 3–64, 2 (GCS Clem. Alex. 3², 46,
1–9). The report about the children of Peter, therefore, can hardly be based on the apocryphal Acts of Peter (ca. A.D. 180–190), which know of the birth of a daughter to Peter
after the Ascension of Jesus (W. Schneemelcher, *Neutestamentliche Apokryphen*, 5th ed., vol.
2 [1989], 256). This section is preserved only in Coptic and hence admits a certain doubt.
On the daughter of Peter, see *Acta Philippi* 142 (81, 11–15, Lipsius and Bonnet 2, 2); *Acta
Nerei et Achillei* 4, 15 (ActaSS May 3, 10F–11A); Jerome, *Adversus Jovinianum* 1, 26 (PL 23²,
257C). R. Gryson, *Les Origines du célibat ecclésiastique du premier au septième siècle*, RSSR.H 2
(Gembloux, 1970), 9f.

³³ *Stromata* 3, 12, 90, 4 (GCS Clem. Alex. 2⁴, 238, 3–5): Ἐπεὶ τούτῳ τῷ λόγῳ οὔθ' οἱ πρὸ
τῆς παρουσίας δίκαιοι οὔθ' οἱ μετὰ τὴν παρουσίαν γεγαμηκότες κἂν ἀπόστολοι ὦσι σωθήσονται.

³⁴ Ibid., 3, 6, 53, 4 (GCS Clem. Alex. 2⁴, 220, 24f.): Ἴσμεν γὰρ καὶ ὅσα περὶ διακόνων
γυναικῶν ἐν τῇ ἑτέρᾳ πρὸς Τιμόθεον ἐπιστολῇ ὁ γενναῖος διατάσσεται Παῦλος.

the curious statement that Paul had been married (cf. Phil 4:3).[35] Like the other apostles, though, he refrained from marital intercourse. Unlike his brethren, he lived completely separated from his wife.[36] And there is a particular reason for that. For if Paul did not have his wife in his company, the suspicion could not even arise that he was not really living continently. Especially those married people who wanted to live continently could be scandalized if an apostle had had his wife with him.[37] Without the example of Paul, many would have "eaten their fill of what was placed before them and as usual lived with their wives",[38] although they would have been quite willing to practice continence. Therefore Paul wished to be an impeccable model and live in perfect continence. In this passage Clement is expressly emphasizing the goodness of creation (1 Cor 10:26).[39] If Paul, then, lived without his wife, he did not intend to reject marriage as such; it was simply to let the virtue of continence (which the other married apostles, too, were practicing) shine forth more brightly, since by its very nature it did not come to light so clearly in a continent marriage.

In later periods this exemplary function was cited repeatedly as the reason for obligatory continence for clerics. The importance of Clement's own argument becomes evident only if it is not viewed against the hypothetical background of an exegetical dispute about the marriages of the apostles. The theme was hardly a clarification of the apostles' circumstances but rather that of the contemporary practice of clerical marriage.[40] For he states that precisely those men who had such an important (apostolic) ministry (οἰκονομία) would have to set an impeccable example.[41] Of course that was probably just as true for

---

[35] Ibid., 3, 6, 53, 1 (GCS Clem. Alex. 2⁴, 220, 16–18); Pseudo-Ignatius, *Ad Philadelphios* 4, 5 (177, 15f. Funk and Diekamp 2). Cf. L. Legrand, "Saint Paul et le célibat", in J. Coppens, ed., *Sacerdoce et célibat: Études historiques et théologiques* (Gembloux and Louvain, 1971), 316–19.

[36] Origen concurs, *Commentarii in epistulam ad Romanos* 1, 1 (FC 2, 1, 80, 10–15).

[37] *Stromata* 4, 15, 97, 4f. (GCS Clem. Alex. 2⁴, 291, 13–25).

[38] Ibid., 4, 15, 97, 4 (GCS Clem. Alex. 2⁴, 291, 20f.): [Μὴ] οἰκοδομουμένοις εἰς τὸ ἀδεῶς τὰ παρατιθέμενα ἐσθίειν καὶ ὡς ἔτυχεν ὁμιλεῖν τῇ γυναικί.

[39] Also at ibid., 3, 6, 52, 1 (GCS Clem. Alex. 2⁴, 220, 2–4).

[40] Therefore it is unimportant whether Paul was really married or whether Clement errs in this. Nor is it important whether the married apostles really lived continently as Clement pictures it. The actual way of life lived by the apostles can be ascertained only from the New Testament. Clement's writings do testify, though, to the kind of life led by ecclesiastical ministers of his day.

[41] Ibid., 4, 15, 97, 5 (GCS Clem. Alex. 2⁴, 291, 21–23).

the clerics, who by their office taught continence to others and thus ought to have lived, like the apostles, in perfect continence.

Having children even after ordination? Nevertheless there is a passage in Clement that seems to maintain exactly the opposite: namely, that married clerics quite often had more children after their ordination. If this were really the case, the thesis of clerical continence would collapse like a house of cards. Hence it is necessary to perform a precise exegesis of the pertinent passage, in order to understand correctly this text, which is often adduced in the scholarly literature as evidence against a discipline of continence celibacy.

> This is why the Apostle himself [says]: "So I would have younger widows marry, bear children, rule their households, and give the enemy no occasion to revile us. For some have already strayed after Satan" (1 Tim 5:14–15). Indeed, he [Paul] does admit the "husband of one wife" (1 Tim 3:2), whether he be a priest, a deacon, or a layman, using his marital rights in an irreproachable (1 Tim 3:2) way: because he [?] "will be saved" by begetting [?] children (1 Tim 2:15).[42]

So Clement wants not only laymen but also higher clerics[43] to "use" their marriage irreproachably and to have children with their wives.[44] Confronted with such clear words, the thesis that Clement knew of a duty for clerics to practice continence within marriage must then seem arbitrary and pointless. But in this passage is Clement really requiring laymen and clerics to beget children? The context concerns the problem of remarriage after the death of the spouse. Should a Christian ever marry again if his partner has died? For the early Church that was an ongoing question, and so it is not surprising if Clement comes to address it. The governing principle for him is to avoid lechery, that is, extramarital sexual relations. It is in this vein that Clement men-

---

[42] Ibid., 3, 12, 89, 3–90, 1 (GCS Clem. Alex. 2⁴, 237, 17–22): Ὅθεν καὶ ὁ ἀπόστολος >βούλομει οὖν< φησὶ >νεωτέρας γαμεῖν, τεκνογονεῖν, οἰκοδεσποτεῖν, μηδεμίαν ἀφορμὴν διδόναι τῷ ἀντικειμένῳ λοιδορίας χάριν· ἤδη γάρ τινες ἐξετράπησαν ὀπίσω τοῦ σατανᾶ.< ναὶ μὴν καὶ τὸν τῆς μιᾶς γυναικὸς ἄνδρα πάνυ ἀποδέχεται, κἂν πρεσβύτερος ᾖ κἂν διάκονος κἂν λαϊκός, ἀνεπιλήπτως γάμῳ χρώμενος· >σωθήσεται δὲ διὰ τῆς τεκνογονίας.

[43] By "priests and deacons", Clement means to include the *sacerdotium* (the episcopal and priestly ministries) and *ministerium* (the diaconal ministry). Contrary to C. Cochini, *Apostolic Origins of Priestly Celibacy* (San Francisco, 1990), 150f.

[44] Similarly *Stromata* 3, 18, 108, 2 (GCS Clem. Alex. 2⁴, 246, 16–20): Τί πρὸς ταύτας εἰπεῖν ἔχουσι τὰς νομοθεσίας οἱ τὴν σπορὰν καὶ τὴν γένεσιν μυσαττόμενοι; ἐπεὶ καὶ >τὸν ἐπίσκοπον τοῦ οἴκου καλῶς προϊστάμενον< νομοθετεῖ τῆς ἐκκλησίας ἀφηγεῖσθαι, οἶκον δὲ κυριακὸν >μιᾶς γυναικὸς< συνίστησι συζυγία.

tions Paul's advice that younger widows should marry again and bear children (τεχνογονεῖν) in marriage and thus avoid incontinence (1 Tim 5:14f.).

Following that is the statement about monogamous men, which is to be understood thus: Priests, deacons, or even laymen may renounce remarriage after the death of their wife, provided that as priests, deacons, or laymen they use their marital rights in an irreproachable way. Paul admits therefore—in an explicit contrast to those widows who remarry and bear children—monogamous men (clerics and laymen), who obviously do not remarry or beget children, who rather have made a promise not to marry again.[45] It was known about these men already when their wives were living that they did not intend to remarry. Such a promise made sense, however, only if the man in question wished to renounce marital intercourse and to do so starting on the day of his promise. The renunciation of remarriage was not, at any rate for Clement, founded on a sense of fidelity to the first and only wife, which would have made it appear improper to remarry. Remarriage was certainly permissible, of course only in the case of an incapacity for continence. Those clerics and laymen who, during the lifetime of their wives, promised to renounce remarriage must therefore from then on have lived continently with their wives.

The following sentence is now decisive. In the usual translation[46] he speaks against a discipline of continence for clerics: "*He*, though, will be saved by *begetting* (τεχνογονία) children." That sounds then like a demand that monogamous clerics and laymen beget children. That cannot be the meaning, however, because the foregoing context uses the same terminology (τεχνογονεῖν) to speak of women's childbearing.[47] Besides, the quoted sentence alludes to 1 Timothy 2:15, where it says concerning "the woman": "[*She*] will be saved by *bearing children*." Then surely the identical quotation in Clement is not making a statement at all about clerics who beget children. It is only said in a general way about the wives of the monogamous men: They will be saved by

---

[45] Such a promise must have been present. For there are also men who may still be living in their first marriage. Paul does not need to "admit" these.

[46] Thus O. Stählin in his translation (BKV, second series, Klemens v. Alex. 3, 312); F. X. Funk, "Cölibat und Priesterehe im christlichen Altertum", in *Kirchengeschichtliche Abhandlungen und Untersuchungen*, vol. 1 (Paderborn, 1897), 146; Cochini, *Origins*, 147, 150.

[47] For begetting children, Clement uses the term παιδοποιία; *Stromata* 3, 12, 89, 2 (GCS Clem. Alex. 2⁴, 237, 17).

bearing children. And the pregnancy referred to can very well have occurred before the ordination of their husbands. This is confirmed by another passage, according to which candidates for the episcopacy are expected to have prepared themselves for governing the church by their years as head of a family.[48] Furthermore the wives of clerics are, just like other wives, "helpers" of their husbands[49] as soon as they have fulfilled their duty of bearing and raising children. Clement uses exactly the same term also for the wives of the apostles who are practicing continence. However, to prevent this continent way of life from being misunderstood as Gnostic hostility to the body, Clement immediately adds: The married woman will be saved by bearing children.

b. Tertullian of Carthage Advocates Continence

Writing at the same time as Clement, farther to the West in the North African city of Carthage, was the Latin-speaking Tertullian (d. after 220), a brilliant orator, but also a theological hothead. Unlike Clement he was a layman. His writings involve a twofold difficulty. On the one hand, they often elude exact interpretation, because they are formulated with such pointed exaggeration that the true meaning is often to be found only by reading between the lines.[50] On the other hand, as of the early years of the third century, Tertullian embraced Montanism. This rigorist prophetic movement of Christians in Asia Minor was looked upon as heretical.

Now the references to clerical continence are found precisely in those writings that date from Tertullian's Montanist period. Nevertheless, these statements are by no means worthless with regard to the mores of the Catholic Church. Montanism and the Church at large were in many respects very close to each other. Thus, if the Catholic Tertullian after a certain time turned to Montanism, then for him it was not much more than a conservative move. His Montanist writings are by no means simply heretical; otherwise they would not have continued to be read and handed down in uncensored form by the Church

---

[48] Ibid., 3, 12, 79, 6 (GCS Clem. Alex. 2⁴, 232, 1f.): Φησὶν ἐπισκόπους δεῖν καθίστασθαι τοὺς ἐκ τοῦ ἰδίου οἴκου καὶ τῆς ἐκκλησίας ἁπάσης προΐστασθαι μελετήσαντας.

[49] Ibid., 3, 18, 108, 1 (GCS Clem. Alex. 2⁴, 246, 10). Cf. ibid., 2, 23, 140, 2 (190, 18–23).

[50] J. P. Audet, *Mariage et célibat dans le service pastorale de l'Église: Histoire et orientations* (Paris, 1967), 21f.

at large—for instance, by the strictly orthodox bishop Cyprian. More-over the real impetus of Montanism was its ethical rigorism, not a re-vision of ecclesiastical ministry.[51] When Tertullian speaks of offices in the Church, he is surely describing generally Catholic conditions that comprised the Montanist milieu as well.[52]

Continence in the ecclesiastical orders. It is advisable to begin with a short comment about the ecclesiastical orders or states. By these "or-ders" (*ordines*) are meant clerics, virgins, and widows who, according to Tertullian's understanding, as a rule practice sexual continence:

> How many men and how many women are numbered among the eccle-siastical orders on account of their continence! They preferred to marry God and reestablished the dignity of [their] flesh.[53]

Roger Gryson translates the first sentence differently: "How many men and how many women—in the orders of the Church—are among those who practice continence"![54] That sounds as if there were within the ecclesiastical orders quite a few who were living continently. But the Latin text—"Quanti igitur et quantae in ecclesiasticis ordinibus de continentia censentur"—does not allow such a diluted interpretation. Continence is nothing short of the decisive and characteristic require-ment for admission to the ecclesiastical orders,[55] among which cler-ics, too, are numbered. This much can be said, then: continence was required of clerics.

But what exactly is Tertullian's concern? With the little book from which the quotation is taken he wants to dissuade a widowed acquain-tance absolutely from entering a second marriage. Therefore he men-tions examples of individuals who did not remarry after the death of their spouse. And from among those who, on the basis of their con-tinence, are numbered in the Church's orders, he then singles out

---

[51] E. Dassmann, *Kirchengeschichte*, vol. 1, *Ausbreitung, Leben und Lehre der Kirche in den er-sten drei Jahrhunderten* (Stuttgart, 1991), 127f.

[52] B. Kötting, *Die Beurteilung der zweiten Ehe im heidnischen und christlichen Altertum*, (diss., Bonn, 1942), 139.

[53] Tertullian, *De exhortatione castitatis* 13, 4 (CCL 2, 1035, 35–37): "Quanti igitur et quantae in ecclesiasticis ordinibus de continentia censentur, qui deo nubere maluerunt, qui carnis suae honorem restituerunt." Cochini's treatment of the passage, *Origins*, 143–46, is inadequate.

[54] Gryson, *Origines*, 22: "Combien d'hommes et combien de femmes, dans les ordres de l'Église, sont parmi ceux qui pratiquent la continence."

[55] Contrary to Gryson, *Origines*, 30.

those who "preferred to marry God and reestablished the dignity of [their] flesh". The way this is formulated reveals that Tertullian has in mind here only widowed clerics and widows[56]—he, with an eye to his widowed friend, is concerned about such cases—who preferred to marry God rather than a second spouse,[57] that is, remained unmarried and thus reestablished the honor of their flesh. By "reestablishing the honor of the flesh" Tertullian means renouncing the sexual relations engaged in previously within marriage. The aforementioned passage can be translated with greater precision, then, as follows: How many men and women—from among those who, on the basis of their continent way of life, are numbered among the ecclesiastical orders—there are who [after the death of their spouse] preferred to marry God and in this way reestablished the honor of their flesh.[58]

Thus this passage from Tertullian fits perfectly into the picture that we have thus far of clerical continence. For Tertullian it is self-evident that clerics practice continence. In this regard he makes no finer distinctions. He does not say: They are all continent except for the married clerics. We must start, then, with the assumption that there was a uniform discipline that comprised continence for both married and unmarried clerics. In any case, however, we may assume that there was a prohibition of marriage for widowed clerics, which is sufficiently well documented anyway in Tertullian's writings (see below, pp. 75–76). He would scarcely have been able to convince his acquaintance not to marry if widowed clerics had been free to remarry. Then his argument could even have been used against him. Hence we can say: Widowed clerics were not allowed to remarry, and that was true for the sake of the continence discipline common to all the ecclesiastical orders.

Such obligatory continence, it is certain, was not imposed arbitrarily. By no means is Tertullian speaking here of a merely ideal situation, the imaginary product of his exaggerated wishful thinking.[59] On the contrary, admission into an ecclesiastical order may have been bound

---

[56] Here are meant all the widowers and widows in the ecclesiastical orders, since Tertullian knows of a fundamental prohibition of remarriage for clerics. Furthermore he would not have been able to persuade his acquaintance of the necessity of not remarrying if widowed clerics had been free to enter a further marriage.

[57] Cf. Tertullian, *Ad uxorem* 1, 4, 4 (CCL 1, 377, 20).

[58] *Qui* refers back to *Quanti et quantae*. This renders superfluous the contorted interpretation of Audet, *Mariage*, 22, and Gryson, *Origines*, 23.

[59] Contrary to Gryson, *Origines*, 26.

up with a formal promise (*votum*) to practice continence,[60] whether or not a public declaration of vows before the bishop and the assembly was required.[61] That is precisely what constitutes an order: a clear and definitive commitment to a form of life recognized and called for by the Church.

The monogamous, continent man. The continence of married clerics and their wives must have been a constant and self-evident practice. It is true that Tertullian nowhere explicitly attests to it. But it can be inferred from his remarks in the work entitled "On the Exhortation to Chastity". Another text should be cited, which has not been sufficiently noted until now and which is closely related to the passage previously discussed. It is addressed, again, to that widowed acquaintance, whom Tertullian wants to deter from entering a new marriage:

> Will you therefore stand in the presence of the Lord with as many wives as you mention in your prayer? Will you make an offering for two of them and commend these two [to God's mercy] through a priest who was ordained while in his *first marriage* or was even sanctified in the *virginal state* and is surrounded by once-married *widows*? And when your offering ascends, will your forehead be free [of care]? And among your other petitions, wondering whether she concurs, will you ask for your [second] wife's chastity as well?[62]

This is not the place to lay out the entire context. It is enough to point out that Tertullian emphasizes the importance of permanent continence.[63] And then he confronts his friend with what it would be like if he, as a digamist—as someone living in a second marriage—were to pray during the Mass for chastity. At the Liturgy are present, too, those monogamous and virginal priests and those widows who, as a sign of their state in life, practice continence. In any case Tertullian means to contrast the unchastity of his marriage-happy fellow Christian

---

[60] The notion of self-consecration is expressed ("quique se iam illius aevi filios dicaverunt").

[61] On the promise of virginity in Tertullian, see H. Koch, *Virgines Christi: Die Gelübde der gottgeweihten Jungfrauen in den ersten drei Jahrhunderten*, TU 31, 2 (Leipzig, 1907), 59–112, at 65–76.

[62] Tertullian, *De exhortatione castitatis* 11, 2 (CCL 2, 1031, 8–14): "Stabis ergo ad dominum cum tot uxoribus, quot in oratione commemores? et offeres pro duabus et commendabis illas duas per sacerdotem de monogamia ordinatum aut etiam de uirginitate sancitum, circumdatum uiduis uniuiris? et ascendet sacrificium tuum libera fronte? et inter cetera, uolutans, <si> bonae mentis, postulabis tibi et uxoris castitatem?"

[63] Ibid., 10 (CCL 2, 1029, 1–1030, 34).

with the continence of the ecclesiastical orders: a digamous man prays in the sight of continent priests and widows. As in the other passage Tertullian holds up before the acquaintance to whom he is writing the continence of the ecclesiastical orders, only this time the married clerics are expressly named.[64] In all probability, then, Tertullian assumes that married clerics and their wives practice continence also.

This is further corroborated by another consideration. That is, when Tertullian enumerates the virginal and monogamous clerics and the widows, he is reiterating a classification that he introduced at the beginning of his treatise. There he distinguished among three kinds of continence: virginity, continence definitively observed by consenting married couples, and the permanent widowed state, freely chosen.[65] Tertullian now wants to encourage his widowed acquaintance to practice the third kind of self-consecration. And so he depicts for him what it would be like to pray for the virtue of chastity for himself. Then he, the widower, would be standing there within the circle of those who are continent according to their state in life: continent married priests, virginal priests, and widows.

The clergy, then, was composed in like manner of married and unmarried men, whose unifying discipline was precisely continence. The fact that this was not explicitly mentioned for married priests most likely indicates that during that period, at least in North Africa, the connection between continence and clerical monogamy was self-evident. The monogamy of the cleric and permanent continence were two sides of the same coin. Such a correlation cannot simply be dismissed out of hand; proof of this is a passage in Origen's writings forty years later, in which this very connection between clerical monogamy and clerical continence plainly comes to light.

---

[64] Contrary to H. Koch, "Tertullian und der Cölibat", ThQ 88 (1906): 407.

[65] Tertullian De exhortatione castitatis 1, 4f. (CCL 2, 1015, 16–1016, 25): "Prima species est uirginitas a natiuitate; secunda, uirginitas a secunda natiuitate, id est a lauacro, quae aut in matrimonio purificat<o> ex compacto aut in uiduitate perseuerat ex arbitrio; tertius gradus superest monogamia, cum post matrimonium unum interceptum exinde sexui renuntiatur. Prima uirginitas felicitatis est, non nosse in totum a quo postea optabis liberari; secunda uirtutis est, contemnere cuius uim optime noris; reliqua species hactenus nubendi post matrimonium morte disiunctum praeter uirtutis etiam modestiae laus est."

3. Men in a Second Marriage Are Not Ordained

With this evidence concerning the apostles' marriages (in Clement) and the ecclesiastical offices (in Tertullian) we have already exhausted the collection of texts referring to clerical continence. But there are other statements that testify indirectly to a discipline of continence celibacy, and these are at least as important if not more so. We came upon this discipline in the pastoral letters on the basis of the monogamy proviso. Now the argument can be turned around to say: If in the second century there really was a discipline of continence for married clerics, then the prohibition against digamy must have continued to be valid for them, too.

a. Why Is Digamy Forbidden Only to Clerics?

This is exactly what proves to be true for the second century: clerical candidates were not allowed to be twice-married, whereas widowed lay persons were free to enter a second marriage. We have already met with this in Clement of Alexandria. His formulation about the monogamy of priests, deacons, or even laymen presupposed that a duty to remain monogamous existed for higher clerics, while lay persons could voluntarily renounce remarriage.[66] Tertullian's statements are quite unequivocal.[67] He speaks of a sanctioned law to which all who have been accepted into the priestly *ordo* are subject; priests who subsequently were known to have married again as widowers were deposed.[68] And for Hippolytus of Rome, too, ordaining a digamous man was unthinkable. With these authors we have a cross-section of the Church in the East and the West. There were difficulties with this, which we have

---

[66] *Stromata* 3, 12, 89, 3–90, 1 (GCS Clem. Alex. 2⁴, 237, 17–22); A. Oepke, "Ehe I (Institution)", in RAC 4 (1959), 662; H. Preisker, *Christentum und Ehe in den ersten drei Jahrhunderten: Eine Studie zur Kulturgeschichte der Alten Welt*, NSGTK 23 (Berlin, 1927), 204f.; Kötting, *Beurteilung*, 155f.

[67] *De monogamia* 12 (CCL 2, 1247, 1–1248, 41). Gryson, *Origines*, 26–32.

[68] Tertullian, *De exhortatione castitatis* 7, 2 (CCL 2, 1024, 10–13): "Inde igitur apostolus plenius atque strictius praescribit unius matrimonii esse oportere qui allegant<ur> in ordinem sacerdotalem. Vsque adeo quosdam memini digamos loco deiectos." *De uxorem* 1, 7, 4 (CCL 1, 381, 19–23): "Quantum detrahant fidei, quantum obstrepant sanctitati nuptiae secundae, disciplina ecclesiae et praescriptio apostoli declarat, cum digamos non sinit praesidere, cum uiduam adlegi in ordinem nisi uniuiram non concedat."

yet to discuss, but they only go to prove the fundamental validity of the prohibition of digamy for clerics.

In this respect clerics were treated differently from lay persons. The monogamy proviso of the pastoral letters was itself a special rule for clerics. Thus, in comparison to the laity, they were subject to a stricter discipline with regard to marriage; lay persons were certainly allowed to marry a second time (1 Tim 5:14). How can this unequal treatment be explained? Most often scholars attempt an explanation to the effect that it was to avoid exposing clerics to reproach, since remarriage was not particularly esteemed in late antiquity. It is true that early Christian theologians as well speak none too favorably of a second or subsequent marriage of lay persons,[69] even though it was allowed. It was considered veiled adultery and hence was disreputable.[70]

Yet one cannot just overlook the deeper connection between the prohibition of digamy and clerical continence. First of all, it holds true quite fundamentally: if the number of marriages was limited for clerics, then one cannot rule out in advance the possibility that engaging in sexual relations in marriage was not simply free. On the contrary, one would suspect that some sexual restriction was imposed on married clerics. Accordingly, Clement sees the high esteem in which Christians hold celibacy as an indication that within marriage, too, spouses may engage in sexual relations only in a limited way.[71] Thus it is taking only a small step to say that the prohibition of digamy for clerics is explained by a discipline of continence for the married clergy.

Actually the rationale for this will not be found in a general devaluation of second marriages, but rather in the concrete duty of the married clerics and their wives to practice continence. Clement's view is that the only persons who in fact enter a second marriage are those not capable of continence; for Paul allowed a second marriage exclusively for this reason (1 Cor 7:8f.).[72] One will then conclude, precisely as

---

[69] Athenagoras, *Supplicatio pro Christianis* 33, 4; Clement of Alexandria, *Stromata* 3, 1, 4, 3 (GCS Clem. Alex. 2⁴, 197, 11–15); 3, 12, 80, 1 (232, 4–9); 3, 12, 82, 4 (233, 25–29); Tertullian, *De exhortatione castitatis* 3, 5 (CCL 2, 1019, 30–34); Origen, *Hom.* 20, 4 *in Ier.* 20:7–12 (GCS Orig. 3, 182, 20–183, 4); Methodius, *Convivium* 3, 12, 83 (GCS Method. 41, 7f.). Justin Martyr, 1 *Apologia* 15, 5 addresses outward and spiritual adultery without forbidding successive digamy as a sin.

[70] Gryson, *Origines*, 30.

[71] Clement of Alexandria, *Paedagogus* 2, 10, 94, 1 (GCS Clem. Alex. 1³, 213, 32–214, 2).

[72] *Stromata* 3, 12, 82, 4 (GCS Clem. Alex. 2⁴, 233, 25f.): Καὶ εἴ τινι ὁ ἀπόστολος δι' ἀκρασίαν καὶ πύρωσιν >κατὰ συγγνώμην< δευτέρου μεταδίδωσι γάμου.

in the pastoral letters, that married clerics had to be in their first marriage because continence was expected of them. Having fulfilled the duty of raising children, the clerics had to live, from ordination day on, together with their wives without sexual intercourse, as though with "women helpers". Clement connects the mention of the clerics' "helpers" explicitly with the "unius uxoris vir".[73]

Tertullian's remarks point in the same direction. The Montanist movement extended the prohibition of digamy to all lay persons. Therefore Tertullian promoted for the laity also the restriction imposed on clerics (marriage only once), on the grounds that the entire discipline of clerics was valid for the laity as well.[74] Tertullian may have wanted to apply to the laity *en masse* the second-marriage criterion (which was actually an impediment to orders), yet he was unable to gain acceptance for his plan, because the prohibition of digamy was inextricably connected with the observance of continence in the *first* marriage. There was no way that such continence could be demanded of laymen. Contemporaries could easily contradict Tertullian: It is nonsense to forbid laypeople to marry a second time; after all, you cannot forbid them to have marital intercourse as though they were clerics. The prohibition of a second marriage was plausible only for someone living continently within marriage. Tertullian sees this contradiction very clearly when he admits that the prohibition against a second marriage ultimately leads to the prohibition of a first marriage as well, since the underlying motive is the ideal of perfect continence.[75] This is the reason that he does not speak explicitly about a particular discipline of continence for married clerics, because it would only damage his argument, which is supposed to dazzle the reader so that he will not notice its weaknesses.[76] It still makes amply clear how closely connected Tertullian understood the prohibition of digamy and continence within marriage to be (for clerics).

---

[73] *Stromata* 3, 18, 107, 5–108, 2 (GCS Clem. Alex. 2⁴, 246, 5–20).

[74] Tertullian, *De monogamia* 11f. (CCL 2, 1244, 1–1248, 41); *De exhortatione castitatis* 7, 2 (CCL 2, 1024, 13–15); *De uxorem* 1, 7, 4 (CCL 1, 381, 19–25).

[75] *De exhortatione castitatis* 9, 4 (CCL 2, 1028, 25f.): " 'Ergo', inquit, 'iam et primas, id est unas nuptias destruis?' " Cf. Kötting, *Beurteilung*, 150.

[76] Thus the objection of Koch falls, "Tertullian", 407–9, where he argues that since Tertullian demands of married lay persons that they observe the clerical discipline, it could have been a matter here of a prohibition of digamy alone and not of a duty of marital continence.

b. Tertullian of Carthage Complains About Digamous Bishops

Clerics, unlike laymen, were not allowed to marry a second time. Here we see in bold relief a particular discipline for clerics that was connected with a general obligation to practice continence. Now against this one could advance an argument based on two passages by Tertullian and the Roman priest Hippolytus. They seem to prove that the prohibition against digamy often went unheeded in the West,[77] indeed, that clerics still married even after ordination. If the ordination of digamists and the marriage of clerics really were possible in the second century, however, then naturally the idea of a continence discipline for married clerics and their wives would be erroneous. In that case there could be no question of a unified discipline of celibacy.

It appears that the two texts of Tertullian and Hippolytus describe the same historical circumstances and thus support each other. But that can be ruled out for both factual and methodological reasons. Tertullian is not speaking about the same state of affairs as Hippolytus.[78] The two texts must be treated separately. A critical reading will reveal, moreover, that they are to a great extent misleading on account of their polemical character. As ostensible testimony against a general prohibition of [clerical] digamy and marriage, in any case, they simply will not do. Let us examine first the passage by Tertullian, which again is from a work written during his Montanist period (around 217):

> The Holy Spirit foresaw that many would say, "All things are permitted to the bishops", just as your well-known Utinensian paid no heed even to the Scantinian law. How many are the bigamists among you, presiding, and thus insulting the Apostle, incapable of blushing when these texts are read in their presence?[79]

If this passage were directed against abuses among the Montanist clergy, that would exonerate the Catholic Church. We would then have fewer difficulties in maintaining that clerical continence was practiced

---

[77] Gryson, Origines, 29, 31, 43.

[78] C. Richert, Die Anfänge der Irregularitäten bis zum ersten Allgemeinen Konzil von Nicäa, StrThS 4, 3 (Freiburg, 1901), 88–92.

[79] Tertullian, De monogamia 12, 3 (CCL 2, 1247, 21–25): "Prospiciebat Spiritus sanctus dicturos quosdam: Omnia licent episcopis, sicut ille uester Vtinensis nec Scantiniam timuit. Quot enim et digami praesident apud uos, insultantes utique apostolo, certe non erubescentes, cum haec sub illis leguntur?"

within the Catholic Church. But we do not want to make it so easy for
ourselves. We will assume that Tertullian here is objecting to Catholic
abuses. He speaks at first about that bishop in the North African town
of Utina who evidently had been found guilty of pederasty, as the remark about the Scantinian laws implies.[80] He is not accused of digamy,
it is true, but the fact that he is mentioned is still illuminating. For this
bishop was no doubt deposed on account of his crime. Tertullian is
being polemical, of course, when he says that everything is permitted to
the Catholic bishops, even pederasty. But that is a grotesque reproach
and merely rhetorical. "Everything is permitted" must be understood
to mean, "It occurs." Just like pederasty, then, it occurred among the
Catholics that digamous bishops held office, and one can assume likewise that they were deposed on that account.[81] As for the digamous
bishops that Tertullian has in view, it is necessarily a matter of "genuine" digamists, those who were living in a second marriage after their
baptism (see the following section). It is moot, though, whether they
were ordained while already in a second marriage or whether they had
married a second time only after their ordination. Neither was permissible, in any case.

Tertullian knew of digamy as an impediment to orders; he discusses
it explicitly in another place. Clerics who married again were deposed
in his day.[82] There is no dispensation from the irregularity of digamy.
Undoubtedly this was not a special Montanist regulation but a practice carried over from the Church at large. At any rate Montanism is
not known to have introduced an innovation in this regard. And the
person to whom Tertullian addresses his treatise is convinced as well
that Paul demands monogamy of the bishops.[83] Therefore there can be
absolutely no doubt that monogamy for clerics was the rule but that
there were a few black sheep who had caused a sensation. Tertullian,
indeed, means to say that the pastoral letters enjoin monogamy upon
clerics in particular only because such lamentable cases were to be expected and ought to be punished immediately.

---

[80] *Realencyclopädie Pauly-Wissowa* 2 A 1 (1921), 352. Cf. Council of Elvira, canon 71;
Council of Ancyra, canon 16f.; John Chrysostom, *Adversus oppugnatores* 3, 8 (PG 47, 360–
63).

[81] An exhaustive and pertinent analysis is found in Richert, *Anfänge*, 83–92.

[82] Tertullian, *De exhortatione castitatis* 7, 2, 5, 6 (CCL 2, 1024, 11f., 1025, 29f., 1026,
39f.).

[83] *De monogamia* 12, 4 (CCL 2, 1247, 26f.).

c. Callistus of Rome Does Not Count
Marriages Contracted before Baptism

Tertullian's Greek-speaking contemporary Hippolytus (d. 235), who worked as a priest in Rome, could be no less polemical. One must of course appreciate his conscientiousness. For however much he scolds, he does not lie; if worse comes to worst, he remains silent about important details, as will be immediately evident. What he heard about Bishop Callistus of Rome (217–222) vexed him greatly. Hippolytus could become quite agitated about the soft line that he took. Scolding the pope is not a modern invention; it traces its ancestors back to the early Church. And this is what it sounded like then:

> Callistus' decree pleased many who suffered pangs of conscience and moreover were driven out of many sects; there were even some among them who had been expelled from the Church by our judgment; so they went over to them and filled Callistus' school. He was of the opinion that a bishop must not be deposed if he sins, even if it be unto death. From this time on, bishops, priests, and deacons who had been married two or three times began to be accepted into the clergy. And even if a member of the clergy gets married he can remain a cleric, as though he had not sinned.[84]

One gets the impression that a vehement argument had flared up in Rome about clerical discipline; it appears that Hippolytus was championing the traditional strict clerical discipline, while Callistus liberally allows clerics to be digamous and to marry. As is well known, Hippolytus was extremely conservative in his entire theological approach and saw Callistus as a compromiser and innovator in all areas of Church discipline. And so he makes him out to be a destroyer of the clerical discipline.

What is true about Hippolytus' statement is that in Rome around the year 200 there was a compulsory clerical discipline. Other writers,

---

[84] Hippolytus, *Refutatio omnium haeresium* 9, 12, 21f. (GCS Hippol. 3, 249, 18–250, 1): Οὐ τῷ ὅρῳ ἀρεσκόμενοι πολλοὶ συνείδησιν πεπληγότες ἅμα τε καὶ ὑπὸ πολλῶν αἱρέσεων ἀποβληθέντες, τινὲς δὲ καὶ ἐπὶ καταγνώσει ἔκβλητοι τῆς ἐκκλησίας ὑφ' ἡμῶν γενόμενοι. Προσχωρήσαντες αὐτοῖς ἐπλήθυναν τὸ διδασκαλεῖον αὐτοῦ. Οὗτος ἐδογμάτισεν ὅπως εἰ ἐπίσκοπος ἁμάρτοι τι, εἰ καὶ πρὸς θάνατον, μὴ δεῖν κατατίθεσθαι. Ἐπὶ τούτου ἤρξαντο ἐπίσκοποι καὶ πρεσβύτεροι καὶ διάκονοι δίγαμοι καὶ τρίγαμοι καθίστασθαι εἰς κλήρους· εἰ δὲ καί τις ἐν κλήρῳ ὢν γαμοίη, μένειν τὸν τοιοῦτον ἐν τῷ κλήρῳ ὡς μὴ ἡμαρτηκότα. Cochini's discussion, *Origins*, 152–54, is inadequate.

too, testify at least to the fact—based no doubt on the pastoral letters—that clerics were prohibited from marrying a second time (Clement, Tertullian).[85] Thus it was not just the conservative wing under Hippolytus that wanted to suppress the clergy and failed because of the bishop. Hippolytus did not want to introduce an ascetical innovation. For him, the traditionalist, that would have been unthinkable. But is it true that Callistus had violated the well-established clerical discipline? Or did he merely deal with it a little more flexibly?

Before answering this question one must be aware of the polemics in the statements of Hippolytus; otherwise one will be taken in by the very distortions with which he tries to discredit his rival. Of course he is not describing the situation soberly but is misrepresenting it in his own favor. For Hippolytus' ambition had been gravely offended. Callistus had deprived him of the prospect of occupying the Roman See. And so Hippolytus had separated himself from the Roman Catholic Church and, as an anti-pope in Rome, had aimed his cannons at the "school of Callistus" in order to settle his personal accounts with his opponent. His statements, therefore, are not to be taken at face value, inasmuch as his interpretation of Callistus' concerns and actions was not made in good faith.

Let us examine first, then, the problem of successive marriages. If one were to believe Hippolytus, one would have to imagine that the situation was as follows. Cases were brought to Callistus, the Bishop of Rome, in which bishops, priests, and deacons were holding office while living in a second marriage. Callistus decided for his jurisdiction not to suspend these clerics. Consequently it could even happen that digamous men might be ordained. Of course Hippolytus saw in this a break with the tradition that evidently had a claim to validity both in Rome and in North Africa.

But is it likely that Callistus, contrary to tradition, abandoned the "unius uxoris vir" of the pastoral letters? After all, that was an unequivocal order from Paul that cannot simply be evaded: clerics should be married only once. In any case, for him to do so would have been to risk vehement opposition, as the attacks by Hippolytus demonstrate. Surely Callistus was not anxious to precipitate a confrontation. We must assume, rather, that he did not interpret the pastoral letters in

---

[85] As for circumstances in Rome, we have negative judgments of digamy; B. Kötting, "Digamus", in RAC 3 (1957), 1030.

the same way as Hippolytus and thus arrived at a divergent view of the given disciplinary situation. Two possibilities present themselves, of which the first variant is hardly worth considering.

Tertullian and Hippolytus applied the monogamy rule of the pastoral letters to the time before ordination: clerical candidates could be married only once.[86] Was Callistus applying this arrangement to the time afterward, claiming that after his ordination the cleric could have only one wife, that is, after the death of his wife he could not marry again—which still did not rule out the possibility of multiple marriages before ordination? Did Callistus then interpret the "unius uxoris vir" merely as a prohibition against marriage for clerics? It is difficult to accept that explanation. The interpretation of Tertullian and Hippolytus corresponds to what was practiced throughout the universal Church. And it is scarcely imaginable that Callistus would have twisted the interpretation of "unius uxoris vir" so radically that it resulted, practically speaking, in the opposite.

More reasonable is another, attractively simple solution. It was proposed already in the nineteenth century by the eminent Church historian in Munich Ignaz von Döllinger, but it was not taken up by celibacy scholarship. Callistus and his theologians presumably justified the ordination of digamists by saying that marriages that took place before baptism were not to be counted.[87] Although it cannot be proved that clerical marriages were viewed in this way in Rome at the beginning of the third century, nevertheless there are detailed discussions of this problem at a later period (see below, pp. 164f.). Even in Callistus' time, however, we find opinions that prebaptismal marriages in general should not be counted. Callistus could have cited Tertullian, for instance. The latter, certainly, would have liked all Christians to be married no more than once, but in applying the prohibition against digamy he did not take into account a marriage that had been entered into and ended before the baptism of the widowed spouse. A person widowed before baptism could marry again after baptism.[88] The same was then true, obviously, for clerics. Hence even in North Africa there

---

[86] Tertullian, *De exhortatione castitatis* 7, 2, 5, 6 (CCL 2, 1024, 11f.; 1025, 29f.; 1026, 39f.).

[87] I. von Döllinger, *Hippolytus und Kallistus oder die römische Kirche in der ersten Hälfte des dritten Jahrhunderts* (Regensburg, 1853), 149f.; cited by Richert, *Anfänge*, 80–83. Cf. Kötting, *Beurteilung*, 179f.

[88] Tertullian, *De monogamia* 11, 9–12 (CCL 2, 1245, 58–1426, 97).

could be digamous clerics, provided that the first marriage dated from before baptism.

This lenient way of counting marriages was, to be sure, disputed. Tertullian applied it, in any case, to the laity (1 Cor 7) and not to the clergy (1 Tim 3:2) and tried, within the framework of a very laborious exegesis, to establish a prohibition of digamy for all Christians. On this subject, then, there was no consensus, especially since the reason Tertullian gave for not counting marriages before baptism is very poor: "For from the moment of faith [that is, at baptism] our life itself begins to be counted, too."[89] Thus there is some latitude in the theological valuation of digamy. Hippolytus and Callistus may have taken different standpoints on the matter. If so, then the polemic of Hippolytus was not entirely without justification.

What consequences does that have for the continence of married clerics and their wives? Continence is, after all, coupled with the monogamy rule. Now, though, if Callistus was ordaining men who were living in a second or a third marriage, could there still be talk of a continence discipline? In those days it was understood that a second marriage was proof of an inability to practice continence. If in fact a second, third, or fourth marriage was now allowed, does that then mean that in Rome continence was not required of married clerics? We can hardly assume that. The decisive factor here is the theological view of baptism.

From the second century on there is documentary evidence on all sides testifying that baptism always communicated a capacity for continence also. The experience of unmarried as well as married converts showed that the grace of their baptism rendered them capable of a continent way of life that before seemed to them impossible.[90] However one may have lived previously, baptism enabled one to practice continence anew. Seen in this way, a marriage before baptism did not tell against one's capacity for continence. Baptism extinguished, as it was thought, the inability to practice sexual abstinence. Thus baptism itself was considered the justification for ordaining digamists. Of course after baptism there could be only one marriage. The meaning and purpose

---

[89] Ibid., 11, 9 (CCL 2, 1245, 62): "A fide enim etiam ipsa uita nostra censetur."

[90] Justin Martyr, 1 *Apologia* 14, 2; Origen, *Contra Celsum* 1, 26 (GCS Orig. 1, 78, 17–28). This view is in contrast with the views of the Syrian Christians, who demanded continence as a prerequisite for the reception of baptism; Chadwick, "Enkrateia", 353.

of the prohibition of digamy (liberally interpreted) would then be for
Callistus as well the continence of married clerics and their wives.

4. Higher Clerics Must Not Marry Again

Circumstances in Rome were disputed not only with regard to the ordination of digamists. There was also the question of whether clerics
could marry after their ordination. Hippolytus maintained that Callistus permitted this. If that were the case, then of course obligatory continence for married clerics would have been untenable. Indeed, from the
monogamy proviso of the pastoral letters we inferred a prohibition of
marriage for clerics who were already ordained. Conversely this means
for the second century: if clerics in Rome were allowed to marry, then
in that diocese continence could not have been required of them. For
what would be the sense of a wedding if it was not permissible to
consummate the marriage? Many scholars therefore consider Hippolytus to confirm their opinion that there was no continence celibacy in
Rome.

It all depends on a critical formulation of Hippolytus: "Even if a
member of the clergy gets married, he can remain a cleric, as though
he had not sinned." Ignaz von Döllinger has suggested that Hippolytus
is probably thinking only of lower clerics beneath the rank of diaconate.
This solution is convincing, because it is as simple as it is obvious. In
contrast to the previous sentence, Hippolytus speaks in a remarkably
undifferentiated way about the "clergy"; included among them are also
subdeacons and lower clerics. With respect to their suitability for marriage, there was in fact no uniform practice in the Church.[91] According to this explanation, Hippolytus wanted to oblige not only higher
clerics but even unmarried subdeacons to renounce marriage.

If this is correct, then higher clerics in Rome were generally not
allowed to marry. Neither Hippolytus nor Callistus questioned such a
prohibition. It becomes evident here for the first time, whereas it can
only be inferred indirectly from the pastoral letters. In fact not one
case is known where a cleric was married after his ordination. Such a
prohibition of marriage was undoubtedly founded upon a discipline of

---

[91] Döllinger, *Hippolytus*, 150–58. Cited by Richert, *Anfänge*, 74f. The same interpretation
is found in G. Bickell, "Der Cölibat eine apostolische Anordnung", ZKTh 2 (1878): 29.

obligatory continence for married clerics and their wives. One is not allowed to proceed to a marriage that cannot be consummated.

Now of course this explanation, which finds in the passage from Hippolytus a reference to lower clerics, is in the final analysis not certain. It could have been intended for higher clerics as well. Is it possible after all that Callistus allowed higher clerics to marry? Hippolytus' polemic gives the impression that only a conservative wing in the Roman Church viewed clerical marriage as a sin, while the moderates under Callistus saw it as something normal. And yet the way he formulates his objection seems to suggest that a prohibition of marriage quite probably existed and that Callistus, too, recognized it in principle. Indications for this are not only the crude generalization Hippolytus makes, but also his expression, "even if a member of the clergy gets married, he can remain a cleric." According to this, there was a regulation in Rome whereby any higher cleric who married after ordination would be deprived of his ministerial rank. We find confirmation of this a hundred years later in canon 1 of the Synod of Neocaesarea (see below, p. 122). Callistus therefore did not abolish the marriage prohibition but merely refrained from deposing clerics in certain cases. The clerics in question continued to be supported, then, by the Church, though they were not permitted to exercise clerical functions. Presumably a concern about providing for the family decided the question about further support for such clerics.

So if Callistus really did retain in the ranks of the clergy higher clerics who had married, then he may have been trying to resolve a case in which a cleric had acted in ignorance of the Church's prohibition. Such a situation would not be unparalleled in a later period. This is demonstrated by the case of a priest with whom Basil the Great had to come to terms because the former had married—in ignorance of ecclesiastical law, to be sure. Basil retained him in the ranks of the clergy, but he was no longer allowed to carry out his priestly functions. According to Hippolytus' formulation, this cleric then "remained a cleric". Callistus, who was noted for his clemency, could have done precisely this in a similar situation. Thus Callistus by no means actively promoted the marriage of clerics, even though Hippolytus wants to convey this false impression. In any case he made allowances, in the financial sense as well, for clerics who, ignorant of the law, had married.

Were the apostles allowed to marry? Aside from Hippolytus, one could still think, on the basis of a statement by Tertullian, that clerics were permitted to marry. Specifically, Tertullian speaks of the right of the apostles, not only to *have* a wife (1 Cor 9:5), but even to *marry*. In fact Tertullian does admit that they have this right, but we must read farther: the point is that the apostles did not avail themselves of this right (Peter was already married). By not marrying, they exhorted others to practice continence. Tertullian says exactly the same thing in another treatise, according to which none of the apostles (with the exception of Peter) had wives.[92]

These two passages cannot be played off against each other because one was written during Tertullian's Catholic period while the other dates from his later Montanist period, as Heinz-Jürgen Vogels claims. In his opinion Tertullian testifies, at least in the one passage, to "the natural right, guaranteed by Scripture, of the apostles to have a wife". But both documents in question here are Montanist. Contrasting the dates of the documents accomplishes nothing. One simply has to know the way in which Tertullian writes. He is noted for twisting and turning every argument as it suits him. When he speaks of the right of the apostles to marry, it is the hot air of a rhetorician who wants to dissuade someone from marrying. Naturally, for Tertullian there was no debate as to whether the apostles married. That is precisely why he mentions the idea in making his argument. His acquaintance, too, has the option of marrying and ought to pass it up. Therefore it is rather ingenuous to believe that Tertullian was in earnest about apostles marrying.

Now if no real right to marry existed even for the apostles, then a right to marry cannot be deduced either for their successors, the bishops. Tertullian is, as one might well imagine, a poor authority to cite on the subject of marrying clerics. The situation remains: in North Africa and in Rome higher clerics were not allowed to marry. This confirms once more a possible discipline of obligatory continence for married clerics. For what was the sense of a marriage prohibition for clerics in this early period? What rationale caused it to be so gener-

---

[92] Tertullian, *De exhortatione castitatis* 8, 3 (CCL 2, 1027, 21f.): "Licebat et apostolis nubere et uxores circumducere, licebat et de euangelio ali. Sed qui iure hoc usus non est in occasione, ad exemplum nos suum scilicet et prouocat, docens in eo esse probationem, in quo licentiae experimentum abstinentiae praestruxit." *De monogamia* 8, 6 (CCL 2, 1240, 36–39): "Non uxores demonstrat ab apostolis deductas, quas et qui non habent, potestatem tamen manducandi et bibendi habent, sed simpliciter mulieres quae illis eodem instituto, quo et Dominum comitantes, ministrabant." H. J. Vogels, *Priester dürfen heiraten: Biblische, geschichtliche und rechtliche Gründe gegen den Pflichtzölibat* (Bonn, 1992), 74f.

ally accepted? A restriction of marriageability becomes plausible only against the background of a general requirement of continence for the higher clergy.

5. Summary

After the pastoral letters it is not until the year 200 in the western and eastern parts of North Africa that we find reasonably clear references to continence celibacy. Clement of Alexandria is of the opinion that clerics, too, are allowed to be married and to have children. But nowhere does he concede that clerics may still beget children after their ordination. We should rather assume the contrary: clerics in their manner of life followed the example of the married apostles. Like them, they conducted themselves in marriage as perfect Christians ("Gnostics"), without sexual intercourse. After their ordination their wives stood at their sides as "helpers". There is good reason, therefore, to conclude that the tradition concerning the apostolic way of life known to Clement also included clerical continence.

Tertullian of Carthage presupposes that there were virginal as well as widowed and married clerics. Bound up with the clerical state, moreover, was a duty of continence, which could be put into practice in various ways. One must consider, accordingly, virginal, widowed, and married clerics living continently. Of course we find no explicit evidence in Tertullian for marital continence practiced by married clerics, though indirect references leave hardly any doubt that such a discipline existed.

A strict discipline of obligatory continence for married clerics and their wives can be inferred also from the prohibition of digamy. In Egypt, North Africa, and in all likelihood in Rome as well, clerics—unlike lay persons—were not permitted to marry a second time. Tertullian speaks, it is true, about many digamous bishops, but at the same time he knows of an explicit prohibition of digamy and of the deposition of digamous clerics. Hippolytus accuses Callistus, the Bishop of Rome, of ignoring this prohibition and ordaining digamists. But Callistus can scarcely have called into question the fundamental prohibition of digamy. He merely adopted a more liberal interpretation in that he, like Tertullian, did not count marriages contracted before baptism. So it could happen that a widowed man, who married a second time after his baptism, was ordained. This in no way affected the requirement of continence.

A further indication of the discipline of obligatory continence is a general prohibition of marriage, which is mentioned for the first time by Hippolytus. Callistus also knows and respects this prohibition, though it may be that, contrary to Hippolytus, he still permits lower clerics to marry. Possibly he refrains also from deposing a higher cleric who (due to ignorance of the Church's law) has married after his ordination. That is not to say, of course, that such a cleric would be allowed to continue to exercise his ministry. We can assume, rather, that he could no longer carry out his clerical duties, although he continued to remain in the ranks of the clergy so as to be assured of the accompanying financial support.

IV. Clerical Continence from the Third Century until Nicaea (325)

In the third century the literary sources attesting to clerical continence become more unequivocal. The time frame of the present chapter extends into the fourth century up to the Council of Nicaea, which was held in the year 325 not far from Constantinople (today Istanbul). It was the first gathering of bishops in the history of the Church to be approved as an ecumenical council. It was an event of worldwide significance. Nicaea marks the glorious period of the state-approved Church, whereas in the third century the Church still showed signs of her cautious, tentative beginnings and was also being sorely tested by persecutions.

If we disregard the Spanish Council of Elvira, then the information that we have for the ante-Nicene period after A.D. 220 concerns the continence discipline in the eastern Mediterranean region exclusively. This might seem surprising, inasmuch as the prevailing notion sees celibacy as a discipline contrived in the West, specifically in Rome. In reality, though, it has its historical and spiritual roots in the East. They go back to a period in which one cannot yet speak of a universal primacy of the pope, in the strict sense. Thus in the East, already in the third century, a discipline of clerical continence was clearly defined, without having been transplanted there or influenced by the pope.

1. At the Time of Origen Continence Is Required

We hear about a discipline of clerical continence in Greek-speaking Syria and Egypt. The two regions had been in close contact from time immemorial. The Syrian *Didascalia* and the writings of the renowned catechist Origen can therefore be seen as closely related to each other.

a. A Syrian Constitution

The Syrian *Didascalia* belongs to the genre of ecclesiastical constitutions. It presents rules and regulations concerning life in the Church community that, of course, are not so much canonically systematic as they are pastorally verbose.[1] The authority and hence the wide dissemination of this ecclesiastical constitution are explained by the fact that it was believed to be instructions from the apostles, and excerpts from it therefore were even read aloud during the Liturgy. Originally composed in Greek, the *Didascalia* dates back to the first half, perhaps even to the first decades, of the third century.

> But it is required that the bishop shall be "a man that has taken one wife, and who has managed his house well" (1 Tim 3:2, 4). And thus let him be proved when he receives the imposition of hands to sit in the position of the episcopacy: whether he is chaste, and whether his wife also is a believer and chaste; and whether he has brought up his children in the fear of God.[2]

The *Didascalia* takes up the requirements in the pastoral letters for candidates to the episcopacy. The qualifications for ordination listed in the pastoral letters are essentially legal matter and therefore were included also in this ecclesiastical constitution. The *Didascalia* thereby attests to what is henceforth the case in almost all opinions about clerical continence: the "unius uxoris vir" is the hinge on which the Church's continence celibacy turns: the bishop must have taken only one wife and must be living chastely together with his wife. Chastity here certainly means more than mere decency; it implies, rather, the capacity to conduct the marriage continently after ordination. It is no accident that the wife is mentioned too, for she was directly affected by her husband's obligation to be continent; it was not enough for him to be able to live in perfect continence; she too had to be capable of it.

The *Didascalia* is in line with our interpretation of the pastoral letters. It, too, understands the profile of the bishop in the First Letter to Timothy as a catalogue of criteria for selecting episcopal candidates. It

---

[1] G. Schöllgen, "Pseudoapostolizität und Schriftgebrauch in den ersten Kirchenordnungen: Anmerkungen zur Begründung des frühen Kirchenrechts", in idem and C. Scholten, eds., *Stimuli: Exegese und ihre Hermeneutik in Antike und Christentum: Festschrift E. Dassmann*, JAC.E 23 (Münster, 1996), 96–121, at 116.

[2] *Didascalia apostolorum* 4 (CSCO.S 176, 45, 15–46, 4).

states also that as a rule the bishop should be at least fifty years old.[3] That also clarifies, then, how it arrives at the demand that the candidate and his wife should live chastely (continently). At the age of fifty it may be assumed that the couple had not had any more children for quite some time. The children should have been grown already and their upbringing completed. Thus the bishop, freed from family demands, could devote himself entirely to his ministry of leadership in the Church. Later on we will hear also from the *Apostolic Constitutions* how it is urged, for the sake of continence, that candidates for orders be of a suitable age (see below, pp. 108f.).

b. Monogamy and Continence

The *Didascalia* makes evident a connection between the "unius uxoris vir" and clerical continence: the bishop should be married once and live chastely (continently). In this very requirement a problem can be seen, which leads us to one of the most influential theologians of the Greek Church and her grand master of spirituality. Origen (d. around 253/254) was a pupil of Clement of Alexandria, from about 203 on his successor in the catechetical school of that city, and, like him, an unmarried priest.[4] His discussions of clerical discipline are important also because he was informed about circumstances in other ecclesiastical regions through his sojourns in Rome and Palestine. The point of departure for his reflections is provided by the pastoral letters. He cannot quite understand why only monogamous men can become clerics. He has come up with some interesting thoughts on this subject in his commentary on Matthew (after A.D. 244):

> Since we see, however, that men married twice can be much better than those who have only married once, we asked ourselves why Paul does not allow twice-married men to be installed in ecclesiastical offices; and this question seemed to me worth investigating. For it is possible that someone has suffered misfortune in two marriages, lost his second wife while still young, and then lived out his remaining years until old age in self-control and purity. Who might not then reasonably ask why, when an ecclesial officeholder is sought, we refuse a digamous man like this on account of what is said about marriage. The monogamous man, however,

---

[3] Ibid. (CSCO.S 176, 43, 25f.).

[4] O. Bardenhewer, *Geschichte der altkirchlichen Literatur*, 2d ed., vol. 2 (Freiburg, 1914), 109.

who perhaps has lived together with his wife into old age, we prefer to admit to office, even if he never had become accustomed to chastity and continence.[5]

As background information we learn that ecclesiastical discipline admitted no digamists to orders. This is undisputed, both in the West and in the East. Even if marriages entered into before baptism are counted differently, a candidate for orders had to be living, nominally at least, in his first marriage. Then Origen came forward as the first Father of the Church to express criticism of the rule. It is very unlikely that he did so in order to raise purely theoretical problems. Origen had plenty of contact with bishops, and he dealt again and again with morally dubious clerics. After ordination there was nothing one can do. It was necessary to choose candidates better before admitting them to orders. Origen advocates, not asking pedantically whether the candidate is once-married, but rather determining whether he really can practice continence.

He designs the following case: two candidates aspire to an ecclesiastical office. One lived in a second marriage but was again widowed young, did not marry again, and has practiced the virtue of continence until old age. The other is once-married, still lives together with his

---

[5] Origen, *Comm. in Mt.* 14:22 (GCS Orig. 10, 337, 19–338, 7): Ἐπηπορομεν δή, ὁρῶντες δυνατὸν εἶναι βελτίους πολλῷ τυγχάνειν τινὰς διγάμους μονογάμων, τί δήποτε οὐκ ἐπιτρέπει ὁ Παῦλος διγάμους εἰς τὰς ἐκκλησιαστικὰς καθίστασθαι ἀρχάς· καὶ γὰρ ἐδόκει μοι ζητήσεως ἄξιον εἶναι τὸ τοιοῦτον, τῷ ἐνδέχεσθαι ἀτυχήσαντά τινα περὶ δύο γάμους, ἔτι νέον ὄντα ἀποβαλόντα τὴν δευτέραν, ἐγκρατέστατα καὶ καθαρώτατα βεβιωκέναι παρὰ τὸν λοιπὸν μέχρι γήρως χρόνον. Τίς οὖν οὐκ ἂν εὐλόγως ἐπαπορήσαι, τί δήποτε ζητουμένου τοῦ ἄρξοντος τῆς ἐκκλησίας τὸν μὲν τοιόνδε δίγαμον οὐ καθίσταμεν διὰ τὰς <περὶ> τοῦ γάμου λέξεις. Τὸν δὲ μονόγαμον καὶ (εἰ τύχοι) μέχρι γήρως συμβιώσαντα τῇ γυναικὶ κρατοῦμεν ἄρχοντα, ἔσθ᾽ ὅτε μηδὲ γυμνασάμενον εἰς ἀγνείαν καὶ σωφροσύνην; correctly evaluated by C. Richert, *Die Anfänge der Irregularitäten bis zum ersten Allgemeinen Konzil von Nicäa*, StrThS 4, 3 (Freiburg, 1901), 78f. The κρατοῦμεν ἄρχοντα must mean "we prefer to admit to office", not "keep in office" (cf. PL 13, 1243A: "principem eligimus"). The translation of H. J. Vogt, *Origenes: Der Kommentar zum Evangelium nach Mattäus*, vol. 2, BGrL 30 (Stuttgart, 1990), 63, gives the impression that married clerics who were still begetting children were allowed to remain in office. But the entire passage of the text deals with candidates for orders before their admission to the higher clergy. The crucial sentence says this explicitly: Ζητουμένου τοῦ ἄρξοντος τῆς ἐκκλησίας. In order to emphasize his point, Origen uses an example in which both the monogamist and the digamist are older candidates for orders, whereby the monogamist, although he did not live continently until he was aged, is preferred to the digamous widower and is ordained. Thus in both instances Origen is comparing to each other men who are expected to be continent after ordination, and that is what gives rise to his criticism.

wife, and even in his later years has not really been able to get used to continence. How can it be that the man widowed after his second marriage is not ordained? He is living in perfect continence. Why is the candidate preferred who has never given proof of his capacity for continence?

It was possible for Origen to ask this in the first place only because a married cleric in his day evidently had to live with his wife in perfect continence. Thus even if a man was ordained who, as was well known, had not been continent previously and who begot children up to an advanced age, he was nevertheless obliged to practice continence after his ordination. An ordination in this case was a risk, because one might doubt whether the candidate was really capable of continence. Precisely therein lies the problem that Origen had with the prohibition of digamy. In the absence of a continence discipline, his criticism would be unintelligible. Because the continence of clerics was for Origen the crucial thing, he considered it questionable for the Church in practice to insist so much upon the monogamy rule.

Moreover, the monogamy rule certainly had its basis in the demand for continence. Origen explicitly allows laymen to enter a second marriage. But still, he concedes it only to those who cannot withstand concupiscence: "Continence is opposed to a second marriage."[6] Now he intends to demonstrate that this association of monogamy and continence is, in practice, questionable. Why should a candidate for orders who is perfectly continent be turned away automatically simply because he is twice-married, while a monogamous man is allowed to apply, although he has never given proof of his ability to live continently? Monogamy is not always a sufficient guarantee of a capacity for continence. Therefore the married man should begin to train himself in chastity, ideally during the lifetime of his spouse, so as not to succumb at a later age to concupiscence in case he is widowed.[7] Conversely Origen does not understand why digamy should always preclude continence; by the death of the second spouse, at latest, a continent way of life is again achieved.

Like the *Didascalia*, Origen's commentary on Matthew also confirms

---

[6] Origen, *Fragmenta* 35 *in* 1 *Cor.* 7:8–12 (504, 16f. Jenkins). H. Crouzel, *Virginité et mariage selon Origène* (Paris and Bruges, 1963), 152–60.

[7] Origen, *Fragmenta* 35 *in* 1 *Cor.* 7:8–12 (504, 35–37 Jenkins); *Hom.* 17, 10 *in Luc.* 2:33–38 (FC 4, 1, 204, 14–20).

our exegesis of the "unius uxoris vir" of the pastoral letters. Origen was quite aware of the intrinsic connection between the monogamy and the continence of a cleric, but for him it was at the same time problematic: the monogamy proviso was supposed to guarantee the future continence of the cleric, but reality sometimes argued against it. Why not widen the circle of potential ordinands, therefore, to include not only monogamists but also continent men? This difficulty was not resolved. Later theologians, too, would deal with it: Jerome and Theodore of Mopsuestia (see below, pp. 157–63). The point of departure for their arguments was the duty of married clerics and their wives to practice lasting continence. That furnishes an additional reason why there can be no doubt whatsoever that Origen already knew of an obligatory continence celibacy.

c. Begetting Spiritually, Not Corporally

In another passage Origen gives his opinion clearly enough about the continence of married clerics and their wives. There he is grappling with the polygamy and the numerous offspring of the Old Testament patriarchs. In the early Church that was perceived as a crude contrast to the high esteem in which the Gospels hold continence. It took some effort to justify the seemingly all-too-casual attitude of the patriarchs toward sexuality. It seemed strangest of all that the priests of the Old Covenant begot children, because evidently this was contrary to the manner of life led by Christian priests. It should be emphasized at the outset that Origen was the first theologian to note the merely occasional continence of the Old Testament priests. They did not always practice continence, but only "as long as they served at the altar".[8] Now Origen is of the opinion that in their case marital intercourse was tolerated at times for the sake of their descendants; indeed, priests could only be taken from the tribe of Levi, and so it had to continue in existence. In sharp contrast to them he sets off the "priests of the Church". They are perfectly free to beget children, too, but only spir-

---

[8] *Hom.* 4, 6 *in Lev.* (GCS Orig. 6, 324, 10–15): "Ante omnia enim sacerdos, qui divinis assistit altaribus, castitate debet accingi, nec aliter purgare vetera et instaurare poterit nova, nisi lineis induatur. De lineis saepe iam dictum est, et tunc maxime, cum de indumentis sacerdotalibus dicebamus quod species ista formam teneat castitatis, quia origo lini ita de terra editur, ut ex nulla admixtione concepta sit." Cf. ibid., 6, 6 (GCS Orig. 6, 368, 23–28).

itual children—that is to say, Christians—through the proclamation of the Word.[9]

Judging from what Origen says here, it certainly appears as if the priests of the Church observed strict continence.[10] Adolf von Harnack correctly notes that only a spiritual begetting is allowed here, but he erroneously concludes that clerics were obliged to be unmarried. For it is self-evident that Origen knows of married clerics, since he speaks of the children of bishops, priests, and deacons.[11] The comparison with corporeal begetting implies, anyway, that Origen is thinking of married clerics. Thus continence is enjoined upon them, too. But if the marital continence of clerics is meant here, then it was evidently permanent, contrary to that of the Levites. Why that was so is also indicated by Origen: The "priests of the Church" must pray without ceasing;[12] that, however, demands uninterrupted continence (see below, pp. 101ff.).

d. Perfect Priesthood

As we have seen, for Origen the continence of married priests and their wives was not a matter of debate. This is not surprising. After all, he

---

[9] Ibid. (GCS Orig. 6, 368, 23–369, 2): "Sed videamus, ne forte, quoniam in superioribus diximus hoc genus indumenti indicium castitatis videri, quo vel femora operiri vel constringi renes videntur ac lumbi, ne forte, inquam, non semper in illis, qui tunc erant sacerdotes, has partes dicat esse constrictas; aliquando enim et de posteritate generis et successu subolis indulgetur. Sed ego in sacerdotibus ecclesiae huiusmodi intelligentiam non introduxerim; aliam namque rem video occurrere sacramento. Possunt enim et in ecclesia sacerdotes et doctores filios generare, sicut et ille, qui dicebat: 'filioli mei, quos iterum parturio, donec formetur Christus in vobis'." Cf. Hom. 5, 6 in Gen. (GCS Orig. 6, 65, 6–13); Hom. 20, 2 in Num. (GCS Orig. 7, 188, 8–18).

[10] A. von Harnack, Der kirchengeschichtliche Ertrag der exegetischen Arbeiten des Origenes, vol. 1, TU 42, 3 (Leipzig, 1918), 61, 77; R. Gryson, Les Origines du célibat ecclésiastique du premier au septième siècle, RSSR.H 2 (Gembloux, 1970), 16; H. Crouzel, "Les Origines du célibat ecclésiastique: À propos d'un Livre recent", NRTh 6 (1970): 652f. cautiously opposes this view on the basis of hermeneutic considerations, which, however, are too vague. In any case the interpretation of the spiritual fatherhood of clerics, as found in the tradition of Origen, points to a clerical discipline of continence (see below, p. 119).

[11] Origen, Comm. 15, 26 in Mt. 19:16–30 (GCS Orig. 10, 426, 13–20): Ἀγὼν δέ ἐστι καὶ καθελεῖν οἴημα διὰ τὸ ἐκ πατέρων <Χριστιανῶν> ἀνατετράφθαι ἐν Χριστιανισμῷ μέγα φρονούντων, καὶ μάλιστα ἐπὰν τύχῃ πατράσιν ἐπαυχεῖν καὶ προγόνοις προεδρίας ἠξιωμένοις ἐν τῇ ἐκκλησίᾳ, ἐπισκοπικοῦ θρόνου ἢ πρεσβυτερίου τιμῆς ἢ διακονίας εἰς τὸν λαὸν τοῦ θεοῦ. T. Schäfer, Das Priester-Bild im Leben und Werk des Origenes, RSTh 9 (Frankfurt, 1977), 132, gives a clumsy misinterpretation of this passage when he takes it to mean that bishops, priests, and deacons married and begot children.

[12] Hom. 6, 6 in Lev. (GCS Orig. 6, 370, 2).

generally esteemed virginity and continence very highly. In this he followed Clement. Now, from a high esteem for continence one cannot
simply infer the existence of a corresponding clerical discipline. For
that, even clearer indications are needed. Besides those already cited
there are interesting statements in which Origen associates priestly activity and sexual continence in a way that admits of only one conclusion: To be a priest means for him, by definition, living continently.
In these statements he has in view, first of all, the universal priesthood
of all the faithful. From that, however, we can then draw inferences
with respect to the ordained priesthood.

Origen acknowledges that married couples "present [their] bodies
as a living sacrifice holy and acceptable to God" when they agree to
abstain from marital relations for a time so as to devote themselves to
prayer.[13] This makes it very clear, however, that the sacrifices offered
by the priest were accompanied by the offering of his body, that is,
continence. The priestly duty of offering sacrifice and continence were
intimately connected with each other from the very beginning. And
Romans 12:1 seems to have been of prime importance for this understanding of ritual purity: "I appeal to you therefore, brethren, by the
mercies of God, to present your bodies as a living sacrifice, holy and
acceptable to God, which is your spiritual worship." Origen sees this
spiritual worship precisely in the continence of virginal believers and
of continent married couples.[14] A passage of his later work "Against
Celsus" (ca. 245–248), in which he defends Christianity against the
literary attacks of the pagan Celsus, throws into bold relief the ordering
of continence to the priesthood.

> On the other hand, those [Christians] who on account of their ignorance
> are despised by them [that is, the Platonic philosophers] and described
> as fools and slavish souls, keep themselves so far removed from lust and
> depravity and all the ugliness of sexual relations, as soon as they have

---

[13] *Comm.* 9, 1 *in Rom.* 12:1f. (FC 2, 5, 28, 8–21): "Videbitur ergo praecipue hostia vivens
et sancta et Deo placens corpus esse incontaminatum. Verum quoniam videmus nonnullos
sanctorum aliquos etiam apostolorum habuisse coniugia, non usquequaque possumus hoc
de sola virginitate sentire, quamvis in huiuscemodi hostiis habere primum ordinem possit,
sicut et in lege alia erat hostia sacerdotis, alia principis, alia synagogae et alia unius animae. Et
quamvis in ecclesia prima post apostolos hostia martyrum, secunda virginum videatur, tertia
continentium, puto tamen, quod neque illi, qui in coniugiis positi sunt et ex consensu ad
tempus vacant orationi velut Nazaraeorum vota solventes, si in ceteris sancte agant et iuste,
negandi sunt 'corpora sua' exhibere posse 'hostiam viventem, sanctam, Deo placentem'."

[14] Ibid.; *Hom.* 1, 5 *in Lev.* (GCS 6, 287, 9–288, 20).

accepted the teaching of Jesus and have entrusted themselves to God, that many of them, in the manner of perfect priests who abhor all sexual relations, remain completely pure, not only with regard to sex. Among the Athenians there is very likely some [pagan] priest who is not considered capable of subduing his masculine drives and controlling them to the extent he wishes. Therefore, according to the views on chastity prevailing among the Athenians, he is regarded as pure only when his sexual parts have been coated with hemlock juice. Among the Christians, however, men can be found who do not need hemlock juice in order to serve the Divinity in purity. For them, instead of hemlock, the Word of God is sufficient to remove all evil cravings from their hearts, so that they can present their prayers to the Godhead.[15]

Christians after baptism refrained from any forbidden sexual relations, while they were still free to have marital intercourse. That is a foregone conclusion. Here, though, Origen is also considering married people who not only gave up extramarital sins but accomplished an even greater conversion and even renounced in principle their marital rights.[16] Origen knows, as Clement before him did, of the permanent renunciation of the use of marriage among Christians.[17] If the total abstinence of many Christians is now being compared with the manner of life of perfect priests, then that says something, first of all, about Origen's idea of perfect priests: they renounce all sexual relations, and do not merely suspend them for a certain time. Tertullian sees it this way as well.[18] This presents, then, a remarkable connection between priesthood in general and continence.

This allows us, though, to draw conclusions in turn about the ordained priesthood. For if there is such a thing as perfect priesthood among Christians, then this cannot be uncoupled from the ministerial priesthood of the Church. There were married priests in their ranks, just as there were married priests among the pagans, whose continence was now being surpassed by the Christians.[19] The Athenian priest mentioned by Origen was the hierophant of the mysteries of Eleusis. As a rule he was married and had children. From the day he took office until his death he had to refrain from sexual intercourse. It is possible that he

---

[15] *Contra Celsum* 7, 48 (GCS Orig. 2, 199, 12–25).
[16] Gryson, *Origines*, 18.
[17] *Contra Celsum*, 1, 26 (GCS Orig. 1, 78, 17–28).
[18] *De monogamia* 8, 1 (CCL 2, 1239, 7).
[19] Tertullian, *De exhortatione castitatis* 13, 1–3 (CCL 2, 1033, 1–1035, 34).

was obliged to practice continence permanently, or it may have been only during the festival periods.[20] With these Origen contrasts those married Christian men who practiced perfect continence without any lust-restraining pharmaceuticals (of the sort that the hierophant used) and so could recite their priestly prayers. What is more obvious than to think of married clerics, who outdid their pagan colleagues on two counts, so to speak: they were always continent and they were so of their own free will.

Another statement of Origen leads into this context of universal and ministerial priesthood:

> Do not think that, as the stomach is made for food and food for the stomach, in the same way the body is made for cohabitation. If you want to understand the argument [of the Apostle] as to why the body was made, then hear: so that it may be a temple for the Lord; so that the soul, which is holy and blessed in the sight of the Holy Spirit, may function as a priest of the Holy Spirit dwelling within it.[21]

This surely is supposed to mean that the body does not exist for sexual relations but rather should be continent and holy, a temple of the Holy Spirit, so that within it the soul can offer sacrifices like a priest. In Origen's opinion the Holy Spirit is absent during the time of marital intercourse.[22] Similar reflections on ritual purity are found in his writings in such great number[23] that there can be scarcely any doubt about a permanent ascetical discipline for married clerics and their wives. Continence is viewed as a universal prerequisite for priestly activity. In a similar way Origen can view continence in general as a necessary condition for the priest who serves at the altar.[24] If one wanted to take this to mean a merely periodic continence at ritually appointed times, one would not do justice to the frequency of the statements. Why

---

[20] H. Strathmann, *Geschichte der frühchristlichen Askese bis zur Entstehung des Mönchtums im religionsgeschichtlichen Zusammenhange*, vol. 1, *Die Askese in der Umgebung des werdenden Christentums* (Leipzig, 1914), 210f. Jerome also favors permanent continence: *Adversus Jovinianum* I, 49 (PL 23², 295f.).

[21] Origen, *Fragmenta 29 in 1 Cor.* 6:13f. (370, 2–6 Jenkins): Μὴ νομίσῃς ὅτι ὥσπερ ἡ κοιλία γέγονεν τοῖς βρώμασιν καὶ τὰ βρώματα τῇ κοιλίᾳ, οὕτω καὶ τὸ σῶμα γέγονε διὰ συνουσιασμόν. Εἰ θέλεις τὸν προηγούμενον λόγον μαθεῖν διὰ τί γέγονεν, ἄκουε ἵνα ναὸς ᾖ τῷ κυρίῳ, καὶ ἵνα ἡ ψυχὴ ἁγία καὶ μακαρία οὖσα τὸ πνεῦμα τὸ ἅγιον ὡσπερεὶ θεραπεύουσα ἱερεὺς γένηται τοῦ ἐν σοὶ ἁγίου πνεύματος.

[22] *Hom. 6, 3 in Num.* (GCS Orig. 7, 35, 16f.).

[23] Crouzel, *Virginité*, 53–60.

[24] *Hom. 4, 6 in Lev.* (GCS Orig. 6, 324, 10–15).

should Origen refer again and again to the continence associated with priestly activity if the continence required of priests was the same kind as was expected of every lay person who participated in the Divine Liturgy?[25] It was not by accident that Origen made a distinction between laymen and priests. Therefore greater continence was required of the priest.

e. Constant Availability of the Priest

Origen of Alexandria. Clerics were subject to a more stringent continence discipline,[26] while laymen had to abstain from marital relations only on the days when the Divine Liturgy was celebrated; we find more detailed information about this situation in a sermon of Origen on the Book of Numbers. In it he speaks about the necessity of unceasing prayer (cf. 1 Thess 5:17). In the same place he refers to Paul's advice that married couples should agree to refuse one another for a certain time in order to pray (1 Cor 7:5). We find here precisely that periodic continence which laymen observed before they attended a Divine Liturgy. But were they not actually supposed to pray constantly? Would they really not have to practice continence all the time, then? Faced with this dilemma, Origen writes:

> [Paul recommends temporary continence for married people,] so it is certain that unceasing sacrifice is impossible for those who are subject to the obligations of marriage. I therefore conclude that only the one vowed to unceasing and perpetual chastity can offer unceasing sacrifice. There are other feasts for those who cannot offer unceasingly the sacrifice of chastity.[27]

This is reminiscent of statements by Clement. A careful approach to the text will note that clerics are not mentioned explicitly. Every Chris-

---

[25] Origen, *Selecta in Ez.* 7 (PG 13, 793B); *Fragmenta* 34 *in 1 Cor.* 7:5 (501, 2⁻502, 33 Jenkins).

[26] Origen, *Fragmenta* 50 *in Jer.* 36:21 (GCS Orig. 32, 223, 21⁻25) refers to the stricter demands made on clerics who celebrate the Eucharist in comparison with the laymen who attend.

[27] *Hom.* 23, 3 *in Num.* (GCS Orig. 7, 215, 11⁻16): "Certum est quia impeditur sacrificium >indesinens< his, qui coniugalibus necessitatibus serviunt. Unde videtur mihi quod illius est solius offerre sacrificium >indesinens<, qui indesinenti et perpetuae se devoverit castitati. Sed sunt et alii dies festi his, qui forte non possunt indesinenter immolare sacrificia castitatis." C. Cochini, *Apostolic Origins of Priestly Celibacy* (San Francisco, 1990), 155⁻58.

tian should offer sacrifice unceasingly.[28] Of course, as Paul says, this is not possible for those who have sexual intercourse. Since evidently only those who have taken a vow of continence can offer sacrifice unceasingly, this is true now in general for widows, virgins, and ascetics, but also a priori for priests, who *ex professo* must pray unceasingly.[29]

Moreover Origen is not speaking in general about prayer but rather about the sacrifice demanded by sexual abstinence. The restrictive formulation ("only the one vowed to . . . chastity can offer") makes it plain that Origen is thinking exclusively of the Eucharistic Sacrifice. Indeed, he is delivering his homily in the course of a eucharistic celebration. So at this point he probably has only clerics in mind. He deliberately speaks of the sacrifice in order to make clear to his listeners the meaning of the clerical discipline: The duty of offering unceasing sacrifice demands of all clerics, whether married or not, permanent continence. In Origen's time, evidently, only those candidates were ordained who had taken a formal vow of chastity.

We must pause here and pursue an objection that is raised against a discipline of continence celibacy in the third century. It must be noted in this regard that, toward the end of the fourth century in the Latin Church, the requirement of perfect continence for married clerics was justified by the daily celebration of the Eucharist: someone who celebrated the Eucharist daily had to be continent daily and ultimately renounce marital intercourse entirely. What would happen, though, if in the third century the custom of daily Eucharist did not yet exist? At least for the place where Origen was living, we must suppose that the Eucharist was celebrated only on Sundays. One might conclude that at this time it was not yet necessary to observe permanent continence.

This objection, however, is not valid. For one thing, Origen in another passage cites, not specifically the Eucharist, but prayer in general as the reason for the sexual continence of the priest.[30] It is true that we do not find the explicit equation: the constant prayer of the priest demands perfect continence in the married cleric. If it were put in those terms somewhere, the search for historical evidence would be considerably easier. And yet this conclusion is absolutely unavoidable.

---

[28] *Hom.* 23, 3 *in Num.* (GCS Orig. 7, 214, 22–27).

[29] *Hom.* 6, 6 *in Lev.* (GCS Orig. 6, 370, 2): "Oret ergo et sacerdos ecclesiae indesinenter." At this precise point Origen is addressing also the chastity of the priests of the Church.

[30] Ibid.

According to Paul's statement, married couples should refrain from sexual intercourse in order to pray (1 Cor 7:5). Therefore, if unceasing prayer is viewed as the duty of the cleric, it necessarily follows that he must refrain from marital relations. Tertullian already gives a radical interpretation of this verse: "Prayer is necessary for men every day, at every moment; and once prayer is necessary, so too is continence."[31] Of course this is true a fortiori for clerics.

More importantly, however, in the homily on Numbers referred to above, Origen speaks of the "unceasing sacrifice". Even if that does not mean that the Eucharist was actually celebrated every day, it still must be an expression for the constant availability of the priest. The priest had always to be ready for service. Therefore he had always to practice continence. At least ideally, there was daily Divine Liturgy already in the third century. Corresponding to the ideal of the priest and according to liturgical rhetoric, a priest had always to pray and offer sacrifice. We have an especially impressive witness for this from Rome in the prayer for the consecration of a bishop, as transmitted to us by Hippolytus around the year 215: "Father, grant . . . that thy servant, whom thou hast chosen for the ministry of bishop, . . . may serve thee blamelessly as high priest day and night and be gracious in thy sight. May he assemble the number of the saved and offer to thee the gifts of thy Holy Church. May he . . . unwavering, blameless and with a clear conscience offer thee the spotless and unbloody Sacrifice."[32] Thus at a time when the bishop in Rome did not yet celebrate daily, he was summoned to pray and sacrifice day and night. Constant readiness, then, sufficed. And so we can determine the ritual purpose for a discipline of clerical continence long before the custom of a daily eucharistic celebration.

Cyprian of Carthage. The question about daily Eucharist leads us to North Africa. For there the Eucharist was actually being celebrated every day at around this period. We know of this through Bishop Cyprian of Carthage (d. 258), a contemporary of Origen.[33] Like an

---

[31] Tertullian, *De exhortatione castitatis* 10, 2 (CCL 2, 1030, 16–18): "Si quotidie, omni momento oratio hominibus necessaria est, utique et continentia, post quam oratio, necessaria est." [The English version has been translated from the Latin.—TRANS.]

[32] Hippolytus, *Traditio Apostolica* 3 (FC 1, 218, 17–28). Cf. *Constitutiones apostolorum* 8, 5, 6f. (SC 336, 146, 28–148, 41).

[33] Gryson, *Origines*, 177; R. Kottje, "Das Aufkommen der täglichen Eucharistiefeier in der Westkirche und die Zölibatsforderung", ZKG 82 (1971): 219f. On the unceasing prayer

anvil, Cyprian withstood the heavy blows of the Christian persecution in the year 250 and, looking beyond all factions, fought for the unity of the Church. Although he was a Latin Father, his theology was in many respects similar to Origen's. He shared with him the same cultic understanding of the priesthood and the Eucharistic Sacrifice. Hence the Divine Liturgy was, for him as well, always connected with sexual asceticism.[34] On this subject he was in agreement with his compatriot Tertullian, whom he greatly revered and whose writings he frequently read. We have heard about Tertullian's views concerning daily prayer and the corresponding observance of continence. From this it is entirely clear that, for Cyprian, too, the daily Divine Liturgy implied permanent sexual abstinence. And that is true not only for celibate clerics like Cyprian himself, but also for the married priests of his diocese, about whom we hear occasionally in his letters.

It may seem unwarranted to infer a discipline of clerical continence from the custom of daily celebration of the Eucharist and to do so for such an early period. Yet our argument here is no different from that of Roger Gryson, who claims to know, based on the daily Eucharist, that continence celibacy was introduced toward the end of the fourth century in Rome.[35] What is true for the fourth century, though, must also be true for the third century: where there is daily celebration of the Eucharist, there is perfect continence of the clergy. Thus Gryson's thesis about a late introduction of a strict continence discipline is refuted by its own presuppositions. There is no way that the connection between daily Eucharist and continence celibacy can be an invention

---

of the priest, see R. Seagraves, *Pascentes cum disciplina: A Lexical Study of the Clergy in the Cyprianic Correspondence*, Par. 37 (Fribourg, 1993), 120f.

[34] *Epistulae* 65, 3 (CSEL 3, 2, 724, 11); *Testimoniorum libri III ad Quirinum* 3, 32 (CSEL 3, 1, 145, 11f.). H. Böhmer, "Die Entstehung des Zölibates", in *Geschichtliche Studien Albert Hauck zum 70. Geburtstag* (Leipzig, 1916), 17: "Thus it should be viewed as a mere accident that, in the fragments of third-century ecclesiastical literature that we still have, no direct statement about the continence of those who serve at the altar has been preserved. All of the ideas from which that demand resulted by a logical necessity were, in any case, present already at that time, and the passages that seemed to authenticate and justify them were, for people like Cyprian, already just as familiar and oft-cited as the well-known Messianic sayings." G. Denzler, "Zur Geschichte des Zölibats: Ehe und Ehelosigkeit der Priester bis zur Einführung des Zölibatsgesetzes im Jahr 1139", StZ 183 (1969): 393; R. Gryson, "Dix ans de recherches sur les origines du célibat ecclésiastique: Réflexion sur les publications des années 1970–1979", RTL 11 (1980): 171.

[35] Gryson, *Origines*, 200f., 203; E. Schillebeeckx, *Christliche Identität und kirchliches Amt: Plädoyer für den Menschen in der Kirche*, (Dusseldorf, 1985), 290.

of Rome. As early as the first half of the third century in North Africa, when Cyprian was writing, there must have been a celibacy discipline. This is really not surprising. For if Origen in Egypt knew of clerical continence, why should it not have existed at that time also in western North Africa?

2. Disputed Canons of the Ecclesiastical Canons of the Holy Apostles

To be free of one's only wife. Indications are that the region of Egypt or Syria was the place of origin for the *Canones ecclesiastici sanctorum apostolorum* [known in German as the *Apostolische Kirchenordnung*], written around the year 300. They cite the apostles as their authority and deal with the qualifications necessary in a candidate for the episcopacy or the priesthood. In doing so they do not contradict the picture we have obtained from the *Didascalia* and from Origen; rather, they confirm these findings. Canon 16 is concerned with the bishop: "It is good for him [that is, the (candidate for) bishop] to be without a wife [ἀγύναιος], but if not, that he be free of his only wife [ἀπὸ μιᾶς γυναικός]."[36] The ἀπὸ μιᾶς γυναικός is difficult. The translation "free of his only wife" is unassailable, though, for internal textual reasons. In this case Roger Gryson produced the decisive arguments against Franz Xaver Funk.[37] The latter wanted to understand the Greek text as though the bishop were supposed to have been married no more than once. Then the canon would say nothing at all about sexual continence. Nevertheless this interpretation fails to account for the wording of the text, which, contrary to the formulation in the pastoral letters, adds an ἀπὸ [= away from, *or temporally* after, since; cf. Latin *ab, abs*]. The ἀπὸ clearly stands in parallel with the ἀ-γύναιος [un-married]. If the text is taken at face value, then ἀπὸ γυναικός means simply: free of a wife (cf. 1 Cor 7:27).

Possibly marital separation (not divorce) is being required here of the married bishop. If so, that would be tantamount to a custom whereby even today a married bishop of the Orthodox Church must send his wife to the convent. The early theologians, it is true, are quite aware

---

[36] *Constitutio ecclesiastica apostolorum* 16, 2 (24, 11–25, 1 Schermann): Καλὸν μὲν εἶναι ἀγύναιος, εἰ δὲ μή, ἀπὸ μιᾶς γυναικός.

[37] Gryson, *Origines*, 94–96.

of Paul's saying, "the husband should not divorce his wife" (1 Cor 7:10f.).[38] But in their view, Paul here is objecting only to a unilateral marital separation, when someone repudiates a spouse against the latter's will. Thus Clement of Alexandria could maintain that Paul himself, for the sake of the apostolate, had separated from his wife, certainly with her consent.

It was by no means acceptable for someone to separate from his wife in order to enter a spiritual marriage with another woman. Eusebius of Caesarea complained about the conduct of Bishop Paul of Samosata (around 260), who separated from his wife under such circumstances.[39] Toward the end of the fourth century the Apostolic Canons explicitly forbid marital separation (see below, pp. 181–83). At the time of Chrysostom we have a few further references for Syria.[40] In the year 400 Chrysostom, as patriarch of Constantinople, took action against Bishop Antoninos of Ephesus, who had separated from his wife but then had gone back to her again and had begotten children.[41] All told, the Ecclesiastical Canons of the Holy Apostles could hardly be speaking of the marital separation of the bishop.

The simplest interpretation of Canon 16 is one proposed by Christian Cochini: The bishop either must never have married (ἀγύναιος = unmarried),[42] or else, if he had married, he must have had one wife in the past (ἀπὸ μιᾶς γυναικός), that is to say, be widowed.[43] In any case, Chrysostom was aware that in his time many wanted to understand the "unius uxoris vir" of the pastoral letters in this way.[44] Accordingly the canon intends that a bishop be selected from among virginal or else widowed candidates. This probably expresses a preference, quite widespread in the East, for celibate higher clergy. On one occasion,

---

[38] Clement of Alexandria, *Stromata* 3, 18, 108, 1 (GCS Clem. Alex. 2⁴, 246, 10–13); 3, 12, 79, 1 (231, 18). For Origen, see Crouzel, *Virginité*, 148–52.

[39] Eusebius, *Historia ecclesiastica* 7, 30, 14 (GCS Eus. 2, 2, 712, 6). See also ibid., 3, 29, 2 (GCS Eus. 2, 1, 260, 13–15): The deacon Nikolaus, who like many apostles was married and had children, was prepared to separate from his wife before his ordination.

[40] John Chrysostom, *De virginitate* 40, 2 (SC 125, 234, 18–21).

[41] Palladius, *Vita Johannis Chrysostomi* 13 (SC 341, 276, 171f.). Cochini, *Origins*, 293f. is inadequate.

[42] For example, Porphyry, *De abstinentia* 4, 17.

[43] Cochini, *Origins*, 203–5.

[44] *Hom.* 10, 1 *in* 1 *Tim.* 3:1–4 (PG 62, 549): Μιας γυναικὸς ἄνδρα; Τινὲς μὲν οὖν φασιν, ὅτι τὸν ἀπὸ γυναικὸς ἠνίξατο μένοντα ἐλεύθερον.

for example, John Chrysostom consecrated six celibate bishops who were to replace an equal number of deposed bishops.[45]

Married bishops, however, were by no means excluded by this preference. For it only states: It is *good* (καλὸν) for a bishop-candidate to be without a wife. Married bishops were also accepted. This does not call into question or make optional the marital continence required of them, also. Previously scholarship has supposed that it did, because it understood the ἀπὸ μιᾶς γυναικός, not as widowhood, but as marital continence. According to that interpretation it would be *good* for the candidate, if he was married, to give up marital relations. That does not sound very binding, then. Marital continence would then be made an option of the cleric. On the contrary, though, the *good* can only refer to the first half of the sentence, the very purpose being to express the preeminence of celibacy over marital continence: It would be wonderful if all bishops were celibate;[46] if they are in fact married, then they have to practice continence.

However one may approach the text, it is self-evident that the marriage was conducted continently. This is not only implied by a similar formula in Epiphanius.[47] It is even more the result of the situation's inner logic. The bishop should be without a wife, if at all possible. Well, why? On account of continence. If he was married (for the first time), then he naturally lived with his wife continently; it was better for continence, though, in the case of the spouse's death, to remain widowed; best, of course, was the virginal state. This presents neatly the same ranking that is then found in very similar terms in Epiphanius[48] and other ecclesiastical writers.

To refrain from relations with their wives. Another canon of the Ecclesiastical Canons of the Holy Apostles confirms our considerations. This canon 18 deals, not with the widowed presbyters, but with those who are still married: "It is necessary that the presbyters be of an advanced age already and experienced; in a certain manner (τρόπῳ τινὶ) they refrain from relations with their wives."[49] In this canon the τρόπῳ is

---

[45] Palladius, *Vita Johannis Chrysostomi* 15 (SC 341, 296, 47, 300, 104).

[46] Cochini, *Origins*, 205, n. 181. The construction "it is good . . .; but if not . . ." is found also in Paul's discussion of staying single and marrying (1 Cor 7:8f.).

[47] Epiphanius, *Panarion LXXX haeresium* 48, 5 (GCS Epiph. 2², 231, 14): Τῶν ἀπὸ μονο-γαμίας ἐγκρατευομένων.

[48] Epiphanius, *De fide* 21, 7f. (GCS Epiph. 3, 522, 8–11).

[49] *Constitutio ecclesiastica apostolorum* 18, 2 (25, 13–26, 2 Schermann): Δεῖ οὖν εἶναι τοὺς

controversial. If it is translated in the form as given above, it appears to express the command that presbyters practice only a certain periodic continence. But that can hardly be convincing, for the simple reason that there is no other contemporary evidence for a discipline of continence at stipulated times. Not until the seventh century do we find the unequivocal demand that clerics should observe sexual continence only on the occasions when they celebrate the Divine Liturgy. Besides, periodic continence is a matter of course, required of and practiced by every married Christian. It would be superfluous to make a special requirement of it for the presbyters. Furthermore the canon would then necessarily cast a very dubious light on Christian marriages. For it would imply that only those at an advanced age could be trusted to conduct their marriages chastely and honorably.

Therefore the question remains, what does it mean that presbyters must refrain *in a certain manner* from relations with their wives? Adolf Harnack and Roger Gryson basically gave the answer when they referred to two similarly worded passages from a later Church document.[50] There it says: The bishop should be no younger than fifty years old, "so that in a certain manner [ὅτι τρόπῳ τινὶ]" he may avoid the inconstancies of youth; the widow enrolled by the Church should be no younger than sixty years old, "so that in a certain manner [ὅτι τρόπῳ τινὶ]" she will not be tempted to marry again. The second part of the canon (the participle ἀπεχομένους) is thus connected to the preceding part as a purpose clause. The τρόπῳ τινί turns out to be not that crucial to the sense of the canon. However τρόπῳ τινί may be translated —"in a certain manner" or, with Harnack, "in a suitable way [that is, appropriate to the ecclesiastical state]" (= κατὰ τρόπον)[51]—in any case we are dealing with a clear, disciplinary purpose, which puts an end to all options. This is true of all three examples. By no means may the

πρεσβυτέρους ἤδη κεχρονικότας ἐπὶ τῷ κόσμῳ, τρόπῳ τινὶ ἀπεχομένους τῆς πρὸς γυναῖκας συνελεύσεως.

[50] A. von Harnack, *Die Quellen der sogenannten Apostolischen Kirchenordnung*, TU 2, 5 (Leipzig, 1886), 9f.; Gryson, *Origines*, 97. *Constitutiones apostolorum* 2, 1, 1 (SC 320, 144, 2–6): Τὸν ποιμένα τὸν καθιστάμενον ἐπίσκοπον εἰς τὰς Ἐκκλησίας ἐν πάσῃ παροικίᾳ δεῖ ὑπάρχειν ἀνέγκλητον, ἀνεπίληπτον, ἀνέπαφον πάσης ἀδικίας ἀνθρώπων, οὐκ ἔλαττον ἐτῶν πεντήκοντα, ὅτι τρόπῳ τινὶ τὰς νεωτερικὰς ἀταξίας καὶ τὰς ἔξωθεν διαβολὰς ἐκπεφευγὼς ὑπάρχει. Ibid., 3, 1, 1 (SC 329, 120, 1–3): Χήρας δὲ καθιστᾶτε μὴ ἔλαττον ἐτῶν ἑξήκοντα, ἵνα τρόπῳ τινὶ τὸ τῆς διγαμίας αὐτῶν ἀνύποπτον βέβαιον ὑμῖν διὰ τῆς ἡλικίας ὑπάρχῃ.

[51] Τρόπῳ τινὶ could also be an abbreviated form of τρόπῳ ᾧτινι (relative adverb construction: "in such a manner as").

bishop pursue a carefree life, as the young are wont to do; therefore he should be at least fifty years old. The widow may not marry again in any case; therefore she should be at least sixty years old. It is true then analogously for the presbyter according to the Ecclesiastical Canons of the Holy Apostles: in no way is he to have marital relations with his wife; therefore he should be at an advanced age. The thought behind this is that it will be easier for an older father of a family to practice perfect continence from now on. One may well suspect that the value judgment implied here was based on experience. It is quite possible that many clerics, ordained all too early, failed to practice marital continence thereafter. Therefore the age for admitting married men to holy orders was raised.

3. The Celibacy Canon of the Spanish Council of Elvira

Much of what has been said thus far indicates that the churches of Syria, Egypt, and North Africa knew the discipline of continence celibacy. Repeatedly the sexual abstinence of married clerics was made a theme. As far as we have been able to tell up to this point, it was never a matter of limited, periodic continence. There may be a question of such a discipline for laypeople who wanted to participate in the Divine Liturgy. This brings us to our next passage, which is disputed on just this point: Are we dealing here with a merely periodic continence, that is, a ritual discipline restricted to appointed times, or is permanent abstinence being required of clerics?

a. Elvira Prohibits Marital Relations for Higher Clerics

With the Council of Elvira (actually Ilíberis, today Granada), which took place around 306,[52] we turn now to Spain. In Elvira bishops, priests, and deacons from almost all the Spanish provinces had gathered. First we must discuss the chronology of the council and of its canons. Most scholars date the council around A.D. 306. Others view celibacy as a late invention of Rome and therefore postpone canon 33

---

[52] T. Ulbert, "Hispania I (landesgeschichtlich)", in RAC 15 (1991), 607–46, at 629, dates the Council of Elvira between 300 and 302.

to the end of the fourth century.[53] In fact Maurice Meigne once suggested a late dating for several of the canons, foremost among them being the celibacy canon (on account of its double negative construction and moreover because of its supposedly anti-ascetical point).[54] But only a year later it was demonstrated that this hypothesis was baseless;[55] it cannot bear the burden of proof. Though several canons may indeed have been added later to the acts of the council, nevertheless any attempt to sort out particular canons remains arbitrary. Hence the point of departure for scholarship now, as before, is the uniform dating of the canons of Elvira around A.D. 306.[56]

Important for us is canon 33. This much-debated celibacy canon is concerned with married ecclesiastical ministers; the double negative should cause neither grammatical nor semantic difficulties:

> We have decreed a general [*in totum*] prohibition for married bishops, priests, and deacons, or also for all clerics who have been appointed to ministry [*vel omnibus clericis positis in ministerio*]: they must not come together with their wives and they must not beget children. Whosoever shall do the same shall be expelled from the ranks of the clergy.[57]

---

[53] Schillebeeckx, *Identität*, 289; H.-J. Vogels, *Priester dürfen heiraten: Biblische, geschichtliche und rechtliche Gründe gegen den Pflichtzölibat* (Bonn, 1992), 38–40; G. Denzler, *Die Geschichte des Zölibats* (Freiburg, 1993), 25f. Gryson, too, "Ans", 164, favors a late dating of canon 33, but that is a *petitio principi* [begging the question]: because in his opinion celibacy originated with the popes, the canon must have been written no earlier than the end of the fourth century. He and the others do not get beyond conjectures ("Je crois").

[54] M. Meigne, "Concile ou collection d'Elvire", RHE 70 (1975): 361–87, assigns to canon 33 of Elvira an anti-Priscillianist dating of around 380. He understands the canon as if it demanded marital intercourse in direct opposition to the ascetical Priscillians. According to this view, it is not a celibacy canon at all. This is said to result from the double negative construction ("prohibere . . . abstinere se").

[55] E. Griffe, "Le Concile d'Elvire et les origines du célibat ecclésiastique", BLE 77 (1976): 123–27. His grammatical considerations are convincing. The text in question is unequivocally a celibacy canon (as Gryson agrees, "Ans", 160–64). Thus an anti-ascetical interpretation of the canon, which is the sole argument for an anti-Priscillianist late dating, is untenable.

[56] R. Garcia Villoslada, *Historia de la Iglesia en España*, vol. 1, *La Iglesia en la España romana y visigoda (siglos I–VIII)* (Madrid, 1979), 82–84; J. Orlandis and D. Ramos-Lissón, *Die Synoden auf der Iberischen Halbinsel bis zum Einbruch des Islam (711)* (Paderborn, 1981), 3–6; E. Reichert, *Die Canones der Synode von Elvira: Einleitung und Kommentar* (diss., Hamburg, 1990), 21–23, 49. Even if a few canons had been added later to the Acts of the Council, there would be no evidence whatsoever for assuming that this was true of canon 33 as well.

[57] Canon 33: "Placuit in totum prohibere episcopis, presbyteris et diaconibus vel omnibus clericis positis in ministerio abstinere se a coniugibus suis et non generare filios.

Thus Elvira did not require celibacy of clerics. It presented no problem at all for the Council Fathers that there were married clerics. Canon 33, in fact, deals exclusively with them. According to the will of the bishops, they should live together in continence with their wives. But here the debate of the historians begins. What sort of continence was required, then: permanent abstinence from the day of ordination on, or should the clerics refrain from relations with their wives only periodically, when they celebrate the Divine Liturgy?

The Paphnutius legend caused many scholars to discover in this canon a limited, ritual continence. For if the Council of Nicaea had rejected perfect continence for married clerics and their wives, then Elvira could only require ritual continence as a preliminary step toward it; Elvira may have introduced such a discipline of periodic continence, or it may merely have confirmed an existing practice. Those who advance this interpretation understand the phrase "clericis positis in ministerio" as follows: On account of their ministry at the altar (*ministerium*), clerics must be continent and may not beget children. If it were a matter of an innovation here, it would fit well into that picture found in celibacy scholarship, according to which clerics, in the beginning, were not restricted at all in their marriages, and ritual continence was not introduced until Elvira, and then eventually, toward the end of the fourth century, total abstinence became accepted on the basis of the daily eucharistic celebration.

This interpretation, however, cannot be allowed for two reasons. First, *ministerium* cannot be interpreted as service at the altar or ritual duty (*sacrum ministerium*). There is no basis whatsoever for that in the text. Such a reading is contradicted by the use of an identical formula (*in ministerio positi*) in canon 18.[58] Therefore continence here does not have a ritual basis at all, as though sexual relations made a person impure and unfit for the Divine Liturgy.[59] *In ministerium ponere* means

---

Quicumque vero fecerit, ab honore clericatus exterminetur" (12f. Jonkers). As to the double negative construction, see Griffe, "Concile", 124–26.

[58] "Episcopi, presbyteres et diacones si in ministerio positi detecti fuerint quod sint moechati" (9 Jonkers) of course cannot mean: "Clerics who during their service at the altar are found guilty of adultery."

[59] Thus J. P. Audet, *Mariage et célibat dans la service pastorale de l'Église: Histoire et orientations* (Paris, 1967), 31–34; Gryson, *Origines*, 40; B. Verkamp, "Cultic Purity and the Law of Celibacy", RfR 30 (1971): 199–217 at 199f.

simply "to appoint someone to his office".[60] Moreover, *omnibus clericis positis in ministerio* then means "to all those who have been appointed to office as clerics", or even more precisely, "all clerics, as soon as they have been appointed to office". Thus it is being required quite bluntly that married clerics must practice perfect continence from the day of their ordination.[61]

To assume that this passage refers to a merely periodic continence is just not possible for a further reason. Around the turn of the fourth century married couples were bound anyway to observe continence on days when the Divine Liturgy was celebrated. Why then should Elvira emphasize such a custom of periodic continence for clerics in particular? Or had this discipline perhaps fallen into disuse among the clerics, of all people, so that it had to be urged upon them again? But that, too, is erroneous. For it would be impossible to verify whether clerics really observed continence on liturgical days and refrained from begetting children. The canon, however, is aimed at a practical administration of justice: Whoever violates continence will be deposed from office. Canon 33 thus deals unequivocally with permanent and lasting continence.[62]

Now was this perfect continence an innovation? In any case the phrase *in totum* indicates that this canon has a history. Perhaps, therefore, instead of a previous custom of limited ritual continence, the canon now begins to require continual abstinence?[63] Before Elvira, then, had the clerics observed abstinence only on liturgical days? Of course that would be plausible if texts predating Elvira could be produced that witness to a clerical custom of periodic continence. For such a discipline, however, there is evidence only for the laity and Old Testament priests, but not for clerics.[64]

---

[60] Cf. K. E. Georges, *Ausführliches lateinisch-deutsches Handwörterbuch*, vol. 2 (Darmstadt, 1992), 1774.

[61] Kottje, "Aufkommen", 226.

[62] Thus G. Denzler, as well, *Das Papsttum und der Amtszölibat*, vol. 1, *Die Zeit bis zur Reformation*, PuP 5, 1 (Stuttgart, 1973), 8.

[63] Thus Gryson, *Origines*, 39.

[64] Neither may canon 29 of the Council of Arles (in 314) be cited as evidence of this, since the canon must be assigned to a date no earlier than the end of the fourth century. "Moreover, [concerned with] what is worthy, pure, and honest, we exhort our brothers [in the episcopate] to make sure that priests and deacons have no [sexual] relations with their wives, since they are serving the ministry every day. Whoever will act against this decision

It will clarify matters if we take a look at the sentence structure of the canon. First the ranks of the clergy are listed: married bishops, priests, and deacons, and afterward the same group of persons is named again: all married clerics.[65] Besides this, the correspondence between *in totum* and *omnibus* signals the scope of the canon: Not only the bishops or only the priests or only the deacons must practice continence, but rather all who have been appointed to serve the Church. Therefore there must have been married clerics (perhaps in remote areas) who were not practicing continence, perhaps on the grounds that they were "only" deacons or "only" priests. No doubt these clerics did not merely break some rule of periodic continence. Rather, they begot children and thereby were proved guilty of having failed in their duty to observe continence.

Elvira, therefore, was not initiating continence celibacy. The reason why the bishops were concerned with married clerics, rather, was to deal with individual abuses. Continence was expected of married clerics and their wives, but a few thought that they could evade this requirement. Perfect continence was not introduced overnight, as a novelty without any theological basis. It would have been impossible to impose that upon a clergy that had received holy orders on completely different terms.[66] Then too, the severity of the punishment (removal from office) would scarcely be intelligible. An innovation of this kind, with such a universal retroactive effect on rights already obtained, would necessarily have called forth a storm of indignation.[67]

How could it have happened that in Elvira, a city at the western limit of the universal Church in that era, a council demanded as a foregone conclusion a discipline of continence that is, moreover, attested to in the East?[68] It certainly causes one to conjecture that in the third century a uniform discipline existed for the higher clergy from East to West. Precisely because this practice was customary in other parts of

---

will be deposed from the honor of the clergy" (CCL 148, 25, 15–18). Gryson, *Origines*, 190. Another viewpoint is presented by Cochini, *Origins*, 161–69.

[65] Research has discovered many instances of an explanatory *vel* in the sense of "that is to say". This is confirmed by the Council of Carthage a. 390 canon 2 (112f. Jonkers).

[66] Cochini, *Origins*, 160.

[67] A. M. Stickler, *The Case for Clerical Celibacy: Its Historical Development and Theological Foundations*, trans. Brian Ferme (San Francisco, 1995), 23.

[68] Canon 27 of the Council of Elvira points to the East with regard to canon 3 of the Council of Nicaea.

the Church as well, Elvira could enjoin continence upon the married clerics and their wives without compromise. Resistance on the basis of customs in other regions was not anticipated.

b. Canon 33 Is the First Formal Celibacy Law

Canon 33 of the Council of Elvira is rightly considered to be the first formal celibacy law, in the sense of a continence requirement. This is not infrequently misunderstood, and it is claimed that here, on the edge of the then-known world, the discipline of continence celibacy first emerged from the waters of baptism. As though there had been no such thing at all previously. Mainly for this reason scholars again and again have had difficulties with Elvira, because it seemed to be situated in the history of celibacy like a foundling exposed to the elements.[69] Meanwhile we have learned, though, that even before Elvira there were numerous references to a continence discipline. To that extent the council only confirms what we already know from Syria, Egypt, and North Africa.

Nevertheless, descriptions of celibacy begin again and again with the claim that explicit legislation concerning continence begins only with Elvira, and therefore no such discipline could have existed before this time. Behind this is, to some degree, the notion that what is not committed to writing cannot exist. But how many customs of the early Church that are taken for granted were never legally formulated and yet existed! The legal historian distinguishes between law and legislation. The unwritten legal norm temporally precedes written legislation. Before something becomes "a law" it is standard practice for a long time.[70] Many examples of this can be cited from the history of secular law, and in the history of the Church it is no different. Therein lies nothing short of an argument from legal theory for the existence of continence celibacy as early as the third century.

Now one might think that there may very well have been continent married clerics before Elvira, who freely decided to observe this discipline in keeping with common ascetical practices, but without having been compelled to do so by any authority. The hypothesis of a voluntary clerical continence, though, is unconvincing. References to

---

[69] Gryson, Origines, 180; idem, "Ans", 160.
[70] Stickler, Celibacy, 17–18.

obligatory continence are found, after all, in canonical contexts as well, which give expression, not to general exhortations or pious wishes, but rather to deliberate and definitive regulations. We should recall here the Syrian *Didascalia* and the Ecclesiastical Canons of the Holy Apostles. The pastoral letters already contain a legal provision with regard to clerical continence, which claims a validity allowing no exceptions. The ordination of digamists and the marriage of clerics, at least, were forbidden long before Elvira. And these very regulations make sense only against a background of a continence discipline for clerics.

A further suggestion must be made here, which will be discussed more fully farther on (see below, pp. 333–47). One should not conclude too quickly from a modern perspective on life, which is characterized by individualism and self-determination, that only voluntary continence could actually have existed when the Church was just beginning and that the rights and the freedom of clerics and their wives were restricted only much later. For could it not be that in the early Church, on the contrary, the majority of clerics—for whatever reasons —accepted and practiced continence as a foregone conclusion? The rationale of the various Church regulations was obviously to guarantee the perfect continence of clerics by means of a framework of prerequisites and conditions. It is evident that obligatory continence itself did not need to be inculcated constantly before Elvira, though, probably because continence for clerics was something taken for granted as a component of their sacred ministry.

4. Eusebius Continues the Tradition of Origen

Let us return from Spain to the Hellenistic Orient. There we meet the theologically and politically influential Eusebius, archbishop of Caesarea in Palestine (263–339). He lived through the time of the last persecution of Christians under the Roman emperor Diocletian in A.D. 304–305. He maintained the best of contacts with the imperial house, particularly with Constantine, the first emperor to promote Christianity. As an esteemed bishop, Eusebius was later present at the Council of Nicaea, at which marital continence for clerics was allegedly rejected. It can be shown how erroneous the Paphnutius legend is on the sole basis of Eusebius' discussions of clerical discipline. A crucial passage can be found in the *Demonstratio Evangelica*, which was written before the Council (around 315–325).

Since we are investigating to what extent Abraham and Jacob begot children, we here refer those who are eager for knowledge to our more detailed statements elsewhere, in which we have discussed the polygamy and the numerous children of the God-loving men of old. Only let this much be said, that even according to the laws of the New Covenant, begetting children is not entirely prohibited. For "it is fitting", according to Scripture, "that a bishop be the husband of an only wife" (1 Tim 3:2). But this being understood, it behooves [προσήκει] consecrated men, and those who are at the service of God's cult, to abstain thereafter from conjugal intercourse with their wives. As to those who were not judged worthy of such a holy ministry, Scripture grants them [conjugal intercourse] while saying quite clearly to all that "marriage is honorable and the nuptial bed is without stain, [and that] God judges profligates and adulterers" (Heb 13:4).[71]

In his own way Eusebius was broaching exactly the same subject as Origen. This is not surprising, since Origen himself had previously lived and studied for years in Caesarea. Eusebius had his library in his possession and made extensive use of it. The polygamy and the abundance of children begotten by the Old Testament patriarchs presented a problem for his concept of morality as well. Christians had an idea of marriage that was substantially stricter. Having noted their positive attitude toward marriage, Eusebius then comes to the topic of married clerics; he mentions more clearly than Origen, though, their duty to observe continence after ordination.

Against this understanding of the text it has been objected that Eusebius here is not speaking of clerics at all. It is true that he speaks somewhat nebulously of "consecrated men . . . who are at the service of God's cult"; they must practice continence. For this reason Roger Gryson thinks that Eusebius is speaking here, not about priests, but about monks.[72] If that were so, the entire excerpt would have no rel-

---

[71] Eusebius, *Demonstratio evangelica* 1, 9, 20f. (GCS Eus. 6, 42, 33–43, 8): Ζητουμένης δὲ τῆς κατὰ τὸν Ἀβραὰμ καὶ Ἰακὼβ παιδοποιίας, ἐν ἑτέροις τὸν λόγον σχολαίτερον ἀποδεδώκαμεν, ἐν οἷς περὶ τῆς τῶν πάλαι θεοφιλῶν ἀνδρῶν πολυγαμίας τε καὶ πολυπαιδίας διειλήφαμεν, ἐφ᾽ ἃ καὶ νῦν τοὺς φιλομαθεῖς ἀναπέμπομεν, τοσοῦτον ἐπισημηνάμενοι, ὅτι καὶ κατὰ τοὺς τῆς καινῆς διαθήκης νόμους οὐ πάμπαν ἀπηγόρευται τὰ τῆς παιδοποιίας, ἀλλὰ κἀν τούτῳ τὰ παραπλήσια τοῖς πάλαι θεοφιλέσιν διατέτακται. Χρῆναι γάρ φησιν ὁ λόγος τὸν ἐπίσκοπον γεγονέναι >μιᾶς γυναικὸς ἄνδρα<. Πλὴν ἀλλὰ τοῖς ἱερωμένοις καὶ περὶ τὴν τοῦ θεοῦ θεραπείαν ἀσχολουμένοις ἀνέχειν λοιπὸν σφᾶς αὐτοὺς προσήκει τῆς γαμικῆς ὁμιλίας· ὅσοι δὲ μὴ τῆς τοσαύτης ἠξίωνται ἱερουργίας, τούτοις ὁ λόγος καθυφίησιν μονονουχὶ διαρρήδην ἅπασιν κηρύττων, ὅτι δὴ >τίμιος ὁ γάμος καὶ ἡ κοίτη ἀμίαντος, πόρνους δὲ καὶ μοιχοὺς κρινεῖ ὁ θεός<.

[72] Gryson, *Origines*, 56f.

evance to clerical discipline. In opposition to such a reading, though, one can make four observations. First, the immediate context concerns bishops (1 Tim 3:2). Second, the passage immediately preceding it (see the next quoted passage below) deals with clerics, as Gryson himself admits. Third, this terminology, which apparently refers to the monastic way of life, is applied by Eusebius in other passages to clerics.[73] Fourth, if it were a question of monks, he would have to be thinking of married monks now separated from their wives. Eusebius would hardly have held up this numerically negligible group as an example of those whose sacred ministry requires continence.[74] Besides, monks refrained from marital relations with their wives, not because of the Divine Liturgy, but simply because they chose continence as a way of life. Eusebius, therefore, is certainly referring here to bishops and priests.

A further objection has to be cleared up. The text gives the impression that Eusebius, in referring to the marriage of bishops, is trying to present evidence that, among Christians, begetting children is permitted; since clerics are allowed to be married, they are also allowed to beget children. Such reasoning would naturally be convincing only if bishops, too, demonstrated the goodness of marriage after their ordination and (zealously) begot children. Therefore Franz Xaver Funk sees Eusebius as an "incontrovertible witness" to the fact that no continence celibacy existed.[75] His reading, though, is on the wrong track. Eusebius is trying to demonstrate, rather, that among Christians begetting children, though not forbidden on principle, is nevertheless restricted. This is because Christianity, which is expanding mightily, no longer needs to multiply in the way that was still necessary for the people of Israel if they were to survive. Both the permissibility and the restriction of the generative powers are evident in the clerical discipline. The goodness of marriage and of procreation stands side by

---

[73] Eusebius, *Comm. 48 in Is.* 8:1–4 (GCS Eus. 9, 55, 10f.); *Demonstratio evangelica* 5, 3, 17–19 (GCS Eus. 6, 222, 1–16); *Vita Constantini* 4, 45, 2 (GCS Eus. 1, 1, 139, 16).

[74] H. Crouzel, "Le Célibat et la continence ecclésiastique dans l'Église primitive: Leurs motivations", in J. Coppens, ed., *Sacerdoce et célibat: Études historiques et théologiques* (Gembloux and Louvain, 1971), 336f., n. 7. Against these arguments, even Gryson's subsequent attempt to justify his view is ineffective: R. Gryson, "Sacerdoce et célibat: À propos d'un ouvrage récent", RHE 67 (1972): 76, n. 1.

[75] F. X. Funk, "Cölibat und Priesterehe im christliche Altertum", in *Kirchengeschichtliche Abhandlungen und Untersuchen*, vol. 1 (Paderborn, 1897), 131.

side with the continence of married clerics after their ordination. In exactly the same way Clement had already argued against the heretics who disdained the body, and Epiphanius will view the matter in the same way, also. Neither teaching excludes the other, and there is no contradiction between them either, because, after all, it was the married cleric who begot children before ordination.

Eusebius speaks of married clerics and says fundamentally the very same thing as canon 33 of the Council of Elvira. Neither Eusebius nor Elvira intends merely an obligation to observe periodic continence on the occasion of the Divine Liturgy. On the contrary, the one who has the duty of celebrating the Divine Liturgy must, from the day of his ordination on (λοιπόν), practice continence. Only "those who were not judged worthy of such a holy ministry"—that is, those who were not ordained and hence could not preside at the Divine Liturgy—had the right (by way of concession) to beget children. Thus Eusebius confirms the custom for Palestine: that married clergy avoided all marital intercourse from the day of ordination on.

Many historians latch on to the προσήκει, "it is fitting, it behooves", in order to prove that the continence of married clerics and their wives could not have been an obligatory ecclesiastical norm but was only felt to be appropriate. Thus each one would have been free to continue begetting children or not.[76] In most cases such a reading is still based on the Paphnutius legend. According to that explanation, at the Council of Nicaea Eusebius had allowed himself to be convinced to leave continence to the choice of the individual. The present state of scholarship has rendered this notion untenable. On the other hand προσήκει must not be construed by narrowly applying schoolboy Greek. Eusebius advocated a kind of rhetoric that was then becoming fashionable, which avoided blunt and direct statements in favor of ambiguous and open formulations. Aside from this, continence still remained appropriate and fitting even if it was an obligation. This is because there were intrinsic reasons for it, and it was by no means a purely compulsory law.

Finally, the statement of the *Demonstratio Evangelica* on the subject of the continence discipline is confirmed by the preceding passage. There Eusebius speaks about clerics in the terminology peculiar to him:

[76] Ibid., 128; J.-C. Guy, "Le Célibat sacerdotal: Approches historiques", *Études* 335 (1971): 93–106 at 99f.; E. Schillebeeckx, *Der Amtszölibat: Eine kritische Besinnung* (Düsseldorf, 1967), 26.

The reason that God-loving men of old had for begetting children is no longer cited because the begetting of children no longer has this meaning for us, since we can observe with our own eyes how, by the help of God, thousands of nations and peoples from cities, lands, and fields come and gather through the evangelical teaching of our Redeemer, to attend together the divine instruction through the evangelical teaching. It is appropriate for the teachers and heralds of the true worship of God that they are now free of all the chains of earning a living and daily cares. Indeed, for these men it is now commanded to distance themselves resolutely from marriage so as to devote themselves to a more important matter. Now they are concerned with a holy and not a carnal begetting of descendants. And they have taken upon themselves the begetting, the God-pleasing education, and the daily care, not (only) of one or two children, but of an indeterminable number all at once.[77]

Very likely Eusebius is referring inclusively to married and unmarried men.[78] They beget no children. Each one in his own way "distances himself from marriage": the unmarried man by renouncing marriage, the married man by practicing continence henceforth. Eusebius indicates between the lines that he is indeed thinking of married clerics, too, when he formulates the idea that clerics do not have (only) one or two (natural) children but many other spiritual children *all at once*. He may well have in mind the fact that married clerics begot children before their ordination, though only a few, and afterward they begot, so to speak, spiritual children only.

This detail is interesting insofar as clerics probably had only few children, as a rule. Of course Eusebius also mentions those Old Testament patriarchs who were married only once and who also begot children —at most one or two—only in their younger years.[79] Immediately

---

[77] Eusebius, *Demonstratio evangelica* 1, 9, 14f. (GCS Eus. 6, 41, 37–42, 12): Ἡ μὲν οὖν αἰτία τῆς τῶν πάλαι θεοφιλῶν ἀνδρῶν παιδοποιίας ἀνείρηται, ἣν οὐκέτι ἐφ᾿ ἡμῶν χώραν ἔχει λέγειν, ὅτε σὺν θεῷ διὰ τῆς τοῦ σωτῆρος ἡμῶν εὐαγγελικῆς διδασκαλίας μυρία ἔθνη καὶ λαοὺς κατά τε πόλεις καὶ χώρας καὶ ἀγροὺς πάρεστιν ἡμῖν ὀφθαλμοῖς ὁρᾶν σπεύδοντα κατὰ τὸ αὐτό, καὶ συντρέχοντα ἐπὶ τὴν κατὰ θεὸν μάθησιν τῆς εὐαγγελικῆς διδασκαλίας· οἷς ἀγαπητὸν δύνασθαι ἐξαρκεῖν τοὺς διδασκάλους καὶ κήρυκας τοῦ τῆς θεοσεβείας λόγου, πάντων ἀπολελυμένους τῶν τοῦ βίου δεσμῶν καὶ τῶν πολυμερίμνων φροντίδων. Μάλιστα δ᾿ οὖν τούτοις ἀναγκαίως τὰ νῦν διὰ τὴν περὶ τὰ κρείττω σχολὴν ἡ τῶν γάμων ἀναχώρησις σπουδάζεται, ἅτε περὶ τὴν ἔνθεον καὶ ἄσαρκον παιδοποιίαν ἀσχολουμένοις, οὐχ ἑνὸς οὐδὲ δυεῖν παίδων ἀλλ᾿ ἀθρόως μυρίου πλήθους τὴν παιδοτροφίαν καὶ τὴν κατὰ θεὸν παίδευσιν τῆς τε ἄλλης ἀγωγῆς τοῦ βίου τὴν ἐπιμέλειαν ἀναδεδεγμένοις. Inadequately explained by Cochini, *Origins*, 179–81.

[78] Gryson, *Origines*, 56.

[79] Eusebius, *Demonstratio evangelica* 1, 9, 16–19 (GCS Eus. 6, 42, 13–32).

thereafter he contrasts them with those men of God who were polygamous and begot numerous children. This distinction between few and
many children manifestly parallels the distinction between clerics and
laymen in the New Covenant: clerics have only a few children from
one marriage before their ordination, while laymen can beget children
throughout their lifetime.

In yet another passage Eusebius speaks of the universal priesthood
in a way that allows us to make inferences about the clerics' manner
of life: for him, renouncing marriage and children, removing oneself
from the daily cares of a household, is plainly serving God in a priestly
activity.[80] This clearly means that, for Eusebius, the clerical priesthood
was inseparably bound up with continence. At the same time we must
assume, based on the excerpt cited previously, that married clerics were
no longer really concerned with family affairs and that they gave up
household matters, because active married life was, in a way, over for
them as of their ordination, and they were completely occupied with
their clerical vocation.

5. Indirect Confirmation of a Continence Discipline

The clerical discipline of the early Church was not limited to a small
number of decrees. There was an entire network of interconnected
regulations. To the extent that they pertained to married clerics and
their wives, they were all intrinsically related, since they had the same
underlying purpose, namely, to guarantee and to safeguard in every
conceivable way the continence of higher clerics.

a. No Cleric May Be Married a Second Time

In the first place, mention should be made of the impediment to orders of digamy. A second marriage was permissible for laymen, but
not for higher clerics. This is how the issue was handled as early as
the Syrian *Didascalia* and the Ecclesiastical Canons of the Holy Apostles, with reference to the pastoral letters. Origen dispels any doubt
about this discipline. No exceptions were tolerated, it seems, since a

---

[80] Ibid., 1, 8, 1–3 (GCS Eus. 6, 39, 11–33).

second marriage, even among laymen, was not viewed kindly.[81] Both the Councils in Asia Minor and also the Spanish Council of Elvira at the beginning of the fourth century admitted no digamous candidate to orders.[82]

What is true already at the beginning of the third century can also be said of the following century: If the digamy prohibition did not exist, that would be evidence against a discipline of clerical continence. The mere fact that digamy has been forbidden unanimously since the time of the pastoral letters points to obligatory continence. For it is a valid inference: whoever married a second time evidently could not practice lasting continence. How would someone who was incapable of practicing continence even as a widower ever be able to do so after his ordination during the lifetime of his second wife? Now, if the prohibition of digamy was so strictly observed, then it must be supposed that a strict discipline of obligatory continence was present as well.[83]

b. The Prohibition of Marriage Applies Also to Deacons

The prohibition of digamy was supposed to disqualify unsuitable candidates before ordination, whereas another regulation had reference to the time after ordination, namely, the prohibition of marriage. This prohibition, too, indirectly confirms the existence of a continence-celibacy discipline for married clerics and their wives. Because in fact married clerics were no longer allowed to have sexual intercourse, a marriage also would have been senseless, since such a marriage could

---

[81] Origen, *Comm.* 14, 22 *in Mt.* 19:3 (GCS Orig. 10, 336, 20–31); *Hom.* 17, 10 *in Luc.* 2:33–38 (FC 4, 1, 204, 22–26); *Fragmenta* 28 *in* 1 *Cor.* 6:12 (370, 13–16 Jenkins).

[82] Richert, *Anfänge*, 68f. Council of Neocaesarea, canon 7 (37 Jonkers): Πρεσβύτερον ἐν γάμοις διγαμούντων μὴ ἑστιᾶσθαι, ἐπεὶ μετάνοιαν αἰτοῦντος τοῦ διγάμου τίς ἔσται ὁ πρεσβύτερος ὁ διὰ τῆς ἑστιάσεως συγκατατιθέμενος τοῖς γάμοις; Council of Ancyra, canon 19 (34 Jonkers): Ὅσοι παρθενίαν ἐπαγγελλόμενοι ἀθετοῦσι τὴν ἐπαγγελίαν, τὸν τῶν διγάμων ὅρον ἐκπληρούτωσαν. If digamy is considered, so to speak, adultery, then for clerics it is unthinkable.

Council of Elvira, canon 38 (14 Jonkers): "Peregre navigantes aut si ecclesia in proximo non fuerit, posse fidelem, qui lavacrum suum integrum habet nec sit bigamus, baptizare in necessitate infirmitatis positum catechumenum, ita ut, si supervixerit, ad episcopum eum perducat, ut per manus impositionem perfici possit." If no bigamous layman is permitted to baptize, then a fortiori no bigamous cleric may.

[83] Gryson, *Origines*, 19, fails to recognize this connection.

not be consummated.[84] Conversely we can say: If a reference to a permission for clerics to marry were ever found, one would have to doubt the existence of obligatory continence.

From Origen, it is true, we hear nothing about a marriage prohibition, but it must have existed nevertheless, since we never hear anything about a permission to marry. There is very little in the Ecclesiastical Canons of the Holy Apostles, either, to suggest a custom of clerical marriage. Canon 33 of Elvira implies a prohibition of marriage.[85] The second clearly articulated marriage prohibition after Hippolytus is not found, though, until around 314–325 in Asia Minor in the decisions of the Council of Neocaesarea. It decrees that every priest who marries after ordination is to be expelled/dismissed from the ranks of the clergy (canon 1).[86] Thereby he is deprived of his ecclesiastical ministry without being excommunicated. This rather mild punishment leads one to suspect that the canon was dealing with cases in which the marriage had been contracted, not in defiance of the rule of clerical continence, but out of ignorance of the Church's prohibition. The prohibition of marriage allows us to infer that a discipline of continence celibacy was in force at the beginning of the fourth century in Asia Minor.

One may wonder why Neocaesarea prohibited only priests from marrying. Could it have been, as the Council of Ancyra (in the year 314) seems to suggest, that a concession was made for deacons to marry once after ordination? That would not be logical. For the marriage prohibition of Neocaesarea did not mention bishops, either. One could have expected, then, that Ancyra would allow one marriage for them, too. Besides, in the same canon of Neocaesarea prohibiting priestly marriage, lewd conduct and adultery are forbidden. Was that also for priests only, or did it apply to deacons and bishops, too? One must be on guard here against making rash judgments. For the time being the finding stands: Priests were not allowed to marry, and with this decision Neocaesarea certainly did not permit the other clerics to do so.

The Council of Ancyra. Now, though, we must consider in greater detail the Council of Ancyra (in Asia Minor, today Ankara), where bishops from Asia Minor and Syria met. It was held in the year 314

---

[84] P.-H. Lafontaine, *Le Conditions positives de l'accession aux ordres dans la première legislation ecclésiastique (300–492)* (Ottawa, 1963), 172f.; R. Cholij, *Clerical Celibacy in East and West* (Herefordshire, 1989), 39f.

[85] Richert, *Anfänge*, 72.

[86] Πρεσβύτερος ἐὰν γήμῃ, τῆς τάξεως αὐτὸν μετατίθεσθαι (35 Jonkers).

and thus preceded the Council of Neocaesarea (around 314–325) by only a short time. To some extent the bishops in attendance were the same ones who would then meet in Neocaesarea also. Since Neocaesarea prohibited (only?) priests from marrying, canon 10 of Ancyra, which has an uncertain textual tradition, has been interpreted as though it permitted deacons to marry.[87]

> Those who are put forward for the diaconate, if, at the time of their nomination, they testified and said that they had to marry and could not live in this way and thereupon married, let them be in the [diaconal] service because the bishop has permitted them to do so. But those who have kept silence and were admitted to ordination while remaining thus [in the celibate state], if they marry subsequently, let them be deposed from the diaconate.[88]

The situation described here is usually pictured as follows: A diaconate ordination is taking place. Everyone has gathered. At the last minute, so to speak, the candidate announces that he does not want to remain celibate but wishes to marry. Just in time: the bishop allows him to marry later, but ordains him without delay, since it is too late to stop the ordination ceremony. So much for the common interpretation of Ancyra. Of course, such permission to marry means also that deacons, once they married, had sexual intercourse with their wives. A wedding only makes sense, after all, if the marriage can also be consummated. And that would affect in a delicate way the thesis concerning continence celibacy.

Taking the permission for deacons to marry as a starting point, one can then reconstruct the course of history. Soon the priests claimed this right for themselves as well, but at that point the bishops did not want to go along with it any more. A little later in Neocaesarea, therefore, they explicitly forbade priests to marry. Hence only the diaconal marriage privilege remained. This was connected with the later clerical discipline in the Eastern Church (still in force today), which allowed deacons and priests to continue without restriction the marriage they

---

[87] Gryson, *Origines*, 86.

[88] Council of Ancyra, canon 10 (64, 6–16 Joannou 1, 2): Διάκονοι ὅσοι καθίστανται, παρ᾽ αὐτὴν τὴν κατάστασιν εἰ ἐμαρτύραντο καὶ ἔφησαν χρῆναι γαμῆσαι, μὴ δυνάμενοι οὕτως μένειν, οὗτοι μετὰ ταῦτα γαμήσαντες ἔστωσαν ἐν τῇ ὑπηρεσίᾳ διὰ τὸ ἐπιτραπῆναι αὐτοὺς ὑπὸ τοῦ ἐπισκόπου τοῦτο. Εἰ δέ τινες σιωπήσαντες καὶ καταδεξάμενοι ἐν τῇ χειροτονίᾳ μένειν οὕτως, μετὰ ταῦτα ἦλθον ἐπι γάμον, πεπαῦσθαι αὐτοὺς τῆς διακονίας.

had contracted before ordination but which forbade them to marry after ordination.

Such a historical reconstruction has its blemishes. For the sources do not agree with it. The later practice of the Eastern Church forbids marriage even for those same deacons. This is quite surprising: the Eastern Church, which is always considered to be the Church with the more lenient clerical discipline, did not take up canon 10 of Ancyra; on the contrary, it repeatedly and explicitly abrogated the permission for deacons to marry.[89] How can that be explained, when Ancyra had allowed it? But canon 10 is not as unambiguous as it may seem. To put it bluntly, it can hardly be marshaled as an argument against the thesis of continence celibacy.

First of all, canon 10 deals with the testing of unmarried candidates for diaconal ordination who still wished to marry. Normally it seems that deacons were forbidden to marry after ordination. Was an exception to this rule now being made if the candidate announced immediately before ordination that he still wished to marry later on? But why, of all people, should the one who decided at the last minute be rewarded? There is nothing plausible about that. Because naturally all the candidates, for safety's sake, would just have pretended to want to marry, so as to keep this back door open for themselves. In practice that would have abolished the prohibition of marriage for deacons. At least one might have expected in this case that an interval would be set, within which time (after ordination) the deacon would have had to marry if he was not to lose his place among the clergy.

Now there is nothing in the text saying that the candidates for orders still had a final chance *during the ordination ceremony* to announce their wish to marry. And neither does it say at all that the bishops in question would nevertheless have ordained these candidates immediately. The Greek text distinguishes clearly between the scrutinies and the ordination ceremony, between κατάστασις and χειροτονία. The desire to marry had to be expressed, therefore, at the nomination to the diaconate (κατάστασις), before the actual ordination by the laying-on of hands (χειροτονία) had taken place. Ordination was preceded by the scrutinies, that is, a careful testing of the candidates, "whether they really fulfill all the demands that are necessarily made of the candidates

---

[89] Funk, "Cölibat", 144f.; Cochini, *Origins*, 169–71; Cholij, *Celibacy*, 75–78. Cochini's interpretation of canon 10, which is not without merit, is based on ὑπηρεσία = subdiaconate.

for an ecclesiastical office".[90] The only thing that the text says about deacons who wanted to marry is that they "may be in the [diaconal] service" if they married later on, and not that they "may continue to exercise their ministry".[91]

The result is the following situation: A deacon-to-be says during the scrutiny that he does not want to remain celibate after all, but wishes to marry. While that in itself puts an end to the ordination planned for him, he can hope, at least, that the bishop will make an exception for him. That can only mean that he postpones the ordination. Thus he remains a candidate for the diaconate, even though he really ought to have been ordained as an unmarried man. It is left to the bishop's discretion whether to admit him later to the diaconate, after his marriage and a certain period of married life.[92]

Canon 10 thus allows, not the marriage of deacons, but of deacon candidates and, therefore, in any case, of lower clerics (subdeacons, and so on). Lower clerics were obliged neither to practice continence nor to renounce marriage. This is also the reason why canon 10 speaks only about deacons. It would be erroneous to think that a concession was made, by way of exception, for them to marry after ordination, because only the diaconate was impending, whereas the discipline for priests and bishops was intentionally more strict. No concession was made for candidates for the priesthood and the episcopacy to marry, either before or after their ordination, because they were already higher clerics (that is, deacons or priests). That meant, though, that they were not allowed to marry, on principle. A candidate for diaconal ordination, too, was no longer allowed to marry. But since he was not yet a higher cleric, a concession could be made for him to marry, of course before ordination. Similarly, apostolic canon 26 (late fourth century) also permitted marriage absolutely to those who were still lower cler-

---

[90] Cyprian, *Epistulae* 29 (CSEL 3, 2, 548, 8f.). Κατάστασις is used often to denote the selection or nomination of a candidate for orders (cf. *Constitutiones apostolorum* 6, 17, 1 [SC 329, 346, 2f.] but also occasionally to refer to ordination; G. W. H. Lampe, ed., *A Patristic Greek Lexicon* (Oxford, 1961), 720.

[91] Gryson, *Origines*, 84, translates the sentence in this way, favoring his interpretation, but without justification for it in the text.

[92] This interpretation is confirmed by Novel 123, 14 to 1, 5, 546 of the *Codex Justinianus*. Before the ordination ceremony the bishop must ask the deacon about his intention with regard to marriage. At the ordination permission is no longer possible for a later marriage (Cochini, *Origins*, 363f.).

ics.[93] If Ancyra had allowed those soon to be deacons to marry even after ordination, one would have had to grant the same to priests and bishops as well.

All of this leads us to infer that there was a continence discipline for deacons, too. A candidate who declared during the scrutinies his desire to marry showed, after all, that he could not practice continence. That made him unsuited for ordination. For if someone until then could not be continent even as an unmarried man, how was he supposed to have the strength to practice continence while living together with his wife? Yet another reflection demonstrates that a prohibition of marriage for unmarried deacon candidates must have been connected with a general discipline of continence. Why, then, were unmarried candidates not allowed to marry at least once? There were, after all, married colleagues, too. Was that not discrimination without justification, merely because they did not marry at the right time? Such a prohibition of marriage would in fact have been an almost unintelligible restriction of the right to marry, if in the background there had not been a duty for married clerics to practice permanent continence.

c. Lewd Conduct Excludes One from Ordination

If continence was demanded of clerics, then naturally lewd conduct before ordination must have weighed rather heavily. And so it did in fact. The time before baptism was overlooked.[94] Just think of the unsettled behavior of the man who later, after his conversion, became Bishop Aurelius Augustinus; he was known to have an illegitimate son. After baptism, however, a lapse in morals was considered a serious offense. For men it even presented an impediment to orders, as Cyprian of Carthage testifies.[95] Naturally a mere rumor did not suffice. There were fundamentally two possible ways that a case could become known. Either the lewd conduct was discovered, causing a public scan-

---

[93] *Constitutiones apostolorum* 8, 47, 26 (SC 336, 280, 83f.): Τῶν εἰς κλῆρον παρελθόντων ἀγάμων κελεύομεν βουλομένους γαμεῖν ἀναγνώστας καὶ ψάλτας μόνους.

[94] Council of Ancyra, canon 12 (32 Jonkers): Τοὺς πρὸ τοῦ βαπτίσματος τεθυκότας, καὶ μετὰ ταῦτα βαπτισθέντας ἔδοξεν εἰς τάξιν προάγεσθαι ὡς ἀπολουσαμένους.

[95] Cyprian, *Epistulae* 66, 1 (CSEL 3, 2, 727, 5–9): "Tu existimes sacerdotes Dei sine conscientia eius in ecclesia ordinari, nam credere quod indigni et incesti sint qui ordinantur quid aliud est quam contendere quod non a Deo nec per Deum sacerdotes eius in ecclesia constitutantur."

dal; or else the man in question had manifested his conscience to the bishop and had accepted a public penance.[96]

Whatever the case may be, such a man was not going to be ordained. However much he may have atoned for his transgression, he might as well have given up his hopes of holding an ecclesiastical office. This is not surprising, since many a Church Father considered even a second marriage, which was in and of itself legitimate, as cloaked incontinence. If even digamy was an impediment to orders, then a fortiori "genuine" incontinence would have been, too. Origen says explicitly: Men who, after becoming Christian, are guilty of lewd conduct are not eligible for any further office in the Church, even after they do penance and are readmitted to the sacraments.[97] As early as the pastoral letters, such men, who after their baptism had to do public penance, were certainly barred from holy orders; for they were no longer "above reproach" (1 Tim 3:2).[98]

But what was the reason for taking such strict measures in examining candidates for orders? Why did they not consider the matter done with after the public penance? Was this meant to be a way of protecting by all means the good reputation of the cleric? That played a role in it, to be sure: to give outsiders no occasion to criticize the representatives of the Church. Indeed, the Church was not yet established, not by far, and she had to fear repeated encroachments by civil authorities. Therefore the hurdles were set especially high. Absolutely no one could be ordained or remain in office who for any reason whatsoever had had to perform the Church's public penance.[99]

There was probably even more behind it. Obviously, the matter at hand suggests that lewd conduct was connected somehow with continence celibacy. It was necessary for lewd conduct to be punished with particular severity because clerical discipline was at stake. This can be seen with unusual clarity in the decrees of Elvira. Married bishops, priests, and deacons, that is, the higher clerics, were forbidden to engage in marital intercourse (canon 33). Moreover the Council of

---

[96] Richert, *Anfänge*, 21f.; Lafontaine, *Conditions*, 161–68.

[97] Origen, *Contra Celsum* 3, 51 (GCS Orig. 1, 248, 3–5); *Hom.* 17, 10 *in Luc.* 2:33–38 (FC 4, 1, 204, 22–24). Cf. Cyprian, *Epistulae* 66, 1 (CSEL 3, 2, 727, 6–9).

[98] Cf. *Didascalia apostolorum* 4 (CSCO.S 176, 43, 24f. 46, 9–11).

[99] Richert, *Anfänge*, 14–26.

Elvira resolved that no man who had committed adultery or fornication after baptism might be ordained to the subdiaconate. The reason given is illuminating: subdeacons were candidates for higher orders (canon 30).[100]

This entire picture is plausible because continence was enjoined upon the higher clerics. Adultery before ordination was evidence of the inability of the man in question to practice marital continence. Naturally that was true even if the transgression became a matter of common knowledge only after ordination. For this reason it had to be punished subsequently as well—indeed, with all possible severity by removal from office (canon 30).[101] Sins of incontinence, therefore, were an impediment to orders for the same reason as second marriages: Whether a man entered another marriage after the death of his wife or had an extramarital affair after baptism, in either case he evidently could not practice continence. Even though penance had been done for the sexual transgression, that still did not remove the inclination to sin. Thus the man in question disqualified himself for the manner of life required of the cleric.

d. The Wives of Clerics Are Duty-bound as Well

Thus far we have been discussing the continence of married clerics. Possibly this gave the impression that the whole matter concerned only men: They decided to apply for the priesthood and then took upon themselves the practice of continence. But were their wives not still around? After all, they were immediately affected by the decision! For they, too, had to practice continence if their husbands were ordained as deacons, priests, or bishops. Indeed, this is a rather problematical point. Ultimately the ordination was at the expense of the wife. She

---

[100] "Subdiaconos eos ordinari non debere, qui in adolescentia sua fuerint moechati, eo quod postmodum in surreptionem ad altiorem gradum promoveantur; vel si qui sunt in praeteritum ordinati, amoveantur" (12 Jonkers). Lafontaine, *Conditions*, 166. Cf. Theophilus Alexandrinus, *Edicta canonica* 5 (PG 65, 37D).

[101] Richert, *Anfänge*, 28f.; Lafontaine, *Conditions*, 162f.; Council of Neocaesarea, canons 9f. (37 Jonkers): 9. Πρεσβύτερος ἐὰν προημαρτηκὼς σώματι προαχθῇ καὶ ὁμολογήσῃ, ὅτι ἥμαρτε πρὸ τῆς χειροτονίας, μὴ προσφερέτω μένων ἐν τοῖς λοιποῖς διὰ τὴν ἄλλην σπουδήν. Τὰ γὰρ λοιπὰ ἁμαρτήματα ἔφασαν οἱ πολλοὶ καὶ τὴν χειροθεσίαν ἀφιέναι. Ἐὰν δὲ αὐτὸς μὴ ὁμολογῇ, ἐλεγχθῆναι δὲ φανερῶς μὴ δυνηθῇ, ἐπ' αὐτῷ ἐκείνῳ ποιεῖσθαι τὴν ἐξουσίαν. 10. Ὁμοίως καὶ διάκονος, ἐὰν ἐν τῷ αὐτῷ ἁμαρτήματι περιπέσῃ, τὴν τοῦ ὑπηρέτου τάξιν ἐχέτω. Theophilus Alexandrinus, *Edicta canonica* 5 (PG 65, 37D–40A).

had to adapt to a situation that, in the first place, pertained, not to her, but to her husband's vocation.

If the matter was viewed this way, before a man was ordained it was necessary to see whether his wife, too, was capable of continence. One could not just be content with the fact that the man was able to practice permanent continence. For what if his wife had problems with it? Would she not then necessarily put him in a difficult position? If he remained firm, though, was it not possible that she might then try to go her own way outside the marriage? In other words, if there really was a continence discipline for clerics, then there must also have been regulations with regard to their wives. That is in fact the case. We find in the Syrian *Didascalia* for the first time the demand that the wife of a clerical candidate be chaste (continent).[102] The wives had to cooperate if their husbands were to renounce sexual relations successfully.

The change in marital life brought about by continence could be altogether advantageous for the wives. In discussing the pastoral letters we have already mentioned that this presented new responsibilities to them. It could open the way for them to a new degree of independence. While the husband was busy with the many needs of the faithful, the wife now had to take care of the house. And this had very little to do with cooking and dusting. That was the job of the servants. It was the wife's duty, rather, to conduct and manage the entire household. Moreover, clerical office was a highly esteemed position. Not without good reason does it say in the First Letter to Timothy, "If any one aspires to the office of bishop, he desires a noble task" (1 Tim 3:1). Authority, dignity, and prestige were bound up with this office. For the sake of this "noble task", both the husband and the wife accepted sacrifices as part of the bargain, including, first of all, continence.

Adultery among clerics' wives. A series of conciliar decrees establish criteria by means of which it could be demonstrated in individual cases that the wives of candidates for orders were, to all appearances, unable to observe continence. One wanted to be sure even before ordination. An aspirant to orders, therefore, could not be married to a wife whose circumstances of life led one to suspect she could not practice continence. Against this background the Council of Neocaesarea (around 314–325), in its eighth canon, forbids the husband of an adulteress to be admitted to orders.

---

[102] *Didascalia apostolorum* 4 (CSCO.S 176, 46, 2f.).

If the wife of a layman has committed adultery, and the fact has been clearly established, the man cannot join the ministry. If she committed adultery after the ordination of her husband, he must send her away. If he continues to live with her, he cannot exercise the ministry entrusted to him.[103]

To begin with, the canon considers a sexual transgression of the wife that can be proved. A woman found guilty of such an offense obviously cannot practice continence. It is quite possible that she would cause difficulties for her husband after his ordination. If the adultery took place after the ordination, her husband must dismiss her. Separation (not divorce) is necessary. Public penance on the part of the wife does not alter the situation. For then the sin is expiated, but the inability to observe continence remains. If the cleric continues to live with his wife when she has been found guilty of adultery, the suspicion arises that they are again having relations with one another. Naturally such a severe regulation did not help women. The ordinance was surely meant as a deterrent. For the council, the irreproachable reputation of the cleric took precedence.

Since Neocaesarea and also Elvira (canon 65)[104] compelled clerics to separate from their adulterous wives, one might think, based on the somewhat unclear formulation of the canons, that they pertained to lower clerics as well, even though they were not subject to a continence discipline. It would appear, then, that clerical continence could not be the determining factor for these regulations. That argument, however, is only partially correct. It is certainly possible that these canons had subdeacons and other lower clerics in view as well. That is because the *cursus honorum* already existed: the lower clerics of today are the deacons, priests, and bishops of tomorrow. Therefore the scope of many celibacy canons was extended to include the lower clerics.[105] Thus, although perfect continence was not yet required of them, still the rul-

---

[103] Canon 8 (37 Jonkers): Γυνή τινος μοιχευθεῖσα λαϊκοῦ ὄντος ἐὰν ἐλεγχθῇ φανερῶς, τοιοῦτος εἰς ὑπηρεσίαν ἐλθεῖν οὐ δύναται. Ἐὰν δὲ καὶ μετὰ τὴν χειροτονίαν μοιχευθῇ, ὀφείλει ἀπολῦσαι αὐτήν. Ἐὰν δὲ συζῇ, οὐ δύναται ἔχεσθαι τῆς ἐγχειρισθείσης αὐτῷ ὑπηρεσίας. [English translation as in Cochini, *Origins*, 178, n. 94.] Cf. Council of Arles, canon 25 (CCL 148, 25, 4–6).

[104] "Si cuius clerici uxor fuerit moechata et scierit eam maritus suus moechari et non eam statim proiecerit, nec in finem accipiat communionem, ne ab his, qui exemplum bonae conversationis esse debent, ab eis videantur scelerum magisteria procedere" (19f. Jonkers).

[105] Cf. Council of Elvira, canon 30.

ing with regard to the eventual adultery of clerical wives was already applied to them.

Roger Gryson interprets canon 8 of Neocaesarea in an entirely different manner, because he does not want to hear of a clerical continence discipline at this early date. He thinks that clerics were allowed to continue their married life without restrictions, provided only that adultery was not a consideration.[106] The purpose was not to guarantee the continence of clerics but only to protect their good reputation. Of course, that is conceivable also. But that could not explain as precisely the severity of the sanction, marital separation.

One might ask why cases of adultery on the part of clerics' wives were increasingly frequent in the first place. Was that not perhaps due to the fact that married clerics had to live with their wives continently? And were not the men, for vocational reasons, much more motivated than the women, who may have accepted continence perforce as part of the bargain? Many wives, evidently, found that they were not in a position to persevere in this renunciation and went astray. We find a similar phenomenon in Asia Minor among the Eustathians, who required marital separation of all Christians. The consequence was that many wives were unequal to this severe ascetical discipline and committed adultery.

Digamy among the wives of clerics. Also illuminating is a further impediment to orders: If a candidate for orders had married a widow, that is, a woman contracting her second marriage, he could not be ordained. This regulation is found from the end of the fourth century on in the West.[107] It was thought that the concern here was for the good reputation of the cleric, especially since a candidate for orders, according to apostolic canon 18, was not allowed to be married to a widow, or to a woman dismissed by her husband, or to a harlot, a servant, or an actress.[108] But in what way were widows supposed to have a bad reputation? Another explanation was sought in the levitical ideas of

---

[106] Gryson, *Origines*, 87.

[107] M. Boelens, *Die Klerikerehe in der Gesetzgebung der Kirche unter besonderer Berücksichtigung der Strafe: Eine rechtsgeschichtliche Untersuchung von den Anfängen der Kirche bis zum Jahre 1139* (Paderborn, 1968), 27f., 31f.

[108] *Constitutiones apostolorum* 8, 47, 18 (SC 336, 280, 63–65): Ὁ χήραν λαβὼν καὶ ἐκβεβλημένην ἢ ἑταίραν ἢ οἰκέτιν ἢ τῶν ἐπὶ τῆς σκηνῆς οὐ δύναται εἶναι ἐπίσκοπος ἢ πρεσβύτερος ἢ διάκονος ἢ ὅλως τοῦ καταλόγου τοῦ ἱερατικοῦ.

ritual purity in the Old Testament (Lev 21:13f.),[109] which are said to assert themselves here. But that, too, is secondary. What was behind it was, rather, the continence of the cleric. For the widow would have been living, after all, in a second marriage with a future cleric. Digamy on the part of the cleric, though, was judged to be a sign of an inability to practice continence. The same was true, then, for the wife as well. Thus she probably could not practice continence.

e. Clerics in So-called Spiritual Marriages

Besides the usual marriages of priests there was yet another type of relationship whereby ministers lived together with women under the same roof. We are speaking here of the so-called spiritual marriage, also referred to as the state of *syneisagein*, a rather curious phenomenon of the early Church. Spiritual marriages came into vogue in the second century, and in the fourth century, despite the beginnings of resistance, they were still not at all uncommon. It is understood to have consisted of a marriage-like partnership between a man and a woman, who were not married and who, moreover, did not want to have sexual intercourse with each other. The purpose of these quasi-marriages was sexual continence. There could be two basic motives for the arrangement. On the one hand, it could be a kind of pragmatic partnership, in which the woman, who wanted to live as a virgin, sought first of all the protection of a secluded life in a household. At that time, indeed, it was quite difficult for an unmarried woman to live alone. Such a *syneisaktos* [the Latin term is *subintroducta*] may have fulfilled more or less the same duties as a housekeeper. On the other hand, the arrangement could be a partnership of like-minded ascetics who want to provide proof of their ability to observe continence.

Whether such an arrangement was healthy and an expression of human maturity need not be discussed here. This book is concerned with clerical continence. The state of *syneisagein* certainly had something to do with it. In connection with the ecclesiastical discipline, it even loses a bit of its scurrility. Spiritual marriages were at first altogether tolerated by the Church, though of course, on account of the obvious

---

[109] Lafontaine, *Conditions*, 181–84; B. Kötting, *Der Zölibat in der Alten Kirche*, Schriften der Gesellschaft zur Förderung der Westfälischen Willhelms-Universität zu Münster, 61 (Münster, 1970), 12.

risks, they were viewed with great skepticism.[110] Interestingly enough, such marriages were entered into by clerics also. This caused various councils at the beginning of the fourth century to deal with the phenomenon in their regulations for clerics.[111] Evidently ambiguities and even flagrant abuses crept in, which furnished the occasion for many a satirical song in the surrounding heathen world.

But we have quarrels within the Church to thank for the memory of a cleric who was talked about in his day because he lived in a spiritual marriage. What is more, he was a bishop, which made him particularly open to criticism: Paul of Samosata. Bishop of Antioch in Syria from around the year 260, he lived, as did many of his deacons and priests, together with virgins, so-called *subintroductae*. The bishops who condemned him at a synod in Antioch in the year 268 on account of false doctrines also mentioned his spiritual marriages, but they were unable to accuse him of any moral lapses. Of course they saw the dangers and the questionable features in such a manner of life. Then came a remarkable comment by the synod Fathers. To wit, they expect Paul to set an example:

> How indeed could he admonish or warn another not to live any more with a woman, and thus guard himself from falling, according to what is written (Sir 9:8f.?), when he has already sent away [*one*] woman, but has brought in with him *two* others, in the prime of life and pleasant to look at?[112]

Thus Paul was supposed to be an example for others. More precisely, he ought to have been able to exhort others "not to live any

---

[110] 1 Cor 7:36–38 (?); *Didache* 11, 11 (?); *The Shepherd of Hermas* 6, 3; 87, 6–88, 8; Irenaeus, *Adversus haereses* 1, 6, 3; Pseudo-Clemens, *Ad virgines* 1/2; Cyprian, *Epistulae* 4; B. Lohse, *Askese und Mönchtum in der Antike und in der Alten Kirche*, RKAM 1 (Munich and Vienna, 1969), 131–33, 154–57, 161f.

[111] Council of Elvira, canon 27 (11 Jonkers): "Episcopus vel quilibet alius clericus aut sororem aut filiam virginem dicatam Deo tantum secum habeat; extraneam nequaquam habere placuit." Council of Nicaea, canon 3 (40 Jonkers): Ἀπηγόρευσε καθόλου ἡ μεγάλη σύνοδος μήτε ἐπισκόπῳ μήτε πρεσβυτέρῳ μήτε διακόνῳ μήτε ὅλως τινὶ τῶν ἐν τῷ κλήρῳ ἐξεῖναι συνείσακτον ἔχειν πλὴν εἰ μὴ ἄρα μητέρα ἢ ἀδελφὴν ἢ θείαν ἢ ἃ μόνα πρόσωπα πᾶσαν ὑποψίαν διαπέφευγε. H. Achelis, *Virgines subintroductae: Ein Beitrag zum VII. Kapitel des I. Korintherbriefs* (Leipzig, 1902), 5, 33–47, 65–68. There may also be an allusion to clerical *subintroductae* in Pseudo-Clemens, *Ad virgines* 2, 15, 6 (49, 11–15 Funk and Diekamp 2).

[112] Eusebius, *Historia ecclesiastica* 7, 30, 14 (GCS Eus. 2, 2, 712, 4–7): Πῶς γὰρ ἂν ἐπιπλήξειεν ἢ νουθετήσειεν ἕτερον μὴ συγκαταβαίνειν ἐπὶ πλέον εἰς ταὐτὸν γυναικί, μὴ ὀλίσθῃ, φυλαττόμενον, ὡς γέγραπται, ὅστις μίαν μὲν ἀπέστησεν ἤδη, δύο δὲ ἀκμαζούσας. [Translation as in Cochini, *Origins*, 191, n. 139, with scriptural citation and emphasis added per Heid.]

more with a woman".[113] It is not said whom he should exhort to perfect continence. It may be that the consecrated virgins and the ascetics were meant. It seems more likely, though, that Eusebius was objecting to marital separation in connection with spiritual marriages. In that case he would actually have been rebuking Paul as follows: How is someone supposed to be able to exhort married people henceforth to practice continence, when he himself separates from his legitimate wife but then enters into spiritual marriages? Presumably Eusebius had a particular group of persons in view, namely, the deacons and priests of the diocese of Antioch, who evidently took their bishop as an example, some of them even entering into spiritual marriages. Whether they were married now or not, they should no longer have joined with a woman but rather lived continently. Their bishop should have persuaded them to do so through his exemplary conduct and manner of life. And he would not accomplish that by having a dubious relationship with several *subintroductae*, but rather by leading an exemplary life together with his *one* legitimate spouse.

We can assume that the Church was at first quite tolerant of this form of living together, as long as it was not combined with abuses such as a previous marital separation. Probably another reason for tolerating spiritual marriage was that it corresponded to the universal clerical discipline, which demanded continence of the married clerics and their wives. And conversely, higher clerics considered themselves entitled to take women into their homes after their ordination and to live with them as brother and sister, because the married clerics, too, lived continently with their wives. The fact that couples who lived together in this way did not marry can be attributed, then, to the prohibition of marriage for clerics.

Hence the clerical custom of *syneisagein* corroborates the thesis that married clerics lived with their wives continently. In any case Christian Cochini has argued plausibly that even the Council of Nicaea in its third canon, which is directed against the *subintroductae*, presupposes a

---

[113] Cyprian, *Epistulae* 4, 3 (CSEL 3, 2, 475, 14–19), writes that he is horrified by a deacon who lives together with a *subintroducta*: "And even though all without exception must maintain decency, nevertheless the presiders and the deacons have a still much greater duty and responsibility for this, since they are supposed to give good example to the others by their manner of life and their morals. For how can they possibly watch over purity and continence when they themselves act as instructors in corruption and vice?"

discipline of clerical continence.[114] If this is correct, then Nicaea designates the spouses of clerics as women who are above all suspicion (of unchastity with their husbands). The fact that the council views as a matter of course the wives' support for their husbands' continent manner of life is indeed high praise for their spirit of self-sacrifice and their solidarity with the vocation of their husbands.

f. We Know Nothing of Legitimate Children Born after Ordination

Someone who disputes the discipline of continence celibacy during the first three centuries will attempt to discover in the historical sources any references at all to the children of clerics who came into the world only after their fathers were ordained to the higher clergy. If obligatory continence did not exist, then it can be concluded a priori that clerics, too, begot children and in doing so met with the approval and sympathy of their faithful. Yet despite the most painstaking investigation, Roger Gryson could not find one single married cleric in the first three centuries who, on reliable testimony and with no evidence to the contrary, had begotten a child after his ordination. He certainly would not have allowed such a find to slip by.[115] The only doubtful passage in Clement of Alexandria must be understood in a different way (see above, pp. 70–72).

This finding is all the more surprising in that the married cleric may have been the norm for the pre-Constantinian period,[116] which in turn could undoubtedly be traced to the wide distribution of the pastoral letters and the way they were interpreted. No texts can be found that mention, sympathetically and approvingly, clerics who besides their priestly ministry also begot children. One could imagine many things that might have been portrayed. But on the contrary, when the wives of the clerics are referred to, which occurs not infrequently, it is always in connection with a reference to strict continence. We do not even hear about a single cleric getting married legally after his ordination. Much less was there any compulsion to marry before ordination.

---

[114] Cochini, *Origins* 185–95. Cf. Cholij, *Celibacy*, 78–85.

[115] As H. Kruse, "Eheverzicht im Neuen Testament und in der Frühkirche", FKTh 1 (1985): 113, very nicely remarks. See also Cholij, *Celibacy*, 73. Gryson, *Origines*, 42, has by means proved his claim, "On voit . . . qu'il y a des clercs qui continuent à user du mariage."

[116] Gryson, *Origines*, 1–44. Catalogue of married clerics in Cochini, *Origins*, 87–123.

Let us assume that there was no continence discipline. Then clerics, too, at one time may well have been proud of their children. Why do we never hear of the wonderful family fellowship of clerics? Why does a bishop while giving a homily never mention the birth of a child? Why do we never hear of a priest baptizing his own child? Nowhere do we find authors who see fatherhood as a duty of the clergy, which benefits both Church and state. Nowhere do clerics complain of sleepless nights because their babies or sick toddlers were crying. One never hears of problems with raising juveniles. Are we to conclude that clerics so thoroughly lost their voices when it came to the joys of child-rearing? Or can their silence be explained simply by noting that they no longer begot children, because they were observing a continence discipline?

This silence is in fact a remarkable phenomenon, of course, only if one disputes the existence of continence celibacy. Not remarkable at all if one takes seriously everything that the Syrian *Didascalia*, Origen, Elvira, Eusebius, and the councils say about clerical discipline. Evidently the Church's practice was much more comprehensive and consistent than these few writings lead us to suppose. Precisely for this reason one must also argue on the basis of an oral tradition, or even a simply lived tradition, that is hinted at in the writings of the second and third centuries but then becomes manifest in a most explicit form from the fourth century on. Clerical continence was in vogue in the ante-Nicene period and evidently was observed by and large.

g. *Disciplinary Infractions Prove the Rule*

Of course there would necessarily be problems with obligatory continence. Infractions were to be expected. Such exceptions would only go to prove the rule. We hear again and again about clerics who violated the high standards of their office, beginning with that Valens mentioned by Polycarp of Smyrna[117] and on to the abuses lamented by Origen.[118] But we hear almost nothing about infractions of the celibacy discipline.[119] The accusation of Hippolytus, that Callistus did

---

[117] *Epistula ad Philippos* 11.

[118] Harnack, *Ertrag* 1:69–87; vol. 2, TU 42, 4 (Leipzig, 1919), 115, 129–41; H. J. Vogt, *Das Kirchenverständnis des Origenes*, BoBKG 4 (Cologne and Vienna, 1974), 3–80.

[119] H. Crouzel, "Une Nouvelle Étude sur les origines de célibat ecclésiastique", BLE 83 (1982): 294–97 at 295f.

not depose bishops when they sinned, even unto death, could refer to
adultery; at least Hippolytus would like to suggest as much. But that is
too vague and cannot stand as evidence.[120] Was there, then, no general
obligation to practice continence after all? By no means can such an
argument be proved conclusively.

Marital continence for clerics was a two-edged affair. Who could
check to see whether the married couples really were practicing continence? Of course the good will and right conduct of the married couples were always assumed, as long as there was no proof to the contrary.
In one passage Origen objects to the secret impurity of many clerics.[121]
He denounces those who preach "strict chastity" while being inflamed
themselves with a "secret lust". On one occasion Origen rails about
those who make an exterior display of chastity and virginity but in
reality lead a dissolute life, and in this connection he names bishops,
priests, and deacons.[122] Thus, even here it was not a matter of an open
breach of celibacy but, at worst, of human weakness and hidden transgressions. In any case, Origen expresses his objections in terms that
certainly sound like a general continence discipline to which all clerics,
including the married ones, were subject.

A breach of celibacy became legal matter under the Church's law only
when a cleric was caught in flagranti or when his wife was expecting a
child. Canon 33 of Elvira speaks explicitly of the latter case and decrees
that offenders shall be deposed from the clerical state. Now one might
think that, if obligatory continence really existed, there would have
to be some mention now and then of illegitimate children of married
clerics. We do in fact find this, hidden at times in other expressions that
do not speak explicitly about children. The Council of Neocaesarea
(canon 1) rules that if a priest after his ordination commits fornication
or adultery, he is to be deposed and excommunicated.[123] The Apostolic

[120] Hippolytus, *Refutatio omnium haeresium* 9, 12, 21 (GCS Hippol. 3, 249, 22f.). The
cleric who commits the "sin unto death" is mentioned also by Basil, *Epistulae* 199, 32.

[121] Origen, *Comm.* 2, 11 *in Rom.* 2:17–24 (FC 2, 1, 244, 21–27): ". . . ut etiam dux et
doctor ecclesiae sit ad illuminandos eos, qui in scientia caeci sunt, et instruendos parvulos
in Christo; ne is, inquam, talis alios quidem velit docere districtius et de his, quos instruit,
summam disciplinam castitatis exigere, ipse vero intemperantiae vitio et cupiditatis urgeatur,
nonnumquam etiam flammis occultae libidinis aestuet."

[122] Origen, *Comm. series* 24 *in Mt.* 23:29–36 (GCS Orig. 11, 2, 40, 15–21). Cf. Jerome,
Adversus Helvidium 21 (PL 23², 216A).

[123] Ἐὰν δὲ πορνεύσῃ ἢ μοιχεύσῃ, ἐξωθεῖσθαι αὐτὸν τέλεον καὶ ἄγεσθαι αὐτὸν εἰς μετάνοιαν

Canons provide for the removal of that bishop, priest, or deacon who is found guilty of lewd conduct (canon 25).[124]

One might object that these canons had only "normal" adultery in view, which was forbidden to every layman as well. The sanction against lewd conduct, then, would have pertained only to extramarital relations; marital intercourse would have been entirely permissible for clerics. Naturally lewd conduct meant adultery, but not exclusively. For lewd conduct was defined as illicit sexual relations; in the case of clerics, though, intercourse with their wives was also illicit.[125] Basil, for instance, determined that a deacon who after his ordination had engaged in lewd conduct ought to be expelled from the diaconate and had to practice perfect continence even after his laicization.[126] This canon applied generally, hence for married deacons as well. We can infer from the punishment that deacons had to practice perfect continence. Jerome and Synesius speak of adultery when a cleric has relations with his wife and begets a child.[127] Thus lewd conduct can very probably be understood to mean incontinence within marriage also.

Occasionally incontinence within marriage may have been less of a problem than extramarital sexual activity, that is to say, adultery. The continence discipline may have led to situations in which one or another cleric pursued extramarital relations. This, naturally, was regarded as being especially worthy of condemnation and was punished with the severest penalties. But it does provide evidence of how, given the strict discipline, so many clerics, both unmarried and married, could become involved in a crisis that was not merely personal but also marital and familial.

As for the illegitimate children of clerics, we do not know what became of them. The information is simply lacking. They probably

---

(35 Jonkers). Cf. Council of Elvira, canon 18 (9 Jonkers): "Episcopi, presbyteres et diacones si in ministerio positi detecti fuerint quod sint moechati, placuit propter scandalum et propter profanum crimen nec in finem eos communionem accipere debere."

[124] *Constitutiones apostolorum* 8, 47, 25 (SC 336, 280, 79–82): Ἐπίσκοπος ἢ πρεσβύτερος ἢ διάκονος ὁ πορνείᾳ ἢ ἐπιορκίᾳ ἢ κλοπῇ ἁλοὺς καθαιρείσθω, καὶ μὴ ἀφοριζέσθω· λέγει γὰρ ἡ γραφή· <Οὐκ ἐκδικήσει Κύριος δὶς ἐπὶ τὸ αὐτό>. Ὡσαύτως καὶ οἱ λοιποὶ κληρικοί.

[125] For example, since the time of Cyprian, breaking a vow of virginity is referred to as adultery; J. Schmid, "Brautschaft, heilige", in RAC 2 (1954), 528–64 at 562. Furthermore, cf. Jerome, *Adversus Jovinianum* 1, 13 (PL 23², 240B).

[126] *Epistulae* 188, 3 (124f. Courtonne 2).

[127] Jerome, *Adversus Jovinianum* 1, 34 (PL 23², 268D); Synesius, *Epistulae* 105 (PG 66, 1485A).

remained with their parents. It was not the practice to allow the fathers to continue serving the Church while insisting that the children be cared for elsewhere. Some of the fathers definitely remained in the clergy and continued to be supported by church funds, so that their families, too, would have security. If that was not the case, then they had no alternative but to earn their own living.

Occasionally there may even have been a sad instance of resorting to an abortion in order to conceal the sin against chastity. Such a case is not to be ruled out even if there is no unequivocal proof of it. In those days one had to reckon at least with the possibility, as is proved by Cyprian's polemic against Novatus, whom he reproaches for having procured such an abortion. Before discussing that incident, let us examine another case from the same period, about which we have more detailed knowledge.

The case of Fortunatianus. There was an uproar in North Africa over Bishop Fortunatianus of Assuras. The eminent but somewhat imperious Bishop Cyprian of Carthage had to come to terms with him. During the previous persecution under the emperor Decius, Fortunatianus had compromised himself by sacrificing to the gods. He was no longer acceptable. In spite of this, when the persecution stopped, he wanted to reoccupy his episcopal see. Cyprian was horrified by this and poured out invective upon Fortunatianus.

> And even now they yearn for feasting and the pleasures of the table, at which they have been overloading their stomachs every day lately, until they would again vomit forth what they had not digested. Thus they prove now quite clearly that previously, too, they did not serve their religion but rather their bellies and that they pandered to their greed in an unholy covetousness. Therefore, as we see and believe, because God put them to the test, punishment overcame them as well, so that they might stand no longer at the altar, so that the lascivious might not continue to come into contact with what is chaste, the apostate with the faith, the unholy with religion, the earthly minded with the divine, the sacrilegious with the sacred.[128]

Cyprian does not mince words: many clerics stand lasciviously at the altar. It has been said that the continence discipline then was in a rather bad way. But Cyprian is not very reliable here. For Cyprian, who observed strict continence himself, since he was preparing for

---

[128] *Epistulae* 65, 3 (CSEL 3, 2, 724, 4–14).

baptism, suddenly was no longer speaking about Fortunatianus alone but apparently about several clerics who dared to stand lasciviously at the altar. This is generalizing, a rhetorical ploy. Cyprian inferred their impurity from the sole fact that they indulged in the pleasures of the table and banqueting: whoever lived that way could readily be assumed to be unchaste as well. Caution is advised with regard to other statements by Cyprian, also. In another passage he is dealing once again with a cleric who is causing him trouble.

The case of Novatus. Cyprian, in a letter to Pope Cornelius (251–253), tells of a priest named Novatus who has committed a series of grave transgressions "against divine law and the Church's discipline". He misappropriated Church funds, let his father starve, and kicked his wife in the abdomen so that she suffered a miscarriage.[129] In this instance Cyprian appears to condemn merely the infanticide and not the begetting of the child per se. Accordingly one could think that it went without saying that priests were allowed at that time to beget children.[130]

The whole affair, of course, does not permit us to make any certain judgment about the existence of a continence discipline. Probably with regard to the infanticide we are dealing with an unfounded accusation. First of all, any one of the three crimes mentioned would have sufficed to have Novatus removed from office immediately, if not excommunicated. But evidently tangible proofs were not presented. At worst accusations were made public, and those about events going back at least two years. At that time in the year 249 the whole business was scheduled to go to trial and was supposed to be cleared up by an investigation that had already begun, but which was not carried out because the persecution started. And before an investigation could be resumed, Novatus left the Church. Consequently the accusations were never proved. And based on the schism in the year 251, Cyprian then concludes that the accused had a bad conscience.

In general one ought to be careful with such accusations. Again and again it happened that clerics were charged with lewd conduct without

---

[129] Cyprian, *Epistulae* 52, 2f. (CSEL 3, 2, 617, 18–619, 16). F. J. Dölger, "Das Lebensrecht des ungeborenen Kindes und die Fruchtabtreibung in der Bewertung der heidnischen und christlichen Antike", AuC 4 (1934): 1–61 at 54f., erroneously relates this to the Deacon Felicissimus.

[130] Thus H. Koch, "Tertullian und der Cölibat", ThQ 88 (1906): 410.

any proof then being produced by later investigation.[131] Besides, the charge of causing a miscarriage is already extremely frivolous in and of itself. For how could that ever be proved? Such a rumor would be easy to keep alive. And even if Novatus was only thought to have begotten a child, Cyprian still speaks of the violation, not only of divine law, but also of Church discipline.[132] This could very well have meant continence celibacy. In that case Novatus would have wanted to conceal his transgression against continence by causing an abortion.[133] Seen this way, Cyprian's accusation, even if unfounded in reality, would indirectly confirm the existence of continence celibacy.

6. Summary

The Syrian *Didascalia* and Origen continued that line of thought in the East which had its beginning with Clement of Alexandria. In Syria a higher cleric was, as a rule, married. At least the bishop, though, had to be clearly advanced in years. The cares about children and their upbringing had to be in the past, so that the husband could devote himself completely to the interests of the Church. Viewed thus, it was an entirely appropriate demand that he should live henceforth with his wife in continence.

Origen of Alexandria was acquainted with a discipline of continence celibacy, as can be deduced from his remarks about the prohibition of digamy. He asks himself: If continence is critical for a married cleric, then why do they not ordain also men who are widowed after their second marriage? After all, they too are practicing continence. These reflections of course did not lead to the abrogation of the digamy prohibition. The Church adhered to the tradition that presented both: monogamy and continence. For Origen, priesthood without perfect continence was absolutely unthinkable.

---

[131] Augustine, *Epistulae* 209, 4 (CSEL 57, 349, 15–17); Theophilus Alexandrinus, *Edicta canonica* 5 (PG 65, 37D); 8 (41BC).

[132] Pseudo Cyprian (= Novatian) *De bone pudicitiae* 4 (CSEL 3, 3, 16, 16–18) speaks of marital continence as a higher degree of the virtue, since here legitimate intercourse is renounced as well.

[133] Clement of Alexandria, *Paedagogus* 2, 10, 96, 1 (GCS Clem. Alex. 1³, 215, 3–5), knows that women, in order to keep their lewd conduct from becoming public knowledge, use abortifacients. Similarly: Council of Elvira, canon 63, 68; Council of Ancyra, canon 21.

The Spanish Council of Elvira at the beginning of the fourth century, which became famous for its celibacy canon, confirmed for the Latin West what was already delineated in Tertullian and Cyprian. Bishops, priests, and deacons, if they were married, had to practice continence within marriage. They were not speaking merely about a ritually determined abstinence on days when the Divine Liturgy was celebrated. Nor can it be said that strict continence was being introduced here for the first time. The purpose was, rather, to put an end to the possible ignorance or uncertainty of many clerics who perhaps lived in remote areas and were not properly informed about this obligation.

In this same theological tradition of Clement and Origen stood Eusebius, archbishop in the Palestinian region of Caesarea. In his writings also we find crucial references to continence celibacy. Connected with the prohibition of digamy according to the pastoral letters was the obligation for ordained men to abstain from conjugal intercourse from the day of their ordination onward.

Finally there are several kinds of indirect evidence for the discipline of continence celibacy. Among these is the prohibition of digamy in the various ecclesiastical constitutions, councils, and in Origen. To be reckoned among these also is the exclusion of incontinent men from orders, a criterion known to Cyprian, Origen, and the councils. In both cases there was the same fundamental consideration: A man who had demonstrated by his conduct (namely, a second marriage or lewd conduct) that he was incapable of practicing continence would not be admitted to a ministry for which the ability to observe continence was a basic prerequisite.

The prohibition of marriage [for clerics] also speaks in favor of continence celibacy. The disputed decree of the Council of Ancyra in Asia Minor is relevant to this line of argument. It dealt with the case of an unmarried candidate for the diaconate who nevertheless before his ordination expressed a desire to marry. There was some room here for the discretion of the bishop. The candidate in question, in any case, was not allowed to marry after ordination, any more than a priest or a bishop would have been. If possible, though, a concession would be made for him by postponing the ordination. The bishop could still ordain such a candidate a few years after his marriage, after admitting him to the group of married candidates for the diaconate.

A discipline of clerical continence is confirmed also by the custom of *syneisagein*: a man and a woman lived together without a formal marriage, but in doing so they expressly forwent sexual contact. It was chiefly clerics who lived in such marriage-like social arrangements. The case of Bishop Paul of Samosata became widely known. Presumably the following reasoning was behind it: If married clerics had to live continently together with their wives, why should an unmarried cleric not then be able to live together with a woman without marriage? Passionate proponents of continence even saw in this an especially shining example of ascetical self-mastery.

The wives of clerics were the subject of another consideration. There were always two parties to the continence of married clerics: man and wife. If there was a celibacy discipline, then continence had to be required of the latter as well. The council decrees confirm precisely this. Candidates for orders could not be married to adulteresses. If wives of clerics had demonstrated by adulterous conduct that they were incapable of continence, their husbands had to separate from them. Besides this, it was not permissible for a cleric to have married a digamous wife. For in the case of wives, too, digamy was thought to be a sign of unsuitability for continence.

Finally it is striking that, even though we have information about numerous clerics who had children, it can never be demonstrated with certainty that they were begotten after ordination. That would be the critical point, however, if one wanted to disprove the existence of obligatory continence. Never was a deacon, priest, or bishop mentioned approvingly because he had begotten a child. Never was a cleric proud of the progeny from his later years. On the other hand, every time there was talk about the unchaste behavior of any cleric at all, it was subject to ecclesiastical sanctions. Sexual intercourse by clerics was not tolerated. Transgressions remained the exception and proved the rule.

Contrary to the oft-repeated opinion that the Church in the East, as opposed to the Western Church, never knew of a continence discipline, we must say exactly the opposite: A universal discipline of clerical continence is attested to with greater certainty in the East than in the West. The strongest evidence is found in Origen and Eusebius. Furthermore, neither author gives the impression that clerical continence was disputed or that they had to expend a great amount of effort in order to establish it. It appears, rather, to be taken for granted as self-evident. Before we look beyond Elvira and examine more closely the situation in the West, however, we can gather still more material from the East and prove the existence there, in the fourth century as well, of an obligation for all clerics to practice continence.

V. Clerical Continence in the Fourth-Century, Post-Nicene Eastern Church

The Council of Nicaea in A.D. 325 marks a turning point in the history of the Church. The terror of the great persecutions of Christians was past. Constantine showed favor toward Christians and promoted the Church, which entered into a close association with the state. Many prefer to view this as the definitive departure from the hale, uncomplicated early Christian world. For them the Church after Constantine, to a certain extent, reverted to the Old Testament period, since we again find laws, houses of God, priesthood, and a sacrifice as in the days of Moses. Naturally the world since Constantine has changed for Christians. But it is not a real break with the past. There is an ongoing continuity in the theological and disciplinary concepts of the ante-Nicene and post-Nicene Church. This applies also to clerical discipline. What we have been able to determine with regard to obligatory continence so far in the first three centuries in East and West continues to be valid and to develop in the fourth century.

In this chapter we are traveling exclusively along the paths of the Eastern Church. It has become customary to maintain that obligatory continence first came into existence in the West toward the end of the fourth century (disregarding Elvira around the year 306), and then only through the influence of authoritarian popes of this period. That such a thesis is untenable can be demonstrated by the fact that there is evidence for the clerical continence discipline in the East at a time before the popes set about promoting it. The separate treatment of the East and the West must not cause us to forget that in the fourth century a real unity still existed in the Church. Among the theologians and the bishops there was still a common language and reciprocal exchange. Only later, at the turn of the fifth century, would the complete Latinization of the West and ecclesiastical-political conflicts lead to a gradual alienation.

1. The Complete Discipline of the Church

The fourth century was the golden age of patristics, the finest hour of the great theologians and bishops. They accomplished the work of building up the Church—in both the organizational and the spiritual sense—during a period of expansion when she went from strength to strength with the wind of the government at her back. Many of the Church Fathers were not only very learned but also left a large corpus of their own writings, far more comprehensive than that of most ante-Nicene authors. No wonder, then, that by the time of Epiphanius and Jerome we find detailed and illuminating opinions on continence celibacy. To a limited extent this is also true for John Chrysostom.

a. *Epiphanius of Salamis*

Epiphanius was born around the year 315 in Palestine in the vicinity of Gaza, where he spent many years. Already at that time thousands of Christian pilgrims were drawn to the "Holy Land". In his day the archbishop of Caesarea in that locality was Eusebius, with whose clear stance on continence we are already acquainted. Epiphanius, however, did not remain in Palestine. From 367 until his death in the year 403 he was bishop of the Cypriot town of Salamis (Constantia) near what is today called Famagusta. His long life covered, therefore, almost the entire fourth century. He distinguished himself by his refined or—depending on the observer's viewpoint—trenchant sense of all things Catholic. In an almost unparalleled effort he investigated what made the Catholic Church different from the innumerable splinter groups and heresies. In his work entitled *The Medicine Chest* [Greek: *Panarion*; Latin: *Haereses*], written from 374 to 377, we find for the first time a rather long treatise on the fact and meaning of the clerical discipline.

> For they [that is, the Novatians] thought that what is fitting to the priesthood because of its preeminent position should be conferred upon all. Thus they heard that "the bishop must be above reproach, the husband of one wife, temperate" (1 Tim 3:2), and "deacons likewise" (1 Tim 3:8) and also the priest, but they did not understand that this was restricted to particular states of life. Since the Incarnation of Christ, the holy Word of God does not admit to the priesthood the monogamists who, after the

death of their wives, have contracted a second marriage; [this] because of
the exceptional honor of the priesthood. And it is observed by the holy
Church of God with great exactitude and without fail. But the man who
continues to live with his wife and to sire children is not admitted by
the Church as a deacon, priest, or bishop, even if he is the husband of an
only wife; [only] he who [abstains from relations with his first wife] or
is a widower; [this is observed] especially where the ecclesiastical canons
are exact.

But in many places, you will surely object, priests, deacons, and subdeacons still beget children. That, however is the result, not of the canonical rule, but rather of human nature, which is just reckless; or else the
reason for it is that, because of the crowds of people (seeking baptism),
no suitable men could be found for the ministry.

Because the Church always looks to what is most appropriate, she
recognized under the guidance of the Holy Spirit that she should have
no scruples about offering to God the service [of worship] and that she
should fulfill her spiritual obligations with an entirely clear conscience.
In my view, it is nevertheless fitting, on account of the service that they
must be ready to perform even unexpectedly, that the priest, the deacon,
and the bishop be free for God. For if the holy Apostle commands even
laymen to keep themselves free for prayer for a time (1 Cor 7:5), how
much more does he prescribe the same for the priest! I am of the opinion
that they must be undisturbed and free to carry out the spiritual duties
of their God-pleasing, perfect priesthood. But in the case of laymen, on
account of the weakness (of the flesh), one can weigh whether those who
are unable to remain monogamous should contract a second marriage after the death of the first wife.[1]

Epiphanius wants to make one thing clear here—and in another passage it is put even more explicitly: The legislation of the entire Church,
for all the particular variations, pursues the same purpose, namely, the
apostolic rule of sexual continence for the higher clergy. Epiphanius
is the first to bring everything together with such clarity: The three
groups of married, widowed, and virginal clerics are bound to observe the same discipline of continence. Thus continence celibacy was
founded on holy orders, and therefore it applied uniformly, regardless
of whether the ordained man was now married or single. And to this
discipline belonged the digamy prohibition as well, inasmuch as the re-

---

[1] *Panarion lxxx haeresium* 59, 4, 1–8 (GCS Epiph. 2², 367, 7–368, 14); C. Cochini, *Apostolic Origins of Priestly Celibacy* (San Francisco, 1990), 226–33.

striction of eligibility for marriage was connected with the continence required of all clerics.

We should mention here another passage by Epiphanius. It is significant in that the discipline of the Church was being defended here explicitly against the Encratite tendencies of the Montanists. In a similar manner Clement of Alexandria had already opposed an exaggerated disdain for the body by referring to the clerical discipline. Whereas the Montanists now were rejecting marriage completely, the Church walked the middle way: beside the "holy priesthood" stood "holy marriage";[2] the Church affirmed marriage but valued continence more highly. Therefore, on the basis of the "ecclesiastical rules [κανών]" going back to the apostles, she reserved the priesthood for those men who were living continently in a first marriage, widowed, or virginal.[3] Therefore Epiphanius, too, sees no contradiction at all between the restriction of the clerics' right to marry and the Church's fundamental affirmation of marriage.

Anyone who disputes that Epiphanius is speaking, to the best of his knowledge, about a binding celibacy discipline, which was valid throughout the Church though perhaps not always consistently enforced, can be suspected of ideological prejudice.[4] When Epiphanius speaks of ecclesiastical canons, that is what he means. And in fact we do

---

[2] *De Fide* 21, 5, 7 (GCS Epiph. 3, 522, 3, 8).

[3] *Panarion lxxx haeresium* 48, 9, 1–6 (GCS Epiph. 2², 230, 26–231, 19): Ἡ δὲ ἁγία ἐκκλησία καὶ παρθενίαν δοξάζει καὶ μονότητα καὶ ἁγνείαν καὶ χηροσύνην ἐπαινεῖ καὶ γάμον σεμνὸν τιμᾷ καὶ δέχεται, πορνείαν δὲ καὶ μοιχείαν καὶ ἀσέλγειαν ἀπαγορεύει, ὅθεν ἰδεῖν ἔστιν τὸν χαρακτῆρα τῆς ἁγίας καθολικῆς ἐκκλησίας καὶ τοὺς παραπεποιημένους τῶν ἄλλων τρόπους, <ὡς> καὶ τὸν δοκιμάσαντα ἀποδιδράσκειν ἀπὸ πάσης πλάνης καὶ σκολιᾶς ὁδοῦ καὶ τρίβου ἀνάντου διακειμένης. Ἔφην γὰρ ἄνω ὡς ἀπὸ τοῦ ἁγιωτάτου ἀποστόλου προείρηται καὶ πάλιν ἐρῶ, ὅτι ἀσφαλιζόμενος ἡμᾶς καὶ τὸν χαρακτῆρα τῆς ἁγίας ἐκκλησίας διαιρῶν ἀπὸ τῆς τῶν αἱρέσεων πλάνης ἔφη, ὡς τολμηρῶς τὰ ἐκ θεοῦ καλῶς τεταγμένα ἀπαγορεύοντες νομοθετοῦσι. Φήσας περὶ τῶν κωλυόντων γαμεῖν καὶ ἀπέχεσθαι βρωμάτων. Καὶ γὰρ συμμετρίᾳ τινὶ * ὁ θεὸς Λόγος ἐν τῷ εὐαγγελίῳ φήσας >θέλεις τέλειος γενέσθαι;<, συγγνωμονῶν τῇ τῶν ἀνθρώπων πλάσει καὶ ἀσθενείᾳ χαίρει μὲν ἐπὶ τοῖς τὰ δόκιμα τῆς θεοσεβείας δυναμένοις ἐνδείκνυσθαι καὶ παρθενίαν ἀσκεῖν αἱρουμένοις καὶ ἁγνείαν καὶ ἐγκράτειαν, τὴν δὲ μονογαμίαν τιμᾷ· εἰ καὶ μάλιστα τὰ χαρίσματα τῆς ἱερωσύνης διὰ τῶν ἀπὸ μονογαμίας ἐγκρατευομένων καὶ τῶν ἐν παρθενίᾳ διατελούντων τῷ κόσμῳ προδιετύπου ὡς καὶ οἱ αὐτοῦ ἀπόστολοι τὸν ἐκκλησιαστικὸν κανόνα τῆς ἱερωσύνης εὐτάκτως καὶ ὁσίως διετάξαντο. Εἰ δέ τις κατὰ ἀσθένειαν ἐπιδεηθείη μετὰ τὴν τελευτὴν τῆς ἰδίας γαμετῆς συναφθῆναι δευτέρῳ γάμῳ, οὐκ ἀπαγορεύει τοῦτο ὁ κανὼν τῆς ἀληθείας, τουτέστιν τὸν μὴ ὄντα ἱερέα.

[4] Funk's arguments about Eusebius are lame, but when he comes to Epiphanius they are simply desparate (Cochini, *Origins*, 228–34).

know about the celibacy canon of Elvira and the Ecclesiastical Canons of the Holy Apostles, about Ancyra and Neocaesarea. Of course in the fourth century there was still no legislation for the Church universal. This means, conversely, that all the decisions of councils and synods at that time had legal force only in a given region. There were areas where no "exact ecclesiastical canons" pertaining to continence existed, yet even in such places there was an unwritten custom, which naturally was easier to evade. And even the regional canons, to be sure, were not always unequivocal, or else they merely dealt with certain aspects of clerical continence—for instance, only with the digamy prohibition. Epiphanius positively admits this.

We must keep in view the situation of the Church in that period. After she gained official recognition during Constantine's reign and was promoted to the state religion under Theodosius in the year 381, the number of Christians increased by leaps and bounds. That necessarily had consequences for clerical discipline, too, and naturally it made the clergy more prone to relax their ascetical practices. The population of enormous territories was now largely Catholic, and clerics had to be ordained quickly; sometimes it was just not possible to make a careful selection. Often, therefore, the reason for offenses against celibacy was not the rejection of continence but simply ignorance of the law or the lack of clergy.

And so there may have been one or another who could not practice continence. By human standards one could not expect it to be otherwise. But that was precisely the obvious exception to the rule, to the "ecclesiastical canon", as Epiphanius puts it. One cannot pretend that this rule did not exist simply because it was not adhered to in many dioceses. Had Epiphanius only spoken about the law of clerical continence without mentioning violations of the rule, one would immediately become suspicious. One would consider Epiphanius untrustworthy and say, "But that is impossible! No rule is without exceptions!" Now Epiphanius does mention exceptions, and so why should that not be taken as a proof of his honesty and the general validity of continence celibacy? He probably would not have spoken merely about exceptions if the continence discipline had been disputed at all and if any earlier bishops (for instance, of the caliber of a Paphnutius) had explicitly pronounced against it. Epiphanius was much too conscientious and conservative. One may regard him, then, as a witness to the clerical discipline in the fourth-century, post-Constantinian period.

The testimony of Epiphanius is important above all because we can credit him with an independent judgment about the conditions in the entire eastern portion of the empire. He is writing before the great papal initiatives, the decretals, and synodal statements of the West, which began to address the theme of clerical continence in the 380s, in the last two decades of the century. Even though his ministry kept him on the island of Cyprus, Epiphanius was, indeed, a thoroughly Rome-oriented bishop. But for simple chronological reasons he could not have been influenced by the continence-euphoria of the Latins. And conversely it cannot be said without further explanation that the popes and the councils had innovated in issuing their celibacy decrees. The East had it earlier, or at least simultaneously.

b. Jerome in Bethlehem

Jerome (347/348 to 419/420), one of the best-known scholarly personages of the early Church, singularly well versed in the Greek and Hebrew Sacred Scriptures, provides many valuable references to clerical continence. One cannot speak about him without also saying something about his character. No one makes as scintillating an impression as he does. Quick-tempered and easily offended, he was consumed with zeal for the Catholic cause, though on many an occasion he was overzealous. In being 100 percent Catholic, he was in no way inferior to Epiphanius, whom he knew personally and with whom he stayed in 382 during a Roman synod. Born in Dalmatia, Jerome actually should be credited to the Latin Church. But biographically as well as spiritually he was at home in the entire world. As a traveler almost without peer, personally acquainted with the conditions in Gaul, Italy, Syria (Antioch), Asia Minor (Constantinople), and Palestine from his sojourns in those places, as the secretary of Pope Damasus thoroughly versed in the ecclesiastical condition of the West, and until the end of his life in contact with innumerable laymen and clerics in East and West (for example with Theophilus of Alexandria and Augustine of Hippo) through a voluminous correspondence, he belonged equally in the West and in the East.

Indeed, what we learn from Jerome about clerical continence dates almost exclusively to the period when he had definitively settled in the Holy Land, in Bethlehem (from 385 on). For methodological reasons, therefore, we must ascribe his statements to the East, even though they are found in writings addressed to Western correspondents and stem from a period when Rome already had clearly taken a strong stance in favor of clerical continence.[5] Jerome would surely not assert things that do not apply in the East. This is all the more true because he was well acquainted with the writings of the Greek theologians. If he had found there objections to an obligatory continence discipline, he certainly would have conveyed them to the West. Besides, he was much too learned, too imbued also with the Oriental sort of scholarship that thought historically and took divergent opinions very much into account. This is demonstrated, for example, by the fact that Jerome records the criticism of the digamy prohibition, which ultimately went back to Origen. But nowhere does he ever mention that a bishop or theologian of the Eastern Church called into question clerical continence per se.

Thus the passages that we will now cite were written during his years in Bethlehem, when clerical continence was also being discussed in Rome. It is certain that Jerome was well acquainted with the developments there. At the very least, the letter from the Spanish Bishop Himerius to Pope Damasus would have been in his hands back in the days when he was papal secretary. This letter caused some concern in Rome about the future of the clerical discipline, as we shall see. But even later, while in Bethlehem, Jerome had his sources of information in Rome. Therefore it is not entirely possible to distinguish, in the literary output of his Bethlehem years, what reflects Western experience and what regards the Eastern realm. One can actually say, therefore, that since Jerome knew of clerical continence and on this subject did not differentiate between East and West, then it had to have been for him a matter concerning the entire Church.

Jerome, a priest himself since his sojourn in Antioch, saw it as the duty of clerics to protect the Church as the Bride of Christ in continence and chastity.[6] He was acquainted with the complete clerical discipline, which consisted of marriage and digamy prohibitions (see below, pp. 170 and 157–59) and of marital continence.[7] He writes

---

[5] It is methodologically objectionable when R. Gryson, *Les Origines du célibat ecclèsiastique du premier au septième siècle*, RSSR.H 2 (Gembloux, 1970), 142f., numbers Jerome among the writers of the West.

[6] *Epistula* 14, 8, 1 *ad Heliodorum* (CSEL 54, 55, 6f.).

[7] *Epistula* 52, 16, 1 *ad Nepotianum* (CSEL 54, 439, 8–12). Written around 394–396.

about the latter in his apologetic work addressed to Pammachius from the year 393:

> Here then is what we have clearly said [against Jovinian]: Marriage is permitted in the Gospel, but women, if they persist in accomplishing the duty that is theirs, cannot receive the reward promised to chastity. Let the husbands, if they grow indignant at this opinion, be irritated not with me but with Holy Scripture, better yet with the bishops, the priests, the deacons, the entire priestly, even Levitical choir, who know that they cannot offer sacrifices if they accomplish the conjugal act![8]

Marital duties and liturgical duties did not go together. Now one might still think that it is a matter here of a continence discipline restricted to liturgical days. Another passage, though, makes everything clear:

> The apostles were either virgins or continent after having been married. Bishops, priests, and deacons are chosen among virgins and widowers; in any case, once they are ordained, they live in perfect chastity.[9]

When one considers, moreover, yet another passage concerning the Vigilantius affair, which states that in the entire region east of Gaul— Egypt and Rome are mentioned *pars pro toto*—the only married men ordained are those who practice continence (see below, p. 269–70), then there can be no more serious objections to this discipline. Every exception only proves the rule. If Jerome in agreement with Epiphanius says that continence is observed everywhere, apart from the (alleged) exceptions in Gaul, then the statement is unassailable. Had they all been sworn, then, to a historical lie? Would someone not have contradicted them, had they merely been claiming that all clerics had the obligation to practice continence? Would not at least one or another theologian have ventured a refutation? At any rate there is plenty of

---

[8] *Epistula* 49, 10, 1 *ad Pammachium* (CSEL 54, 365, 4–10): "Ecce perspicue nuptias diximus concedi in euangelio, sed tamen easdem in suo officio permanentes praemia castitatis capere non posse. Quod si indigne accipiunt mariti, non mihi irascantur, sed scripturis sanctis, immo episcopis, presbyteris et diaconis et uniuerso choro sacerdotali et Leuitico, qui se nouerunt hostias offerre non posse, si operi seruiant coniugali." Cochini, *Origins*, 296–98. [Translation as in Cochini, *Origins*, 296–97.]

[9] *Epistula* 49, 21, 3 *ad Pammachium* (CSEL 54, 386, 20–387, 3): "Apostoli uel uirgines uel post nuptias continentes; episcopi, presbyteri, diaconi aut uirgines eliguntur aut uidui aut certe post sacerdotium in aeternum pudici."

evidence that the public by no means simply accepted every statement by theologians.[10]

c. John Chrysostom

Epiphanius belonged on Cyprus, Jerome in Palestine, John Chrysostom (d. 407) in Syria. John testified as well to the full discipline of the Church, even if not quite so clearly as the other two. He was not only one of the most important figures of the Eastern Church, but also personally one of the most convincing. As of 386 he worked as a priest in Antioch. His sermons quickly made him famous. And so eleven years later his career led him against his will to the patriarchal see of Constantinople.

In his view the higher ministry of the Church formed a unity, even though it was divided into three degrees. Bishops, priests, and deacons were subject to the same discipline.[11] Consequently, what Chrysostom says only about deacons or only about bishops was true, then, for priests as well, and vice versa. The higher ecclesiastical ministries were all treated in the same way, also with respect to marriage and continence. As a bishop, Chrysostom refused to ordain men who had remarried.[12] Accordingly, the digamy prohibition applied for all higher clerics. There is no question either about his predilection for unmarried clerics. This was obviously a consequence of his sympathy for monasticism. During his episcopacy in Constantinople he assigned a whole series of ordained ascetics to pastoral work.[13]

At the time of Chrysostom there was a married clergy, as is evident from his commentaries on the pastoral letters. Chrysostom, however, did not understand "the husband of one wife" (1 Tim 3:2) as though a cleric were required to have a wife and children. He saw marriage as a possibility for those who were already married and as such were

---

[10] Thus Jerome met with vehement opposition when he deprecated marriage in his writings to Eustochium (*Epistula* 52, 17, 1 *ad Nepotianum*) and against Jovinian.

[11] Gryson, *Origines*, 67f.

[12] Ibid., 71.

[13] I. Auf der Maur, *Mönchtum und Glaubens verkündigung in den Schriften des hl. Johannes Chrysostomus*, Par. 14 (Fribourg, 1959), 105–41; M. Lochbrunner, *Über das Priestertum: Historische und systematische Untersuchung zum Priesterbild des Johannes Chrysostomus*, Hereditas 5 (Bonn, 1993), 86 n. 40.

called to the episcopacy.[14] Moreover we have information from other sources about a series of married bishops in the Eastern dioceses.[15] But did they practice continence? Roger Gryson thinks that a discipline of obligatory continence cannot be discovered in the writings of Chrysostom. There is in fact no direct order to observe continence.

And yet Chrysostom on several occasions gives us a glimpse of clerical continence. In any case he connects the continence of married clerics with the "unius uxoris vir", exactly as Jerome and the Western authors do. This emerges from his commentary on the Letter to Titus:

> The candidate, says Saint Paul, must be "blameless, the husband of one wife", and his children must be "believers and not open to the charge of being profligate or insubordinate" (Tit 1:6). Why does he want such a man? He stops the mouths of the heretics who reject marriage and shows that this institution is not accursed, but rather so honorable that a married man can even ascend to the holy throne [of the bishop]. And at the same time he condemns those who are uncontrolled [ἀσελγεῖς]. He does not admit them, since he refused this position of honor to those who are twice-married. How could someone who cannot watch over the memory of his deceased wife ever be a good leader? What accusations will he not be exposed to? For you all know very well that, although the laws do not forbid it, a second marriage is nevertheless open to many reproaches.[16]

Chrysostom marshals here the classical arguments that Clement of Alexandria had already used against the heretics contemptuous of marriage: The Church neither rejects marriage—that is said probably to

---

[14] *Homiliae in 1 Tim.* prol. (PG 62, 503f.): Καὶ γὰρ περὶ ἐπισκόπων διαλεγόμενος, καὶ πολλὰ περὶ αὐτῶν εἰπών, οὐδαμοῦ περὶ τῆς ἡλικίας ἀκριβολογεῖται. Εἰ δὲ λέγοι γράφων, *Τέκνα ἐν ὑποταγῇ ἔχοντα*, καὶ, *Μιᾶς γυναικὸς ἄνδρα*, οὐ τοῦτό φησιν, ὡς ἀναγκαῖον καὶ τέκνα ἔχειν καὶ γυναῖκα, ἀλλ', εἰ συμβαίη ποτὲ ἀπὸ κοσμικῶν ἄγεσθαι, ἵνα τοιοῦτοι ὦσιν, ὡς καὶ οἰκίας εἰδέναι προεστάναι καὶ παίδων καὶ τῶν ἄλλων ἁπάντων.

[15] Gryson, *Origines*, 67.

[16] *Hom.* 2, 1 in *Tit.* 1 (PG 62, 671): Εἴ τις, φησὶν, ἀνέγκλητος, μιᾶς γυναικὸς ἀνὴρ, τέκνα ἔχων πιστά, μὴ ἐν κατηγορίᾳ ἀσωτίας, ἢ ἀνυπότακτα. Τίνος ἔνεκεν καὶ τὸν τοιοῦτον εἰς μέσον παράγει; Ἐπιστομίζει τοὺς αἱρετικοὺς τοὺς τὸν γάμον διαβάλλοντας, δεικνὺς ὅτι τὸ πρᾶγμα οὐκ ἔστιν ἐναγές, ἀλλ' οὕτω τίμον, ὡς μετ' αὐτοῦ δύνασθαι καὶ ἐπὶ τὸν ἅγιον ἀναβαίνειν θρόνον· ἐν ταυτῷ δὲ καὶ τοὺς ἀσελγεῖς κολάζων, καὶ οὐκ ἀφιεὶς μετὰ δευτέρου γάμου τὴν ἀρχὴν ἐγχειρίζεσθαι ταύτην. Ὁ γὰρ πρὸς τὴν ἀπελθοῦσαν μηδεμίαν φυλάξας εὔνοιαν, πῶς ἂν οὗτος γένοιτο προστάτης καλός; τίνα δὲ οὐκ ἂν ὑποσταίη κατηγορίαν; Ἴστε γὰρ ἅπαντες, ἴστε ὅτι εἰ μὴ κεκώλυται παρὰ τῶν νόμων τὸ δευτέροις ὁμιλεῖν γάμοις, ἀλλ' ὅμως πολλὰς ἔχει τὸ πρᾶγμα κατηγορίας. See also *De virginitate* 37–39. The dating of the homilies on the Pastoral Letters is uncertain.

counter the Eustathians in Asia Minor—nor subscribes to unbridled sexuality. Both teachings are illustrated in the clergy: clerics are married and have had children, but after their ordination they live in perfect continence. Chrysostom says it quite clearly: Incontinent men are not admitted to holy orders. He finds the requirement of continence implicit in the "unius uxoris vir". To his way of thinking, anyone living in a second marriage gives cause for suspicions and accusations, because it is possible that he might not be practicing continence after his ordination, either. In his opinion a widower marries only because he cannot or does not want to practice continence;[17] the first marriage is "a sign of great holiness and continence", whereas the second is an sign of insufficient self-control.[18]

Thus Chrysostom expected continence after ordination. The text goes on to confirm this. For a married candidate to the priesthood or the episcopacy, indeed, child-rearing was already a thing of the past. He must already have proved himself in that, so that his abilities could be judged on that basis.[19] For the future, after ordination, there was no prospect of further family life. This is corroborated again in another homily from the Antiochene period. "Let deacons be the husband of one wife" (1 Tim 3:12). You see how he demands the same virtue from deacons, too! Even if they do not have the same dignity as a bishop, they still must be equally blameless, equally chaste [ἀγνοί] (cf. 1 Tim 3:8).[20] Roger Gryson, in discussing this passage, overlooks the crucial point, that is, that the deacons' conduct had to be, in comparison to that of the bishops, "equally chaste [continent]".[21] Therefore Chrysostom can serve very well as a witness to a discipline of continence celibacy in the Eastern Church.

Angelic purity. Chrysostom had a lasting influence on the sacerdotal image in the East through his book about priests. He thereby set standards. It was the first treatise ever "On the Priesthood". Chrysostom composed it at the beginning of his priestly ministry, around the year

---

[17] *De non iterando coniugio* 1 (SC 138, 162, 27f.).

[18] Ibid., 2 (SC 138, 168, 84–86).

[19] *Hom.* 2, 1 *in Tit.* 1 (PG 62, 671f.).

[20] *Hom.* 11, 1 *in* 1 *Tim.* 3 (PG 62, 553): Διάκονοι ἔστωσαν μιᾶς γυναικὸς, φησὶν, ἄνδρες. Ὁρᾷς πῶς τὴν αὐτὴν ἀπαιτεῖ καὶ παρὰ διακόνων ἀρετήν; Εἰ γὰρ καὶ μὴ τῆς αὐτῆς εἰσιν ἀξίας τῷ ἐπισκόπῳ, ἀλλ' ὅμως ὁμοίως ἀνεπίληπτοι, ὁμοίως ἀγνοὶ ὀφείλουσιν εἶναι. Cf. Pelagius, *Expositio in* 1 *Tim.* 3 (PL 30, 880B): *Pudicos* (1 Tim 3:8). *Continentes scilicet.*

[21] Gryson, *Origines*, 66f.

385. In it he depicts in the brightest possible colors his image of the dignity and responsibility of the priestly office. Since Chrysostom, before his ordination, grappled for some time with the ideals of monasticism, he tries to put them to use in his perspective on the priesthood.[22] Above all he would like to see the virtues of monks in the clergy as well, and therefore when testing candidates for the priestly ministry one should pay attention to the purity characteristic of monks; indeed, priests should be even purer than hermits. This imperative addresses the sexual realm in particular, which presents a real danger to the priest who is involved in pastoral ministry.[23]

Thus Chrysostom very likely expected complete, indeed monastic continence from the priest. And when he writes, "The soul of the priest must be even purer than the rays of the sun", that does not mean a merely spiritual purity of the soul, but rather a perfect purity that is quite corporeal as well.[24] This is a deliberate generalization with no nuancing. In this view of the priest as cultic minister, the requirement of continence is fundamentally self-evident.[25] Chrysostom includes in it the married clergy, as well.[26]

Now one might think that, for married priests, this chastity that is so highly esteemed would consist in ritual purity. It would apply, then, only for days when the Divine Liturgy was celebrated. If one reads the entire treatise "On the Priesthood", though, and sees the extraordinarily high esteem in which Chrysostom holds the sacred ministry, how he demands from men who serve at the altar virtues surpassing those of all other states in life, how he exalts them to the sphere of the angels, then it becomes simply unimaginable that he would have been content with periodic continence. He has in mind nothing less than perfect, angelic purity.[27] He finds the reason for the requirement of perfect purity, not in the eventual celibacy or virginity of the priest, but rather in the priestly ideal as such. The priesthood demands perfect purity inasmuch as the priest stands at the service of the faithful every

[22] Lochbrunner, *Priestertum*, 84–90.
[23] John Chrysostom, *De sacerdotio* 6, 2 (SC 272, 306, 1–308, 21); 6, 4 (318, 69–320, 75); 6, 8 (330, 9–15).
[24] Ibid., 6, 2 (SC 272, 306, 6); 6, 4 (316, 39f.).
[25] G. Denzler, *Die Geschichte des Zölibats* (Freiburg, 1993), 66.
[26] Gryson, *Origines*, 71.
[27] John Chrysostom, *De sacerdotio* 3, 4 (SC 272, 142, 1–10).

day[28] and the Eucharistic Sacrifice is offered daily.[29] The perfect priest-hood of the New Covenant thus demands perfect purity, whether the ordained man is married or not. Here his thinking is completely in line with Origen's, and from the perspective of this tradition it really can-not be doubted that the married clerics and their wives also practiced perfect continence.

Even if Chrysostom did not explicitly include the continence of married priests and their wives in his discussion, the inner logic of his concept of priesthood makes this conclusion compelling. He could not have afforded the inconsistency of praising unmarried priests to the skies on account of their absolute purity, while applying lower stan-dards to married priests. That would have meant a two-class system: the celibates would be praiseworthy, but the married clerics really would no longer be acceptable. The former would do justice to the priestly state, whereas the latter would only obscure the whole matter. If the high theology of the priesthood sees the specifically priestly excellence in the sacrifice of chastity, then that very fact makes possible a uniform discipline assigning equal dignity to married and unmarried clerics.

2. Obligatory Continence Despite Criticism of the Digamy Prohibition

According to the pastoral letters, married men can be ordained only if they are living in their first marriage. That is what the phrase "unius uxoris vir" means. At first glance that seems to have nothing to do with obligatory continence. By now, though, we have had several occasions to learn better. For the manner in which the theologians of the first three centuries treated the impediment to orders of digamy soon makes it clear that this was an essential approach to continence celibacy. Re-call Tertullian, Clement, and Origen. The texts of the fourth century corroborate this finding.

---

[28] *Hom.* 2, 4 *in* 2 *Tim.* 1:8–10 (PG 62, 612).
[29] *Hom.* 17, 3 *in Hebr.* 9:24–26 (PG 63, 131); *Adversus Iudaeos* 3, 4 (PG 48, 867).

a. Can Digamists, Too, Not Practice Continence?

Let us return once more to Origen. In his writings the connection between the digamy prohibition and continence-celibacy is particularly clear: The obligation of married clerics and their wives to abstain completely from sexual relations was for him not a problem. But why, then, were those men ineligible for ordination who after a second marriage had been widowed, who were therefore practicing continence at least as well as other candidates? No plausible answer to this question occurred to him. Epiphanius of Salamis, too, appears to have been acquainted with the dispute about why men who were living in a second marriage, or else had been widowed after a second marriage, were not ordained. He, too, could only answer that this had always been the case.[30]

On all sides, then, perplexity prevailed, although this problem had been taken up again and again. Certainly the pain felt by many digamists who would have liked to see themselves at the altar played its part, too. And then people naturally became upset about such a Church ordinance, which was perceived to be unjust. Many a digamist living an exemplary life must have felt discriminated against when he saw that now and then questionable characters were given preference over him, only because they were fortunate enough not to have contracted a second marriage. Perhaps the people of God applied a certain pressure, also, because the prohibition of digamy seemed somehow arbitrary to them. That explains, then, why the topic remained so divisive. This is apparent in two detailed texts. They are so similar to each other that one must assume there was a common theological tradition.

Jerome. Jerome is the preeminent exegete in the Latin tongue. He composed his commentary on the Letter to Titus around 387–389 in Bethlehem. The passage that is of particular interest to us is obviously related to the theology of Origen. But it is not impossible that another influence may have been that of Theodore (see the following discussion), with whom he could have become acquainted during his stay in Antioch in the years 374–375. Jerome writes:

---

[30] Epiphanius, *De fide* 21, 8 (GCS Epiph. 3, 522, 11–13).

Let us see, then, what sort of man can be ordained a priest or a bishop. "If any man is blameless, the husband of one wife, and his children are believers and not open to the charge of being profligate or insubordinate" (Tit 1:6). . . . The fact that he says "the husband of one wife" we must understand in this way: Not because we ought to think that every monogamist is preferable to a digamist; rather, that man ought to be capable of exhorting others to monogamy and continence who presents his own example along with the instruction.

Let us assume for a moment that a young man lost his wife and, giving in to the urges of the flesh, took a second wife, whom he likewise lost shortly thereafter. And from then on he practiced continence. Another, though, has lived as a married man until old age and has had—in the opinion of most people—happy marital relations with his wife, without ever having abstained from sexual intercourse. Which of the two seems to you to be better, more chaste, more continent? That one, to be sure, who in unfortunate circumstances entered a second marriage but later led a chaste and holy life, and not the one who even at an advanced age did not renounce his wife's embrace. Therefore it is no reason for self-praise if a man is chosen as a monogamist, as though he were superior to that digamist, because in the case of the latter, fecundity counts more than the will [to practice continence].

Some reason as follows about this passage: It corresponded to Jewish custom to have two or more wives. We read this in the Old Law, too, about Abraham and Jacob. And now they claim to see in this law a prohibition, that no one may be chosen to be a bishop who has two wives at one and the same time.

Many think—and this view is even pettier, although by no means any more true—that even those who as pagans had a wife but lost her, and after their baptism married another, are not allowed to be selected as priests. If that is how the situation is to be handled, then one would sooner have to exclude from the episcopacy those who previously (without the bond of marriage) indulged their lust with various women, but after their rebirth had only one wife. It would be much more reprehensible if a man had committed adultery repeatedly [before baptism] than if he had entered into a second marriage [after baptism]. For in the one case marriage proves to be a disadvantage, while in the other case an unbridled propensity for sin prevails.[31]

Jerome corroborates and approves of the Church's practice of ordaining only monogamists, or digamists as well if their first marriage

---

[31] *Comm. in Tit.* 1:5f. (PL 26, 598A–599A).

was before baptism. In any case, the digamy prohibition was valid, regardless of whether one accepted the strict or the broad interpretation of it.[32] That does not prevent him, though, from addressing Origen's critique with regard to widowed digamists. He wonders why a continent digamist is excluded from orders, while an unchaste man who has been married once can be admitted to the Church's ministry. Jerome speaks just as Origen did about unchaste men in a first marriage who are ordained. That does not mean, though, that there was no obligatory continence. The unchaste men, after all, were not ordained with permission to continue leading an unchaste life. Exactly the opposite should be said: Why were men ordained who had never practiced continence and had never grown accustomed to it, although continence was required of them after ordination? Would such a man after ordination not in all probability become unchaste? And why, on the other hand, were respectable men excluded from holy orders from the start, even though they had already put to the test their ability to practice continence?

All of this presupposed that holy orders were denied to digamists because in their case, a priori, the "will [to practice continence]" was not present. But that is precisely the question. For, very likely, there were digamists who wanted to and could practice continence. And nevertheless, Jerome was still aware somehow that the digamy prohibition of the pastoral letters was laid down for the sake of the future continence of clerics. This presupposition was the foundation for the Church's discipline of not ordaining digamists. Jerome, however, also saw that in reality it could be vice versa. Therefore the monogamy rule, in his opinion, must not be understood as a purely formal preference; otherwise it would quickly become senseless.

Theodore of Mopsuestia. Theodore (ca. 350–428), a slightly younger contemporary of Jerome, was one of the most important commentators on Sacred Scripture in the Greek Church. At one time in Antioch he was a fellow student of John Chrysostom, with whom he later maintained contact as well; from 392 on he served as bishop in Mopsuestia in Cilicia (Asia Minor). In his commentary on the First Letter to Timothy, written perhaps around 410–415, Theodore considered himself obliged to discuss the phrase "unius uxoris vir" at great length.

---

[32] *Adversus Jovinianum* 1, 14 (PL 23², 244C): "Digamus in clerum eligi non potest." Ibid., 1, 34 (268D).

It is quite ridiculous what one finds in many authors. For instance when a man has contracted a second marriage, he is not admitted to the clergy, even if he practices continence. But if someone who has legitimately taken only one wife has lived indecently, he is admitted, although Saint Paul has unequivocally permitted remarriage, whereas all relations outside of a legitimate marriage are adulterous. And do not forget that a man living in a second marriage, too, is admitted to the clergy after baptism, in those cases where notice is taken only of the second, as though baptism would cause him no longer to have lived with two wives.

Often, however, they do the same with entirely unworthy men and consider themselves justified in baptizing such a one and then admitting him to the clerical ministry, although he has in no way demonstrated virtue or piety. To say nothing of the actual meaning of baptism, which most of them do not want to see at all! But they must know that Saint Paul gives guidelines as to how a bishop, in his opinion, ought to have lived and that he is by no means speaking about the sins that are remitted through the grace of baptism. If such a practice were correct and Paul had permitted a man to be admitted to the clergy immediately after his baptism, regardless of his earlier life-style, then all of his guidelines would be superfluous. But Paul forbids that (cf. 1 Tim 3:6). He wants someone who is admitted to the episcopacy to be able to give evidence of his former righteousness and either to have been righteous at all times or else to show with complete remorse that he has turned his life around for the better, which should be evident in the period following. Indeed, things are now going well for many who have committed a very great crime [in the past].

Some have understood "the husband of one wife" as I, too, am inclined to interpret it. Because at that time many legitimately had two wives at once, which they were permitted to do even according to the Mosaic Law. Many had only one lawful wife but did not content themselves with that and joined with other women, whether their slaves or women who manifestly lived in sin. That happens even today among those who are not at all concerned about continence. According to their interpretation, Paul said that that man should be selected for the episcopacy who has taken one wife and lived chastely with her, has remained true to her, and with her has kept lust in check. In their opinion, a man who has lived thus, and after the loss of his first wife has lawfully married a second time and has lived in the same manner with his second wife as well, according to the guidelines of Paul cannot be refused access to the episcopacy.

I take it that this is what Saint Paul said. I do not believe that he would have permitted the second marriage just like the first, provided that it was entered into lawfully, if he had wanted to exclude the twice-married man from the episcopacy. For he said: "To the unmarried and the widowers I say [. . . if they cannot exercise self-control, they should marry]" (1 Cor 7:8), took both groups together and placed them under the same law, because he evidently considered the two to be the same. And rightly so. For what difference does it make, with respect to natural concupiscence, if one has never had a wife or if one had a wife but lost her through her death? That is not a matter of free will but of fate. For one man may have had a wife for a long time and enjoyed her as it pleased him, whereas another man may have lost his wife after a short time and considered himself compelled to marry again. Those are matters of fate. Saint Paul, however, is listing matters of free will, one by one, because he thinks that the candidate for bishop must be tested, above all, with respect to such things. For it is ridiculous, actually, to think that Paul is giving guidelines, not to test free-will decisions, but to make a selection on the basis of fate. For if someone were to say that he [Paul] indeed cared very little about fate, but precisely in the case of the bishop was more exacting and wished him to have joined hitherto with only one wife, then he ought to understand that, for the same reason, there would be no justification for accepting such a candidate even after baptism. For obviously a subsequent baptism does not bring it about that he did not have two wives, nor does it cause everyone to assume that he has only joined with one wife. A fortiori, a man who, though lawfully married to only one wife, gave himself licentiously to innumerable others and whose way of life became public knowledge, for the same reason cannot be admitted to the episcopacy, just because he has received baptism. For if someone says that the man who was lawfully wed to two wives and lived with them chastely may not be admitted to the episcopacy, because careful attention must be paid to his free-will decisions, how much less reason is there, then, to admit the other man who lived licentiously simply on the grounds that he has been baptized.

And this [in summary] is what ought to be said about the phrase "the husband of one wife". We thought that we should speak more clearly about this, because we set no store by the interpretation of it that most other writers give.[33]

Theodore's sober exegesis is hardly light fare. Let us attempt to outline the situation in the Church and to retrace the main steps of his argument. In Theodore's day the phrase "unius uxoris vir" was predominantly interpreted as a digamy prohibition. This is corroborated by Basil of Caesarea, for whom digamy fundamentally excluded a candi-

---

[33] *Comm. in* 1 *Tim.* 3:2 (99, 13–106, 24 Swete 2).

date from ecclesiastical ministry (that is, from the diaconate upward).[34] Theodore, too, seems to recognize this as the general practice in the Church: Only men who were living in a first marriage were ordained. Of course in many places the situation was handled in such a way that a marriage that took place before baptism was not counted. We will return to this in the next section. In any case Theodore takes a negative stance toward the digamy prohibition. In doing so he is more radical than Origen and Jerome. He considers the digamy prohibition sense-less and antiquated. But does he therefore reject obligatory continence as well?[35] If that were the case, obligatory continence in general would be called into question for the East around the year 400.

But we must look to the reasons that Theodore gives for his neg-ative stance toward the digamy prohibition. Of prime importance is the same practical consideration that Origen has already brought up. There are, to be sure, potential candidates for orders who have married a second time and moreover practice continence, possibly even because the second wife, too, has died. Why should they be prevented from receiving holy orders? Theodore views being widowed and remarrying as something like a natural phenomenon, which happens to a man but which contains no moral indication about the suitability of a candi-date for orders. The crucial datum that we derive from this argument, however, is that perfect continence was required of the married cleric and his wife.[36] It is precisely for this reason that the monogamy rule became problematic.

Therefore it is simply not the case that Theodore, if he criticizes so harshly the Church's practice of prohibiting digamy, could not possibly know of a continence rule. The opposite is true. Precisely because he adheres to obligatory continence, it is for him a decisive factor in se-lecting aspirants that the candidate has put to the test before ordination his ability to practice continence. However, if it can be demonstrated that a twice-married man is capable of continence, then in Theodore's eyes he is to be preferred to a monogamous man who thus far has not managed to control himself. It is precisely for the sake of continence that Theodore wishes to dispute the validity of the monogamy rule.

---

[34] *Epistulae* 188, 12 (130 Courtonne 2).

[35] Thus Gryson, *Origines*, 73.

[36] In another passage Theodore speaks of priests as "spiritual fathers"; *Comm. in Ps.* 44:17a (298, 24 Devreesse).

In recommending that the digamy prohibition be revoked, Theodore places himself in opposition to the Church's practice. He admits this explicitly in his concluding sentence. It does not seem, though, that as bishop he therefore simply disregarded the digamy prohibition. Rather, it is a question, as it was in Origen's case, of his theological opinion. Evidence against a repeal of the monogamy rule is furnished by the events surrounding the removal from office of the digamist bishop Irenaeus of Tyre in the year 448. We learn about them in a letter of Theodoret (d. around 466), bishop of Cyrrhus, which is not far from Mopsuestia. According to this letter, many digamists were ordained in the Church of Syria, Palestine, and Asia Minor at the beginning of the fifth century.[37] But it is inconclusive whether the first marriage in each case took place before baptism. One would assume that that was indeed the situation, based on Theodore's statements, which indicate that this rule was generally observed. Of course the rule appears to have been disregarded in this one documented instance of Irenaeus because of partisan interests, which were rendered more legitimate by theologians like Theodore and Theodoret. Otherwise the emperor would not have been able to depose Irenaeus on the pretext of digamy. At the same time that goes to show that such abuses were not simply tolerated. All in all, this is corroborated by Jerome when he says that throughout the world there are numerous digamist clerics. At the same time he leads one to believe that in these situations a marriage that took place before baptism is not taken into account.

b. Mitigation of the Digamy Prohibition, but Not of the Continence Discipline

As may be supposed, the continual and persistent criticism of the digamy prohibition furthered a development that ultimately led to a mitigation of the digamy prohibition. And indeed, in the case of candidates for orders who were married more than once, the marriages that had taken place before baptism were not counted. Thus at least a certain group of digamists could be considered monogamous and could be ordained. Such a concession found adherents throughout the Church but ultimately could continue only in the East, since in the West the

---

[37] *Epistulae* 110 (SC 111, 40, 20–42, 8).

papacy, at latest during the reign of Pope Innocent, pronounced an unequivocal *non placet*.

Now this development, whereby the digamy prohibition was softened—a development that the West, however, avoided in the long run—can be misunderstood. Thus far we have emphasized the idea that a second marriage in and of itself demonstrated the inability to practice continence. Nevertheless, men who had married repeatedly were now being ordained—though of course, counting from the day of their baptism on, they were living in a first marriage. Do we not have to assume that continence was not required of these candidates? On the other hand, did the West not interpret the digamy prohibition strictly because (since the time of Popes Siricius and Innocent) it did require continence? Put another way: If there was no agreement about interpreting the digamy prohibition in the East and West, did that not remove the foundation for a consensus with regard to the continence discipline of married clerics?

To get to the bottom of these questions, we must examine again the statements of Jerome and Theodore cited above, to the effect that digamous men, too, were ordained if they were living in their first marriage since baptism. This practice in the East is corroborated elsewhere, too. Apostolic canon 17 from the end of the fourth century excludes from the higher clergy only those men who have entered into a second marriage after baptism.[38] Thus they acted as though baptism effaced a previous marriage.

Theodore, however, finds such a practice ridiculous in every respect. He categorically rejects it. In this he agrees with Ambrose of Milan and Pope Innocent. But he has somewhat different arguments. First of all: Baptism does not cancel out a first marriage, for a very pragmatic reason. If baptism in fact simply canceled out everything, what would be the sense, then, of making any requirements at all for aspirants to holy orders? Paul could have spared himself the trouble of discussing the matter in the pastoral letters. In that case one would only have to make sure to ordain men after their baptism. Not to mention that baptism does not undo the fact of having had sexual relations. Therefore it is just as unreasonable to baptize unchaste men and then ordain them

---

[38] *Constitutiones apostolorum* 8, 47, 17 (SC 336, 278, 60–63): Ὁ δυσὶ γάμοις συμπλακεὶς μετὰ τὸ βάπτισμα ἢ παλλακὴν κτησάμενος οὐ δύναται εἶναι ἐπίσκοπος ἢ πρεσβύτερος ἢ διάκονος ἢ ὅλως τοῦ καταλόγου τοῦ ἱερατικοῦ.

immediately. All told: Baptism in and of itself does not make someone suitable for ordination, otherwise Paul would not have forbidden ordination right after baptism, "ordaining neophytes"; only continence that has been put to the test can recommend someone for holy orders.

Jerome is, unlike Theodore, not in favor of abolishing the digamy prohibition completely, but he does propose mitigating it. He may well owe this view to Tertullian, whose ascetical writings he had studied thoroughly. Furthermore, Jerome defends the liberal interpretation of the rule with precisely the reasoning criticized by Theodore: If lewd conduct is eradicated by baptism, then why should the impediment to orders of digamy not be removed by baptism as well? Jerome says the same thing in greater detail in his letter to Oceanus, written around 400.[39]

The theology of baptism provided a background for Jerome and the other proponents of a liberal interpretation of the monogamy proviso. Baptism not only granted the forgiveness of sins; it also bestowed the power of grace and thus a new capacity to observe continence.[40] That is why holy orders could indeed be conferred, on account of baptism, not only upon digamists whose first marriage took place before baptism, but also upon candidates who before their baptism were known to lead unchaste lives. And in fact people must have referred to such cases as they were demanding the ordination of digamists. They simply could not understand why a lawful marriage that took place before baptism should be an obstacle to ordination, while the licentious and wicked life of an unmarried man presented no problems.[41] Although remarriage was considered a proof of the inability to practice continence, nevertheless this ability was thought to be restored by baptism, until the contrary was proved. In this instance one could speak of a dispensation, grounded in sacramental theology, from the Pauline prohibition of digamy.

With that we have confirmed the fact that the mitigation of the digamy prohibition had nothing to do with a mitigation of the continence discipline. On the contrary, the authors go so far as to cite the

---

[39] See also *Adversus Jovinianum* I, 15 (PL 23², 244D–245A).

[40] Jerome, *Epistula* 69, 2, 4f. 7, 1–6 *ad Oceanum* (CSEL 54, 681, 10–19; 692, 10–694, 2).

[41] Ambrose, *De officiis ministrorum* I, 50, 247 (PL 16², 104AB); Jerome, *Epistula* 69, 3–5 *ad Oceanum* (CSEL 54, 682, 14–689, 2). In an analogous way, Jerome distinguishes between two kinds of virginity: the first as of the day of birth, the second as of the day of rebirth (*Epistula* 49, 20, 3 *ad Pammachium*).

continence requirement in order to justify this concession. That explains how Jerome, one of the most unyielding advocates of continence celibacy, simultaneously interpreted the digamy prohibition liberally.

c. Do the Pastoral Letters Merely Forbid Polygamy?

We have examined the difficulties that the "unius uxoris vir" caused for Eastern theologians. In their discussions, again and again, we found references to an existing discipline of obligatory continence. One objection, however, could be brought against such a connection. For in the writings of early Christian theologians there is another interpretation of the "unius uxoris vir" that seems to have nothing whatsoever to do with continence. If the pastoral letters say that the cleric should be the husband of only one wife, then that could still mean that he is not supposed to be living together with several wives at the same time. This would then be directed against polygamous candidates. Today's exegetes are not the first to ponder this possibility; early theologians have already pursued this line of thought.

Theodore of Mopsuestia proposes the most radical interpretation in this regard; we have already cited above the pertinent passage in the larger context. In his opinion the pastoral letters, when they mention the "one wife" of the cleric, are not at all concerned about asking in which consecutive marriage a candidate for orders may be living. Paul would consider a second or a third marriage just as possible and unobjectionable for priests as it was for laymen (1 Cor 7:8f.). His intention, rather, was to forbid polygamy or else concubinage.

John Chrysostom. Theodore knows that other exegetes, too, agree that polygamy is far from irrelevant here. Think, for instance, of Jerome and Chrysostom. Both of them present the reflection that Paul could be rejecting in the case of clerics the kind of polygamy that may have been encountered among the pagans and the Jews. According to Chrysostom, Paul is not teaching compulsory marriage for bishops but rather is forbidding polygamy.

> "Now a bishop", he [Paul] says, "must be above reproach, the husband of one wife" (1 Tim 3:2). He does not say this as a law, as though it were the only thing allowed, but rather he restrains immoderation thereby. It was in fact permitted to the Jews to marry a second time and to have two wives at the same time. Honorable is marriage (cf. Heb 13:4). But

some think that this is being said: that a man ought to be the husband of a wife.[42]

Jerome. A similar argument is found in Jerome's writings, not only in his commentary on the Letter to Timothy cited earlier, but also in his letter to Oceanus.

> For the saying of the Apostle, that he [the priest] should be "the husband of one wife" (1 Tim 3:2), one could advance another interpretation. The Apostle was a descendant of the Jewish people; the Church of Christ in her first beginnings was built from the remains of Judaism. He knew that it was permitted according to the Law, as was well known from the example of the patriarchs and of Moses, for a man to have several wives and to beget children with them. Even the [Jewish] priests were allowed to claim this freedom as their own. Now the Apostle wanted to prevent the priests of the Church from demanding for themselves the same freedom to have two or even three wives at the same time; rather they were supposed to have only one wife at any time.[43]

If the pastoral letters simply mean to exclude polygamous men from the clergy, then naturally the entire argument about continence is inapplicable. In that case the phrase "husband of one wife" would have no relevance to the aptitude for continence. The only concern then would be that each cleric be true to one wife and not have other wives on the side. It would be a question of leading a good married life, not of restricting eligibility for marriage and therefore not of obligatory continence, either. Paul would then be saying: The cleric should not cohabit with several women at the same time, but rather should have lawful relations with only one wife.

At this point the central pillar of the argumentation thus far threatens to collapse. Therefore it is important to examine very closely who is making the statement with regard to polygamy and what else he has to say about continence. After all, doing without polygamy does not necessarily involve doing without marital continence. The exegete who finds a polygamy prohibition in the pastoral letters merely finds himself

---

[42] *Hom.* 10, 1 *in* 1 *Tim.* 3:1–4 (PG 62, 547): Δεῖ οὖν, τὸν ἐπίσκοπον ἀνεπίληπτον εἶναι, μιᾶς γυναικὸς ἄνδρα. Οὐ νομοθετῶν τοῦτό φησιν, ὡς μὴ ἐινὰ ἐξὸν ἄνευ τούτου γίνεσθαι, ἀλλὰ τὴν ἀμετρίαν κωλύων· ἐπειδὴ ἐπὶ τῶν Ἰουδαίων ἐξῆν καὶ δευτέροις ὁμιλεῖν γάμοις, καὶ δύο ἔχειν κατὰ ταυτὸν γυναῖκας. Τίμιον γὰρ ὁ γάμος. Τινὲς δὲ ἵνα μιᾶς γυναικὸς ἀνὴρ ἢ φασὶ τοῦτο εἰρῆσθαι.

[43] *Epistula* 69, 5, 1f. *ad Oceanum* (CSEL 54, 686, 18–687, 5).

unable any more to deduce obligatory continence from the "unius uxoris vir". Now we know for a fact that all the writers who considered
the polygamy interpretation as a possibility were also acquainted with
clerical continence. We have seen this both for Jerome and also for
Theodore. The same is true for Chrysostom. From today's perspective, then, one cannot maintain that the early theologians understood
the pastoral letters to be guarding only against polygamous clerics, so
that clerics were permitted to have sexual intercourse with their lawful
wedded wives without any further considerations.

Theodoret of Cyrrhus. This is altogether confirmed by yet another
writer in Syria: Theodoret (ca. 393 to 466), later the bishop of Cyrrhus.
The period of his literary production, it is true, continued into the fifth
century. But like Theodore and Chrysostom, he enjoyed the advantage
of a theological education in Antioch and thus was in the mainstream
of the Antiochene exegetical tradition; hence there is good reason to
cite him in this regard. His remarks, too, are found in an exegetical
commentary on the pastoral letters, in particular on the First Letter to
Timothy (1 Tim 3:2).

> "The husband of one wife", Paul begins his teaching. For virginity was
> not practiced among the Greeks, and the Jews rejected it because for them
> begetting children was a blessing. Since at that time, consequently, it was
> not easy to find virginal candidates, he commands [Timothy] to ordain
> such married men as held continence in esteem.
>
> Many writers, it seems to me, have interpreted well the phrase "the
> husband of one wife". Once, in fact, it was customary among Greeks
> and Jews to live together in marriage with two, three, or more wives at
> the same time. Even today, many still have concubines and mistresses, al-
> though the imperial laws forbid having two wives simultaneously. Hence
> these exegetes think that the godly Apostle said: A man who lives con-
> tinently together with only one wife can be ordained a bishop. For in
> their opinion he did not refuse a second marriage, since on the contrary
> he often commanded such a thing: "A wife is [legally] bound to her
> husband", he says, "as long as he lives. If the husband dies, she is free to
> be married to whom she wishes, only in the Lord" (1 Cor 7:39). And
> again: "To the unmarried and the widows I say. . ." (1 Cor 7:8). And by
> mentioning both states of life together, he places them under the same
> law. For the preeminent concern is with continence. And digamy is not
> a matter of free will. To be sure, if a man dismisses his first wife himself
> in order to marry a second, he must be rebuked and should be called
> to account. If death, however, dissolved the first marriage by force, it

is nature that compels the man to join in wedlock with a second wife. Thus the second marriage does not result from free will but from adverse circumstances. When I look at everything this way, then I concur with the opinion of these exegetes.[44]

Theodoret is very much dependent upon the arguments of Theodore. Everything that we have said about the latter is borne out here. Theodoret, too, favors the view that in the pastoral letters Paul is not pronouncing a digamy prohibition at all but is dealing with a prohibition of polygamy. But at the same time he is speaking explicitly about the obligatory continence of married clerics. When there is an ecclesiastical office to be occupied, then married candidates are only the second choice—standbys, as it were, for unmarried men. From this it is quite clear: married clerics had to practice continence, just as it was expected of virginal men and widowers also.

We have heard about Theodore's opposition to the digamy prohibition, and now about Theodoret's as well. In the final analysis it remains unclear whether their influence actually led to its abandonment in principle (aside from the question about the date of baptism). What Theodoret writes also remains just a personal theological opinion: he is only copying out Theodore's commentary. Whatever the situation may have been, continence remained in any case the preeminent criterion in the selection of candidates. As late as the fifth century the Syrian Church adhered unswervingly to the continence discipline, and

---

[44] *Interpretatio in* 1 *Tim.* 3:2 (PG 82, 804D–805B): <Μιᾶς γυναικὸς ἄνδρα.> Ἀρχὴν εἶχε τὸ κήρυγμα. Τὴν δὲ παρθενίαν οὔτε Ἕλληνες ᾔσκουν, οὔτε Ἰουδαῖοι μετῄεσαν· εὐλογίαν γὰρ τὴν παιδοποιίαν ἐνόμιζον. Ἐπειδὴ τοίνυν κατ’ ἐκεῖνον τὸν καιρὸν, οὐχ οἷόν τε ἦν ῥᾳδίως εὑρεῖν τοὺς τὴν ἁγνείαν ἀσκοῦντας, τῶν γεγαμηκότων τοὺς τὴν σωφροσύνην τετιμηκότας κελεύει χειρο-τονεῖν. Τὸ δὲ, *μιᾶς γυναικὸς ἄνδρα*, εὖ μοι δοκοῦσιν εἰρηκέναι τινές. Πάλαι γὰρ εἰώθεισαν καὶ Ἕλληνες καὶ Ἰουδαῖοι, καὶ δύο, καὶ τρισὶ, καὶ πλείοσι γυναιξὶ νόμῳ γάμου κατὰ ταυτὸν συνοικεῖν. Τινὲς δὲ καὶ νῦν, καίτοι τῶν βασιλικῶν νόμων δύο κατὰ ταυτὸν ἄγεσθαι κωλυόντων γυναῖκας, καὶ παλλακῖσι μίγνυνται καὶ ἑταίραις. Ἔφασαν τοίνυν τὸν θεῖον Ἀπόστολον εἰρη-κέναι, τὸν μιᾷ μόνῃ γυναικὶ συνοικοῦντα σωφρόνως, τῆς ἐπισκοπικῆς ἄξιον εἶναι χειροτονίας. Οὐ γὰρ τὸν δεύτερον, φασὶν, ἐξέβαλε γάμον, ὅγε πολλάκις τοῦτο γενέσθαι κελεύσας. <Γυνὴ γὰρ, φησὶ, δέδεται νόμῳ ἐφ’ ὅσον χρόνον ζῇ ὁ ἀνὴρ αὐτῆς· ἐὰν δὲ ἀποθάνῃ ὁ ἀνὴρ, ἐλευθέρα ἐστὶν ᾧ θέλει γαμηθῆναι, μόνον ἐν Κυρίῳ.> Καὶ πάλιν· <Λέγω δὲ ταῖς ἀγάμοις, καὶ ταῖς χήραις·> καὶ συνάψας ἑκάτερον τάγμα, ἕνα τέθεικε νόμον. Τῷ ὄντι γὰρ ὑπερκειμένης τῆς ἐγκρατείας, οὐ τῆς γνώμης ἡ διγαμία. Εἰ μὲν γὰρ αὐτὸς τὴν προτέραν ἐκβαλὼν ἑτέρᾳ συνεζύγη μέμψεως ἄξιος καὶ κατηγορίας ὑπεύθυνος. Εἰ δὲ τὸ βίαιον τοῦ θανάτου διέζευξε τὴν προτέραν, ἡ δὲ φύσις ἐπικειμένη δευτέρᾳ ζευχθῆναι κατηνάγκασε γυναικί, οὐκ ἐκ γνώμης, ἀλλ’ ἐκ περιστάσεως ὁ δεύτερος γεγένηται γάμος. Ταῦτα καὶ τὰ τοιαῦτα σκοπούμενος ἀποδέχομαι τῶν οὕτω νενοη-κότων τὴν ἑρμηνείαν.

did so even though many an authority entirely rejected the digamy prohibition or reinterpreted it as a polygamy prohibition.[45]

3. The Trend toward a Celibate Clergy

What we are ascertaining, then, is anything but an undermining of obligatory continence. There are even indications that in many places voices were calling for clerical discipline to be more strictly interpreted and enforced. All in all, the prevailing factor was certainly the ascetical tradition in favor of a celibate clergy. Contributing to this, especially at the fringes, were also heretical movements like the Eustathians in Asia Minor.

a. After Ordination No One May Marry Any More

If higher clerics were forbidden to have sexual intercourse with their wives, then it follows that marriage was prohibited. We hear about this explicitly from Hippolytus of Rome and at the Council of Neocaesarea in Asia Minor. Finally, the references become more and more numerous in the second half of the fourth century for the region of Syria and Asia Minor. Two ecclesiastical constitutions deal with this subject. The Apostolic Canons decree that only lower clerics may still marry after their ordination.[46] Accordingly, then, in the Apostolic Constitutions it says that marriage is forbidden to bishops, priests, and deacons (see below, pp. 173–74). Jerome, too, testifies indirectly to the marriage prohibition when he says that Peter and the other apostles had been married, but had married before they were called and subsequently gave up their marital relations.[47] The Paphnutius legend in the first half of the fifth century is not all that far off track, then, when it calls the marriage prohibition an ancient ecclesiastical tradition.[48]

For this reason alone it would necessarily have been very surprising if Basil, of all people, who since 370 had been archbishop of Caesarea in Asia Minor and one of the chief defenders of orthodoxy in the Eastern

---

[45] Contrary to Gryson, *Origines*, 77.

[46] *Constitutiones apostolorum* 8, 47, 26 (SC 336, 280, 83f.): Τῶν εἰς κλῆρον παρελθόντων ἀγάμων κελεύομεν βουλομένους γαμεῖν ἀναγνώστας καὶ ψάλτας μόνους.

[47] *Adversus Jovinianum* 1, 7. 26 (PL 23², 230C; 256C).

[48] Socrates Scholasticus, *Historia ecclesiastica* 1, 11, 5 (GCS Socr. 42,19f.).

Church, had viewed the marriage of priests as a normal occurrence. Many think that a statement in his second canonical letter, which he probably wrote in the year 375, must be understood in this way. This letter contains a series of canonical regulations. Basil also mentions sanctions he is imposing upon a priest who unwittingly entered an illicit marriage.

> As to the priest who was bound unknowingly in an illicit marriage, I have already decided what has to be done, that is, he would keep his place in the sanctuary but would abstain from any other function; a simple pardon would suffice for him. It would not be reasonable to let a man who has to bind his own wounds bless others; for blessing is a communication of grace, and he does not have it because of the fault he committed un-knowingly. How then could he communicate it to another? Let him not bless therefore, neither publicly nor privately, nor distribute the Body of the Lord to others, nor fulfill any other ecclesiastical function; but let him be content with precedence and implore the Lord's pardon for the iniquity he committed in his ignorance. (Canon 27)[49]

First we must clarify what is understood by an illicit marriage. Then too, it is not clear whether the priest in question married before or after his ordination. Let us assume for the moment that the marriage took place before the ordination. Perhaps the priest married a widow or a prostitute. In the second half of the fourth century explicit pro-hibitions were issued to this effect.[50] On this hypothesis, Basil has in view a priest married to a woman who, to their way of thinking at that time, cannot guarantee the discipline of priestly continence.[51] The marriage remains valid. Basil does not require a separation. But the cleric is not allowed to continue exercising his ministry, even though he is not removed from the ranks of the clergy and thus does not forfeit his claim to support.

---

[49] *Epistulae* 199, 27 (159 Courtonne 2): Περὶ τοῦ πρεσβυτέρου τοῦ κατ' ἄγνοιαν ἀθέσμῳ γάμῳ περιπαρέντος ὥρισα ἃ ἐχρῆν· καθέδρας μὲν μετέχειν, τῶν δὲ λοιπῶν ἐνεργειῶν ἀπέχεσθαι. Ἀρκετὸν γὰρ τῷ τοιούτῳ ἡ συγγνώμη. Εὐλογεῖν δὲ ἕτερον, τὸν τὰ οἰκεῖα τημελεῖν ὀφείλοντα τραύματα, ἀνακόλουθον. Εὐλογία γὰρ ἁγιασμοῦ μετάδοσίς ἐστιν. Ὁ δὲ τοῦτο μὴ ἔχων διὰ τὸ ἐκ τῆς ἀγνοίας παράπτωμα πῶς ἑτέρῳ μεταδώσει; Μήτε τοίνυν δημοσίᾳ μήτε ἰδίᾳ εὐλογείτω, μήτε τὸ σῶμα τοῦ Χριστοῦ κατανεμέτω ἑτέροις μήτε τι ἄλλο λειτουργείτω, ἀλλὰ ἀρκούμενος τῇ προεδρίᾳ προσκλαιέτω τῷ Κυρίῳ συγχωρηθῆναι αὐτῷ τὸ ἐκ τῆς ἀγνοίας ἀνόμημα. Cochini, *Origins*, 219–22. [English translation of citation as in Cochini, *Origins*, 221.]

[50] *Constitutiones apostolorum* 8, 47, 18 (SC 336, 280, 63–65).

[51] R. Cholij, *Clerical Celibacy in East and West* (Herefordshire, 1989), 96.

It is also conceivable, though, that the marriage followed the ordination. When Basil speaks of an illicit marriage, this is a far cry from saying that he knew also of licit marriages after ordination. This is ruled out on the basis of the Council of Neocaesarea, which punished every marriage attempted by a priest with removal from the ranks of the clergy. Accordingly, every marriage attempted by a cleric was illicit, but the priest in question had not been aware of that fact. In Basil's time there was terrible confusion in Asia Minor about the Church's canons because of the influence of Arianism. It is therefore quite conceivable that Basil, by way of exception, refrained from deposing a priest who evidently married out of ignorance of the Church's laws. Possibly the bishop was adhering to procedures followed by Callistus in similar cases.

This matter of ignorance of the law remains plausible for both hypotheses, whether the marriage occurred before or after the ordination. In the fourth century we hear repeatedly about the neglect of the continence discipline through ignorance. Hence if there were violations, it cannot be concluded that these were conscious protests against the rule of clerical continence. That may have been the case here and there. But in Asia Minor and elsewhere there were extensive, almost inaccessible territories in which the Church's discipline could very easily have begun to slip or even fall into oblivion. Furthermore it should always be taken into account that schismatic groups abandoned the continence rule and thereby caused confusion among the less well informed.

To be sure, at that time there were also voices, at least among the learned exegetes, who read into the "husband of one wife" phrase in the pastoral letters an obligation for bishops (clerics) to be married, which of course was not an obligation to marry.[52] That must be considered as a minority opinion, though, probably stemming from an aversion to the exaggerated views of the Eustathians. Opponents of celibacy could hardly have been behind it, for a marriage after ordination was not the intent. These exegetes simply advanced the opinion that a cleric ought to have proved his worth in the married state. Chrysostom, of course, rejects such thinking. For him it is clear that virginal men are also admitted to the priesthood.

---

[52] John Chrysostom, *Hom. in 1 Tim.* prol. (PG 62, 503f.), cited above, p. 153, n. 14. *Hom.* 10, 1 *in 1 Tim.* 3:1–4 (PG 62, 547), cited above, p. 167, n. 42.

b. Must Married Candidates for Orders Be Widowed?

Apostolic Constitutions. We have already mentioned the marriage prohibition in the Apostolic Constitutions. We must now examine the
corresponding excerpt more closely. It gives an interesting insight into
a broader interpretation of the "unius uxoris vir" of the pastoral letters.
Besides the prohibition of digamy and polygamy, a further possibility
was discussed around the year 380 in Syria or Constantinople:

> We have said that one must institute as bishops, priests, and deacons
> monogamists (cf. 1 Tim 3:2), whether their spouses be still alive or
> whether they be dead; if these men were celibates it is no longer permit-
> ted that after the imposition of hands they contract marriage, or if they
> were married enter to contract another marriage; let them be content to
> approach the imposition of hands while having a wife.[53]

It has been thought that this passage is authorizing married higher
clerics to have sexual intercourse with their wives.[54] That, however,
cannot be taken as a point of departure. The sole intent of the constitution is to derive a marriage prohibition from the monogamy rule
for clerics.[55] If only those men may be ordained who have been married only once, then this involves a marriage prohibition for all clerics
without exception: no cleric may marry, whether he is now virginal,
widowed, or (still) married.

Thus marriage of any sort is being forbidden to higher clerics as a
group. This looks very much as though the marriage prohibition is
being introduced here for the first time ever, or at least is being defended against considerable resistance. In the heartland of the Byzantine Church had it come to a crisis of clerical discipline? Were there
clerics everywhere who wanted to marry after their ordination? If that

---

[53] *Constitutiones apostolorum* 6, 17, 1 (SC 329, 346, 1–6): Ἐπίσκοπον καὶ πρεσβύτερον καὶ
διάκονον εἴπομεν μονογάμους καθίστασθαι, κἂν ζῶσιν αὐτῶν αἱ γαμεταί, κἂν τεθνήκασιν, μὴ
ἐξεῖναι δὲ αὐτοῖς μετὰ χειροτονίαν ἢ ἀγάμοις οὖσιν ἔτι ἐπὶ γάμον ἔρχεσθαι, ἢ γεγαμηκόσιν
ἑτέραις συμπλέκεσθαι, ἀλλ' ἀρκεῖσθαι ᾗ ἔχοντες ἦλθον ἐπὶ τὴν χειροτονίαν. [English translation as in Cholij, *Celibacy*, 138.] Taking the last sentence in the interpretation of Cochini,
Origins, 308f.

[54] P.-H. Lafontaine, *Les Conditions positives de l'accession aux ordres dans la première législation
ecclésiastique (300–492)* (Ottawa, 1963), 174, 194.

[55] Hence this does not concern the problem of a second marriage before ordination, in
which the first marriage took place before baptism, or else continence was practiced within
a second marriage.

were the case, then one could scarcely maintain that the married clergy observed obligatory continence. We cannot exclude this possibility, but it is not probable.

John Chrysostom. There is another possibility. And that has to do with the aforementioned third explanation of the "unius uxoris vir". John Chrysostom leads us into this train of thought. He lived in the same vicinity as the compiler of the Apostolic Constitutions. In a sermon on the First Letter to Timothy, probably given in Antioch (around 386–397), we come across a remark that helps us along. Chrysostom refers in one passage to a (then) novel interpretation of the "unius uxoris vir", which he approaches critically:

> "(The bishop should be) not greedy for gain, but hospitable, not quarrelsome, and no lover of money, managing his own household well, keeping his children submissive and respectful in every way" (Tit 1:7; 1 Tim 3:3). If, then, the married man has worldly concerns (1 Cor 7:33), and if, on the other hand, a bishop should not have them, how can the Apostle say, (the bishop should be) "the husband of an only wife"? Some say that we are dealing here with the case of a man who has been freed (from his ties with) his wife; if such is not the case, it is permissible that he be a man having a wife (on condition that he live) as if he did not have one (1 Cor 7:29). At that time this was indeed rightly permitted because of the prevailing situation. For it [is] possible to lead such a life honorably if one wishe[s] to do so. Indeed, though it is difficult for a rich man to enter the kingdom of heaven (Mt 19:23), there have frequently been rich people who did so; the same is true for marriage [or: the married man].[56]

It appears that there are shrewd commentators who claim to have tracked down a contradiction in Paul's thought about clerics. On the one hand, he says in the First Letter to the Corinthians that a married man cannot be anxious about the affairs of the Lord (1 Cor 7:32–34). On the other hand, in the pastoral letters he allows for married cler-

---

[56] *Hom.* 10, 1 *in* 1 *Tim.* 3:1–4 (PG 62, 548f.): Μὴ αἰσχροκερδῆ, ἀλλ᾽ ἐπιεικῆ, ἄμαχον, ἀφιλάργυρον, τοῦ ἰδίου οἴκου καλῶς προϊστάμενον, τέκνα ἔχοντα ἐν ὑποταγῇ μετὰ πάσης σεμνότητος. Εἰ τοίνυν ὁ γαμήσας μεριμνᾷ τὰ τοῦ κόσμου, τὸν δὲ ἐπίσκοπον οὐ δεῖ τὰ τοῦ κόσμου μεριμνᾶν, πῶς φησι, Μιᾶς γυναικὸς ἄνδρα; Τινὲς μὲν οὖν φασιν, ὅτι τὸν ἀπὸ γυναικὸς ἠνίξατο μένοντα ἐλεύθερον· εἰ δὲ μὴ τοῦτο εἴη, ἔνεστι γυναῖκα ἔχοντα, ὡς μὴ ἔχοντα, εἶναι. Τότε μὲν γὰρ καλῶς τοῦτο συνεχώρησεν, ὡς πρὸς τὴν τοῦ πράγματος φύσιν τὴν τότε οὖσαν. Ἔνεστι δὲ αὐτὸ μεταχειρίσασθαι καλῶς, εἴ τις βούλοιτο. Ὥσπερ γὰρ ὁ πλοῦτος δυσχερῶς εἰσάγει εἰς τὴν βασιλείαν τῶν οὐρανῶν, πολλαχοῦ δὲ οἱ πλουτοῦντες εἰσῆλθον· οὕτω καὶ ὁ γάμος. [English translation as found in Cochini, *Origins*, 292.] Cochini, *Origins*, 292f. Cf. Pseudo-Chrysostom, *Serm.* 2, 2 *in Iob* (PG 56, 569).

ics (cf. above, pp. 52–55).[57] How can this contradiction be resolved? Some reason as follows: It is true that bishops should be the husband of one wife; that means, though, that they should be freed from their ties with their wives and should remain so.

But what is that supposed to mean: to be free of one's wife (ἀπὸ γυναικός) and to remain so? Two interpretations present themselves. Christian Cochini thinks that, besides virginal men, widowers are being considered here; only those monogamous men whose wives have already died and who have not remarried are allowed to be ordained to the episcopacy (and to the other higher ranks of the clergy). It is also conceivable that only that married candidate is to be ordained who has definitively separated from his wife and now lives alone. This is how Roger Gryson sees it.[58] All in all, though, the first possibility is more likely. It is also suggested by the Ecclesiastical Canons of the Holy Apostles (see above, pp. 105ff.), which probably expect that candidates for the episcopacy, if already married, be widowed. Besides, we can suppose that Chrysostom would have condemned marital separation, since it was being promoted by the Eustathians, who were in formal schism.

We can say with certainty, then: In Chrysostom's time there were people who accepted married men for ordination only on the condition that they were widowed. Chrysostom would rather not be so strict. He considers it right to ordain married men, too, who are still living with their wives. That is how Paul, too, dealt with the situation. It was justified then because Paul depended upon having the episcopal sees occupied. It was appropriate to ordain married men as well, because there were not enough celibates to appoint to all of the episcopal sees.[59] Jerome takes a similar view.[60] While saying this, Chrysostom might very well have preferred to select widowed candidates, just as the Ecclesiastical Canons of the Holy Apostles did.[61] Certainly he had nothing against widowers, but he did not want to restrict the "unius uxoris vir" to such candidates.

Now some have been of the opinion that if Chrysostom is support-

---

[57] See also John Chrysostom, *Hom.* 10, 2 *in 1 Tim.* 3:1–4 (PG 62, 550).

[58] Gryson, *Origines*, 65.

[59] John Chrysostom, *Hom.* 10, 2 *in 1 Tim.* 3:1–4 (PG 62, 550).

[60] *Adversus Jovinianus* 1, 34 (PG 23², 268B).

[61] Cf. ibid., 1, 35 (PG 23², 270B): "Oportet ergo episcopum irreprehensibiliem esse, ut nulli vitio mancipatus sit; unius uxoris virum, qui unam uxorem habuerit, non habeat."

ing married clerics here, it is not very likely that he knew of obligatory continence. But that is jumping to conclusions. He does not emphasize in particular that clerics have to practice continence within marriage. But that is clear; it is enough for Chrysostom merely to allude to it in the formula taken from Paul's writings, "to have a wife as though one had none".[62] The cleric by all means can be married; nevertheless, in actuality he ought to have his wife no longer. That can only mean continence on the part of the cleric. And this is not just the expression of a pious wish,[63] but a hard and fast rule, as the agreement of the entire Antiochene tradition on this point demonstrates.

Against this background we can now understand without further ado the Apostolic Constitution cited at the beginning of this section (b). It does not introduce a brand new marriage prohibition for higher clerics at all; rather it demarcates the existing prohibition from exaggerated demands. Many people, indeed, wish to go beyond the marriage prohibition, which is already in effect anyway, and see only virginal or widowed men in the clergy. The Constitutions defend against this, just as Chrysostom does. Married clerics do not have to be widowed. Monogamous men should be ordained regardless of "whether their spouses be still alive or whether they be dead". That, however, cannot mean that a marriage after ordination would still be allowed. Married men ought to be glad in the first place that they are ordained notwithstanding their marriage. Thus the Constitution corroborates what was generally the custom in the Eastern Church at that time: candidates for orders were sought first among virginal men, then among widowers, and lastly among married men.

If this reasoning is correct, then important conclusions follow from it concerning the continence discipline. For it was then by no means in the middle of a crisis in Syria. Then too, there were no clerics who wanted to marry. On the contrary, many wanted to see an even stricter application of the continence discipline. They wanted to admit only virginal and widowed men to holy orders. In opposition to this, however, the more moderate course was taken, the traditional line of thought that always recognized that there were bishops, priests, and

---

[62] Similarly Jerome, *Epistula* 52, 16, 1 *ad Nepotianum* (CSEL 54, 439, 8-12): "Praedicator continentiae, nuptias ne conciliet. qui apostolum legit: superest, ut et qui habent uxores, sic sint, quasi non habentes, cur uirginem cogit, ut nubat? qui de monogamia sacerdos est, quare uiduam hortatur, ut δίγαμος sit?"

[63] Thus Gryson, *Origines*, 77.

deacons who lived together with their wives, of course in strict continence.

c. Celibate and Ascetical Clerics Are Preferred

Ignatius of Antioch. Before we examine the fact that, besides widowed men, celibate and ascetical aspirants to ecclesiastical ministry were preferred in the fourth century, a passage from Ignatius of Antioch should be interpolated. He was a bishop in Syria, corresponded with the Christian communities and the bishops of Asia Minor, and became famous for his spectacular martyrdom in Rome under the emperor Trajan (98–117). Ignatius speaks about a loss of respect among bishops who were married; at the very least this is how the passage must be understood.

> If anyone can remain chaste in honor of the Lord's flesh, then let him do so without boasting. For if he boasts of it, he is lost; and if he thinks himself for this reason better than the bishop, he is ruined.[64]

There were celibate men who felt superior to the bishop[65] because they led a virginal life, while he was married. That, however, is a far cry from saying that this married bishop—possibly the addressee, Polycarp of Smyrna—had not been practicing continence with his wife; he was, of course, not virginal and so had not "remained in chastity". Thus, already in the second century there were currents of thought within the Church that preferred celibate to married bishops. The Church's line, though, remained secure: Marriage was licit for clerics, also.

Now let us return to the fourth century. The Ecclesiastical Canons of the Holy Apostles, too, would prefer bishops without wives and in this regard considers unmarried or widowed men. There is a remark to the same effect in Epiphanius stating that clerics are selected in the first place from virginal candidates and then also from the monks.[66] However, since there were not always enough candidates available in these groups, they also had recourse to continent married men and

---

[64] *Epistula ad Polycarpum* 5, 2 (220, 5–7 J. A. Fischer, *Die Apostolischen Väter*, 9th ed., SUC, 1 [Darmstadt, 1986]): Εἴ τις δύναται ἐν ἁγνείᾳ μένειν εἰς τιμὴν τῆς σαρκὸς τοῦ κυρίου, ἐν ἀκαυχησίᾳ μενέτω. Ἐὰν καυχήσηται, ἀπώλετο, καὶ ἐὰν γνωσθῇ πλέον τοῦ ἐπισκόπου, ἔφθαρται. Cochini, *Origins*, 139–41.

[65] Conceited comparisons with clerics took many forms. Cf. *Didache* 15, 1f.; Clement of Rome, *First Letter to the Corinthians*, 35, 2; 38, 2; *Apocalypsis Petri* NHC 7, 2, 79.

[66] For monks ordained as priests and bishops, see Athanasius, *Epistula ad Dracontium* (PG 25, 524–33); Palladius, *Historia Lausiaca* 1; 11; 49.

widowers.[67] At the time of Epiphanius, then, a preference in favor of unmarried clerics can already be recognized. Chrysostom, too, notes the sequence: celibates, widowers, and married men.[68] A three-tiered system of clerical prestige had developed.

We can discern here a tendency toward a more rigorous and sometimes even exaggerated application of the Church's continence discipline. The part played by the influence of monks and ascetics was not insignificant. The monastic movement had its roots and greatest achievements in the East, principally in Egypt, Palestine, and Syria. Tens of thousands of men and women resolutely renouncing the world could not fail to have had an influence on the life of the Church. Normally these people sought solitude. But more and more often the demands of the faithful led these ascetics to become involved with the care of souls. Both civil and ecclesiastical law promoted the employment of monks in the Church's ministry. The bishops relied on them in great numbers.

Gregory Nazianzen. The results were predictable. Monks were considered to be something better, the spiritual ones, specially qualified to direct souls. This disparity exists in the Eastern Church to a certain extent to this day between the celibate *startsi* and the married secular priests (*popy*). This shows, then, how deeply rooted in history such mentalities are. Gregory Nazianzen (d. around 390), one of the leading theologians of Asia Minor, demonstrated a keen awareness of erroneous developments in which people began to disdain married priests and to avoid them. He was not ready to accept that. In a discourse held in 381 in Constantinople he warns:

> Do not say: "Let a bishop baptize me, and let him be a metropolitan or the bishop of Jerusalem (since grace does not depend on a place but on the Spirit), and let him be of good birth. For I do not wish to risk an offense to my noble birth by the one who confers baptism." Or, "If he is a priest, then let him be unmarried or among those who are continent and lead an angelic life."[69]

---

[67] *De fide* 21, 7f. (GCS Epiph. 3, 522, 8–11).

[68] John Chrysostom, *De non iterando coniugio* 2 (SC 138, 166, 75f.).

[69] *Oratio* 40, 26 (SC 358, 256, 10–16): Μὴ εἴπῃς· <ἐπίσκοπος βαπτισάτω με, καὶ οὗτος μητροπολίτης ἢ Ἱεροσολυμίτης—οὐ γὰρ τόπων ἡ χάρις, ἀλλὰ τοῦ Πνεύματος—, καὶ οὗτος τῶν εὖ γεγονόντων· δεινὸν γὰρ εἰ τῷ βαπτιστῇ τὸ εὐγενές μου καθυβρισθήσεται> ἢ· <πρεσβύτερος μέν, ἀλλὰ καὶ οὗτος τῶν ἀγάμων καὶ οὗτος τῶν ἐγκρατῶν καὶ ἀγγελικὴν τὴν πολιτείαν.

The last sentence could be understood to mean that Gregory was declaring to be legitimate a clerical marriage in which continence was not practiced, as if one ought to respect equally, besides the clerics who are continent, those who are not. But the Greek text means something different. The "angelic life" is a technical term for the celibate way of life of ascetics and monks.[70] Among the adherents of this very ideal were also Gregory and his friends. Gregory was familiar with the monastic movement chiefly through his acquaintance with Basil, who in turn knew Eustathius of Sebaste. The phrase "those who are continent", too, does not refer to married clerics but to the circle of ascetics.[71]

As a result the entire passage is a clear statement that in no way calls continence celibacy into question but rather confirms it: In the opinion of certain candidates for baptism, it was not enough for a bishop to administer the sacrament to them, he had to be a metropolitan or come from Jerusalem and, moreover, had to be a nobleman; and if it was only going to be the usual priest, then he had to be at least unmarried, but optimally a representative of the ascetical or monastic state. This reflects not only the high esteem in which asceticism was held by the faithful but also the lower opinion of married clerics as opposed to unmarried clergy.

This observation is noteworthy because one would actually not expect it to be so. Today in the Orthodox Church there are innumerable married priests, while the Latin Church is familiar only with celibate priests, with few exceptions. In the early Church the situation seems to have been different. In the East, too, the prevailing trend was strongly in favor of exclusively unmarried or else widowed clerics. This trend was at least as strong as it was in the West, where toward the end of the fourth century clerical cloisters were erected at many cathedral churches, which, so to speak, brought the Latin model of a monastic clergy into general currency.

Hence, throughout the entire Church, the trend was going in the direction of a celibate clergy. Now one should not impute false moti-

---

[70] Theodoret, *Historia religiosa* 4, 3 (SC 234, 294, 13f.); Gerontius, *Vita Melaniae iunioris* 8 (SC 90, 140); Leontius Neapolitanus, *Vita Johannis Eleemosynarii* 46 (100, 1 H. Gelzer, ed., *Leontios von Neapolis: Leben des heiligen Johannes des barmherzigen Erzbischofs von Alexandrien* [1893]); Johannes Moschus, *Pratum spirituale* 168 (PG 87, 3036A). Auf der Maur, *Mönchtum*, 143f., n. 12.

[71] Cochini, *Origins*, 241. This is corroborated by the sentence structure as well (divided into several parts by καὶ οὗτος).

vations for this development. It certainly had nothing to do with contempt for marriage. In any case Epiphanius in the East would firmly reject that. Indeed, he saw in the very custom of clerical marriage a proof for the goodness of marriage. As the great contender with heretics, he defended marriage against all manner of Encratite calumny. As for the West, we will hear parallel arguments in connection with the Jovinian affair. Apart from this, monks were simply considered to be the spiritual men, the proven charismatics, who often had at their disposal also a minimum of biblical training and thus were suited for the preaching ministry.

d. Ascetical Clerics May Not Dismiss Their Wives

We have already spoken repeatedly about the ascetical-monastic movement in Asia Minor associated with the name of Eustatius of Sebaste. It is difficult to obtain an accurate picture of it. We probably should view the Eustathians as an ascetical reform movement, originally, which then quickly met with opposition and was accused of heretical views.[72] To what extent this was justified may be impossible to say.

The Council of Gangres. We learn about this movement in connection with the Council of Gangres. In this locality in central Asia Minor the bishops gathered in the year 340 to bring a much-disputed situation under control. In canon 4 they clearly cast a vote in favor of married priests: "If anyone affirms that one should not receive communion during the holy sacrifice celebrated by a married priest, let him be anathema."[73]

It is not without reason that the Council of Gangres defended the legitimacy of the married clergy. As is apparent from the synodal document (the introduction to the canons), it is directed against a specific group: the Eustathians. These Christians promoted a radical asceticism, citing as their authority a man named Eustathius, though their claim was, in any case, not entirely justified. For if Eustathius had advocated the same views as his supposed adherents, he would scarcely have become archbishop of Sebaste in Armenia in the year 356.

---

[72] J. Gribomont, "Saint Basile et le monachisme enthousiaste", *Irénikon* 53 (1980): 123–44.

[73] Canon 4 (82 Jonkers): Εἴ τις διακρίνοιτο παρὰ πρεσβυτέρου γεγαμηκότος, ὡς μὴ χρῆναι λειτουργήσαντος αὐτοῦ προσφορᾶς μεταλαμβάνειν, ἀνάθεμα ἔστω.

The Eustathians rejected marriage in principle (cf. canons 1 and 9). Hence they demanded continence and marital separation of all Christians. Accordingly, they accepted the Eucharist only from priests who were unmarried or who had at least separated from their wives. They were not content with the practice of continence within marriage; those who were married had to dissolve their marriage formally. The bishops were not ready to accept such a tightening of clerical discipline motivated by contempt for marriage. Therefore they resolutely defended the married clergy. In doing so, however, it was not their intention to demand that married clerics, too, have sexual intercourse with their wives, nor were they tolerating such behavior.

Apostolic canon no. 5. What is known about the time and place in which the Apostolic Canons originated allows us to cite canon 5 of this ecclesiastical constitution in connection with the Eustathians. This decree is the expression of an ascetical enthusiasm that had spread among the clergy but that had become seriously exaggerated: "A bishop, priest, or deacon may not dismiss his wife on the pretext of piety. If he dismisses her, let him be suspended, and if he persists, let him be deposed from office."[74] In this connection we must consider a further decree, canon 51:

> If any bishop or presbyter or deacon, or anyone at all on the sacerdotal list abstains from marriage, or meat or wine, not on account of personal discipline [mortification] but out of abhorrence, forgetting that all things are exceedingly good, and that God made man male and female, but blasphemously misrepresents God's work of creation, either let him mend his ways, or let him be deposed from office and expelled from the Church.[75]

Evidently there were overzealous clerics who left their wives and, so to speak, sent them into the desert. If the authorities were now turning against such conduct, that could be evidence against a continence-celibacy discipline, especially in light of a further passage in Chrysos-

---

[74] *Constitutiones apostolorum* 8, 47, 5 (SC 336, 276, 17–19): Ἐπίσκοπος ἢ πρεσβύτερος ἢ διάκονος τὴν ἑαυτοῦ γυναῖκα μὴ ἐκβαλλέτω προφάσει εὐλαβείας· ἐὰν δὲ ἐκβάλῃ, ἀφοριζέσθω, ἐπιμένων καθαιρείσθω.

[75] Ibid., 8, 47, 51 (SC 336, 294, 252–58): Εἴ τις ἐπίσκοπος ἢ πρεσβύτερος ἢ διάκονος ἢ ὅλως ἐκ τοῦ καταλόγου τοῦ ἱερατικοῦ γάμου καὶ κρεῶν καὶ οἴνου οὐ δι' ἄσκησιν, ἀλλὰ διὰ βδελυρίαν ἀπέχεται, ἐπιλαθόμενος, ὅτι· <Πάντα καλὰ λίαν> καὶ ὅτι· <Ἄρσεν καὶ θῆλυ ἐποίησεν ὁ Θεὸς τὸν ἄνθρωπον>, ἀλλὰ βλασφημῶν διαβάλλει τὴν δημιουργίαν, ἢ διορθούσθω ἢ καθαιρείσθω καὶ τῆς Ἐκκλησίας ἀποβαλλέσθω. [English translation of the canon from Cholij, *Celibacy*, 98–99.]

tom, where he says, "Indeed, many wives for love of continence have left their husbands, thinking that they were performing a pious deed, but they drove them to adultery."[76] The introduction to the canons of Gangres speaks of similar cases among the Eustathians. In this instance men and women separated from their spouses unilaterally but then could no longer practice continence themselves and committed adultery. Accordingly, canon 5 could be saying: Clerics should not separate from their wives but should carry on sexual relations with them so that they will not become adulterous. Then, too, one might even wonder whether this decree were not intended to bar the door against the contemporary efforts of the Latin councils and popes to legislate celibacy.

Support for this thesis has been sought in the Council of Nicaea in the year 325 and in the Second Council of Trullo in the year 691. This late council, in opposition to Rome and citing the apostolic canon, explicitly allowed Byzantine clerics to continue their use of marriage (canon 13). But the reference to Trullo immediately diminishes the value of this argument. For this council took place 300 years after canon 5 was framed. In the three intervening centuries it had never occurred to anyone to make capital out of this canon against Rome; in fact criticism of continence celibacy was completely unheard of (except among the Novatians and the Arians).[77] Besides this, Trullo and canon 5 are not even formulated along the same lines. For the Council of Trullo authorizes marital relations for deacons and priests only, but not for married bishops. Therefore we should reject the attempt to interpret apostolic canon 5 as an anti-celibacy law, based on that much later legislation.

The second point adduced, at least in the past, was the Paphnutius legend. If it were authentic, then the first historically documented opposition to a discipline of continence celibacy would have been at Nicaea, and canon 5 would have taken up this subject again fifty years later. Now, though, that the legend has been identified as a legend, there is not one single testimony from any ecclesiastical source well into the fourth century that questioned obligatory continence for higher clerics in principle; on the contrary, all of the sources now available presup-

---

[76] *Hom.* 86, 4 *in Mt.* (PG 58, 768): Ἀλλὰ τινες ἔρωτι δῆθεν ἐγκρατείας ἀποστᾶσαι τῶν ἰδίων ἀνδρῶν, ὡς εὐλαβές τι ποιοῦσαι, ὤθησαν αὐτοὺς ἐπὶ μοιχείαν.

[77] Cochini, *Origins*, 311f., 418f.

posed the existence of this practice or else explicitly and strongly recommended it. There were also Eastern theologians in this period who
reasoned along these lines: Jerome and Epiphanius. Hence it may be
said that within this historical context an anti-celibacy law is extremely
unlikely.

Let us recommend another solution. Concretely, as Roger Gryson
correctly notes, canon 5 has in view those clerics who "on the pretext of piety" wish to safeguard their chastity even further and hence
separate from their wives.[78] It deals therefore with clerics who practiced strict continence with their wives but who wished to guarantee
it completely by means of marital separation. This is corroborated by a
decree of the *Codex Theodosianus* from the year 420: "Love of chastity
does not suggest the abandonment of those women who, before the
ordination of their husband, were worthy (of being united to him)
by legitimate marriage."[79] Remarkably, a marital separation is being
sought here on the occasion of priestly ordination. This can only be
in connection with the clerical obligation to practice continence. The
Codex, therefore, intends to say that love of chastity can be practiced
within a continent marriage as well.[80] Apostolic canon 5, accordingly,
in no way disputes the continence discipline for married clerics and
their wives but rather presupposes it as a general practice.

This fits well into the picture of the Eustathians in Asia Minor.
Against them the Church resolutely defended clerical marriage. Viewed
thus, the canon presupposes the marital continence of clerics yet opposes an exaggerated asceticism that would show contempt for marriage and, on the pretext of piety, would renounce marital obligations
and forsake the wife against her will. Indeed, one who is married can
no longer practice a form of chastity that is suited only to the unmarried; he has to satisfy the obligations of his marriage. The only thing
that is being forbidden, therefore, is a unilateral separation. Abandoned
wives of clerics, no doubt, could become a problem if the Christian
community had to take responsibility for their support.

---

[78] Gryson, *Origines*, 101; Lafontaine, *Conditions*, 195.

[79] *Codex Theodosianus* 16, 2, 44 (851, 6–9 Mommsen 1, 2). Cited below, p. 305, n. 52.

[80] Precisely this was said as early as Clement of Alexandria, *Stromata* 3, 6, 46, 4 (GCS
Clem. Alex. 2⁴, 217, 20–22).

4. Did Clerics Really Have to Practice Continence?

For the fourth century there is unequivocal evidence for a discipline of obligatory continence. On the other hand, though, there is no clear indication that married clerics were permitted to continue begetting children. And yet we find a couple of cases where there is doubt. The texts in question are such that the reader could infer or suspect that married clerics were positively allowed to engage in sexual intercourse. On this basis it was thought that obligatory continence could be disproved for Asia Minor, Palestine, and Egypt, that is, for the far greater part of the Eastern Church. Nevertheless, a proof relying on these texts ultimately lacks validity; indeed they cannot even begin to disturb the picture of the situation in the Eastern Church that we have managed to attain thus far.

a. Gregory Nazianzen the Elder

We have heard already that Gregory Nazianzen the Younger, the theologian, came to the defense of married clerics vis-à-vis their unmarried or ascetical colleagues. Perhaps this position had something to do with his family situation. For his father was a bishop and could look back on a long married life. He was also named Gregory and was bishop in Nazianzus. In the year 361 he ordained to the priesthood his son Gregory, who later, as a bishop, took over the administration of his father's diocese, if only for a short time. To that extent we are dealing here with an interesting case of clerical succession by inheritance.

In two much-debated verses of his poem, "De Vita sua" [On his life], Gregory the Younger seems to imply that he was born after the ordination of his father.[81] In that passage he has his father say:

> Thou [that is, Gregory the Younger] hast not yet lived so long
> as the time of sacrifices which I [that is, Gregory the Elder] have
>   gone through.[82]

---

[81] Gryson, *Origines*, 80f. But there are doubts; see Cholij, *Celibacy*, 73. He refers to Cochini, *Origins*, 94, 126, 242–44.

[82] Gregory Nazianzen, *Carmina* 2, 1, 11 (78, 512f. Jungck): Οὔπω τοσοῦτον ἐκμεμέτρηκας βίον, ὅσος διῆλθε θυσιῶν ἐμοὶ χρόνος.

These verses are full of obscurities, which need not be recounted in-dividually.[83] Here we will shed more light on just one argument. The verses originated at a time when Gregory's father was already over eighty years old and was urging his son to consent to be ordained, so as to relieve him of his pastoral duties. The father's old age forms a part of the background, in that the father wants to see his son in the ministry at last. Gregory the Elder means to allude in a very general way to his advanced age, for which his son ought to show considera-tion. Thus the "sacrifices" do not necessarily refer to the Eucharistic Sacrifice at all. They can simply mean the day-to-day sacrifices, the renunciations of life.[84] Gregory the Elder, therefore, wants to say that his son has not yet been through as much as he has.

Probably the verses do contain a reference to eucharistic celebrations after all. But that does not mean that Gregory the Elder had offered his sacrifices as a priest. It is equally possible that he is referring to his participation in the Eucharist as a layman.[85] There are many indications that Gregory the Elder received baptism in the year 325, whereas his son was born a little later, around 326.[86] In that case the father would have been participating in the Sacrifice of the Mass for a longer time than Gregory the Younger had been alive. At any rate Gregory the Elder was already fifty years old when he was consecrated a bishop in the year 329. His wife Nonna was just as old.[87] It is difficult to suppose that she bore her son at that age. Gregory does testify that his mother bore him when she was already advanced in years, but that would also have been the case long before the ordination of her husband.[88] Even if no final clarification can be reached, it is still more likely that Gregory had already been born a few years before the ordination of his father.

Priestly dynasties. The story of the two Gregories is not an isolated case. We find not infrequently in ancient literature references to priests whose fathers are priests or bishops themselves. The sons followed in the footsteps of their fathers, from whom they received their training.

---

[83] C. Jungck, ed., *Gregor von Nazianz: De vita sua* (Heidelberg, 1974), 231f.

[84] Cochini, *Origins*, 244, n. 242.

[85] Cf. Tertullian, *Exhortatione castitatis* 11, 2 (CCL 2, 1031, 10–14): "et offeres . . . et as-cendet sacrificium tuum" refers to a layman.

[86] Jungck, *Gregor*, 232; B. Wyss, "Gregor II (Gregor von Nazianz)", in RAC 12 (1983), 793–863 at 794.

[87] Gregory Nazianzen, *Oratio* 18, 41 (PG 35, 1040C).

[88] Cf. *Oratio* 2, 77 (SC 247, 190, 8f.); 8,4 (SC 405, 252, 1–6).

And thus one generation of priests provided directly for the next. Of course that could have degenerated into a precarious nepotism. One finds the beginnings of clerical dynasties, in which the son succeeded the father or the nephew the uncle. Origen condemns this.[89] Bishop Polycrates of Ephesus toward the end of the second century had seven relatives in the episcopacy.[90] Julian (d. after 454), son of a bishop in southern Italy, as a lector married the daughter of a bishop (around 400–405). Thus there was a match between two children of priests. Paulinus of Nola wrote a wedding song for the young couple, in which it says: Either Julian and his wife Titia [a.k.a. Ia] would decide to live in virginal unity with one another, comporting themselves as one body that knows nothing of the flesh, or else they should be acceptable to one another in the body so that they may transmit the gift of life to holy virgins, or their chaste offspring may form a priestly race.[91] That is to say that the two should renounce continence in order to raise children who later would practice continence as virgins or priests. But nothing came of it. In any case we do not know of any children. Nevertheless, for Julian there was clerical advancement. He became his father's successor and finally bishop of Eclanum near Benevento. Apparently he lived together with his wife. At least for his time as a bishop he made a vow of continence. It is possible that his wife was dead or had retreated to a cloister when he was ordained a deacon in the year 408 and was consecrated a bishop around 416.[92]

Father-to-son successions in the priestly ministry do not necessarily mean that the sons were begotten after their fathers were ordained. There is not one case in which such a suspicion can be verified. One must guard against drawing hasty conclusions, as is clearly demonstrated by an example from the Armenian Church of the fourth cen-

---

[89] Origen, *Hom.* 22, 4 *in Num.* (GCS Orig. 7, 208, 8–14). A. von Harnack, *Der kirchengeschichtliche Ertrag der exegetischen Arbeiten des Origenes*, vol. 1, TU 42, 3 (Leipzig, 1918), 77f.

[90] Eusebius, *Historia ecclesiastica* 5, 24, 6 (GCS Eus. 2, 1 492, 10f.). Bishop Eustathius of Sebaste was probably the son of Bishop Eulalius of Sebaste. Pope Damasus was a priest's son. Deacon Evagrius Ponticus was son of a choir-bishop. The Novatian bishop Chrysanthus was son of the Novatian bishop Marcian; Socrates Scholasticus, *Historia ecclesiastica* 7, 12, 1 (GCS Socr. 356, 20–22). See also Ambrose, *De officiis ministrorum* 1, 44, 217 (PL 16², 94C) and C. Pietri, *Roma Christiana: Recherches sur l'Église de Rome, son organisation, sa politique, son idéologie de Miltiade à Sixte III (311–440)* (Paris and Rome, 1976), 1: 711.

[91] Paulinus, *Carmina* 25, 233–237 (CSEL 30, 245, 233–37).

[92] Cochini, *Origins*, 105; P. Brown, *Die Keuschheit der Engel: Sexuelle Entsagung, Askese und Körperlichkeit am Anfang des Christentums* (Munich and Vienna, 1991), 418f.

tury. For four generations the episcopal see of the Katholikos (major archbishop) was passed down from father to son. But a closer examination of the facts shows that the son in each instance was begotten before the ordination of the father.[93]

b. Gregory Nazianzen the Younger

Gregory the Younger was a sensitive soul, humanly speaking, and as a theological mind he was equally subtle. In the course of his life he had to swallow the bitter pills of many injuries and defeats. He was able to work through these things to some degree by writing poetry. In the year 381 he committed his unhappy experiences to writing in the poem "About Himself and the Bishops",[94] in which he settles accounts with "bad bishops" in a polemical and pessimistic tone. What happened? In the year 379 Gregory assumed leadership of the small orthodox community in Constantinople. A long-lasting theological dispute had split the Church into Arians and Nicenes. This only ended with the victory of the Nicenes at the Council of Constantinople in 381. Hence Gregory could now be formally enthroned as patriarch of Constantinople. But then began the difficulties with the Council Fathers. It came to acrimonious disputes. Gregory finally resigned and returned, sick and disillusioned, to Nazianzus. In his grand autobiographical poem he is quite outspoken: Not one of the uneducated, narrow-minded bishops who brought about his downfall[95] remained unscathed.

Before we examine the portrayal of this den of thieves and what it has to say about clerical continence, let us fast-forward for a moment to Theodore of Mopsuestia, who became a bishop in Asia Minor at about the time of Gregory's death. Theodore criticized the digamy prohibition, along with many other rules concerning the appointment of clerics. "Often, however, they do the same with entirely unworthy men and consider themselves justified in baptizing such a one and then admitting him to the clerical ministry, although he has in no way demonstrated virtue or piety." Because Theodore, in all of his various criticisms, was concerned about continence, he objected to the practice of recommending for ordination unbaptized men who for years

---

[93] Cochini, *Origins*, 129; Cholij, *Celibacy*, 73.

[94] Greek-German edition by B. Meier, ed., *Gregor von Nazianz: Über die Bischöfe: (Carmen 2, 1, 12)*, SGKA N.F. 2, 7 (Paderborn, 1989).

[95] Gregory Nazianzen, *Carmina* 2, 1, 12, 21–25.

had led unchaste lives but who were then baptized shortly before their ordination. Who could ever accept that as a guarantee of future continence? The ordination of a newly baptized man was generally forbidden, anyway (1 Tim 3:6).[96] But once in a while exceptions were made, for instance in the case of Ambrose, who was baptized and ordained, so to speak, in one stroke.[97] To be sure, until then he had led a blameless life.

Gregory was grappling with a similar case. In his conflicts with his competitors and envious confreres, one person especially among his fellow bishops appeared to be a thorn in his side,[98] one who had received baptism only a short time before. He himself, who was well qualified for such an office because of his life-long studies and "philosophical", that is, ascetical, manner of life,[99] could not comprehend how a man without any preparation whatsoever of this sort, though admittedly having excellent leadership qualities,[100] could drive him out of Constantinople. He held it against his competitor that he aimed for the episcopacy right after his baptism, without any training and after leading previously a life of dissolution given over to carnal pleasures.[101] Gregory describes it in great detail:

> . . . a house, a plump [that is, pregnant] wife, the desire for children, property, a household steward. . . . Others, though, who are full of the innate drive, madly in love, aroused, sprucing themselves for the female sex—to put it mildly—without having opened the bridal chamber, or who even live together with a beloved to whom they are not yet wed, and this even before their cheeks are covered with the manly adornment of a beard, still decked out in their first fluff, young in body, in character still younger, or else already marked with the vices of older days, these, *these* then, are the leaders of the children not by the flesh, of those who

[96] John Chrysostom, *De sacerdotio* 2, 8.

[97] The contrary command from the pastoral letters was not taken in a strict sense by fourth-century Christians. The fact that they considered themselves justified in this can probably be explained by the change in baptismal practices. At that time baptism, viewed as the sole chance to be cleansed of sins (Gregory Nazianzen, *Carmina* 2, 1, 12, 453, 493), was postponed to the end of one's life.

[98] Ibid., 2, 1, 12, 660f., 682–84.

[99] Ibid., 2, 1, 12, 48–59, 71–74, 576–609.

[100] Ibid., 2, 1, 12, 709–12, 734.

[101] Ibid., 2, 1, 12, 60–63. All this applies to the man who, at the Council, was elected Gregory's successor, Nectarios, who at this point in time had not yet been baptized and who was altogether more of a politician than a churchman.

are begotten by the Spirit, to whom the flesh is entirely foreign; these, who have learned to do homage to the passions of others, to which they themselves have succumbed, advocates for their own sins in the sins of others, tolerating unbridled behavior just as they lay claim to it for them-selves.[102]

Gregory also mentions notorious lewd conduct, namely premarital sexual relations, but essentially he is upset about the house, family, children, property, and former occupation of his episcopal competitor, which disturb him per se, because he himself, thanks to his ascetical conduct and celibate way of life, has never known all these things. And even if it is admitted that his adversary led a dissolute, scandalous life, this was in any case still before he was baptized.[103] He has not been guilty of misconduct since his baptism. Even Gregory has to admit that.[104] The only rhetorical device remaining is an insinuation that his opponent will not mend his ways and that, given his former way of life, the power of a patriarch's office will corrupt him.[105]

If we assume, therefore, that Gregory's competitor led an utterly dissolute life, then he evidently justified his episcopal consecration by referring to the power of baptism, which, through the Holy Spirit, had worked in him an immediate transformation,[106] which Gregory polemically caricatures: "Now you are the master of modesty for vir-gins and wives. How dubious is your decency after your former con-duct."[107] And those responsible in Constantinople accepted this way of viewing the qualities of the candidate, on which so much depended, too, with respect to an episcopal see that was so important in Church politics. Gregory writes: The candidate's past was not examined, but it was at once deemed worthy of the bishop's throne.[108] He sees here an overly great confidence in baptism, which only eradicates sin but does not necessarily change the character as well, the disposition to sin.[109] Therefore someone to whom the office of bishop is offered immedi-ately after his baptism should first put his Christian life to the test for

---

[102] Ibid., 2, 1, 12, 610–33. [English text translated from the German version of B. Meier.]
[103] Ibid., 2, 1, 12, 535f.
[104] Ibid., 2, 1, 12, 68–70, 541f., 710, 734f.
[105] Ibid., 2, 1, 12, 382f., 634–36.
[106] Ibid., 2, 1, 12, 395, 400, 442.
[107] Ibid., 2, 1, 12, 428f.
[108] Ibid., 2, 1, 12, 380f.
[109] Ibid., 2, 1, 12, 449f.

a while and postpone his candidacy,[110] as canon law itself provides.[111] This coincides with Theodore's opinion.

Certainly Gregory's poem accords us an interesting insight into the disappointed soul of its author and into many episcopal biographies; contrary to the first impression that it gives, however, it in no way proves the existence of morally dissolute clerics in Constantinople.

c. Cyril of Jerusalem

Occasionally it is thought, on the basis of a remark by Cyril, that the existence of obligatory continence in Palestine can be disputed. Cyril (d. 386), who since 348 had occupied the renowned episcopal see of Jerusalem, gave conferences in the Church of the Holy Sepulcher for the adult candidates for baptism. In the course of one of these he made the following remark (around 350):

> To the Most Pure and the Master of Purity it was fitting to be born from a pure bed. For if the one who serves Jesus well [καλῶς] as a priest abstains from [relations with] women, how could Jesus himself be born of [the union between] a man and a woman?[112]

Obviously Cyril is not speaking of the universal priesthood of the faithful but of the cleric's perpetual self-restraint with respect to women. The sense is probably: If the married priest of Jesus does not beget children, how then could Jesus himself have been begotten by a man? A merely periodic continence on the part of the priest would run counter to the argument and, besides, would not be worth mentioning, since married laypeople abstained periodically from having relations as well, so as to participate in the Divine Liturgy.[113] Hence, in this passage the renunciation of conjugal relations is required of the married priest, with no ifs, ands, or buts.[114]

The word καλῶς is a stumbling block. Some read into it the implication that there were, after all, priests who begot children. Is Cyril, then, distinguishing between the priests who were good, that is, the

---

[110] Ibid., 2, 1, 12, 444–47.

[111] John Chrysostom, *De sacerdotio* 2, 6 (SC 272, 134, 30–34).

[112] *Catecheses* 12, 25 (34 Reischl and Rupp 2): Ἔπρεπε γὰρ τῷ ἁγνοτάτῳ καὶ διδασκάλῳ τῆς ἁγνείας ἐξ ἁγνῶν ἐξεληλυθέναι παστάδων. Εἰ γὰρ ὁ τῷ Ἰησοῦ καλῶς ἱερατεύων ἀπέχεται γυναικός, αὐτὸς ὁ Ἰησοῦς πῶς ἔμελλεν ἐξ ἀνδρὸς καὶ γυναικὸς ἔρχεσθαι.

[113] Ibid., 4, 25 (116 Reischl and Rupp 1). Contrary to Gryson, *Origines*, 58.

[114] Denzler, *Die Geschichte*, 28.

virginal ones, and those who were not, who were married and begot
children? Besides the good, celibate priests, there would then be, in a
manner of speaking, the less respectable, average priests who had relations with their wives. It would certainly be very surprising if Cyril
were to make himself unpopular with many of his clerics by using such
a discriminating distinction. Even greater would be the damage among
the faithful, who necessarily would be divided into adherents of good
and "bad" priests. If in fact clerics did have the option to continue
having marital relations, then such discrimination would be entirely
out of place.

Christian Cochini has offered a better interpretation of the καλῶς.[115]
He calls attention to the train of thought in the sermon as a whole,
which constantly attempts to refute Jewish opinions challenging the
true birth of Jesus of the Virgin Mary. Taking into consideration also
that this sermon was given in Jerusalem, where the Jewish rituals were
once celebrated in the Temple, "the one who serves Jesus well [that
is, correctly] as a priest" can be seen in opposition to the false [merely
provisional] Jewish priesthood. For indeed, the Levites were married,
too, but they practiced continence only during those weeks when it
was their duty to serve in the Temple. Even after the destruction of
the Temple by the Romans, there were still Jewish priests, whom
Chrysostom, for instance, describes in harsh terms in his Antiochene
sermons.[116]

d. Athanasius of Alexandria

Another frequently discussed passage is a statement of the eminent
bishop and patriarch Athanasius of Alexandria (d. 373). It is found in
a letter to the monk Dracontius, dated 354/55. He had been elected
bishop but had evaded his new responsibility by taking flight. At that
time this was a completely honorable course of action. Athanasius, to
be sure, was very concerned about appointing someone to occupy the
episcopal see. Hence he did not want to allow the monk just to run off
like that. So he wrote to him and tried to make the episcopal ministry
more palatable to him. He pointed out that asceticism is a concept not
at all foreign to the episcopacy, either.

---

[115] Cochini, *Origins*, 208–10.

[116] Cf. the impurity of "priests today" among the Jews, in John Chrysostom, *Adversus Iudaeos* 6, 5 (PG 48, 911f.).

We indeed know bishops who fast and monks who eat to satiation. We know bishops who drink no wine, and monks who drink it. We know bishops who perform miracles and monks who do not. Many bishops never married, and some monks had children; in the same way [we know] bishops who have children and monks who have their own descendants. And we know, on the other hand, clerics who drink wine and monks who fast. It is indeed permitted to act in this way and not forbidden to act in that way.[117]

So there we have the words, "Many bishops never married, and some monks had children; in the same way [we know] bishops who have children and monks who have their own descendants." Therefore there are married bishops. As bishops, are they still begetting children? Answering this question has been rather difficult, because the entire passage is confused, and the Greek textual tradition is problematic as well. But since the exhaustive discussion of Christian Cochini it can no longer be taken as evidence that clerics, with permission, still begot children after ordination. Even Franz Xaver Funk is convinced that the passage does not say that bishops still carried on marital relations during the time of their ministry.[118] When Funk, on the other hand, claims to state with certainty that at least deacons and priests (who are not mentioned in the text) still begot children, then that is purely wishful thinking.

Athanasius is interested only in the episcopal office. Bishops no longer begot children. That necessarily follows from the text. For when Athanasius speaks of monks who have children, then they begot their children while they were still married and before they withdrew into solitude. Athanasius would never have tolerated monks who begot children. He is not speaking about abuses by clerics and monks, that is, about the possibility of monks and bishops begetting children; he is speaking, rather, about the distinct and permissible ways of life of monks and clerics. Therefore, since he compares bishops with the mar-

---

[117] *Epistula ad Dracontium* 9 (PG 25, 533AB): Οἴδαμεν γὰρ καὶ ἐπισκόπους νηστεύοντας, καὶ μοναχοὺς ἐσθίοντας. Οἴδαμεν καὶ ἐπισκόπους μὴ πίνοντας οἶνον, μοναχοὺς δὲ πίνοντας· οἴδαμεν καὶ σημεῖα ποιοῦντας ἐπισκόπους, μοναχοὺς δὲ μὴ ποιοῦντας. Πολλοὶ δὲ τῶν ἐπισκόπων οὐδὲ γεγαμήκασι, μοναχοὶ δὲ πατέρες τέκνων γεγόνασιν· ὥσπερ καὶ ἐπισκόπους πατέρας τέκνων, καὶ μοναχοὺς ἐξ ὁλοκλήρου γένους τυγχάνοντας. Καὶ πάλιν οἴδαμεν κληρικοὺς πεινῶντας, μοναχοὺς δὲ νηστεύοντασ. Ἔξεστι γὰρ καὶ οὕτως, καὶ ἐκείνως οὐ κεκώλυται. Cochini, *Origins*, 211–16.

[118] F. X. Funk, "Cölibat und Priesterehe im christlichen Altertum", in *Kirchengeschichtliche Abhandlungen und Untersuchungen*, vol. 1 (Paderborn, 1897), 146.

ried monks, by analogy it must be true that the bishops begot their children before their ordination. Thus Athanasius means to say: Bishops and monks are not all that different. Married men with children and unmarried men without children are called to both states; there are ascetical and less ascetical representatives of each. So Dracontius can continue his monastic way of life as a bishop, without having to trouble himself about the married bishops, just as he did not trouble himself about the formerly married monks.

Hence the text does refer to a continence discipline. Specifically, just as there are monks who had children before they set out on the ascetical way, so too there are bishops with families, who nevertheless—and that is part of the intended meaning—after ordination have practiced continence as a matter of principle, exactly as the monks do.[119] And there are virginal monks just as there are virginal bishops.

e. Synesius of Cyrene

A particularly instructive case concerning clerical continence occurred in the year 410 in Egypt, when Theophilus was bishop of Alexandria and thus patriarch over a large part of the North African Church (385 to 412). Synesius, from the Libyan town of Cyrene, a highly educated, politically well versed and humane man, was supposed to become bishop of nearby Ptolemais and thus metropolitan of the province of Cyrenaica. Although he was already forty years old, he had not been married for long and had three small sons aged six and five years.

Synesius was elected bishop. But before the consecration could take place, the election still had to be approved by the Alexandrian patriarch. Like Dracontius, he used this time to avoid taking the office. He fought tooth and nail for over half a year. "With all his might and every possible machination" he tried to dissuade the priests of Ptolemais who had elected him.[120] Among them is to be reckoned a letter he wrote to his brother Euoptios, which was meant, however, to be an open

---

[119] Palladius, *Historia Lausiaca* 44 tells of a priest at the beginning of the fourth century who had a grown son; finally he withdrew to the desert. For a later instance, see Brown, *Keuschheit*, 265.

[120] *Epistula* 11 (PG 66, 1348C): ἁπάσῃ ῥώμῃ, καὶ μηχαναῖς ἐκκλίνας ἱερωσύνην. Such restraint with regard to the office of bishop is entirely in keeping with the Antiochene-Cappadocian tradition. Recall, for example, the guile with which Chrysostom is said to have eluded the priesthood.

letter, tacitly addressed to the patriarch himself.[121] As fate would have it, Theophilus himself had married him and his wife. In this famous letter 105, then, Synesius formulates his ideas about the episcopacy:

> God, and the law and the anointed hand of Theophilus have given me a wife. Well, I confess before all men and I freely admit: I do not want to be separated from her forever, or to live with her in secret, like an adulterer. For the first attitude would be contrary to love, and the second unlawful. But I would hope and pray to have lots of fine children. Without fail the bishop responsible for the ordination should know this.[122]

If we take these lines in isolation, then Synesius is self-confidently insisting that he will continue to live together with his wife and to beget many more children, even in the near future as bishop.[123] Synesius makes his appearance, so to speak, as a second Paphnutius, as an advocate of marital rights. Since he was finally consecrated a bishop, one would have to assume that he got his way and was allowed to have marital relations with the permission of his bishop. This is the conclusion frequently drawn.[124] In any case that is sheer speculation. For we do not know whether permission was actually granted to him to continue engaging in marital intercourse. We hear nothing about subsequent children, either, which is all the more surprising because his three sons died not long after his ordination. But even if he did continue to have conjugal relations, there can still be no doubt as to the fundamental validity of clerical continence. In any case a dispensation from the discipline was granted in rare cases. But such a dispensation is nevertheless improbable. Even the critic Roger Gryson says in summarizing that at the beginning of the fifth century married men who

---

[121] *Epistulae* 105 (PG 66, 1484D–1485A).

[122] Ibid. (PG 66, 1485A): Ἐμοὶ τοιγαροῦν ὅ τε Θεὸς, ὅ τε νόμος, ἥ τε ἱερὰ Θεοφίλου χεὶρ, γυναῖκα ἐπιδέδωκε. Προαγορεύω τοίνυν ἅπασι, καὶ μαρτύρομαι, ὡς ἐγὼ ταύτης οὔτε ἀλλοτριώσομαι καθάπαξ, οὔτε ὡς μοιχὸς αὐτῇ λάθρα συνέσομαι. Τὸ μὲν γὰρ ἥκιστα εὐσεβές· τὸ δὲ ἥκιστα νόμμον. Ἀλλὰ βουλήσομαι τε καὶ εὔξομαι συχνά μοι πάνυ καὶ χρηστὰ γενέσθαι παιδία. Ἐν δὴ τοῦτο δεῖ τὸν κύριον τῆς χειροτονίας μὴ ἀγνοῆσαι. A German translation of the entire letter is found in J. Vogt, *Begegnung mit Synesios, dem Philosophen, Priester und Feldherrn* (Darmstadt, 1985), 9–13, 94–98. Brief mention should be made here of Isidore of Pelusium (d. 431), who also speaks of not observing continence celibacy (*Epistulae* 3, 75 [PG 78, 781C]; Cochini, *Origins*, 299–303). Of course it is suspected that in the case of Isidore's correspondence we are dealing with a forgery.

[123] Brown, *Keuschheit*, 303.

[124] Denzler, *Die Geschichte*, 27f.

assumed the office of bishop gave up conjugal relations and also that there were no exceptions to this regulation.[125]

One could even say that Synesius did not even dream of asking for a dispensation. For if it had been granted to him, he would have had to become a bishop. But that is exactly what he wanted to prevent at all costs. This is the only way in which the sentences cited above can be understood. Repeatedly Synesius would emphasize later on that he had accepted the office against his express wishes, indeed, that he would have preferred death to the title of bishop.[126] For this reason he devised all sorts of "machinations" before his ordination to oppose Theophilus and to escape his destiny. And in fact the open letter, which was calculated to produce an effect, was a final attempt, summoning all of his rhetorical and persuasive skills, to evade the office.

Thus Synesius erects insurmountable obstacles to make it impossible for Theophilus to accept the election. This involves central dogmatic points like the Resurrection. Synesius knows, after all, that Theophilus is an unyielding guardian of the faith in precisely this area. Synesius pretends to view the Resurrection as ultimately a folk myth. Contrary to form, he poses as the arrogant philosopher who, if need be, could make an outward show of teaching such myths, but who in his philosophical chamber entertains quite different thoughts on the matter. He does not want to dissemble to such an extent, however, and therefore he ought to be exempted from the episcopacy. In this connection Synesius says that he wants to live with his wife as before and beget children. He shows the bishop, as it were, the ghostly handwriting on the wall: There would be reason to fear that, as a bishop, he would lead a double life because of his attachment to his wife, which would no doubt violate the law.

This sloganeering does not mean, however, that Synesius intended to knock down the wall and to insist upon the blessing of the highest authority upon his dogmatic and disciplinary idiosyncrasies.[127] In no way did he want to bring about the downfall of obligatory continence —neither in his own case nor in general. That would have run exactly contrary to his personal interests. Theophilus was not supposed

---

[125] Gryson, *Origines*, 48f.

[126] *Epistulae* 11 (PG 66, 1348C); *Epistulae* 57 (PG 66, 1389A, 1397B); *Epistulae* 95 (PG 66, 1464D).

[127] Thus Vogt, *Begegnung*, 104f.

to make any exceptions for him, otherwise he would have had to become a bishop after all. Certainly, then, Synesius was not an opponent of celibacy. He was simply not the cool, arrogant challenger who was somewhat conceited about his academic qualifications and who considered his preferences more important than regard for the office or the will of the Church. Rather, as is apparent from the entire context of letter 105, he was honestly convinced of his own unworthiness, without questioning whether obligatory continence was right.[128]

Synesius had a high ideal of the episcopacy, completely in agreement, for instance, with John Chrysostom's book on the priesthood. The office of bishop was godly and had to be untouched by earthly pleasures. The bishop had to be blameless, set apart from other men, so as to be able to cleanse them of their stains. He speaks about a law that he does not wish to violate by having marital relations with his wife even after ordination. Now Synesius says outright that he would like to have more children and that he wants to continue having conjugal relations; this, however, is simply to make clear to his bishop the responsibility that would be his and that he should not make the decision carelessly but rather ponder what he would be demanding if he were to ordain him. Synesius does not want to force his way into office, but he does say explicitly that he will accept the bishop's decision as the will of God with a clear conscience.[129]

Synesius testifies that an ecclesiastical law obliged the bishops of Cyrenaica to observe perfect continence. Therefore a married cleric who had conjugal relations with his wife was deemed an adulterer. And we can assume that this law was associated with a formal promise of continence. We may even be able to derive the exact formula from the wording of Synesius' letter. When he writes, "I confess before all men and I freely admit: I do not want to be separated from my wife forever", then this probably quotes (almost) exactly the vow of continence: "I confess before all men and I freely admit: I want (!) to be separated from my wife for ever."

It is incomprehensible that Gryson does not wish to recognize the testimony of Jerome from the year 406, in which the latter, speak-

---

[128] Cochini, *Origins*, 303–7. See also Synesius, *Epistulae* 57 (PG 66, 1384A–1400A).

[129] *Epistulae* 105 (PG 66, 1488C): "If . . . the man whom God has given the power to elevate me to the episcopate decides to go ahead with making me a bishop, I will obey because it is necessary, and I will accept it as a word that comes from God. . . . But one must obey God freely." [English translation as in Cochini, *Origins*, 304.]

ing about the Egyptian Church, explicitly states that she ordains only
those married men who are willing to practice continence with their
wives. Moreover, the great champions of clerical continence, Jerome
and Epiphanius, corresponded regularly with Theophilus. It is scarcely
imaginable that the clerical discipline in Egypt should have changed
in any way since the time of Origen; furthermore Cyril of Alexandria
(d. 444) explicitly attests to this discipline in Libya and the Pentapo-
lis: that a candidate for orders, if married, must abstain from marital
relations.[130] Then too, the legal action of Chrysostom against Bishop
Antoninos of Ephesus is sufficient proof that the non-continence of a
bishop—in Asia Minor, in this instance—was punished with removal
from office.[131]

f. The Canons of Hippolytus

The situation in Egypt in the late fourth and early fifth centuries, since
it was of importance for Synesius, gives us good reason to examine
briefly the Canons of Hippolytus. They are often cited as proof that in
the middle of the fourth century in Egypt (or Asia Minor) there was
no discipline of clerical continence. For canon 8 reads:

> If someone asks for ordination, saying "I have received the gift of heal-
> ing", let him not be ordained until the matter is clear and whether the
> healing he accomplished came from God.
>   As to the priest whose wife has a child, he will not be excluded.[132]

It cannot be assumed that we are dealing here with a deliberately
anti-celibacy regulation. Attention must be given to the negative formulation. It does not say, "A priest who begets a child may continue
to exercise his ministry", but rather, "he will not be excluded." This
statement, then, expresses the mitigation of a punishment. A married
priest who has not observed continence should not be excommunicated but should in that case remain in the ranks of the clergy. Natu-

---

[130] *Epistulae* 79, 3 (283, 9–14 Joannou 2): Καὶ εἰ μέλλοι τις χειροτονεῖσθαι κληρικός, περιερ-
γαζέσθω τὸν βίον αὐτοῦ, καὶ πότερόν ποτε γαμετὴν ἔχει ἢ οὔ, καὶ πῶς ἢ πότε ἡγάγετο, καὶ εἰ
ἀπέσχετο. In the Migne edition (PG 77, 365B) the crucial phrase καὶ εἰ ἀπέσχετο is missing.
Cochini, *Origins*, 306f., n. 103.

[131] Palladius, *Vita Johannis Chrysostomi* 13 (SC 341, 276, 171f.). Gryson, *Origines*, 66f.,
gives no valid argument that would justify dismissing the unanimous witness of the sources.

[132] "Le prêtre, lorsque sa femme a enfanté, ne sera pas retranché" (PO 31, 2, 361); W.
Riedel, *Die Kirchenrechtsquellen des Patriarchats Alexandrien* (Leipzig, 1900), 205.

rally this implies that he no longer may perform priestly functions. We have encountered a similar ruling already in Callistus and Basil. Thus this canon testifies to a discipline of obligatory continence.[133]

5. Summary

All in all we have enough evidence concerning clerical continence in the Eastern Church of the fourth century. From a historical perspective, more cannot be expected. We can accept as given an obligation of higher clerics to practice perpetual continence, whether they were virginal, widowed, or married. For the island of Cyprus we have the testimony of Epiphanius of Salamis, for Palestine and Egypt that of Jerome, and for Syria and Asia Minor that of John Chrysostom, Theodore of Mopsuestia, and Theodoret of Cyrrhus. Epiphanius states explicitly that continence celibacy constitutes a universally valid and binding norm. This cannot be doubted, since he also frankly admits violations against celibacy.

Furthermore, the permanent validity of the digamy prohibition strongly suggests a continence celibacy rule. Origen's question, whether there might also be twice-married, widowed men who can practice continence reliably, does not allow the Eastern theologians to rest. Jerome and Theodore argue along these lines, which only goes to confirm: the joint requirements of monogamy and continence for the married cleric were the norm that was in force in Eastern Church discipline. From Theodoret we know that, well into the fifth century, there was no change in this. Despite the criticism, it appears that things never came to an abandonment of the digamy prohibition in principle. It is just that marriages that took place before baptism were not counted.

One innovation is a different interpretation of the pastoral letters that can be gleaned from Chrysostom, Jerome, Theodore, and Theodoret:

---

[133] In addition, the Canons are of very limited value for the history of the fourth century. For they are preserved only in an Arabic version of the twelfth century, which in turn goes back to a lost Coptic translation of a likewise lost Greek original (Gryson, *Origines*, 98). The text we have today, then, is from a repeatedly broken tradition, which furthermore spans many centuries. It would contradict all historical methodology to treat it as a reliable source for the fourth century. It may well have been altered and revised many times. Particular caution is called for when such a document is handed down within a national church such as the Coptic Church. In that case deviations from the practice of other Churches are always to be expected.

Is it possible that with the phrase "the husband of one wife" Paul intended to forbid clerics to practice polygamy? In that case one could think: If Paul was only prohibiting polygamy, then surely, in the opinion of the theologians mentioned, he was permitting sexual intercourse with the one wife remaining to the cleric. But on this subject, also, the sources are unanimous: Whether or not polygamy was the question, there had to be continence in any case. The theologians do nothing to undermine that.

Furthermore we encounter the marriage prohibition, the second constant sign of obligatory continence. In force already before Nicaea in Asia Minor, it was formulated anew in the second half of the fourth century in the region of Syria and Asia Minor. There is also a text of Basil of Caesarea indirectly affirming it, which is only to be expected since the prohibition had a claim to validity at least into the early fifth century (Paphnutius legend).

Another interesting development was heralded as early as 300 in the Ecclesiastical Canons of the Holy Apostles. Going beyond the marriage prohibition, many people wanted to see only virginal or widowed men in the clergy. But Chrysostom and the Ecclesiastical Canons of the Holy Apostles were opposed to that. It was in keeping with the Church's tradition to ordain also men who were still living together with their wives. This, however, was without detriment to the marriage prohibition and the continence rule.

In general the trend toward a celibate priesthood is unmistakable. In the selection of candidates, unmarried men were preferred. Only when these are not available does one have recourse to married men. Statements to this effect are made by Chrysostom and Epiphanius. In this development the growing influence of the ascetical movement played an important role. For among the celibate candidates were many monks, who gained entrance into the clergy in increasing numbers. Even though celibacy in the sense of being unmarried may have been an invention of the West, the gradual preponderance of unmarried clergy as opposed to married ministers was nevertheless a phenomenon in the East as well. This development took place at approximately the same time as the monastic model of community life for clerics gained a footing in the West.

The ascetical trend was not without its erroneous developments. The so-called Eustathians in Asia Minor around the middle of the fourth century should be mentioned. They rejected marriage and demanded that anyone who was already married should divorce. The same was then required of the clergy. Laymen were not allowed to have recourse to married priests. The hierarchy moved decisively against these abuses. It forbade clerics to resort to marital separation under the pretext of piety. The fact that they were not permitted to dismiss their wives does not mean, however, that they were allowed to have sexual intercourse. The intention was merely to put a stop to an exaggerated asceticism that was contemptuous of marriage.

In order to call into question a universally valid continence celibacy, at least for Asia Minor, Palestine, and Egypt, scholars have repeatedly cited Gregory Nazianzen, Cyril of Jerusalem, Athanasius of Alexandria, and Synesius of Cyrene. Nevertheless, it is unlikely that Gregory was born after the ordination of his father. Indeed, the biographical data suggest instead a previous birth. Cyril, too, expects perfect continence of the married priest and his wife, in contrast to the Jewish priests. Athanasius knows of married bishops and monks who after their ordination or monastic profession [termed in Latin *conversio*] ceased having marital relations. When Synesius is recommended for the episcopacy, he insistently expresses his desire to beget many more children with his wife. That, however, is a ruse, since he knows that he cannot become a bishop while harboring this intention. And that is precisely what he wants to avoid. He was ordained after all, and it would seem that he loyally observed obligatory continence.

It is unclear how Roger Gryson, after evaluating all these texts, can come to the conclusion that no restriction of any kind was imposed in the East upon married clerics with regard to how they should conduct themselves within marriage, while in the West the higher clerics were required to abstain from conjugal relations with their wives. "This law first saw the light of day in Rome, toward the end of the fourth century. The papacy subsequently has not slackened in its efforts to maintain it and to have it prevail over the old, more liberal customs."[134] Against this view stand very clear attestations from the first four centuries to a widespread discipline of continence celibacy in the East, which was repeatedly advocated and called for by the Church. Of course, the second part of Gryson's claim must be examined now. Did clerical continence really develop in the West only toward the end of the fourth century? And what role did the popes play in this?

---

[134] Gryson, *Origines*, 127.

VI. Clerical Continence in the Western Church of the Fourth and Early Fifth Centuries

We return once more to the beginning of the fourth century so as to trace now the development in the West. After periods in which the Christian religion was savagely persecuted, the reign of Constantine marked a turning point that was to bring about final and lasting peace (at least with regard to threats from without) and so began an unprecedented rise and a swift propagation of the Christian faith. There was a tremendous rise in the number of clergy as well. In antiquity there was no priest shortage at all; instead we must note a priest surplus.[1]

Of course, celibate men were not always available in sufficient numbers, as Jerome and Epiphanius observed and reported.[2] As in the East, virginity was highly esteemed in the West also. Exemplary proponents of celibacy were Ambrose and Augustine, two of the most capable and influential bishops of that period. That in turn had consequences for the selection of clerics. This was clearly manifested in the cathedral chapters (secular priests living in a quasi-monastic community headed by their ordinary), which became popular in the Western Church from around the middle of the fourth century: in Italy under Eusebius of Vercelli, Paulinus of Nola, and Ambrose of Milan; in Gaul under Victricius of Rouen and Martin of Tours, and in North Africa under Augustine.

The lack of celibate candidates probably would have been noticeable only in the rural areas. To this extent we can follow the analysis of Peter Brown when he writes, "Only metropolitan churches, such as Rome and Milan, could attract large numbers of unmarried young men and encourage them to grow up from childhood on as celibates, under the shadow of the altar (as did John Chrysostom and the young Theodoret in Antioch). The average provincial church, however, was chronically short of recruits to the clergy. It could not dispense with

---

[1] E. Dassmann, *Ämter und Dienste in den frühchristlichen Gemeinden*, Hereditas 8 (Bonn, 1994), 178–87.

[2] Jerome, *Adversus Jovinianum* 1, 34 (PL 23², 269A): "Non sunt tanti virgines, quanti necessarii sunt sacerdotes."

the services of married persons [*sic*]."³ They simply compensated for the lack of virginal candidates by ordaining married men.

Overall the supply was greater than the demand. Unworthy candidates became a problem when ambition drove them to seek office, with the remarkable statement from the First Letter to Timothy on their lips: "If any one aspires to the office of [overseer, that is] bishop, he desires a noble task" (1 Tim 3:1). Bishops repeatedly complained about this abuse.⁴ They depended on having clerics in great quantity, and an adequate preparation of the candidates was not always secured. This need gave rise to *Klerikerkollegien* in the West. For the same reason, a great number of monks were admitted to the clergy, especially in the East; despite many a bad experience, the Church could not do without their spiritual and ascetical training.⁵

Given this momentous phase of expansion, it is surprising that in the West, over the course of many decades, we hear nothing about a discipline of clerical continence. In the fifty years after Nicaea there was not one single reference, either enjoining or rejecting it. Then, however, there was an abrupt change. As of the pontificate of Pope Damasus—himself the son of a priest—who occupied the episcopal see of Rome in the year 366, there was in the West no end to the opinions about clerical continence. There were not just council decrees and papal documents in the downpour. For the first time a discipline of obligatory continence also became the subject of detailed theological discussions.

The impression given by these texts, some of them quite extensive, has often led to the suspicion that continence celibacy was being introduced here for the first time. Having developed in a special environment of ascetical zealotry, it was suddenly translated into action in Rome by resolute pontiffs. That would explain the colossal effort ex-

---

³ P. Brown, *The Body and Society: Men, Women, and Sexual Renunciation in Early Christianity* (New York: Columbia Univ. Press, 1988), 357.

⁴ M. Lochbrunner, *Über das Priestertum: Historische und systematische Untersuchung zum Priesterbild des Johannes Chrysostomus*, Hereditas, 5 (Bonn, 1993), 52–56; C. Baur, *Der heilige Johannes Chrysostomus und Seine Zeit*, vol. 1 (Munich: M. Hueber, 1930), 151–53; Stefan Heid, "Isidor von Pelusium und die Schrift 'Über das Priestertum' des Johannes Chrysostom" FKTh 7 (1991): 196–210.

⁵ Lochbrunner, *Priestertum*, 84–90; A. M. Ritter, *Charisma im Verständnis des Joannes Chrysostomos und seiner Zeit: Ein Beitrag zur Erforschung der griechisch-orientalischen Ekklesiologie in Frühzeit der Reichskirche*, FKDG 25 (Göttingen, 1972), 93–96, 158f., 166.

pended on decrees and position papers justifying the discipline, which can all somehow be traced back to Roman chambers. Contrary to this hypothesis, of course, our investigation thus far has made clear that clerical continence was not originally of Roman vintage. According to everything the historical sources yield, the East was acquainted with an earlier and better-attested continence discipline than the West. But continence celibacy existed in the Latin Church also, well before Damasus. Traces of it are found in Tertullian, Cyprian, and Elvira. Pope Siricius, too, maintained that it had been an uninterrupted tradition (decretal *Cum in unum*), and his testimony in this regard should not be doubted a priori.

Let us examine now the individual texts of the Latin West. They can be arranged according to the ecclesiastical regions of North Africa, Spain, Italy, and Gaul. In doing so we are abandoning a strictly chronological presentation in favor of a regional division. Again and again we will have to deal in the first place with Rome, which was in the process of guaranteeing for itself a position of undisputed preeminence in the Western world. Whatever occurred at the periphery had its consequences in Rome. Rome was the stationary pole in a momentous, unsettled era. As though it were the most self-evident thing in the world, it held high the banner of clerical continence as a signal and a guide for all who had ever had any doubt.

1. The Situation in North Africa and Spain

We have already spoken about the North African and Spanish Church in connection with the Carthaginian theologians Tertullian and Cyprian and the Synod of Elvira in southern Spain. A certain spatial proximity between the two regions allows us to assume that there was a reciprocal influence.[6] North Africa and Spain go together well also because in the fourth century clerical continence was discussed in both places against

---

[6] Cf., for example, Cyprian, *Epistulae* 67. Canon 65 of the Council of Elvira (20 Jonkers): "Ne ab his (sc. clericis), qui exemplum bonae conversationis esse debent, ab eis videantur scelerum magisteria procedere", could be referring to Cyprian, *Epistulae* 4, 3 (CSEL 3, 2, 475, 17–19): "Quomodo enim possunt integritati et continentiae praeesse, si ex ipsis incipiant corruptelae et uitiorum magisteria procedere?" For a general overview, see R. Garcia Villoslada, *Historia de la Iglesia en España*, vol. 1, *La Iglesia en la España romana y visigoda (siglos I–VIII)* (Madrid, 1979), 120–49.

the background of a severe crisis in the Church. Putting an end to this crisis then became in both countries the motive for a reform of the clergy and of the celibacy discipline.

a. The Schism in North Africa Endangers Clerical Continence

Western North Africa, where Tertullian and Cyprian worked, once possessed a proud, flourishing Church. Its subsequent history helps us to understand the later conflict over clerical continence. The history of North Africa was so extraordinary that clerical discipline was necessarily affected by it. Throughout the entire fourth century the worm of division gnawed at the Church. Fritz van der Meer, in his book about Augustine, has depicted with unsurpassed skill the scarcely imaginable disturbances of this period.[7]

The protracted struggle with the Donatists. The Donatists, followers of a certain Donatus, had split off. And they were successful. Their church surpassed the Catholic Church in size, influence, and number of bishops, which approached four hundred. In this North African region there was a complete anti-Church. The remaining Catholic bishops administered the wretched holdings of a bankrupt institution. Here, contrary to what we have heard thus far, a severe priest shortage was prevalent.[8] The rescue came at the last minute, when an extremely capable leader appeared at a priestly ordination in the year 391: Aurelius Augustinus, and "by virtue of a gift from God, the Catholic Church in Africa, which for so long had lain prostrate—torn asunder, intimidated, and oppressed by the heretics who had the upper hand —once again began to lift up her head."[9] United with Aurelius, the Carthaginian bishop of the same name, Augustine organized synods for the North African bishops that were held almost yearly starting in 393. Only in this way did the Catholic Church manage to regain her self-confidence, to reorganize her efforts, and to overcome the Donatist schism after a protracted struggle.

Numerous references point to the very important consequences that this century-long schism had for clerical discipline. It led to daily skirmishes between the Catholic and the Donatist clergy, in which every-

---

[7] *Augustinus der Seelsorger: Leben und Wirken eines Kirchenvaters* (Cologne, 1953), 98–146.
[8] Ibid., 105f.
[9] Possidius, *Vita Augustini* 7 (PL 32, 39).

one accused the other side of moral lapses.[10] A lot of dirty laundry was washed in the course of these exchanges, starting with the deacons and going all the way up to the bishops. Each side triumphantly kept count whenever the career of an immoral cleric on the opposing side went up in flames. The Donatists had a sort of guerilla movement, the so-called Circumcellions, among whose ranks immoral and downright criminal clerics used to hustle as well. Two such bishops were conspicuous for their grossly indecent behavior: they are said to have impregnated nuns and a juvenile.[11] This attests to the widespread degeneration of morals. On the Catholic side, too, we have information about many incidents. But it would be rash to conclude on this basis that there had been a complete breakdown of the Catholic clergy. For the Donatists often remonstrated with the Catholics about the moral turpitude of clergymen living abroad, so that the charges could not be verified at all in Africa. Between the two lines of fire were the Donatist clerics who had gone over to the Catholic Church. The Donatists particularly liked to look for black sheep among this group.

Against this background the development of celibacy in North Africa can be pictured as follows: a discipline of obligatory continence had presumably existed since Cyprian's day. Precisely at this time, though, the Donatists split off from the Church, indeed, while claiming to be the Church of the pure, the undefiled, the saints. Thus it was an elite church with the highest standards. Naturally this made demands, in the first place, of the Donatist clergymen. They had to stand in the presence of the Lord in spotless white garments, and at the same time that meant that they had to observe continence in an exemplary manner. For the Donatists had the same clerical discipline as the Catholics. Therefore it must have been particularly enticing for them to denounce the moral transgressions of the Catholic clerics. Certainly the latter provided plenty of opportunity for criticism. In the long run the Catholics ended up in the minority anyway, and that made the bishops' position even more difficult. Everything was not always at its best, and the priest shortage contributed to this less-than-ideal situation, because it was precisely the capable people who were going over to the Donatists.

---

[10] R. Crespin, *Ministere et sainteté: Pastorale du clergé et solution de la crise Donatiste dans la vie et la doctrine de saint Augustin* (Paris, 1965), 106–10, 113.

[11] Optatus, *Milevitanus* 2, 19 (CSEL 26, 54, 13–20). Cf. Augustine, *Epistulae* 105, 2, 3f.

It is extremely unlikely that the African Church could have prevailed by her own strength over the Donatist majority had not the eminently resolute, morally unimpeachable, and spiritually towering figure of Augustine appeared. By all means, though, any reform would have had to make sure that the Donatists did not have the slightest pretext for accusing the Catholic clergy of any sort of disciplinary violations. Indeed, even the former Donatists, who had come over to the Catholic Church, were shocked by the fact that the clergy there left much to be desired. All this, to be sure, compelled the bishops to take action. And that is also the concrete historical background for the celibacy provisions at the Councils of Carthage. These are not to be understood as an innovation but as the necessary inculcation of an old discipline that was practiced by the Donatists, too, and held by them in particularly high esteem.

The Council of Carthage. In the midst of this crisis—the decline of the Catholic Church in North Africa—and a few years before the long-awaited turning point, comes the first report that we have about clerical continence. It deals with a gathering of bishops held on June 16, 390, in Carthage, presided over by the primate of North Africa, Genethlius. We will go now to the debate in the council hall:

> Epigonius, bishop of Bulla Regia, said, "As was established in a previous council with respect to continence and chastity, I demand that those three degrees which by ordination are strictly bound to chastity, that is, bishops, priests, and deacons, be instructed again in detail to maintain purity."
>
> Bishop Genethlius said, "As was previously said, it is fitting that the holy bishops and priests of God, as well as the Levites [that is, deacons], that is, those who are in the service of the divine sacraments, observe perfect continence, so that they may obtain in all simplicity what they are asking from God; what the apostles taught and what antiquity itself observed, let us also endeavor to keep."
>
> The bishops declared unanimously: "It pleases us all that bishops, priests, and deacons (that is, those who touch the sacraments), guardians of purity, abstain from conjugal intercourse with their wives, so that those who serve at the altar may keep a perfect chastity."[12]

---

[12] Canon 2 (112f. Jonkers): "Epigonius episcopus Bullensium Regiorum dixit: 'Cum in praeterito concilio de continentiae et castitatis moderamine tractaretur, gradus isti tres, qui constrictione quadam castitati per consecrationes annexi sunt, episcopus, presbyter et diaconus, tractatu pleniore, ut pudicitiam custodiant, doceantur.'

The Council Fathers agreed unanimously that married bishops, priests, and deacons were not allowed to have sexual intercourse with their wives. They said that this had already been established by an earlier council; moreover, that it had been taught by the apostles and had been observed since antiquity.

Probably the celibacy initiative did not originate with the African bishops alone. Someone else was behind it, too: Pope Siricius. The schism in the North African Church, which was always something of an outer courtyard of Rome, could not leave the Pope unscathed. The contacts between the Churches of Rome and North Africa had a long, if not always untroubled, history.[13] One thing, more than anything else, suggests the intervention of Rome: A few years before the Council of Carthage, Pope Siricius himself held a council on the subject of clerical continence and communicated its decrees to the bishops of North Africa. In these Roman decrees as well, continence celibacy was enjoined upon married clerics. They are found in the decretal *Cum in unum* (see below, pp. 241–44).

This decretal of Siricius reached Africa, though we do not know exactly when (at the latest in the year 418). Presumably, however, this was the case even before the Council of Carthage. For another council had taken place previously that had already dealt with clerical continence. So says Epigonius, a participant in that council. Presumably the decretal of Siricius was the subject of discussions even at this earlier council. Therefore we can assume that, as early as the 380s, the bishops of North Africa had broached the subject of the continence discipline in consultations with Pope Siricius. At the Council of 390, then, there were voices in favor of promulgating anew the earlier decisions.

The Donatist Bishop Macrobius in Rome. Thus the particular circumstances in which the issue of clerical continence was raised had to do both with Rome's intervention (*Cum in unum*) and also with the Do-

---

"Genethlius episcopus dixit: 'Ut superius dictum est, decet sacrosanctos antistites et Dei sacerdotes nec non et Levitas vel qui sacramentis Divinis inserviunt, continentes esse in omnibus, quo possint simpliciter, quod a Deo postulant, impetrare, ut quod Apostoli docuerunt et ipsa servavit antiquitas, nos quoque custodiamus.'

"Ab universis episcopis dictum est: 'Omnibus placet, ut episcopi, presbyteri et diaconi [another version adds: vel qui sacramenta contrectant], pudicitiae custodes etiam ab uxoribus se abstineant, ut in omnibus et ab omnibus pudicitia custodiatur, qui altari deserviunt.' "

[13] C. Pietri, *Roma Christiani: Recherches sur l'Église de Rome, son organisation, sa politique, son idéologie de Miltiade à Sixte III (311–440)*, 2 vols. (Paris and Rome, 1976), I: 773–76.

natist schism. It was not by chance that Siricius was interested in North Africa. For there were Donatists in his city, too, and so the celibacy issue spilled over from North Africa to Italy. Like many other sects, the Donatists, too, had a branch of their church in Rome. One of their bishops resided there. Around the year 365, under Pope Damasus, the fourth Donatist bishop, Macrobius, came from North Africa to Rome. It is possible that he was originally a Catholic priest. The Berlin scholar Adolf von Harnack has tried to demonstrate that this bishop composed the document "On the Celibacy of Clerics" (*De singularitate clericorum*), which over the centuries was handed down anonymously, and sent it from Rome to a group of Donatist clerics in Numidia and Africa.[14] If that should prove to be correct, it would be an extremely interesting contribution to the celibacy debate in Rome and North Africa.

Macrobius was certainly not sent to Rome by accident. He had already proved himself in North Africa as a particularly exemplary and steadfast proponent of Donatist doctrines. Therefore it was all the more horrifying for him to hear about moral transgressions of Donatist clerics in Africa, since he felt that he was called to watch over the morals of clerics,[15] whom he liked to consider the "brilliant white Senate of the Church".[16] Throughout the entire treatise there are unmistakable indications of the conflict with Catholics, which makes any transgression of the "disciplinary rule that is universally to be observed" so disgraceful in his opinion.[17] What did the Donatist clerical discipline look like, then? By all means, it stood for chastity in the first place. Protecting it and guaranteeing that it remained above suspicion was Macrobius' chief concern. Concretely, it was a matter of the *syneisaktoi*: clerics,

---

[14] A. von Harnack, *Der pseudocyprianische Traktat De singularitate clericorum ein Werk des Donatistischen Bischofs Macrobius von Rom*, TU 24, 3 (Leipzig, 1903), 1–72. Agreeing with this hypothesis are O. Bardenhewer, *Geschichte der altkirchlichen Literatur*, vol. 3 (Freiburg, 1912), 490, W. H. C. Frend, *The Donatist Church* (Oxford, 1952), 186f.; opposed are H. Koch, *Cyprianische Untersuchungen*, AKG 4 (Bonn, 1926), 426–72; M. Schanz, C. Hosius, and G. Krüger, *Geschichte der römischen Literatur bis zum Gesetzgebungswerk des Kaisers Justinian*, vol. 3, 3d ed. (Munich, 1922), 379. But even if the treatise has to be attributed to a third-century Catholic bishop (thus Koch), it still fits best into the African situation caused by Donatism. Cyprian had already opposed the *syneisaktoi*. It is all the more surprising that the author of the treatise does not cite him. Later the Council of Hippo in the year 393, canon 16 (CCL 149, 38, 103–10), took action against *syneisaktoi*.

[15] *De singularitate clericorum* 1 (CSEL 3, 3, 173, 5–10).

[16] Ibid., 45 (CSEL 3, 3, 220, 9): "ut semper in clericis ecclesiae senatus candidus constet".

[17] Ibid., 1 (CSEL 3, 3, 173, 7f.): "quaecumque uniuersis clericis generaliter ad dirigendam regulam competunt disciplinae".

with bishops among them, were living together with virgins [*subintroductae*] in the absence of a marriage bond.[18] Perhaps, though, the problem was merely a matter of housekeepers; unmarried clerics had women to help with household duties. In any case, Macrobius limits himself to addressing those who do not want to marry and therefore live as celibates. Many who try, however, end up "in disgrace". Macrobius uncompromisingly demands straightforward continence of the single clerics, without loopholes of any sort, and he threatens the false "preachers of chastity"—Jerome praises Pope Damasus as "herald of modesty"—with excommunication, on the authority of apostolic instruction and divine interdict.[19]

Unfortunately he said nothing explicit about married clerics; he knows of them, at least.[20] He speaks in general of many married Christians who, for the sake of continence, separate from their spouses and move into different houses:[21]

> This is true love, which separates while maintaining the marriage bond, so as to be united in chastity. This is holy love, which imposes continence upon the spouses for the sake of praising [God] together. They, certainly, love one another inseparably who part from one another in order to triumph over themselves. Neither accusation, nor nature, nor the law, nor the Lord, nor the Apostle has forbidden them or rescinded their right to live together, but rather, so that they might keep their vows, charity has persuaded them to agree to stay away from one another.[22]

Macrobius speaks here, not about marital continence, but about the more radical separation of spouses, because he is exclusively concerned about the aspect of living alone. Naturally, it is self-evident that he also

---

[18] The fact that Macrobius seems to be calling for marriage (ibid., 7 [CSEL 3, 3, 179, 25f.]) does not mean that clerics were permitted to marry; this pertains only to those lay men who lived together with virgins (ibid., 4 [177, 27]).

[19] Ibid., 27 (CSEL 3, 3, 204, 2–5): "Eant nunc praedones pudoris et plagiarii castitatis mulierculis suis exponere molestias querelarum. Apud sanctos nostros non habent omnino suffugium, quibus misceri ecclesia auctoritate Pauli apostoli prohibetur." Ibid., 29 (205, 14).

[20] Ibid., 44 (CSEL 3, 3, 219, 10).

[21] Ibid., 31 (CSEL 3, 3, 207, 3–9).

[22] Ibid., 32 (CSEL 3, 3, 207, 20–26): "Ecce uera dilectio quae in coniugalitate diuidit, ut in castitate coniungat. Ecce sancta dilectio quae coniugalibus ad communem laudem inducit absentiam. Hi pro certo sese inseparabiliter diligunt, qui ut triumphos sibi inferant a se ipsi discedunt: quibus nec crimen nec natura nec lex nec Dominus nec apostolus potestatem unius conuersationis interdixit aut tulit, sed pro tuendis paribus uotis semota unanimitate absentari caritas persuasit." This comes very close to the radical ascetical requirement of the Eustathians in Asia Minor.

advocates the observance of continence within marriage.[23] In that case, though, one must assume that continence was obligatory for married clerics and their wives. For Macrobius writes in another passage:

> Contemplate what it is to be set over the holy people, and consider what it means to be in the service of the divine sacraments. Those who live from the altars must please the altars, and such a solicitude for purity is fitting for those who have been made holy, just as those mysteries which they humbly serve are holy; so that in the presence of the Lord they themselves might not offend the very thing that they are accomplishing nor, in the presence of the people, obstruct what they are preaching.[24]

The formulation of this argument conspicuously recalls the second canon of Carthage, cited above, concerning the continence of married clerics. When Macrobius speaks of the perpetual sacramental ministry and the exemplary role of the clergy, then that undoubtedly applies to all members of the clergy, including those who are married. We can hardly expect that, of all people, the bishop of the Donatist "church of the saints" did not require continence of his married clerics and their wives, when his counterpart Pope Damasus no doubt considered it a matter of course. Therefore we will have to assume that the Donatists in Rome, too, were intent on stirring up a debate about celibacy. Although they may have had some trouble in their own ranks, they still would not have missed a chance to play up any violations of celibacy committed by Catholic clerics. Yet the holiness of the Church was enormously important not only for Donatism but also for the Novatians, another sect that was strongly represented in Rome at the time. It claimed just as insistently to be the holy elite.

The fact that Rome was living under the scrutiny of this critical public had its advantages, too. Awareness of the discipline of clerics was heightened. Therefore Siricius and Ambrose were seeing to it that

---

[23] Ibid., 10 (CSEL 3, 3, 184, 25–27): "si mariti et uxores desideria coniugalia cotidie gerentes non sibi sufficiunt", does not contradict this. Macrobius is saying, rather: If even married persons commit adultery, then how much more likely is it that *syneisaktoi* will become adulterers. That does not mean, though, that all married people would commit adultery or that it would be utterly impossible to live continently.

[24] Ibid., 38 (CSEL 3, 3, 213, 27–214,3): "Contemplamini quid sit populo sancto praeesse et considerate quale sit diuinis sacramentis insistere. Altariis placere debent qui altariis uiuunt [= vivunt], et talis conuenit sinceritatis cura sacratis qualia sunt sacra ipsa quibus exhibent officia seruitutis, ne circa Dominum offendant ipsi quod tractant aut circa populum incipiant inpedire quod praedicant."

the monogamy rule—which was particularly sacred to the Novatians, too—was strictly observed.[25] And most assuredly, the conduct of the Church's ministers was watched even more carefully. Not only Siricius but also the bishops of North Africa tightened the discipline and insisted on its observance. At the Roman Synod in the year 385 the perpetual continence of married clerics was an important item on the agenda. It is remarkable that this point was treated precisely in relation to the conflict with the Novatian and Donatist schismatics.[26] Siricius wanted to be able to confront these self-designated pure and holy ones with an exemplary clergy. Hence he attached great importance to the purity of clerics: "By what guarantee, by what merit does he [that is, the unchaste cleric] believe that he will gain a hearing, when it is said, 'To the pure all things are pure, but to the corrupt and unbelieving nothing is pure' (Tit 1:15)?" With this the Synod addresses the very ideal of the schismatic churches. Purity and holiness should not be the domain of the schismatics, but ought to be at home, indeed, among the Catholic clergy as well.

This topic was pertinent now for North Africa, too, since many of the Roman Donatists came from there. They set themselves up there as the guardians of the mores of the Catholic clergy. And therefore it was appropriate here, too, that the bishops take action and emphatically remind their subordinates of the continence discipline. Siricius makes it clear to his North African colleagues that they must tackle this problem resolutely if they want to reform their dioceses and finally overcome the Donatist schism. Exactly as in the decretal, therefore, the thought appeared at the Council of Carthage also: The prayer of the priest has no power if he does not lead a life of purity. After all, it was purity that the Donatists claimed to have a monopoly on.

Is continence celibacy in North Africa an innovation? The foregoing sketch may well be a true picture of the causes for the North African celibacy initiatives. Nevertheless, we ought to weigh again the other argument that is often brought up, namely, that clerical continence was introduced for the very first time during the proceedings of the Council of Carthage. Is it at all possible to say that on this occasion Siricius'

---

[25] Epiphanius, *Panarion lxxx haeresium* 59, 4, 1 (GCS Epiph. 2², 367, 7–10); Council of Nicaea. canon 8. H.J. Vogt, *Coetus Sanctorum: Der Kirchenbegriff des Novatian und die Geschichte seiner Sonderkirche*, Theoph. 20 (Bonn, 1968), 211.

[26] Siricius, *Epistulae* 5, 2–4 (PL 13, 1159A–1161B); cf. Jerome, *Comm. in Tit.* 1:6 (PL 26, 599A), Crespin, *Ministère*, 34; Pietri, *Roma*, 2:890.

obsession with celibacy drove the North African bishops and the entire clergy into a discipline of obligatory celibacy that had never before been heard of? That is difficult to imagine, for many reasons. First of all, our discussions of Tertullian and Cyprian reached a contrary conclusion. With the memory of this glorious period of the undivided North African Church, a high esteem for priestly continence was surely kept alive also. There is a further consideration. The wording of the celibacy law is strikingly reminiscent of canon 33 of Elvira.[27] Like Elvira, Carthage also speaks about the continence of those who "serve the altar" or "the divine sacraments". It is just as unlikely as it was in Elvira that these expressions paper over a merely periodic continence that was observed only while the clerics had duties at the altar. Rather, these circumlocutions, which have the higher clerics in view, are phrased in such a way as to distinguish them from the lower clerics who do not serve at the altar.[28] Thus if Carthage really is connected with Elvira, then the contact between the Church in southern Spain and the North African Church may well have led to an identical continence discipline even before the fourth century.

We must assume for Africa an independent continence discipline not initiated by Rome. Gradually, though, it left more and more to be desired. And since the Catholic Church, in her conflict with the schismatics, sought to keep close to Rome, the initiative of Siricius was followed. The North African Church had always been marked by a strong orientation toward Rome and was always careful to bring her discipline into conformity with that of the Roman Church. Nevertheless she was a self-confident and in many respects independent Church; recall the divergent views of Rome and Carthage in the debate about rebaptizing heretics. Here Carthage dissented, because it felt more strongly bound to its own tradition than to Rome.

In this respect it is difficult to believe that North Africa would have introduced new laws at the intervention of Siricius. Such an attempt would necessarily have set off at least a controversial debate. But all the bishops at the Council of Carthage speak explicitly about the ob-

---

[27] In particular: "Omnibus placet, ut episcopi, presbyteri et diaconi vel qui sacramenta contrectant, pudicitiae custodes etiam ab uxoribus se abstineant, ut in omnibus et ab omnibus pudicitia custodiatur, qui altari deserviunt" (E. Reichert, *Die Canones der Synode von Elvira: Einleitung und Kommentar* [diss., Hamburg, 1990], 139).

[28] As in Elvira, the explicative *vel* appears twice.

servance of continence "from time immemorial". They could scarcely make that claim unless this ancient tradition had been known in their churches. It is also perfectly clear to the bishops that they are dealing with a thoroughly uniform discipline: continence is obligatory "by reason of holy orders", regardless of whether a man is married or not.[29] If, however, the duty to observe continence derives from ordination, then it cannot be an innovation, since ordination has always been part of the faith.

Certainly there was a need to inculcate this continence discipline anew. A fresh start was needed so that "we, too", that is, the present generation, too, would keep continence. The Council of 345–348 that preceded the Council of 390 had already reminded the clergy of this duty, and the later Council of Carthage did so once again. But it seems that all the fine words did not help. More rigorous measures had to be taken. Until this point they had tried to make do without penalties. But eleven years later the time was finally ripe for sanctions. Perhaps another factor was that meanwhile more and more Donatist clerics were changing over to the Catholic Church and new problems were arising. The bishops gathered on the thirteenth of September, 401, in Carthage and passed the following resolution.

> Furthermore: even if it is reported of some clerics that they do not live continently with their wives, nevertheless the bishops, priests, and deacons, according to the earlier statutes, still must refrain from relations with their wives. If they do not, they are to be removed from ecclesiastical office. The other [that is, lower] clerics, though, are not compelled to do this, but each should observe the respective custom.[30]

Naturally the marriage prohibition, too, applied to higher clerics, as was discussed at a further synod in Carthage in the year 397. The concern here was with children who had said that they wished to become clerics. According to this canon, anyone admitted to the lower clergy as a child, who had then ascended to the order of lector, had to decide upon reaching the age of puberty either to marry or else to

---

[29] C. Cochini, *Apostolic Origins of Priestly Celibacy* (San Francisco, 1990), 6.

[30] Council of Carthage a. 401, canon 3 (CCL 149, 356, 21–26): "Praeterea cum de quorumdam clericorum quamuis erga uxores proprias incontinentia referretur, placuit episcopos, presbyteros et diaconos secundum priora statuta etiam ab uxoribus continere. Quod nisi fecerint ab ecclesiastico remoueantur officio. Ceteros autem clericos ad hoc non cogi, sed secundum uniuscuiusque consuetudinem obseruari debere."

remain celibate.[31] In this way enough time remained until the age of ordination to examine the uprightness of the candidate and his ability to observe continence. If even lower clerics at a certain age had to decide either for or against married life, then undoubtedly marriage was no longer permitted for higher clerics.[32]

There is a further point of interest in relation to the Council of 397. It speaks quite openly about children of the higher clergy (canons 12, 14, and 17), even though the clergy had been strictly obliged to practice continence since the previous synod at the very latest. This demonstrates how erroneous it would be to conclude, from the existence of children of clerics, that there was no continence celibacy. The children in question were in fact begotten before ordination.

If there was a crisis about continence among the clergy in Africa, that was not due to an indifferent or a negative attitude of those in the ministry. It was due, rather, to the overall crisis in the Church, caused by the Donatist schism. The general disruption affected the continence discipline as well—but it was neither forgotten nor ended, nonetheless. And so it was very quickly restored just as soon as ecclesiastical life had recovered. When Jerome in the year 406 declared that the married clergy throughout the West and the East practiced continence, he named Egypt and Rome *pars pro toto*. He could just as easily have mentioned Africa, too. This is proved by the way in which Augustine, writing around 420, takes for granted the continence of married clergymen, who were often recruited to the ministry against their will:

> Hence, when we inspire these [married!] men, for whom the superiority of their sex means the freedom to sin, with the fear of eternal ruin if they contract adulterous marriages, we usually present to them as an example the continence of these clerics who were frequently forced against their wills to carry such a burden. Nevertheless, once they have accepted it, with the Lord's help they carry it faithfully to their destination. Thus we tell these men: What if the violence of a pious people were to compel you [to assume this same burden]? Would you not chastely fulfill the duty imposed upon you? Would you not turn immediately to God to ask him for a strength that you had never thought of before? But, they say,

---

[31] Ibid., a. 397, canon 18 (CCL 149, 333, 133f.). R. Cholij, *Clerical Celibacy in East and West* (Herefordshire, 1989), 55f.

[32] P.-H. Lafontaine, *Les Conditions positives de l'accession aux ordres dans la première legislation ecclésiastique (300–492)* (Ottawa, 1963), 174f.

honor is a handsome consolation for those clerics! We reply, fear ought to rein you in even more effectively. Indeed, if many of the Lord's ministers accepted the yoke suddenly and unexpectedly imposed on them, in the hope of receiving a more glorious place in Christ's inheritance, how much more should you guard against adultery and embrace continence, for fear, not of shining less in the kingdom of God, but of burning in the fires of Gehenna! This we say and similar things, as we are able, to those men who, when their wives have left them or have been dismissed because of adultery, would like to marry other women at any cost.[33]

The word "frequently" in the first sentence does not mean that continence was optional, as though it did not oblige all married clerics; it refers, rather, to the fact that married candidates were frequently selected against their will. Similarly, the statement that "many of the Lord's ministers" took up the burden of marital continence that had been suddenly and unexpectedly imposed on them does not imply that there were others who did not practice continence. It emphasizes instead that many clerics assumed this burden *suddenly* and *unexpectedly*. The contrast is with others who had been trained over a longer time for their ministry and the duties connected with it.

b. *The Reform Movement in Spain Includes Clerical Continence*

In Spain, the first time after Elvira that we hear again about clerical continence is around the year 380. History is silent about the intervening eighty years. At any rate, canon 33 of Elvira proves that continence celibacy cannot be the invention of the late fourth century. It was known already in the time before Constantine. Furthermore, the idea of introducing obligatory continence would scarcely have occurred to the authorities in Spain, at the farthest limit of the universal Church at that time, if it had not been known already in other ecclesiastical territories. At the Council of Elvira, Bishop Hosius (Ossius) of Córdoba in southern Spain was present also; later, as the trusted advisor of the emperor Constantine, he sojourned for many years in the East and played an important part in the Council of Nicaea. He has always been suspected of being the one who—according to the

---

[33] Augustine, *Adulterinis coniugiis* 2, 20, 22 (CSEL 41, 409, 9–410, 3). [The quotation was translated into English from the German version of J. Schmid, *Aurelius Augustinus: Die ehebrecherischen Verbindungen: Zwei Bücher an Pollentius* (Würzburg, 1949), 72f., with reference to the English version in Cochini, *Origins*, 289–91; cf. the discussion there.]

Paphnutius legend—at Nicaea demanded that married clerics observe continence. It is more likely, though, that he became acquainted with the continence discipline of the East and then, after his return to his Spanish homeland, promoted clerical continence even more resolutely until his death around 357–358.[34]

The situation in the Spanish Church during the course of the fourth century can be compared to a certain extent with North Africa. The entire Church was involved in a crisis, a major cause of which was the dissension resulting from the disputes with Arianism.[35] A schism developed here, too, as a consequence. In this instance it was the followers of a wealthy, aristocratic layman named Priscillian. The British historian Henry Chadwick was the first to examine the connection between the influence of his ideas and his further career upon the Spanish Church and the discipline of clerical continence.[36] Priscillianism was a reform movement within the Church that got under way in the second half of the fourth century. The reformers wanted to remedy the crisis with a new austerity and seriousness. Therefore they committed themselves to chastity at the time of their baptism.[37] The clergy, too, recognized the need for spiritual renewal.[38] Thus the Priscillians were able to bring quite a number of ascetically minded bishops and priests over to their side. Priscillian himself was consecrated the bishop of Avila. He and the bishops Instantius and Salvianus were married and undoubtedly lived in marital continence.[39]

The strict notions of the Priscillians missed the mark, however, and polarized the clergy into opponents and proponents of the reform. A division in the clergy, always a cause for alarm, is in the final analysis unacceptable. After a while there was no stopping the resistance of a few bishops. The situation quickly came to a head.[40] Bishop Hydatius of Emerita, metropolitan of Lusitania and the chief opponent

---

[34] See the biography in J. Ulrich, *Die Anfänge der Abendländischen Rezeption des Nizänums*, PTS 39 (Berlin and New York, 1994), 111–35.

[35] H. Chadwick, *Priscillian of Avila: The Occult and the Charismatic in the Early Church* (Oxford, 1976), 5–7.

[36] Ibid., 29–31; D. Callam, "Clerical Continence in the Fourth Century: Three Papal Decretals", TS 41 (1980): 16–24.

[37] Cf. Priscillian, *Canones in Pauli epistulas* 33 (CSEL 18, 124, 8–12).

[38] Cf. ibid., 45 (CSEL 18, 129, 1–4); Council of Saragossa, canon 6.

[39] W. Schatz, *Studien zur Geschichte und Vorstellungswelt des frühen abendländischen Mönchtums* (diss., Freiburg, 1957), 122.

[40] For the following developments, see Pietri, *Roma*, 1:754–63.

of Priscillian, sent an inquiry to Pope Damasus, who may have been
of Spanish descent himself. With that, Rome was involved. As things
developed, on October 4, 380, in Saragossa, not far from Tarragona,
a council was held—the first to deal with the new movement. Many
of the Spanish and Aquitanian bishops in attendance sympathized with
Priscillian. Only a minority repudiated him. The Spanish clergy, in
any case, accepted the ascetical ideals in a manner that would remain
uncontested, even at the anti-Priscillianist Council of Toledo (in the
year 400).

Nevertheless the crisis intensified. Now the pressure was on Hydatius. The Priscillianists brought action against him, and he found
himself forced by a faction within his ascetically minded diocesan clergy
either to clarify the accusations that had been raised about him or else
to give up his episcopal see. It is not known specifically what he was
accused of. Chadwick suspects that Hydatius got into difficulty when
he returned from Saragossa to his diocese and learned there that his
wife was pregnant. That was insupportable for a bishop, and it must
have played into the hands of the reformers. If Chadwick's suspicion
is correct, then the Priscillianists were strict adherents to the later
celibacy policy of Siricius. Hydatius was still able to get his head out
of the noose. He charged Priscillian with Manichaeism. Rome stepped
in later. Finally Priscillian traveled around 381/382 to Italy, intending,
on the spot, to win over the most important men in the Italian Church,
Damasus and Ambrose, to his side. They probably kept their distance
and left further decisions to the Spanish episcopacy. Thereupon Priscillian defended himself in a detailed letter to the Pope against the accusations that, from his perspective, were unjustified (*Liber ad Damasum*).

This situation was the backdrop against which we now must view
the further developments pertaining to clerical discipline. Sometime
around 380 Bishop Himerius of Tarragona in northeast Spain wrote a
detailed letter to Pope Damasus in Rome. In it he asked how to deal
with clerics who did not observe continence. Damasus was not able to
answer the letter before his death in the year 384. But the matter did
not rest for long. His successor to the See of Peter, Siricius, seized the
opportunity and discussed it with his entire *presbyterium*, that is, with
his priests and deacons.[41] Thereupon he sent a long letter to Himerius
on February 10, 385, in which he answered all of the bishop's inquiries.

---

[41] Ibid., 671.

This famous decretal, named after its first word, *Directa*, is a milestone in the history of celibacy. Besides various other themes it concerns monastic and clerical discipline. From it we can draw several inferences as to the general conditions in Spain at the time:

7. Furthermore, you [Himerius] state that there are monks and nuns who have cast aside their resolution to be holy and are sunk so deep in licentiousness that after first meeting stealthily under cover of the monasteries in illicit and sacrilegious passion, they have then . . . begotten children freely in these illicit relations, a thing condemned both by civil law and by the rules of the Church. We direct you to expel these shameless and abominable persons from the company of the monasteries and the congregations of the churches. Should they, however, withdraw to their cells and mourn their terrible crime with constant lamentation, they can attain, through the purifying fire of repentance, forgiveness at the moment of death, out of pure compassion, by the grace of communion.

8. Let us now proceed to the most holy orders of the clergy, who, we learn upon your information, beloved, are so oppressed and demoralized throughout your provinces, to the injury of our venerable religion, that in the words of Jeremiah we might say: "Who will give water to my head or a fountain of tears to my eyes? And I will weep day and night for this people" (Jer 9:1). If the blessed prophet says that his tears cannot suffice to bewail the sins of the people, how great must be the grief that smites us when we are forced to deplore the crimes of those who are a part of our body, especially since, as blessed Paul says, to us belong the daily supervision and unceasing care of all the churches! "For who is weak and I am not weak? Who is made to fall and I am not indignant?" (2 Cor 11:29). For we are told that many priests and Levites [= deacons] of Christ, after long years of consecration, have begotten offspring with their own wives as well as in disgraceful adultery and that they are defending their sin on the ground that we read in the Old Testament that priests and ministers [= Levites] were allowed the privilege of begetting children.

9. Now let any man who is addicted to lust and inculcates vice explain to me why, if he thinks that in the law of Moses the Lord relaxed occasionally the reins on loose living for the priestly orders, the Lord also instructed those to whom he was committing the holy of holies, saying: "Be ye holy, even as I, your Lord God, am holy" (Lev 11:44; 20:7). Why were the priests bidden to take up their dwelling in the Temple, far from their homes, during their year of service? Why but for the purpose that they might have no carnal intercourse even with their wives but in the radiance of an upright conscience offer an acceptable gift unto God? When their time of service was fulfilled, they were permitted association

with their wives but solely for the sake of progeny, because it had been commanded that no man from any tribe but that of Levi should be allowed in the ministry of God.

10. Now the Lord Jesus, when he illumined us by his appearing, declared in the gospel that he had come to fulfill the law, not to destroy it. And so he desired that the visage of the Church, whose bridegroom he is, should shine with the splendor of chastity, so that in the day of judgment, when he comes again, he might find her without spot or blemish, as he taught by his apostle (Eph 5:27). Hence all we priests and Levites [= deacons] are bound by the unbreakable law of these instructions to devote our hearts and bodies (to God) in sobriety and chastity from the day of our ordination, that we may be wholly pleasing to our God in the sacrifices we offer daily. "Those who are in the flesh", says the vessel of election, "cannot please God. But you are not in the flesh, you are in the Spirit, if the Spirit of God really dwells in you" (Rom 8:8f.). And where but in holy bodies, as we read, can the Spirit of God have a dwelling place?

11. Inasmuch as some of the men of whom we speak protest sorrowfully, as your holiness reports, that they fell in ignorance, we direct you not to refuse them mercy, on condition that they remain as long as they live, without any advancement in honor, in the office in which their guilt was detected, provided, however, that they undertake to live in continence hereafter. As for those who unwarrantably rely upon the excuse of the privilege that they maintain was granted them by the Old Law, let them understand that they are deposed by the authority of the Apostolic See from every ecclesiastical position that they have abused and that never again may they handle the venerable mysteries [that is, the Eucharist], of which they deprived themselves by clinging to their obscene passions. And inasmuch as present warnings teach us to be on our guard in the future, if any bishop, priest, or deacon is hereafter discovered in such crime, as we hope will not happen, let him now and at once understand that every way to leniency through us is barred. For wounds that do not heal by the application of compresses must be cut out by the knife.

12. We learn, furthermore, that men of untrammeled and unknown lives, who have had many wives, are aspiring to the aforesaid offices in the Church, just as they fancy. For this we do not blame so much those who obtain these positions through immoderate ambition as the metropolitan bishops in particular, who close their eyes and ears and despise the commandments of our God, to the extent that the responsibility is theirs. We pass in silence over our deeper suspicions, but where is that ordinance of our God, established when he gave the law through Moses, saying: "My priests shall marry only once"? And in another place: "A priest shall take

to wife a virgin, not a widow, or one divorced woman, or a harlot" (cf. Lev 21:13f.; Ezek 44:22). Accordingly, the apostle who changed from persecutor to preacher charged both the priest and the deacon that they should be the husbands of one wife (1 Tim 3:2). But all these precepts are scorned by the bishops of your districts, as if they rather meant the opposite. Now we must not overlook transgressions of this kind, lest we be smitten by the just voice of the indignant Lord, saying, "You saw a thief and went with him and kept company with adulterers" (Ps 50[49]:18). Therefore we here by general announcement decree what must hence-forth be observed by all the churches and what must be avoided.[42]

The definitive, unmistakable decision reads as follows: "All we priests and deacons are bound by the unbreakable law of these instruc-tions to devote our hearts and bodies to God in sobriety and chastity from the day of our ordination." That is exactly what Himerius wanted to hear; in this decision he saw a vote of confidence for his own po-sition. The fact that he had recourse to Pope Damasus is interesting in and of itself. An appeal is made from Spain to Rome as to a higher authority, which once again consolidates the supremacy of the latter over the Latin Church. But, on the other hand, the call for help from Rome is not that surprising, considering that the sagacious actions of Damasus in the Priscillian affair had strengthened the bonds between the Spanish episcopacy and Rome.[43] Damasus was very well acquainted with the situation in Spain. As he viewed it, the inquiry of Himerius had to be decided against the background of the Priscillianist trou-bles, even though Priscillian himself is not mentioned in the decretal *Directa*.[44] At the time when this document was written, the conflict between the opponents and the proponents of the reform was at its height. Still, Saragossa, the location of the council, belonged to the ec-clesiastical province of the archdiocese of Tarragona. Himerius would even be numbered among those who adopted the ascetical ideals of Priscillian.[45]

Obviously the condition of the Church in Spain was so muddled that Himerius could hope for clarification only from Rome. It was openly

---

[42] Siricius, *Epistula* 1, 6, 7–8, 12 *ad Himerium* (PL 13, 1137B–1142A). [English version based on the translation in *The See of Peter*, ed. James T. Shotwell and Louise Ropes Loomis (New York: Columbia University Press, 1991), 702–5.

[43] Pietri, *Roma*, 1:763.

[44] Ibid., 2:1046–49.

[45] Callam, "Continence", 25.

admitted that the Spanish clergy were prostrate and that irremediable disorder prevailed. Concretely, the situation was as follows: Married clerics begot children with their wives or else committed adultery, digamists applied for admission to clerical orders and were ordained, many clerics were married to widows or to women of dubious reputation. Himerius describes the unflattering situation quite candidly for the Pope. We deliberately cited above the first passage as well, which concerned the abuses in monastic life. Here, too, observance of the rule was being trampled underfoot. They were dealing in actuality with a general crisis in the Church, which was not limited to the clergy. The description by Himerius just goes to show that the Priscillianists were right in calling for renewed stringency and asceticism.

But then why did Priscillian not figure in the correspondence between Himerius and Rome? Why was he not mentioned? This is not surprising, since even the Council of Saragossa condemned a series of Priscillianist practices without naming names. Probably it was prudent ecclesiastical policy. Then too, it was those very abuses decried by the reform bishops that prompted Himerius to turn to Rome. But their good intentions meanwhile had been disastrously complicated by the dispute about Priscillian. On the one hand, the positive concern of the reformers needed to be addressed and the abuses in the clergy had to be done away with. On the other hand, a sharp division was appearing in the Church between opponents and adherents of Priscillian. Hence it was better to leave him out of the picture, so as not to endanger the cause of reform.

Even Pope Damasus and Ambrose, the bishop of Milan, whom Priscillian tried to win over during his visit to Italy, no doubt were glad to see the effects of his reform movement upon the clergy, but otherwise they remained aloof. Thus Himerius had the right strategy in turning to Damasus. He would never have done that if he had not known that Rome was on his side in matters of clerical continence. Of course the death of Damasus intervened; his secretary Jerome went to Bethlehem. So it was up to Siricius to reply to the call for help from Spain. He, too, made every effort in his decretal, which was issued in the same year in which Priscillian was condemned, not to establish any connection between clerical continence and Priscillian.

On the other hand, since the adherents of the reform were increasing in number, Siricius made use of the favorable time and supported their requests. He wanted to avoid the impression that Catholics willing to reform were to be found only among the schismatics. In much the same way as it happened during the North African dispute with the Donatists, it was true in this case, too: in order to counter successfully the overly stringent morality of the schismatics and reform the Church, one had to surpass them in holiness and in giving good example. That explains the severity with which Siricius pleaded for clerical continence and held the Spanish bishops responsible for its observance. Himerius and Siricius were not isolated figures fighting against the rest of the world. The Spanish clergy as a whole had become more sensitive about asceticism since the appearance of Priscillian. Part of this was an appreciation for celibacy and continence. The theological arguments of Priscillian in this regard may well have been absolutely orthodox and perhaps were essentially no different from the discussions of Jerome.[46] All in all, therefore, the Spanish clergy reform proceeded from the local clergy itself.

If Elvira is taken seriously, then obligatory continence had already existed for a long time. We can look at this, and at the worsening abuses in the Spanish monasteries that Siricius speaks about, in the same way. No one would claim that monastic observance was first introduced there as a result of his decretal. Analogously, great confusion prevailed among the clerics, too. But it is confusion with respect to a discipline that was valid in and of itself. The movement surrounding Priscillian had the effect of reminding the clergy of their tradition. A shock went through the clergy that released new energies for reform. Priscillian was no more responsible for inventing obligatory continence than Himerius was. Of course, that would go nicely with the cliché, since Priscillian was accused even then of Manichaeism, and he used to have Encratite apocryphal works read alongside the canonical Scriptures. One could then portray the Spanish celibacy movement as the product of heretical influences contemptuous of the body. But the source material does not allow us to reproach Priscillian with a contemptuous attitude toward the body. Henry Chadwick, especially, has undertaken to rehabilitate him. If clerical continence had really been the accomplishment of Priscillian himself, then by condemning him in the year 385 the Church would also have swept aside that clerical discipline. She would then have been hopelessly compromised.

---

[46] Cf. ibid., 22f.

Himerius decries not only the fact that clerics are having children but also that digamists are being ordained as well as those whose wives are remarried or have a dubious reputation. Those are points that also play a role in the Eastern celibacy discipline. This shows an agreement between East and West that can only be interpreted in one way: For Spain, too, the clerical discipline was an institution that was already established and clearly defined, the individual regulations of which were ordered to continence. Incidentally, it is not necessarily the case that the digamy prohibition actually was disregarded in Spain; perhaps they merely followed the more liberal practice, whereby baptism eradicated the impediment to orders of digamy. Evidence of this is found in the Gallic Council of Valence in the year 374, which categorically rejects the ordination of digamists, regardless of the date of baptism or marriage; apparently a contrary practice had crept in there.[47]

Himerius, too, assumed that absolutely everyone ought to be acquainted with this discipline. And yet he knew that many a cleric was not practicing continence because he had not been informed about the duties of his state in life. Obligatory continence had not been canonically established everywhere. In many localities it was customary law. And in distant Spain there were districts in which many were still completely ignorant of the discipline that was in force.[48] Himerius explicitly refers to such cases. Later on, too, there was still a need for enlightenment. The decretal of Siricius, according to his wishes, was published throughout Spain and put into effect,[49] as the Council of Toledo in Central Spain (in the year 400) demonstrates.

But even this Council still speaks of clerics who knew nothing about a continence requirement.

> We command that the deacons be either virginal or chaste and that those who practice continence, even if they have wives, be established in the ministry; provided, however, that those [that is, deacons] who, before the interdict was pronounced by the Lusitanian bishops, lived with their wives incontinently, shall not be clothed with the honor of the priest-

---

[47] Canon I (CCL 148, 38, 20–24): "Sedit igitur, neminem post hanc synodum, qua eiusmodi illicitis uel sero succurritur, digamos aut internuptarum maritos ordinari clericos posse; nec requirendum utrumne initiati sacramentis diuinis, anne gentiles, hac se infelicis sortis necessitate macularint, cum diuini praecepti certa sit forma."

[48] See also Siricius, *Epistula* I, 15, 19 *ad Himerium* (PL 13, 1145A).

[49] *Epistula* I, 15, 20 *ad Himerium* (PL 13, 1146A).

hood. If in fact one of the priests begot children before the interdict, let him not be admitted to the episcopate.[50]

From this first canon of Toledo we can reconstruct the following situation: The bishops of Spain had meanwhile become acquainted with a canonical continence rule for their region, and they supported it. It was introduced there with difficulty at first. Transgressions, to all appearances, were punished with removal from office, as the decretal *Directa* provided. There was of course a *terminus ad quem* regulation, which probably originated from the president of the Council, the Lusitanian metropolitan Petruinus. Accordingly, any married deacon or priest who begot children before the interdict of the Lusitanian bishops was not to be deposed; he could remain in the ministry, but he would not be promoted to any higher order. This regulation, too, corresponded to the decretal *Directa*. Evidently, quite some time before Toledo, a provincial council in Lusitania (between 385 and 400) adopted the directives of Siricius. This gave the bishops assembled in Toledo the opportunity to enact now a more rigorous version of the continence requirement.

2. Conditions in Italy under Pope Damasus

The Spanish crisis cannot have been without consequences in Rome. Through the inquiries of the bishops Hydatius and Himerius it was drawn into the situation there, and it had to attend to the conditions in Spain. As far as clerical continence is concerned, Siricius was not the first to give it much thought. Even from the time of his predecessor Damasus, two detailed position papers on this subject are extant. We are dealing here with the earliest Roman texts on clerical continence since Hippolytus. In them can be discerned a connection with the events in Spain.

---

[50] Canon 1 (20 Vives): "Placuit, ut diacones vel integri vel casti sint et continentes vitae, etiam si uxores habeant, in ministerio constituantur, ita tamen ut si qui etiam ante interdictum, quod per Lusitanos episcopos constitutum est, incontinenter cum uxoribus suis vixerint, presbyteri[i] honore non comulentur. Si quis vero ex presbyteris ante interdictum filios susceperit, de presbyterio ad episcopatum non admittatur."

a. *Ambrosiaster Testifies to the Acknowledgment of Clerical Continence*

Damasus, from 366 to 384 the pope in Rome, could very well have been a strong supporter of clerical continence, just like his temporary secretary Jerome (from 382 to 384). The latter praised the Pope as "the virginal teacher of the virginal Church" and as "the friend of chastity and the herald of modesty".[51] At any rate, no opinion of Damasus himself with respect to clerical continence has been preserved. The decretal *Dominus inter*, which has been ascribed to him, presumably dates from the time of his successors, Siricius or Innocent.[52]

Be that as it may, living during the reign of Damasus in Rome there was a writer from whose pen we have two votes in favor of clerical continence. Who this writer was, we do not know. He is usually called Ambrosiaster. Presumably he belonged, together with Jerome, to the Roman presbyterium [priestly rank of the clergy]. In any case he would scarcely have written without the Pope's knowledge. Since it is quite probable that both texts reflect the Spanish crisis, they must have been written between the letter of Himerius and the death of Damasus, that is, sometime between 380 and 384.[53] That is precisely the time when Jerome was secretary. First the excerpt from the commentary on the Letter of Paul to Timothy:

> "Let deacons be the husband of one wife, and let them manage their children and their households well; for those who serve well as deacons gain a good standing for themselves and also great confidence in the faith which is in Christ Jesus" (1 Tim 3:12–13). He [Paul] elaborates now on what he had said before with regard to the ordination of deacons. He shows that deacons must also be husbands of one wife [that is, married once], so that only those may be chosen for the service of God who did

---

[51] Jerome, *Epistula* 49, 18, 2, 3 *ad Pammachium* (CSEL 54, 382, 6, 9).

[52] Pietri, *Roma*, 1:764–72, refers it to Damasus. This is contradicted by the author's statement that he has already addressed numerous letters about clerical continence to the various churches. That would be more in keeping with Siricius or Innocent. Furthermore, Siricius, in his reply to the inquiry of Himerius to Damasus (*Directa*), would certainly have referred to the decretal of his predecessor. Callam, "Continence", 36, declares himself definitively in favor of Siricius. R. Gryson, "Dix ans de recherches sur les origines du célibat ecclésiastique: Réflexion sur les publications des années 1970–1979", RTL 11 (1980): 165–67, is more cautious and leaves the question open, while excluding the possibility of authorship by Damasus.

[53] Several indications favor composition of the *Quaestiones* in the year 382; A. Souter, *The Earliest Latin Commentaries of the Epistles of St. Paul* (Oxford, 1927), 42.

not go beyond the limits set by God. Indeed, God intended for man only one woman with whom he would be blessed; no one with a second wife receives the blessing.

If they have raised their children properly and taken good care of their households, that is, have proved themselves in private and public life, they can be deemed worthy of the priesthood and have assurance in the presence of God; let them know that they will obtain what they ask if they abstain henceforth from conjugal relations with their wives. In the old days, indeed, Levites or priests were allowed to have relations with their spouses because they did not devote much time to their ministry or priestly duties. There were a multitude of priests and an abundance of Levites, and each one of them would ensure the fulfillment of the divine ceremonies at a given period of time, according to the ordinance of David (1 Chron 6:31–32), who instituted twenty-four classes of priests each doing their duty in turn. . . . Consequently, during the periods when they did not have to serve at the altar, they took care of their households. But when the time of their ministry came, they purified themselves for several days, then went to the Temple to sacrifice to the Lord. Now there should be seven deacons, several priests—two per church—and just one bishop for each city; this is why they must abstain from any conjugal intercourse: they have to be present in church every day, and they do not have the necessary time to purify themselves after conjugal union, as the priests of old used to do. They have to offer the sacrifice every week, and even if the liturgy is not offered every day in foreign lands [*peregrinis in locis*], it is at least twice a week for the local population. And furthermore, there is no lack of sick people to baptize nearly every day. Marital relations were permitted to the ancients because much of their time was not spent in the Temple and they had a private life. If he [Paul] orders laymen to abstain temporarily [from marital relations] in order to attend to prayer, how much more is it incumbent on Levites [= deacons] and priests, who must pray day and night for the people entrusted to them! Therefore they have to be purer than the others, for they are the representatives of God [*actores Dei sunt*].[54]

Here it says that no deacon may be living in a second marriage. Besides that, the bishop, the priest, and the deacon must avoid all sexual intercourse with their wives. There we have the complete celibacy discipline. Only the marriage prohibition is not spelled out. We should realize that we are not dealing here with a papal or synodal docu-

---

[54] Ambrosiaster, *Comm. in 1 Tim.* 3, 12f. (CSEL 81, 3 268, 17–270, 2). Cochini, *Origins*, 222–24.

ment intended to enjoin clerical continence authoritatively. This is, rather, a sober and completely unpretentious commentary on First Timothy, which says: Married clerics and their wives practice continence, whereby deacons, priests, and bishops are subject to the same discipline.[55] The author leaves no doubt about this, and his viewpoint presupposes that the reader is in agreement. There is no indication that he is countering critics of celibacy or that obligatory continence has yet to be propagated.

The second celibacy text by Ambrosiaster will be discussed farther on in the chapter about Manichaeism. Let it be mentioned here that it is evident from this text, too, that clerical continence is an established fact of life in Rome. Furthermore, Ambrosiaster is unaware of any place where the matter is officially handled in a way any different from the discipline in Rome.

Nevertheless one could say that the fact that during the pontificate of Damasus there were two detailed position papers on the subject of clerical continence indicates that there were doubts about its legitimacy. What, then, concretely was the occasion for Ambrosiaster's discourses? He reinforced the continence discipline theologically in two directions: against those who rejected it while referring to the Old Testament and against those who saw in it a Manichaean connection. Then there were, after all, opponents of clerical continence? In a certain sense, yes; but probably fewer of them in Rome than in Spain. Rome, though, considered itself obliged to respond to the questions raised in Spain with a theological treatment of the subject.

b. The Opponents of Clerical Continence in Spain Are Not Convincing

With peace of mind and complete confidence Ambrosiaster declares himself in favor of clerical continence. In Rome he seems to have no opponents. That does not mean, however, that Ambrosiaster is writing without polemics. They are concealed behind the cool, dogmatic presentation of the theologian. Ambrosiaster does not mean to establish an ecclesiastical policy of obligatory continence; that is the province of popes and bishops. His ambitions are purely theological. He emphatically distinguishes the perfect continence of the Christian priesthood from the merely periodic continence of the Old Testament priests.

---

[55] *Comm. in* 1 *Tim.* 3, 10 (CSEL 81, 3 267, 10–27).

The married priest of the Old Covenant was allowed to beget children because he was not constantly ministering to the Lord; the Church's clerics are not allowed to do so, because they must be ready day and night to perform their religious duties.

This topic was being discussed at that time in Spain. There we hear, for the first time in the history of the Church, of outspoken opponents to continence celibacy. Himerius complained bitterly about them. These opponents of celibacy were married clerics who—presumably in reaction to the Priscillianist reformers—refused to practice permanent continence and continued to beget children. Since this went against the discipline, they were challenged, and to justify themselves they cited the Old Testament,[56] which permitted married priests and Levites to beget children. Such a biblical-theological argument was by no means misguided. For a long time before that, theology had been comparing the Christian priestly ministry with the Old Testament priesthood: The deacons and perhaps even the priests were the Levites of the New Covenant.[57] Origen had anticipated this line of thought but also saw that such a comparison was problematic. For the Levites knew only a ritual, limited form of continence. Origen put the following spin on it: The Levites were allowed to beget children in the flesh, while the priests of the New Covenant were permitted only to beget children in faith (see above, pp. 96–97). The Spanish opponents of celibacy were not content with that. They did not see why they had to live more continently than their Old Testament predecessors.

It is surprising that Ambrosiaster took up the arguments of the Spanish opponents of celibacy. Presumably he was informed about them by Damasus. Perhaps he was the theological advisor of the Pope, albeit one whom Jerome did not tolerate very well.[58] In his commentary on the First Letter of Paul to Timothy, Ambrosiaster addresses the arguments of the Spanish opponents of celibacy without mentioning them explicitly. There is a reference to the conditions in Spain also in the remark that in foreign lands (*peregrinis in locis*) liturgies are infrequent.

---

[56] It is expressly a discussion about the Old Testament; G. Bickell, "Der Cölibat eine apostolische Anordnung", ZkTh 2 (1878): 34f.

[57] E.g., Clement of Rome, *Epistula ad Corinthios*, 1, 43f.; Hippolytus, *Traditio apostolica* 3 (FC 1, 216, 26–218, 4); Cyprian, *Epistulae* 1, 1 (CSEL 3, 2, 465, 18–466, 15); Origen, *Hom.* 12, 3 *in Ier.* 13:12–17 (GCS Orig. 3², 89, 21–24); *Hom.* 9, 5 *in Ies. Nav.* (GCS Orig. 7, 350, 26–351, 5).

[58] H. Vogels, "Ambrosiaster und Hieronymus", RBen 66 (1956): 14–19.

This does not mean the rural areas outside of Rome, as is usually assumed, but rather the distant regions of the Iberian peninsula.[59]

The Spanish priests, then, argued as follows: We (like the laymen) are prepared to observe continence on liturgical days; but since we do not celebrate the liturgy daily, we can engage in marital relations on the other days, just as the Levites used to do. The reference to the Old Testament Levites, therefore, originally came, not from Ambrosiaster at all, but from the Spanish opponents of celibacy, who meant to say: Back then under the Old Covenant, too, priests had to practice continence only "as long as they were serving at the altar"; and even Origen says as much. So we only have to practice continence when we celebrate the Eucharist. To circle only the Eucharistic days as continence days on the calendar of a cleric—such pettiness would surely have taken Origen's breath away.

Ambrose of Milan. In this connection let us consult Ambrose, too, another papal theologian, for advice. Ever since 374 Ambrose had been the [arch]bishop of the metropolis of Milan; the policies of which had an influence that extended to the Church throughout northern Italy. In his ecclesiastical province there was no doubt about it: all clerics, whether married or not, had to practice perfect continence.[60] Ambrose was in close contact with the popes. On the subject of clerical continence, too, he has to be considered one of their authoritative advisors. This is immediately evident when the following text is compared with the decretals of Siricius. The passage is taken from *De officiis ministrorum* (On the duties of clergymen), which Ambrose composed for his priests (datings vary between 377 and 391). In all likelihood the book presupposes to a large extent the conditions in Milan. The passage in question also speaks, however, about those priests "in a great many more distant places" (*in plerisque abditioribus locis*) who do not observe continence.

> But what shall I say about chastity, when only one and no second union is allowed? As regards marriage, the law is, not to marry again, nor to seek union with another wife. It seems strange to many why impediment

---

[59] The phrase *peregrini loci* refers unequivocally to foreign lands in Ambrose, *Bono mortis* 2, 7 (CSEL 32, 1, 707, 17f.), and Jerome, *Hebraicae quaestiones in libro Geneseos* 12, 15f. (CCL 72, 16, 22f.). Cf. *Epistola Romani concilii sub Damaso habiti ad Gratianum et Valentinianum imperatores* 9 (PL 13, 581A/B): "in longinquioribus partibus"; Ambrose, *Epistulae* 181, 1 (CSEL 44, 702, 11): "disiunctis remotisque provinciis".

[60] R. Gryson, *Le Prêtre selon saint Ambroise* (Louvain, 1968), 308.

should be caused by a second marriage entered on before baptism, so as
to prevent election to the clerical office, and to the reception of the gift
of ordination; seeing that even crimes are not wont to stand in the way,
if they have been put away in the sacrament of baptism. But we must
learn, that in baptism sin can be forgiven, but law cannot be abolished.
In the case of marriage there is no sin, but there is a law. Whatever sin
there is can be put away, whatever law there is cannot be laid aside in
marriage. How could he exhort to widowhood who himself had married
more than once?

But ye know that the ministerial office must be kept pure and unspotted, and must not be defiled by conjugal intercourse; ye know this, I say,
who have received the gifts of the sacred ministry, with pure bodies, and
unspoilt modesty, and without ever having enjoyed conjugal intercourse.
I am mentioning this, because in [a great many] out-of-the-way places,
when they enter on the ministry, or even when they become priests, they
have begotten children. They defend this on the ground of old custom,
when, as it happened, the sacrifice was offered up at long intervals. However, even the people had to be purified two or three days beforehand, so as
to come clean to the sacrifice, as we read in the Old Testament (Ex 19:10).
They even used to wash their clothes. If such regard was paid in what was
only the figure [that is, prefiguration], how much ought it to be shown in
the reality! Learn then, Priest and Levite, what it means to wash thy
clothes. Thou must have a pure body wherewith to offer up the sacraments. If the people were forbidden to approach their victim unless they
washed their clothes, dost thou, while foul in heart and body, dare to make
supplication for others? Dost thou dare to make an offering for them?[61]

---

[61] Ambrose, *De officiis ministrorum* I, 50, 247f. (PL 16², 104A–105A): "De castimonia tes-
timonia autem quid loquar, quando una tantum nec repetita permittitur copula? Et in ipso
ergo conjugio lex est non iterare conjugium, nec secundae conjugis sortiri conjunctionem.
Quod plerisque mirum videtur, cur etiam ante baptismum iterari conjugii ad electionem
muneris et ordinationis praerogativam impedimenta generentur; cum etiam delicta obesse
non soleant, si lavacri remissa fuerint sacramento. Sed intelligere debemus quia baptismo
culpa dimitti potest, lex aboleri non potest. In conjugio non culpa, sed lex est. Quod culpae
est igitur in baptismate relaxatur: quod legis est in conjugio non solvitur. Quomodo autem
potest hortator esse viduitatis qui ipse conjugia frequentaverit?

"Inoffensum autem exhibendum et immaculatum ministerium, nec ullo conjugali coitu
violandum cognoscitis, qui integri corpore, incorrupto pudore, alieni etiam ab ipso consortio conjugali, sacri ministerii gratiam recepistis? Quod eo non praeterii, quia in plerisque
abditioribus locis cum ministerium gererent, vel etiam sacerdotium, filios susceperunt: et
id tanquam usu veteri defendunt, quando per intervalla dierum sacrificium deferebatur; et
tamen castificabatur etiam populus per biduum aut triduum, ut ad sacrificium purus acced-
eret, ut in Veteri Testamento legimus; et lavabant vestimenta sua. Si in figura tanta observan-
tia quanta in veritate? Disce, sacerdos atque Levita, quid sit lavare vestimenta tua ut mundum
corpus celebrandis exhibeas sacramentis. Si populus sine ablutione vestimentorum suorum

Ambrose, too, speaks here about the Spanish opponents of celibacy. He mentions clerics in a great many "out-of-the-way places" (*plerisque abditioribus locis*). It has always been thought that this referred to rural clergymen of Milan who were still having children. That would mean that, even at the gates of Rome, all was not well with the celibacy discipline. Some read even more into Ambrose's remarks: Obligatory continence was being called into question in principle by his clergymen. For then it says that they wanted to defend their conduct "on the ground of old custom, when, as it happened, the sacrifice was offered up at long intervals". That has been understood as follows: As these clerics saw it, previously there had been no obligatory continence; the "old custom" was, rather, that even priests were still permitted to beget children. Finally, this hypothesis was joined with the Paphnutius legend, according to which continence was of a rather recent origin and until then clerics may well have practiced continence only on liturgical days.

If all this were correct, then we would have stalwart opponents of celibacy even in Italy. It might create the impression that a worldwide opposition to the celibacy initiatives of the popes was being announced. And furthermore one would have explicit proof of the fact that clerical celibacy in Italy was first introduced at the time of Ambrose. Nevertheless, we cannot agree with that hypothesis. When Ambrose writes that in keeping with "old custom" some priests had begotten children, then he does not mean the time before obligatory continence was introduced. What is meant, rather, is the time of the Old Testament.[62] This becomes even more clear from the similar formula in Ambrosiaster that was mentioned earlier. The opponents of celibacy were not saying at all that obligatory continence was an innovation and should

---

prohibeatur accedere ad hostiam suam, tu illotus mente pariter et corpore audes pro aliis supplicare, audes aliis ministrare?" [English translation by Rev. H. De Romestin et al., from *Nicene and Post-Nicene Fathers of the Christian Church*, second series, vol. 10, (reprint, Grand Rapids, Mich.: Wm. B. Eerdmans, 1969), 41.]

[62] Contrary to D. Callam, "The Frequency of Mass in the Latin Church ca. 400", TS 45 (1984): 637–40. Callam thinks that "the sacrifice was offered up at long intervals" cannot refer to the OT, since it does not correspond to any Old Testament cultic practice. But on this point he is mistaken (E. Schürer, *Geschichte des jüdischen Volkes im Zeitalter Jesu Christi*, vol. 2 [Leipzig, 1907], 336f.). On the other hand, it is unclear where *Directa* and *Dominus inter* got their idea of a yearly rota for the Levites. Besides, the intervals of several days are probably mentioned by Ambrose in relation to "the people" who brought their sacrificial offerings. Thus the "old custom" means, in any case, the Old Testament.

therefore be rejected. They appealed, rather, to the ritual continence of the Old Testament Levites and were only willing to practice the periodic continence of the laity ("even the people").

The fact that the clergymen of Milan had no problems with a continence discipline is indicated by Ambrose when he reminds them, to be sure, of their duty to keep their ministry unspotted, but adds, "I am mentioning this, because in a great many out-of-the-way places. . . ." Notice how he apologizes for broaching this subject at all. It is only the incidents in foreign lands that prompt him to do so. Thus Ambrose has in view the same opponents of celibacy with whom Himerius had already come into conflict. The parallels between Ambrose and Ambrosiaster are interesting, too, inasmuch as both of them saw in monogamy a divine law. Both writers dealt with those married clerics who begot children while appealing to the example of the Levites. Ambrose and Ambrosiaster seem to be disputing with the same people, no doubt with the opponents of celibacy in Spain.

Both are concerned, not with the Spanish priests themselves, but with their arguments. Ambrose stayed in close contact with Siricius. When the latter was occupied with the inquiry from Himerius, he most likely exchanged views with Ambrose, too, about clerical continence and about those priests in Spain who justified their critique on the basis of the Old Testament. If Ambrose, in his handbook for the clergy, De officiis, spends a few lines on the duty to observe continence, then it certainly does not imply that he was forced to address the issue by some concrete incident in his metropolitan province. Ambrose merely intended to remind his readers of this duty, which existed, after all, and which could not simply be passed over in silence.[63]

Sometimes the opinion is advanced that Rome had brought the Old Testament Levites into the discussion in order to justify a continence discipline for clerics. As a result, Old Testament notions of ritual purity made their way into the theology of holy orders. However, the argument for clerical continence based on the Old Testament Levitical practices in Ambrose and probably earlier in Ambrosiaster was a reaction to the critics of celibacy.[64] They were the ones who brought up the business about the Old Testament. Ambrose and Ambrosiaster

---

[63] Lafontaine, Conditions, 214.
[64] Cochini, Origins, 236.

adapted themselves to their arguments: It was quite true that one should be continent for the liturgy, but the liturgy included not only the Eucharist but also prayers and baptisms; the cleric, therefore, had to be prepared at all times.

c. Is Daily Celebration the Origin of Clerical Continence?

Scholarship was quick to note that both Ambrosiaster and Siricius mention, as a reason for clerical continence, the daily liturgy. The priest, in contrast with the Old Testament Levite, had to practice perfect continence because he had to be ready every day to celebrate the liturgy. Hence it has been thought that a celibacy discipline was introduced for the first time toward the end of the fourth century in Rome or Milan, when the custom started there of celebrating the Eucharist daily. According to this view, continence for married clerics was limited at first to liturgical days and only gradually developed into a discipline of perfect continence.[65] In contrast, the Eastern Church retained the practice of celebrating Mass sporadically and thus also the discipline of merely periodic continence.

After this thesis there ought to be a big question mark. For one thing, all attempts to find documentary evidence for a merely periodic continence of married clerics and their wives in the first centuries have failed. Rather, it is very likely, both for the East and the West, with greater certainty in the East, that there was a duty to observe perpetual continence and that it existed even before the fourth century, thus at a time before anyone had thought of celebrating daily. Furthermore, the practice of celebrating Mass daily is indeed attested to in the East, namely, by Eusebius of Caesarea, Cyril of Alexandria, and John Chrysostom. That is the same group of bishops who were also acquainted with a clerical continence discipline.[66] Thus the argument

---

[65] H. Böhmer, "Die Entstehung des Zölibates", in *Geschichtliche Studien Albert Hauck zum 70. Geburtstag* (Leipzig, 1916), 11–14; R. Gryson, *Les Origines du célibat ecclésiastique du premier au septième siècle*, RSSR.H 2 (Gembloux, 1970), 60 (idem, "Ans", 168, n. 29, refers to the central importance of the connection between daily Eucharist and celibacy for his thesis in *Origines*); W. Gessel, "Resakralisierungstendenzen in der christlichen Spätantike", in H. Bartsch, ed., *Probleme der Entsakralisierung* (Munich and Mainz, 1970), 101–22 at 111; G. Denzler, *Die Geschichte des Zölibats* (Freiburg, 1993), 66.

[66] Callam, "Frequency", 649. Cf. Jerome, *Comm. in Tit.* 1:8f. (PL 26, 603B); Theophilus Alexandrinus, *Homilia de paenitentia et abstinentia* (224 E. A. W. Budge, ed., *Coptic Homilies in the Dialect of Upper Egypt* [1910]).

about daily Eucharist confirms, instead, for the East the existence of a celibacy discipline long before the initiatives of the popes.

Conversely, toward the end of the fourth century there was no daily celebration of the liturgy in Rome—or in Gaul, or in Spain—and that remained the case for a long time.[67] Ambrosiaster himself says that in his time Mass was not celebrated daily. Northern Italy and North Africa alone were the exceptions. Under the influence of Ambrose and Augustine a distinctive practice arose of daily celebration for the bishops, though perhaps not necessarily for the rank and file priests. Therefore, a celibacy discipline of the sort being discussed in the West toward the end of the fourth century can hardly have had its basis in the daily celebration of the liturgy, since this was found practically nowhere. In the West there was no connection between daily celebration and obligatory continence (as of Cyprian's time, in any case [see above, pp. 103ff.]).

It is not at all true that Rome propagated obligatory continence in its sphere of influence on the grounds that the liturgy was celebrated daily. It would be content, for a long time to come, with the practice of infrequent celebration of the Mass. Siricius did speak euphorically about daily celebration. But that was a hyperbolic manner of speech.[68] And that is why he did not send a decree to Spain, either, saying: If you celebrate daily, then you must observe perfect continence. If Siricius had really wanted to introduce continence celibacy, then it would have made no sense at all to support it with that kind of argument. That would have played right into the hands of the Spanish opponents of celibacy. For in their view, indeed, the sporadic celebration of the Eucharist made it possible for them to come together with their wives.

Therefore Ambrose and Ambrosiaster did not counter the Spaniards with the argument about daily Eucharistic celebration, because that would have been convincing only in places where the Eucharist was in fact being celebrated daily. They used the a fortiori argument, the only one that would have a strong appeal: Laymen and clerics or, alternatively, Old Testament and Christian priests cannot be bound to the same discipline. The Christian priesthood requires total availabil-

---

[67] Callam, "Frequency"; idem, "Continence", 3f.

[68] Cf. Epistulae 5, 3 (PL 13, 1160A): "Quanto magis sacerdos utique omni momento paratus esse debet, munditiae puritate securus, ne aut sacrificium offerat, aut baptizare cogatur?" Although he does not mention daily Eucharist, Ambrosiaster speaks in a similar way about the daily duties of the priest (prayer, sacrifice, baptism).

ity and permanent continence. The question about the frequency of worship is beside the point.[69] Continence celibacy was the discipline in the Western Church long before a daily Eucharistic celebration was heard of. In any case this practice then presented a new argument for the already established discipline of clerical continence.[70]

d. Clerical Continence Comes under the Suspicion of Manichaeism

When the Spanish clerics pointed out that they did not celebrate the Eucharist daily, that was not an argument against continence celibacy that could be taken seriously. It was, however, the first time that a deliberate stance had been taken against strict clerical continence, and so a reply was sent by return post thanks to Ambrosiaster and Ambrose. There was another, much weightier objection with a theological basis: the claim that a continence discipline followed in the wake of Manichaean doctrine. Manichaeism was, especially in the fourth century, throughout the Mediterranean region, a virulent religious movement characterized by a profound pessimism. The world, in its eyes, was wicked, bad through and through, and inimical to God. Consequently, strict continence and celibacy were required, so as to guard the body from every dangerous taint of matter and, ultimately, to rescue the soul from the body.

It could very quickly come to pass that the clerical discipline, too, would be suspected of Manichaeism. Indeed, one might jump to the conclusion that the sexual abstinence of clergymen was an expression of contempt for the body. This objection does not seem to have been raised, however, at least in Rome. At the time of Ambrosiaster, vehement discussions were going on there about how the virginity of Mary should be interpreted. It was possible to mistake this doctrine for a consequence of Manichaean contempt for the body.[71] No one wanted to be considered a Manichaean, though. For this reason Helvidius, an educated layman, wanted to deprive this charge of its foundation. And so he depicted Mary as an example of bountiful motherhood. By analogy that would have meant, in terms of clerical discipline, giving up con-

---

[69] In response to R. Kottje, "Das Aufkommen der täglichen Eucharistiefeier in der Westkirche und die Zölibatsforderung", ZKG 82 (1971): 222, 224.

[70] Ibid., 228: Celibacy "in many instances already as a rule for higher clerics".

[71] D. G. Hunter, "Helvidius, Jovinian, and the Virginity of Mary in Late Fourth-Century Rome", *Journal of Early Christian Studies* 1 (1993): 47–71.

tinence so as not to be suspected of Manichaeism in this department, either. But the polemic did not reach that point. Helvidius, it is true, argued that virginity and the married state were of equal value. But in this dispute, clerical continence appears not to have come into the line of fire,[72] and this goes to prove that it was generally accepted in Rome.

In contrast, the Spanish crisis over Priscillianism presumably did bring the charge of Manichaeism against clerical continence. For Priscillian was accused (we need not discuss here how accurately) of Manichaeism. It is quite remarkable, though, that Ambrosiaster, who disputed with the Spanish opponents of celibacy, came to the defense of clerical continence against the suspicion of Manichaeism as well. Recall that the Spanish celibacy reform was very much concerned about not being connected with the ascetical demands of Priscillian. For that could have given the celibacy reform the reputation of being Manichaean. Once that had happened, it would necessarily have had unforeseeable consequences for the universal Church. For Manichaeism was a worldwide phenomenon, which even had its adherents in Rome. Thus it was important to take the wind out of the sails of any opponents of celibacy that might be found right at their own doorstep, before the Spanish bacillus could start to spread.

Therefore it was in Rome's interest to proceed against the objections theologically, to check them at the very outset, and so to safeguard the Spanish celibacy reform for the long haul. Now Ambrosiaster appears to have done precisely this by his energetic resistance to the suspicions of Manichaeism. Already in his commentary on the First Letter of Paul to Timothy one can discern a rejection of the Manichaean contempt for marriage.[73] The anti-Manichaean concern appears openly in the "Questions on the Old and New Testament". In this work Ambrosiaster treats exegetical questions. In the course of question 127, which explicitly counters the Manichaeans' contempt for marriage and the body by citing the Catholic doctrine,[74] we find the following remarks:

> 35. But people might say: If it is permissible and good to marry, why are priests not permitted to take wives? In other words, why are ordained men no longer permitted to have relations with their wives? Is anyone

---

[72] Callam, "Continence", 5. Contrary to Pietri, *Roma*, 2:893.
[73] *Comm. in 1 Tim.* 4:5 (CSEL 81, 3, 272, 19–21).
[74] *Quaestiones veteris et novi testamenti* 127, 18 (CSEL 50, 406, 23–407, 9).

unaware of the fact that every particular office and position of honor has a corresponding rule of conduct? Naturally there are things that are forbidden to all, without exception, but there are also things that are permissible for some but not for others. And there are things that are permitted at certain times but not at others. Fornication is never permitted to anyone; to do business, though, is at times licit and at times illicit. Indeed, before entering the clerical ministry, a man may do business; once he is a cleric, he is not permitted to do so. And for a Christian it is at times permitted to have relations with his wife, while at other times it is not. On account of the liturgical days it is not permitted to have marital relations, since one must abstain then even from licit things so as to gain more easily a hearing for one's petitions. This is why the Apostle tells married couples that they should agree to abstain for a while from relations so as to free themselves for prayer (1 Cor 7:5).

36. Is everything that is permitted in the presence of other people also permitted in the presence of the emperor? All the more so in matters concerning God! This is why his priest must be more pure than the others. For he acts as God's representative. He is his vicar; so that what is permissible for others is not permissible for him, because every day he must take the place of Christ, either by praying for the people or by offering sacrifice or by baptizing. Not only to him are conjugal relations forbidden, but also to his minister (the deacon); he, too, must be purer since he is in the service of Holy Things. Compared to the light of lamps, the darkness is not only obscure but sordid; compared to the stars, the light of a lamp is only fog; while compared to the sun, the stars are obscure; and compared to the radiance of God, the sun is only night. Even so, the things that for us are licit and pure are, so to speak, illicit and impure when compared to the dignity of God. However good they may be, they are not commensurate with the dignity of God. Is not the tunic good and suitable enough for the average man, whereas for the emperor it would be improper and illicit? . . . That is why the priests of God must be purer than others, since they take the place of Christ, and why the ministers (deacons) of God must be purer. For no one serves the emperor in improper garb. That is why they perform their ministry in pure, white garments. Because God, indeed, is by his very nature the most radiant, his ministers must be pure in their nature more than in their garments.[75]

Ambrosiaster deals with the objection that continence celibacy detracts from the goodness of marriage: "If it is permissible and good to marry, . . . why are ordained men no longer permitted to have re-

---

[75] Ibid., 127, 35f. (CSEL 50, 414, 24–416, 7). Cochini, *Origins*, 224–26.

lations with their wives?" We can assume that this question was not raised by the author himself and that, instead, a reproach coming from the other side was behind it ("But people might say"). The passage here does not go so far as to say: Continence celibacy is Manichaean. It only says: It could be taken as an argument for the Manichaeans. An active campaign against clerical continence is not yet discernible in the argument that the discipline is Manichaean. But of course this remains up in the air somehow. The problem has been defined, and Ambrosiaster reacts to it by clearing the clerical discipline of the charge of being antithetical to marriage.

This is worth noting. Even today celibacy is often interpreted as a vestige of a Manichaean antipathy toward marriage. Some suppose that it originated directly from the doctrines of Manichaeism.[76] Such a claim presupposes that no celibacy discipline at all had developed until the end of the fourth century. For it was precisely in this period that the heyday of Manichaeism occurred. Nevertheless, this hypothesis cannot be correct, because clerical continence can be traced back much farther to the period well before Constantine. This discipline was upheld later, despite all suspicions of Manichaean influence.

From Ambrosiaster we gather that the Church did not drift heedlessly into Manichaeism. With her eyes wide open she addressed the accusation of Manichaeism and dismissed it decisively. This consideration alone makes it highly implausible that a celibacy discipline would have been introduced at precisely this time, when the Church was firmly defining her position over against the Manichaean phenomenon. It probably would not have been feasible, either theologically or as a matter of policy. The saying applies here: You don't change horses midstream. The old discipline is left in place, even when it is contrary to the spirit of the age, so as not to cause even more confusion.

Roger Gryson correctly observes that the great papal documents on clerical continence toward the end of the fourth century are remarkably verbose in justifying the ecclesiastical discipline. Was it therefore an innovation after all? Was it necessary to counter resistance with arguments first in order to institute it?[77] Our discussions thus far point in another direction. If obligatory continence had indeed come under the suspicion of being Manichaean, it had to be justified anew. Am-

---

[76] E.g., Vogels, *Priester*, 45f.
[77] Gryson, *Origines*, 198.

brosiaster makes a good start with arguments similar to those used a little later by the popes. Clerical continence had to be kept above all suspicion by being portrayed as the ancient tradition of the Church, which was quite independent from the spirit of the age—and Manichaeism certainly was that—and looked to its own history and reason for existence. Still, its intelligibility lay in the concept of purity that was current then, which forbade those who served at the altar to engage in sexual intercourse.

Thus clerical continence had, from Ambrosiaster's point of view, nothing to do with antipathy toward sex: marital intercourse was good and pure. But it was perceived as not in keeping with the Divine Liturgy. The priority and propriety invoked here were simply with respect to the majesty and transcendence of God: The cleric should always be ready for prayer, not just periodically like the laity. The demands made upon him were constant. That is why, for example, he was not allowed to conduct business or have marital relations any more. His duty was to reserve himself in a special way for the Divine Liturgy. And to do that he renounced certain legitimate rights. The ultimate reason for the continence discipline was not contempt for the body but rather the fitting ritual preparation of the priest. Once it was formulated thus in the decretal to Himerius (*Directa*), this topic had to be taken up in other places, too, and propagated, as for example at the Roman synod in the year 386 (*Cum in unum*) and in the decretals of Pope Innocent (*Etsi tibi; Consulenti tibi*).

It took no great theological effort to keep clerical continence from drifting into Manichaean contempt for the body. For the discipline was, in principle, nothing new. Already in the second century the continence discipline had become the subject of discussions, in which arguments antithetical to marriage and the body also played a role. Manichaeism was in part a revival and a transformation of the early Christian Encratite movement, which Jerome therefore also mentions in the same breath with Manichaeism.[78] Encratism had already been overcome successfully without in any way implicating clerical continence. In his day Clement of Alexandria had pointed to the marriages and the children of the apostles. The answers that had been given then were available now as well.[79] Thus Ambrosiaster refers to the marriages and the children

---

[78] *Epistula* 49, 2, 5 *ad Pammachium* (CSEL 54, 352, 17–19).
[79] Cf. Jerome, *Adversus Jovinianum* 1, 23 (PL 23², 254A).

of the apostles, especially of Peter; and his marriage did not prevent Peter from being entrusted with the primacy.[80] Christians everywhere knew and acknowledged the weighty fact that Peter, a married man, was called to follow Christ:[81] Rome never forgot its Petrine tradition. It pointed proudly to the marriage of Peter, who of course had lived continently with his wife after his calling. Ambrosiaster confirms what was already clear in Clement: that the affirmation of marriage can go together very well with a discipline of continence within clerical marriage. Neither excludes the other. On the contrary: clerical marriage is acquainted with both parenthood and also the decision to practice perpetual continence.

3. Conditions in Italy under Pope Siricius

Ambrosiaster wrote under Pope Damasus. After the latter's death and Jerome's departure, clerical continence remained a topic of discussion in Rome. This is already evident from a first glance over the next few years. The answer to Bishop Himerius was still outstanding. In the year 384 Siricius moved into the Lateran, and he would remain there for the next fifteen years. The letter to Spain (*Directa*) and a Roman synod on the subject of the celibacy discipline date from his very first year in office, that is, from 385. At the same time a monk named Jovinian arrived and made himself the talk of Rome. In this affair the continence of clerics also played a role. And even when Jovinian was formally condemned by the Pope in the year 390, the discussion went on, because then Jerome, writing from Bethlehem, entered the scene.

a. A Synod in Rome Insists on "The Chastity of the Church"

Not without reason did Himerius portray the conditions in Spain so dramatically. For Rome, all that was rather far away. But the crisis there was by no means taken lightly. Not only Ambrosiaster and Ambrose considered themselves challenged. Alarmed by the Spanish conflagration, Siricius may very well have looked around at his own clergy and

---

[80] *Quaestiones veteris et novi testamenti* 127, 33f. (CSEL 50, 414, 3–23); Jerome, *Adversus Jovinianum* I, 26 (PL 23², 258C).

[81] Cochini, *Origins*, 66–67.

at the other dioceses of Italy. In doing so he then heard of abuses. How could Rome dispense recommendations to Spain when on its own doorstep the laws of continence were being neglected? What was "to be followed by all the Churches (in Spain)" (*Directa*), of course, also had to be observed by "all the Catholic bishops (of Italy)" (*Cum in unum*)!

But not enough: In Rome were stationed, as already mentioned, Donatists and Novatians. They believed that they had gained a monopoly on purity and holiness, and now they were sure to drag every moral lapse of a Catholic clergyman into public view. They saw each incident as proof that they were right in despising Catholics. Every new clerical misstep that was announced automatically stirred up again the discord and division between the Churches. That is the concrete background against which Siricius decided to take action. He did not want "heresies and divisions" to develop for the sole reason that the clergy of the universal Church was giving scandal by their lax discipline. Thereby he was by no means introducing obligatory continence for the first time, as if to show those purists who were the ones really capable of the greater self-renunciation. The continence discipline was in no way a result of the competition between Catholic and Novatian moral claims. Siricius merely reminded his personnel of something that even outsiders were rightly pleading for: the existing discipline—however painful it might be to observe—of clerical continence.

All told, the situation of the Catholic clergy in Rome was by far not so dramatic as in Spain. But there were indications that called for vigilance. Thus, a few months after sending his letter to Himerius, Siricius made it the subject of discussion at a synod in the Vatican Basilica of Saint Peter. Present there were eighty Italian bishops of the region referred to as suburbicarian Italy. Hence almost the entire episcopacy of central and southern Italy was represented, which at that time numbered around one hundred bishops. A little later Siricius published the decrees in a document addressed to all the bishops. Consequently, this papal decretal *Cum in unum* dated January 6, 386, was in reality a synodal document. It was not simply issued by the Pope but rather reflects the thought and the legislative decisions of all the bishops. The essential ordinances of this decretal, which also reached other provinces, in any case Africa and probably also Gaul (cf. the "apocryphal" canons erroneously attributed to the Council of Arles in the year 314), are as follows:

1. . . . Chiefly for the sake of those who recently . . . could not be present,
we are sending letters, as has long been the custom, which do not command new precepts but through which those precepts that have been
neglected because of ignorance and sloth might be observed. These precepts, nevertheless, go back to the apostles and were established by the
Fathers, as it is written: "Stand firm and hold to the traditions which
you were taught by us, either by word of mouth or by letter" (2 Thess
2:15). . . . Hence, because we are obliged to render an account not only
for ourselves but also for the faithful, we must instruct the people about
the divine discipline. There are in fact many who, ignoring the statutes
of our forefathers, have violated the chastity of the Church by their presumption and have followed the will of the people, not fearing the judgment of God.

2. Therefore, so that we may not seem to connive in like manner by
silence or to consent to such things, whereby we could incur the pains
of hell according to the Lord's saying, "You saw a thief and you ran with
him, and you cast your lot with adulterers" (Ps 50[49]:18): these are the
rules that, in view of divine judgment, all Catholic bishops must keep:
. . .

IV. That a cleric must not marry a woman who is widowed.[82]
V. That a man who, as a layman, took a widow [to be his wife] shall
not be admitted to the clergy.
VI. That no one may claim to ordain a cleric from another Church.
VII. That another Church may not admit a cleric who has been deposed.
VIII. That those who come from the Novatians or the "Mountain People" [that is, the Donatists] are to be received by the imposition
of hands, with the exception of those whom they rebaptize.

3. Moreover, we advise what is worthy, chaste, and honest: that the
priests and Levites have no intercourse with their wives, for the clergy
are occupied with the daily duties of their ministries. Paul, writing to
the Corinthians, says: "Abstain from one another so as to be free for
prayer" (1 Cor 7:5). If continence is commanded for lay people so that
their prayers may be heard, how much more must the priest be ready

---

[82] "Ut mulierem, id est, viduam clericus non ducat uxorem." That does not mean that
clerics were in principle allowed to get married, as long as it was not to a widow. The higher
clerics were not allowed to get married at all, and of course not to a widow, while the lower
clerics were allowed to get married, but still not to a widow. By the very nature of the subject, then, the ruling was directed only to the lower clergy, which is also addressed in the
following sentence (ibid., PL 13, 1159A): "Ut is, qui laicus viduam duxerit, non admittatur
ad clerum."

at any moment, in perfect purity and confidence, to offer sacrifice or to baptize? If he were stained by carnal concupiscence, what would he do? Would he excuse himself? What modesty, what peace of mind could he appeal to? By what guarantee, by what merit does he believe that he will gain a hearing, when it is said, "To the pure all things are pure, but to the corrupt and unbelieving nothing is pure" (Tit 1:15)? For this reason I am exhorting, admonishing, beseeching: that this disgrace be done away with, which even the pagans can rightly hold against us. Perhaps it is believed (that the prayer of the impure will be heard) because it is written: "the husband of one wife" (1 Tim 3:2). Yet [Paul] did not say this so that [a cleric] might persist in his desire to beget, but rather for the sake of future continence (that he should henceforth observe: *propter continentiam futuram*). Nor did he [Paul] refuse to admit even virginal candidates, for he said, "I wish that all were as I myself am" (1 Cor 7:7). And he stated his opinion even more clearly when he said: "Those who are in the flesh cannot please God. But you are not in the flesh, you are in the Spirit" (Rom 8:8–9).

4. If these things, my brothers, are observed with utmost vigilance by all, then factions shall cease and dissension shall be quieted, heresies and schisms will not arise, the devil will have no room to rage. . . . If we follow all of these precepts faithfully, the Lord will preserve our bodies and our souls until the day when each one shall be rewarded according to his works. If, however, anyone proud of his carnal way of thinking tries to evade this canonical decision, he must know that he is excluded from communion with us and that he risks the pains of hell.

5. And yet mercy must accompany judgment. For it is right to stretch out a hand to those who are stumbling, as long as this does not cause the downfall of those who are living according to the discipline.[83]

The theme of the document, aside from other rulings, is in the first place "the chastity of the Church". This includes not only the continence of married clerics but also the digamy prohibition with respect to the wife. Infractions against this discipline were occurring. When this document is compared with the letter to Himerius, certain differences in focus and emphasis can be identified. The condition of the clergy in Italy appears to be unlike the situation in Spain. One indication of this is the varying degree of detail with which Siricius treats the individual regulations of the discipline. Although Siricius, in writing to Himerius, treated the digamy prohibition for clerics at great length,

---

[83] *Epistulae* 5, 1–5 (PL 13, 1156A–1162A). [The citation was translated into English from Latin with reference to the German version.—Trans.]

the synodal document says nothing about it. There seems to be no problem with that in Italy, which Jerome, too, indirectly confirms.[84] It is merely stated tersely that the digamy prohibition applies also to the wife of a cleric.

Common to both *Directa* and *Cum in unum*, however, is the extensive treatment given to the continence of married clerics. It seems, then, to have been disputed in Italy, too, in various places—but probably not so much among the bishops who participated in the synod in Rome as among their clerics in the rural areas. Many a word of explanation was probably needed there. To help them through these conflicts, Siricius gives the bishops arguments with which to counter possible objections. Many bishops may not have had the confidence to take action against unchaste deacons and priests and "followed the will of the people". Perhaps they lacked arguments or were themselves unsure about the meaning of this discipline. And so a few of them neglected the Church's laws "through ignorance and sloth". Therefore Siricius supplies them with two helpful arguments. The first and more important refers to the daily liturgical duties of clerics. The other fends off a false interpretation of Paul. The pastoral letters with their formula "unius uxoris vir" do not speak against continence. The monogamy rule is aimed precisely at "future continence" (*propter continentiam futuram*). Otherwise Paul would not have expressly permitted and even preferred virginal men in the ministry.

In any case, one cannot speak of an organized opposition to clerical continence in Italy. There were possibly priests who, when challenged about their conduct, excused themselves by saying that they had known nothing about a discipline of obligatory continence. The same process was taking place here as in Spain: the transition from an unintelligible status quo of local laws to a unified canonical legislation. Although it may at first seem as though the continence of married clerics and their wives were only a recommendation, an urgent desire[85] on the part of Siricius, this caution was nothing but an expression of tactful eccle-

---

[84] For Oceanus, a Roman, a digamous bishop was something entirely unprecedented. He complains about such a case in Spain. Jerome, *Epistula* 69, 2, 1 *ad Oceanum* (CSEL 54, 680, 6–11).

[85] Siricius, *Epistulae* 5, 3 (PL 13, 1160A): "Praeterea quod dignum et pudicum et honestum est suademus." Innocentius, *Epistula* 2, 9, 12 *ad Victricium* (PL 20, 745C) formulates it in a significantly more pointed way: "Praeterea quod dignum et pudicum et honestum est, tenere Ecclesia omni modo debet."

siastical policy.[86] By no means was a hitherto unknown obligation to practice continence being introduced here warily for the first time. The conclusion of the letter, with the utmost severity, threatens excommunication, which is comprehensible only if in fact no new discipline is being imposed, but rather an old custom—granted, one that has fallen into oblivion in many places—is being inaugurated once more.

A glance in the direction of Milan at Ambrose confirms this finding. We have already cited above his book *On the Duties of the Clergy*, in which Ambrose rejects digamy and incontinence in married clerics. If at that time obligatory continence had just been introduced, or if it had been the subject of wide-ranging criticism, then one could expect to find here a comprehensive justification of the discipline. But in this voluminous work Ambrose speaks only briefly about clerical continence. It seems to require no special emphasis. Nor is there any talk about a relaxation of discipline in the rural areas. Ambrose mentions the reasoning of the Spaniards with regard to the merely periodic continence in the Old Testament only because it was being discussed in Rome. He wanted to prevent the argument from unsettling anyone or possibly from providing an occasion to call the celibacy discipline into question.

b. Jovinian Precipitates No Crisis of Clerical Discipline

With the synod called by Pope Siricius, the continence discipline for Rome had been fundamentally settled. The Italian episcopacy followed a clear, uniform line. Now, however, just after the synod, we encounter in Rome a person who has always been regarded as an uncompromising opponent of celibacy: Jovinian (d. before 406). He was a monk who after 385, in any case after the departure of Jerome, had been making propaganda in word and in writing for his views, which were as simple as they were effective.[87] They started up a stormy discussion, which did not remain just a monastic quarrel but churned its waves higher and higher until they reached the Pope and the bishops.

Especially well received was his thesis, which was known already in a similar form by Helvidius: In the sight of God it does not matter whether one lived as a virgin, a widow, or a married person—what

---

[86] Gryson, *Origines*, 142, 158.
[87] According to Gryson, *Origines*, 143, n. 2, Jovinian first appeared around 392.

was decisive was baptism, which assured the same salvation for all.[88] In a certain sense Jovinian rejected the justification-through-works approach of his ascetical colleagues (one could formulate his view as "sola gratia baptismatis", by the grace of baptism alone), which is why he has been compared with the Augustinian monk Martin Luther. Jovinian declared that marriage and celibacy had the same degree of merit,[89] while he himself was unmarried and wished to remain that way.[90] He appeared to be accusing the priests of the Roman Church, concretely, of despising marriage and of exalting virginity at the expense of marriage.[91] Jovinian found adherents, but also opponents, so that the bishops considered themselves compelled to take a position. His doctrine was condemned at a synod under Pope Siricius in the year 390, and again a little later at a synod in Milan under Bishop Ambrose.

What was behind all this? Were the ecclesiastical powers uniting to eliminate a disagreeable opponent of clerical celibacy? The reason we listen so attentively is that Jovinian appears at precisely the same time as the celibacy initiative of Siricius. A connection suggests itself: Did Jovinian precipitate a crisis in asceticism, so that the Roman ecclesiastical leadership, as a counter-move, imposed obligatory continence, possibly for the first time? Many see it that way;[92] they suppose that only now was the banner of asceticism being raised against the friends of the flesh. Peter Brown suspects that there were even stalwart interest groups behind it. According to his interpretation, Siricius wanted to strike a balance between two irreconcilable positions. On the one side stood the virginity ideal of Ambrose, together with his unmarried clerics; on the other side were Jovinian and those bishops who viewed virginity less euphorically and preferred a fruitful, multiplying clergy. The decretal of Siricius sought a compromise solution by leaving the married clergy in place, while imposing on it the duty of continence.[93]

[88] Jerome, *Adversus Jovinianum* 1, 3 (PL 23², 224B); Ambrose, *Epistulae* 42, 2 (CSEL 82, 3, 303, 14–19).

[89] Ambrose, *Epistulae* 15, 2f. (CSEL 82, 3, 303, 14–21).

[90] Augustine, *De haeresibus* 82 (CCL 46, 337, 12f.); W. Haller, *Iovinianus: Die Fragmente seiner Schriften, die Quellen zu seiner Geschichte, sein Leben und seine Lehre*, TU 17, 2 (Leipzig, 1897), 123.

[91] Siricius, *Epistulae* 41a, 5f. (CSEL 82, 3, 300, 52–60); J. G. Nolan, *Jerome and Jovinian* (Washington, 1956), 22.

[92] E. Schillebeeckx, *Der Amtszölibat: Eine kritische Besinnung* (Düsseldorf, 1967), 29f.; he, however, confuses Jovinian with Vigilantius.

[93] Thus P. Brown, *Die Keuschheit der Engel: Sexuelle Entsagung, Askese und Körperlichkeit am Anfang des Christentums* (Munich and Vienna, 1991), 364–68.

That is, of course, a version of history so slippery as to be untenable, combined with a daring notion of the Church's aptitude for compromise. Brown can cite only one piece of evidence that there were bishops who wanted their priests to beget children: the well-known passage in Jerome's letter against Vigilantius; however, it is dated twenty years after the decretals of Siricius, and anyway, because of its blatantly polemical nature, it is to be enjoyed with the utmost caution (see below, pp. 269–70).[94] Furthermore, it speaks of conditions in Gaul. Therefore one cannot cite them in reference to a celibacy crisis in Italy. Besides, the papal documents were published at the very beginning of the Jovinian affair. It is improbable that Jovinian could have precipitated a celibacy crisis within such a short time. Siricius was sending his decretal *Directa* to Spain when Jovinian had just appeared in Rome. Therefore we must assume that the two decretals of Siricius did not yet come to terms with Jovinian.

Let us see what is chronologically possible and what the historical source texts actually yield. Right at the beginning of his pontificate, Siricius cemented the discipline of clerical continence for the Roman ecclesiastical province. It is conceivable, then, that in the aftermath Jovinian, disturbed by the decisions of the Roman synod, brought forward his theses and thus protested against the synod. He, the monk from Rome, would then have stood up like another Paphnutius, so to speak, so as not to allow the Pope and the bishops of Italy to have their way with such a bold innovation. As the spokesman of a disconcerted clergy, he would have unleashed a wide-ranging public discussion and thus stirred up a really good celibacy crisis. Siricius, forced into a corner, saw that the only thing he could do was to condemn Jovinian at the synod of 390 and thus to silence the opposition.

That kind of thing makes a good read: The upright monk goes forth into battle against unscrupulous bishops and is defeated. But can it actually be proved that there was a celibacy crisis? One could only speak about a crisis if in fact clerics had gone over to Jovinian's side and had given up continence. Jerome's remark about the Gallic bishops is not relevant to this question. From Augustine, who was still around to see Jovinian in Rome (before 388), we know that Jovinian attacked "the holy celibacy [*caelibatus*] of the holy men". But he adds right away that

---

[94] For a similar chronological imprecision, see ibid., p. 384 (Ambrosiaster's works date from before 385 and so cannot be considered as a reaction to Jovinian, who was active in Rome after 385).

the Roman clerics did not allow themselves to be led astray.[95] The only thing that Jovinian called into question, therefore, was the celibate state of the unmarried clerics; yet none of them married as a result of his influence. Jovinian cannot have found any following among the clergy, because ultimately, at the aforementioned synod in the year 390, the entire priesthood and diaconate of Rome condemned his doctrines.[96] He may well have had a following even after this condemnation, but not among the clergy. That might also explain why he did not manage to start his own church: he did not have the clergy to do it.[97]

If anyone wanted to speak about a celibacy crisis, he could always point to cases of unchastity that we know about from other sources at the time of Jovinian's activity in Rome. One could then infer that his preaching had an influence. But that remains pure conjecture. There is no substantial basis for it. Next we should mention some deacons in northern Italy who had begotten children. The successor of Ambrose, Bishop Simplician, had them punished at a synod in Turin on September 22, 398. Presumably they had violated the laws unwittingly.[98] In another incident married priests were involved. As a result Pope Innocent sent a letter around 401–407 to two Calabrian bishops.

> No priest should be unaware of the rule of ecclesiastical canons. It is quite disgraceful when a bishop does not know it, especially when pious lay people know it and insist that it should be observed. Recently, indeed,

---

[95] Augustine, *Retractiones* 2, 22, 1 (CCL 57, 107, 2–108, 1f.): "Iouiniani haeresis sacrarum uirginum meritum aequando pudicitiae coniugali tantum ualuit in urbe Roma, ut nonnullas etiam sanctimoniales, de quarum pudicitia suspicio nulla praecesserat, deiecisse in nuptias diceretur. . . . Hoc modo etiam uirorum sanctorum sanctum caelibatum commemoratione patrum coniugatorum et praedicatione frangebat." *De haeresibus* 82 (CCL 46, 337, 8–18): "Virginitatem etiam sanctimonialium et continentiam sexus uirilis in sanctis eligentibus caelibem uitam coniugiorum castorum atque fidelium meritis adaequabat, ita ut quaedam uirgines sacrae prouectae iam aetatis in urbe Roma, ubi haec docebat, eo audito nupsisse dicantur. Non sane ipse uel habebat uel habere uolebat uxorem, quod non propter aliquod apud deum maius meritum in regno uitae perpetuae profuturum, sed propter praesentem prodesse necessitatem, hoc est, ne homo coniugales patiatur molestias, disputabat. Cito tamen ista haeresis oppressa et exstincta est, nec usque ad deceptionem aliquorum sacerdotum potuit peruenire."

[96] Siricius, *Epistulae* 41a, 6 (CSEL 82, 3, 300, 59–301, 63).

[97] Nolan, *Jerome*, 32. Jerome, *Epistula* 49, 2, 3 *ad Pammachium* (CSEL 54, 352, 3–5) does speak of clerics and monks who advocated Jovinian's theses. But in reality those are former friends of Jerome's, who have distanced themselves from him and whom he therefore brands as supposed followers of Jovinian. Contrary to D. G. Hunter, "Resistance to the Virginal Ideal in Late-Fourth-Century Rome: The Case of Jovinian", TS 48 (1987): 48f.

[98] Canon 8 (CCL 148, 58, 91–93): "Qui contra interdictum sunt ordinati uel in ministerio filios genuerunt". Gryson, *Origines*, 175.

our son Maximilian while dealing with such matters filed a complaint; his writ is enclosed. Guided by zeal for the faith and for discipline, he cannot stand to see the Church being defiled by unworthy priests who, as he affirms, have begotten children while in orders. I would not allow myself to talk about this if I did not know that you in your prudence have knowledge of the entire law. That is why, dearest brothers [that is, the bishops, Maximus and Severus], the written complaint is enclosed, so that you may examine the text and order all those who are said to have committed such actions to be summoned. If, after a discussion of the accusations made against these priests, they are convicted, let them be removed from the priestly office, for those who are not holy cannot touch holy things. Let them have nothing more to do with the ministry that they have defiled by their illicit way life. We marvel, though, that your bishops overlook this. It must be concluded that they either shut their eyes to it or else do not know that such a thing is not allowed.[99]

Jovinian, then, has hardly precipitated a crisis among the clergy. The only remaining explanation is that his theses have led to a crisis of vows in ascetical circles. Of course his intention is not to reject them categorically.[100] But there were a few virginal individuals in Rome who came under his influence and gave up their vows.[101] Jovinian saw to it that there was unrest in Milan, as well. Ambrose reports that he had difficulties with monks but not with clerics. After his condemnation in Rome Jovinian showed up in Milan. Thereupon two monks from the Milanese monastery left their community as a result of his influence,[102] and in the year 396 they went to Vercelli. At the top of their lungs they denied, while there, the grace of virginity and the value of widowhood.[103] Virgins ought to marry and have children, widows

---

[99] *Epistulae* 38 (PL 20, 605BC). [The citation was translated into English from Latin with reference to the German version.—TRANS.]

[100] Jerome, *Adversus Jovinianum* 1, 5 (PL 23², 228A): "Facit (sc. Iovinianus) apostropham ad virginem, dicens: <Non tibi facio, virgo, injuriam: eligisti pudicitiam propter praesentem necessitatem: placuit tibi, ut sis sancta corpore et spiritu: ne superbias: ejusdem Ecclesiae membrum es, cujus et nuptae sunt>."

[101] Augustine, *De haeresibus* 82 (CCL 46, 337, 10–12); *Retractiones* 2, 22, 1 (CCL 57, 107, 2–7); *De peccatorum meritis et remissione* 3, 7, 13 (CSEL 60, 139, 20–24); Jerome, *Adversus Jovinianum* 2, 36 (PL 23², 350A).

[102] Ambrose, *Epistulae* 63, 8 (CSEL 82, 3 239, 75) describes both of them as Epicurians; Jerome, *Adversus Jovinianum* 2, 36 (PL 23², 349A), calls Jovinian "our Epicurus". Haller, *Iovinianus*, 130.

[103] Ambrose, *Epistulae* 63, 7 (CSEL 82, 3, 238, 63). Their critique of *abstinentia* pertains to moderation in food and drink.

should remarry.[104] So there we see fugitive monks zealously bringing the theses of their master to the streets.

The fact is that Jovinian's critique was directed exclusively against virginity and thus against the new asceticism, whose herald and apostle in Rome, as is generally known, was Jerome.[105] A whole series of strange-looking characters from the Orient had spread out through Rome and, for want of suitable monasteries, were wandering around the city on their own like vagabonds, always on the look-out for patrons and benefactors. Jerome's ascetical propaganda was not directed to a clerical audience but to wider circles of well-to-do noblemen. He had remarkable success among them. Influential noble families allowed themselves to be won over to the ideal of the celibate life. Then, when Jovinian showed up in Rome, there was a sudden change of mood, which was fatal to Jerome and the "monkish rabble", because an aristocratic Roman lady named Blesilla, who had been taken with enthusiasm for Jerome, went to an early grave, presumably as a result of exaggerated fasting. The entire city rose against Jerome. He could not stay there any longer and, much worse for the wear, left the Eternal City in the year 385. The humiliation that he had undergone kept him from returning ever again. But then, as if that were not enough, Jovinian knew how to profit from the anger of the populace.[106] Intending to annihilate Jerome's cause with a decisive blow, he accused the high esteem for virginity of being a downright Manichaean denigration of marriage.

In the course of the polemics, then, we learn Jovinian's position with respect to the clerical discipline. Like Helvidius, he equates marriage and celibacy, and probably even values marriage more. In his estimation, the phrase "unius uxoris vir" of the pastoral letters refers to at least the equivalence of marriage and celibacy. Is Paul not explicitly favoring a married clergy here? Thus Jovinian would like to exclude unmarried men from holy orders. Furthermore, he considers it possible for ascetics to marry and to beget children. He does *not* derive from the pastoral letters, however, any obligation for already-ordained

---

[104] *Epistulae* 63, 22 (CSEL 82, 3, 247, 244–248, 247). Cf. Jerome, *Adversus Jovinianum* 2, 36 (PL 23², 350A).

[105] Pietri, *Roma*, 1:638–45.

[106] Jovinian rejects a distinction between fasting and the partaking of food, probably occasioned by the death of Blesilla; Jerome, *Adversus Jovinianum* 1, 3 (PL 23², 224B); Ambrose, *Epistulae* 63, 7 (CSEL 82, 3, 238, 62).

unmarried clerics to marry.[107] That would have been senseless, anyway, since married men already made up the majority of the Church's
clergy.[108] Besides, he had no objections at all to obligatory continence
for married clerics, as Jerome expressly testifies in his treatise against
Jovinian (around 392–393).

> He [Jovinian] writes, "It is futile for you to say that, because the Apostle
> appointed bishops, priests, and deacons who were the husbands of one
> wife and had children" (1 Tim 3:2). The Apostle does say, though, that he
> has no command of the Lord about the virgins, but he gives his opinion
> as one who by the Lord's mercy is trustworthy [1 Cor 7:25]. And so
> throughout his treatment of the subject he prefers virginity to marriage
> and recommends what he does not dare to command, to avoid setting a
> snare and so as not to impose more on human nature than it is able to bear.
> And so, too, while instituting the ecclesiastical ministry in the Church
> of the Gentiles, which was still very young, he gave easier commands to
> those who first converted, so that they would not be frightened off. . . .
>
> But even the passage about selecting bishops supports my position.
> [The Apostle] did not say: Let us choose as a bishop a man married to
> one wife and siring children, but: a man who has had only one wife and
> keeps his children in perfect submission (1 Tim 3:2, 4; Tit 1:6). You
> surely admit that he who goes on siring children during his episcopate
> cannot be a bishop. For if people find out about it, he will not be consid-
> ered a husband but condemned as an adulterer. Either you allow priests
> to exercise their nuptial activity so that there is no difference between
> virgins and married people; or, if priests are not allowed to touch their
> wives, they are holy, precisely because they imitate virginal purity.
>
> But let us go farther. If a lay person, any member of the faithful, cannot
> devote himself to prayer without setting conjugal intercourse aside, the
> priest who must offer the sacrifice at all times has to pray unceasingly.
> If he must pray unceasingly, he must continually renounce the marriage
> bed. Even under the Old Law, those who presented sacrificial offerings
> for the people did not remain in their own homes but purified themselves
> by living temporarily apart from their wives; neither did they drink wine
> or fermented beverages, which generally excite concupiscence.
>
> I will not deny that married men are chosen for the priesthood; the
> reason is that there are not as many virginal men as are needed for the
> priesthood. . . . How is it, then, you will ask, that a virginal candidate for

---

[107] Haller, *Iovinianus*, 150.

[108] *Adversus Jovinianum* 1, 23 (PL 23², 253B): "Quasi non hodie quoque plurimi sacerdotes habeant matrimonia."

priestly orders is often passed over and a married man is taken? Perhaps because he does not have other qualities that ought to accompany his virginity, or because he is thought to be virginal but is not. Or his virginity is a disgrace to him [self-mutilation], or his virginity itself has made him arrogant, and while he is conceited about the chastity of his body, he forgets the other virtues. . . . Many are selected, not because they are loved, but because the other one is hated. Most often honesty carries off the victory, while strategems and cunning in the other are resented. Once in a while the people judge wrongly. In the matter of approving priests, each one acts according to his own habits, because he does not so much want a good presider as one who resembles himself. Now it happens that married people, who are in the majority in the populace, to a certain extent applaud themselves in the married [candidates], so as not to have a lesser standing in comparison to those who are virginal; and therefore they prefer the married men to the celibates. I wish to say yet another thing, which will perhaps offend many; but the good people may not be angry with me, for their conscience will not accuse them of any sin. Hitherto even the popes have been guilty of admitting to the clergy not the better candidates, but those who are proud, while considering simple and naïve souls as unsuitable, or else of assigning offices to their cousins and relatives as though in some worldly knighthood, or even of being at the beck and call of the rich.[109]

Jovinian, too, did not permit married clerics to continue having marital relations. In the words of Jerome: "You (that is, Jovinian) surely admit that he who goes on siring children during his episcopate cannot be a bishop."[110] Jovinian, then, cannot have demanded either that clerics ought to marry. They would not have been allowed to consummate their marriage. He probably does say that, according to the pastoral

---

[109] Ibid., 1, 34 (PL 23², 268A–270A): "Sed et ipsa episcopalis electio mecum facit. Non enim dicit: Eligatur episcopus, qui unam ducat uxorem, et filios faciat; sed qui unam ducat uxorem, et filios in omni subditos disciplina (1 Tim 3:2, 4; Tit 1:6). Certe confiteris non posse esse episcopum, qui in episcopatu filios faciat. Alioqui, si deprehensus fuerit, non quasi vir tenebitur, sed quasi adulter damnabitur. Aut permitte sacerdotibus exercere opera nuptiarum, ut idem sint virgines quod mariti: aut si sacerdotibus non licet uxores tangere, in eo sancti sunt, quia imitantur pudicitiam virginalem." Cf. Cochini, *Origins*, 294–96. *Adversus Jovinianum* must have been written after the Roman condemnation of Jovinian (cf. Jerome, *Epistula* 49, 2, 2 *ad Pammachium* [CSEL 54, 351, 17]; contrary to Hunter, "Resistance", 45). On abuses in the selection of priests, see John Chrysostom, *De sacerdotio* 3, 11 (SC 272, 188, 1–190, 23).

[110] "Certe confiteris non posse esse episcopum, qui in episcopatu filios faciat." Callam, "Continence", 13; Gryson, *Origines*, 153; Bickell, "Cölibat", 30. Naturally, besides the bishop the deacon and the priest are also meant (Callam, "Continence", 16, n. 62).

letters, only married men should be admitted to holy orders. In order to prove the equivalence of marriage and celibacy, Jovinian pointed to the pastoral letters, which speak of married clerics. His thought was probably this: If Paul really had placed celibacy above marriage (1 Cor 7), why then did he not demand celibacy even of the clerics (1 Tim 3:2)? Paul even says expressly that he wants married men in the clergy.

But Jerome then does see a priority given to celibates, indeed, based precisely on the "unius uxoris vir" of the pastoral letters. This is not the expression of a marriage obligation for clerics, but rather an exhortation to continence: the bishop should *have* children, as Jovinian himself says,[111] not *sire* them. Thus Paul is speaking of a restriction of marital rights: After ordination clerics may neither marry nor beget children. With that, Jerome is taking up the same argument that the Roman celibacy synod under Siricius had formulated: The phrase "unius uxoris vir" is valid *propter continentiam futuram*, and not as an invitation to beget children. And: Married couples should imitate virginal chastity.[112] Jerome, then, sees the Roman clergy as confirming his interpretation, that is, that the continence of the married clergy implies the relatively greater excellence of virginity.

Decisive for us is Jerome's indication, which we have already mentioned, that even Jovinian fully accepted clerical continence. That has two important consequences for a correct evaluation of Jovinian's role in the Roman celibacy debate. First, obligatory continence for married clerics and their wives could not be a consequence of the euphoria for virginity in the fourth century. Had continence only then been made an obligation, so as to conform the married clerics to the ascetical example of their celibate colleagues, then Jovinian would have put up a fierce resistance. Second, Jovinian in no way intended to call into question obligatory continence as such. His criticism was restricted to the celibate portion of the clergy. In Rome, at any rate, his views met with little or no enthusiasm.

As Jerome sees it, the more exalted position of virginity in comparison to marriage is confirmed by the continence of married clerics. We find this connection between clerical continence and celibacy again in Ambrose. In one letter he comes to terms with the aforementioned monks who fled to Vercelli. He may well have been prompted to write

---

[111] *Adversus Jovinianum* 1, 34 (PL 23², 268A).
[112] Cf. Jerome, *Adversus Helvidium* 21 (PL 23², 214D).

by the fear that one of them might become heir to the vacant episcopal see of Vercelli. Against the followers of Jovinian he defends the
priesthood of the celibate, as it is lived in the clerical community of
Vercelli. In this regard he cites the pastoral letters.

> The Apostle and teacher of virtue [that is, Paul] patiently refutes those
> who contradict him and commands that he [that is, the bishop] must be
> "the husband of an only wife" (1 Tim 3:2). He does not mean by this to
> exclude the unmarried [that is, from holy orders]—for celibacy is above
> the law of precept—but [he says this] so that he [that is, the bishop]
> might preserve the grace of his baptism by conjugal chastity and so that
> he might be invited, by apostolic authority, to stop begetting children
> now that he is a priest—he said, after all, that he *has* children (not that
> he *begets* them)—and to stop having marital relations. [113]

Ambrose takes an approach similar to Jerome's in opposing Jovinian's
theses. The latter wanted to exclude unmarried men from holy orders.
Ambrose counters by saying: The intention of the pastoral letters is
not to make marriage obligatory but to safeguard future continence.
Therefore we must not misinterpret Ambrose's remarks. Jovinian did
not want priests to go on begetting children. Rather, Ambrose says:
The "unius uxoris vir" can never under any circumstances mean compulsory marriage, because it is obviously aimed at continence, which
Jovinian also accepts.

Thus the main point of Siricius' celibacy initiative, that is, the continence of married clerics and their wives, was in no way attacked by
Jovinian. In this matter he, the Pope, Jerome, and Ambrose were all
in agreement. Jovinian also accepted celibate clerics, strictly speaking,
provided that they were ordained as single men. If Augustine says, in
spite of this, that he had attacked the celibacy of the holy men, that
probably means that Jovinian would have liked to see only married
men be ordained in the future.

Jovinian resolutely rejects an exaggerated esteem for celibacy. To
this extent he torpedoes Jerome's efforts to favor unmarried rather
than married clerics. Jerome, following the path of Eastern exegesis,

---

[113] *Epistulae* 63, 62 (CSEL 82, 3, 267, 630–37): "Virtutum autem magister apostolus est
qui cum patientia redarguendos doceat contradicentes, qui *unius uxoris virum* praecipiat esse,
non quo exsortem excludat coniugii—nam hoc supra legem praecepti est—, sed ut coniugali castimonia servet ablutionis suae gratiam neque iterum ut filios in sacerdotio creare
apostolica invitetur auctoritate; habentem enim filios dixit, non facientem neque coniugium
iterare." [The English version has been translated from the Latin.—TRANS.]

sees in the ordination of married men a concession of Paul that was
justifiable in the early period of the Church (see above, pp. 167–68).
Now, however, when choosing candidates, preference really ought to
be given in all cases to the celibate man. This is the same trend toward a celibate clergy that we discovered in Chrysostom and in other
Greek theologians. And just as Epiphanius had done, Jerome sees as
the reason for continuing to accept married candidates at all the fact
that there are not enough virginal candidates and that those who do
apply are not necessarily suitable.

How little Jovinian is challenging the continence discipline of the
married clergy can be seen also from another of Jerome's remarks in
a letter to his Roman friend Pammachius. To understand it we must
sketch briefly the events of the years 392 and 393. Jerome had been living in Bethlehem for quite some time. But he still had an ear for what
was happening in Rome; his old friends kept him up to date through
a voluminous correspondence. So with fear and trembling he learned
about the campaign that Jovinian was conducting against the virginity
he held so sacred. After the latter's condemnation, Jerome saw that his
hour had now arrived. For he had been asked by Rome to refute again
in writing the teachings of Jovinian, which had already been officially
condemned by the Church. The scholar from Bethlehem did not have
to be told twice. After all, for him it was a belated triumph over that
man who had cost him so many sympathetic supporters in Rome.

But in his excess of zeal he botched the work. To the great dismay of
the author, his treatise "Against Jovinian" met with vehement objections from, of all people, his friends who were opposed to Jovinian. For
many it was intolerable, the way Jerome denigrated marriage so as to
exalt virginity to the skies. The rumor circulated, "He has condemned
marriage."[114] Jerome was expected to justify his views. So he wrote
an explanatory letter to Pammachius. In it he recalls the condemnation
of Jovinian by the Roman clergy synod and then continues:

> That worldly people take offense when their state is said to be less im-
> portant than the virginal state, I can understand. But I have to marvel
> at the fact that clerics, monks,[115] and those who practice continence
> do not stand up for their own way of life. They abstain from relations

---

[114] Jerome, *Epistula* 50, 5, 4 *ad Domnionem* (CSEL 54, 394, 13): "damnauit nuptias".
[115] Cf. Haller, *Iovinianus*, 128f.

with their wives so as to practice the virtue of chastity as the virgins do, and now they want married life and virginity to be esteemed equally? Then they ought to join again with their wives, whom they have renounced. But if they continue to practice continence, then they tacitly admit by their conduct that they have exchanged marriage for something more valuable.[116]

Jerome, in his inconsiderate zeal against Jovinian, fell into the trap of Manichaeism. Of course the entire Roman clergy had condemned the anti-ascetical ideas of Jovinian. But it was no doubt precisely the married clerics who found it unsupportable that Jerome should vilify marriage (and not for the first time).

Roman Christians were shocked by Jerome's assertion that even first marriages were regrettable, if pardonable, capitulations to the flesh, and that second marriages were only one step away from the brothel. He went on to suggest that priests were holy only in so far as they possessed the purity of virgins. The married ministers were mere raw recruits in the army of the Church, brought in because of a temporary shortage of battle-hardened veterans of lifelong celibacy. It was a memorable statement of the ascetic viewpoint at its most unpleasant and impracticable.[117]

Jerome had painted his subject in black and white. That was not how married clerics understood their ministry. Nor was it how they viewed the marriages of lay people. Therefore they kept their distance from Jerome. He had made himself rather unpopular anyway with the Roman clergy ten years previously, when he branded their black sheep for the whole world to see.[118] Nevertheless, the clerics did not call continence celibacy into question on that account. They adhered to the Roman decrees just as Jovinian probably did. The continence discipline for married clerics and their wives was not a matter for discussion. That is precisely why Jerome could see in it an argument for the superiority of virginity and why he still attempted in this way to convince the married clerics of Rome that his view was correct.

---

[116] *Epistula* 49, 2, 3 *ad Pammachium* (CSEL 54, 352, 3–9).

[117] Brown, *Body*, 377.

[118] H. Hagendahl and J. H. Waszink, article "Hieronymus", in RAC 15 (1991), 117–39 at 125.

c. Once Again: Clerical Continence Is Not Manichaean

The Jovinian phenomenon cannot be explained without considering Manichaeism as well. In the second half of the fourth century, Manichaeism was part of the atmosphere. Its fundamental tenet was the dualism between spirit, which is good, and matter, which is evil. Was clerical continence a spiritual child of Manichaeism? Priscillian was suspected of being a Manichaean, and, as a result, people were apt to take a dim view of the Spanish celibacy reform. Ambrosiaster defended the continence discipline of married clerics and their wives against such an accusation. Jovinian, too, took part in the discussion. Just like all the other theologians of the Church, he firmly rejected the Manichaean world view and its concept of man.[119] Still: where did Manichaeism begin and where did it leave off? On this question the great minds parted ways. Together with Roman theology, Jovinian defended the goodness of marriage. Earlier on, Ambrosiaster had opposed the Manichaeans by citing the examples of Abraham and Anna, and also of the priest Zechariah [cf. Lk 1], who "with God's consent" (!) begot another son.[120] Jovinian argued in exactly the same way when he pointed to the marriages of Sarah, Anna, and also of Zechariah.[121]

Above and beyond that, however, Jovinian turned against a Manichaean exaggeration of the Church's ideal of virginity. The catalyst here was a positively epidemic enthusiasm for virginity and monasticism in those days, such as had previously been known only by hearsay from the East.[122] Jovinian himself was a monk. He warned against making this movement a trap-door for Manichaeism and thus seems to have criticized the enthusiasm of the likes of Ambrose and Jerome as a Manichaean aberration. Jovinian was fighting against the view that virginity is superior in principle and also against a call for all Christians to live as celibates if possible. Behind this stood a theological concern that was aimed at the Manichaeans' contempt for marriage: Baptism alone guarantees salvation.

---

[119] Hunter, "Resistance", 50–61.

[120] *Quaestiones veteris et novi testamenti* 127, 32 (CSEL 50, 413, 11–27).

[121] Augustine, *Retractiones* 2, 22, 1 (CCL 57, 107, 6–8); Jerome, *Adversus Jovinianum* 1, 26 (PL 23^2, 256B).

[122] F. H. Dudden, *The Life and Times of St. Ambrose*, vol. 2 (Oxford, 1935), 397f.

Jovinian was looking only at marriage per se, not at marital relations. He cared, strictly speaking, only about the question "marriage or celibacy", but not about the possibility of continence within marriage, to which he had no objection. That is interesting, once again, with regard to the thesis that a celibacy discipline was introduced only toward the end of the fourth century on the basis of Manichaean influences from Rome. If Jovinian accused Rome of Manichaeism but at the same time accepted clerical continence, then the latter could hardly have been a consequence of Manichaean influence. Jovinian would have seized upon that immediately and said: Rome is Manichaean because it requires continence of the clerics. But that was far from his mind. Ambrosiaster had already acquitted continence of any suspicion of Manichaeism. Jovinian had no reason to view it any differently.

Jovinian's anti-Manichaean thrust explains why it did not occur to him to cast doubt on the continence of married clerics and their wives. After all, ever since the days of Clement and Epiphanius, and on down to Ambrosiaster, the Church's theologians had always kept within bounds the Encratite movements that were contemptuous of the body, precisely by referring to the clerical discipline. Married clerics were married and remained so, and they had children, though of course they practiced continence after their ordination. For Jovinian, then, they presented no problem; on the contrary, as we have seen, they could serve as proof of the fundamental equivalence between marriage and virginity.

If anyone was a problem for him, then it was the unmarried clerics. Jovinian's views were capable of endangering the celibacy of the unmarried clerics, but not the continence of those who were married. But it did not come to that because of the decisive intervention of Siricius. Of course, Jerome still could have spoiled things with his overzealous book against the already condemned Jovinian. Manifest here was an ascetical drive that actually confirmed Jovinian's fears and that ultimately would also give a Manichaean twist to the clerical discipline. With his boundless enthusiasm for virginity and his blunt denigration of marriage, he almost did a disservice to the worthy cause. Were the most zealous advocates of clerical continence, then, really downright foes of marriage, tough-as-nails ascetics? Did the married cleric's obligation to live in continence with his wife not necessarily give marriage a bad name now? If that were the case, then the Spanish bacillus really had broken out. But what Jerome wrote from his cell met with no approval at all in Rome, and we might assume that even Siricius did not find it very edifying. His relations with Jerome were rather strained anyway. To be sure, no one condemned Jerome, the former secretary of Pope Damasus, but he had marginalized himself by writing as he did.

Taken to their logical conclusion, Jerome's statements would drive a wedge between the married and the unmarried clergy and would necessarily lead to a two-class clerical system. The strength of the early Christian continence discipline, though, lay precisely in its uniformity: All clerics, whether married or not, were subject to the same discipline. In keeping with mainstream theology in the East, on the other hand, Jerome defined various degrees: The couple who practiced continence were respected, but the widowed were more highly esteemed, and the virginal still more highly.[123] Such an arrangement would make tensions among the clergy inevitable. Jerome even accused the popes of being responsible for the ordination of so many married men, when they ought to have preferred unmarried men. Here the popes were being out-distanced on the right and held their ground as advocates of married clergy. In reality, no one in Rome was even thinking of restricting clerical candidates to celibates or widowers. Among the people, too, married men found approval again and again when they aspired to the ministry. Jerome complained bitterly about it, but he had no lobby left. His whole ascetical style did not fit into the Roman landscape.

d. Does Baptism Remove the Impediment to Orders of Digamy?

The dispute with Jovinian did not endanger clerical continence; rather, it ultimately consolidated it. It was necessary to come to terms with it anew and to set it off clearly from every sort of antipathy to marriage. Marriage and celibacy were equally valid Christian ways of life. This did not affect the continence practiced within marriage by married clerics.

The Manichaeism discussion surrounding Jovinian may have led to a theological clarification of the Church's celibacy discipline in one further respect. For a long time uncertainty had prevailed in the question of the Pauline impediment to orders of digamy. Did a marriage that ended in widowhood before baptism count, when a man, who was now married a second time, aspired to clerical office? Or was this first

---

[123] *Epistula* 49, 9, 3, 11, 2 *ad Pammachium* (CSEL 54, 364, 13-18. 366, 4-6); *Epistula* 123, 10, 1 *ad Geruchiam* (CSEL 56, 83, 13-17); *Adversus Jovinianum* 1, 40 (PL 23², 281B).

marriage "canceled" by baptism, so that he was no longer considered a digamist? The earlier writers Callistus and Hippolytus had different opinions on the subject, as one might well assume. Thus, Callistus did not count a marriage occurring before baptism, while Hippolytus included it in his reckoning. On this point there was no consensus among the theologians even in the fourth century. Ambrose's judgment[124] was different from Jerome's,[125] and Augustine's[126] was different from Theodoret's.[127] Whereas in the East there were various arguments for interpreting the digamy prohibition less strictly, a relaxation of the rule was generally rejected in the West.

It seems to be no accident that Jerome, who argued so ineptly against Jovinian and exposed himself to the charge of Manichaeism, advocated the view that a first marriage was canceled by baptism. Thus if a candidate for holy orders had already been widowed before his baptism and then remarried, he could be considered monogamous and become a cleric. Jerome makes such statements around 387–389 in his commentary on the Letter to Titus and before 402 in his letter to Oceanus. Possibly his personal animus against Ambrose and Siricius prompted him to adopt this interpretation, since they were of the contrary opinion.[128] What Jerome wrote did not go unnoticed. A certain Chrysogonos tried to blacken his reputation in Rome by claiming that he was favoring heretics. Presumably he meant that Jerome, with his interpretation, was supporting the Manichaeans and, ultimately, Jovinian. For if baptism canceled a previous marriage, then marriage had to be understood as a sin, since only sins are forgiven in baptism. Jerome, who even with his treatise against Jovinian provided more fuel for the charge of Manichaeism, inevitably cast the shadow of Manichaeism on the Church's marriage doctrine with his stance on digamy as well: The sin of marriage is wiped out by baptism. Such a statement surely made

---

[124] De officiis ministrorum 1, 50, 247 (PL 16², 104AB); Epistulae 63, 63 (CSEL 82, 3, 268, 638–51).

[125] Comm. in Tit. 1:6 (PL 26, 599A).

[126] De bono coniugali 18, 21 (CSEL 41, 214, 1–215, 19). He does not ground the monogamy rule in continence, as Siricius does, but rather ecclesiologically, in the unity between the one Church and the one Christ. He sides with those who count the marriages before baptism as well, because a marriage is not a sin and hence is not wiped away by baptism, either.

[127] Theodoret, Epistulae 110 (SC 111, 40, 20–42, 8).

[128] G. Grützmacher, Hieronymus: Eine biographische Studie zur Alten Kirchengeschichte, vol. 2 (Berlin, 1906), 192–95.

it even more difficult for the Romans to overcome the ideas of Jovinian that were still in currency.

In this respect it is not surprising that Ambrose, who was above all suspicion of Manichaeism, rejected Jerome's position, while still opposing the followers of Jovinian, by making the clear distinction: Baptism wipes out sins only, not the marriage bond. That also meant, then, a strict application of the digamy prohibition (1 Tim 3:2).

> I have not passed over this point, because many persons contend that the husband of one wife has reference to the time after baptism, so that any impediment which would ensue would be washed away in baptism. Indeed, all faults and sins are washed away, so that, if one has polluted his body by many whom he has not bound to himself by the marriage law, these are all forgiven him. But the marriages are not done away with (by baptism) if he has made a second contract, for sin, not the law, is loosed by the laver [of baptism]. There is no sin in marriage, but there is a law. Whatever is of law, therefore, is not remitted like a sin, but it is retained, like a law. Therefore, the Apostle laid down the law saying: "If anyone is without reproach, the husband of one wife." Whoever, then, is without reproach, the husband of one wife, is included among those held by the law to be qualified for the priesthood, but he who entered a second marriage has not the guilt of pollution, though he is disqualified from the privilege of the priesthood.
>
> Having stated what is lawful, let us state in addition what is reasonable. Let us understand, first of all, that not only did the Apostle lay down rules covering a bishop and priest, but the Fathers, also, in the Council of Nicaea, added the mandate that no one who has contracted a second marriage should be admitted to the clergy.[129] How can he console or honor a widow, or urge her to preserve her widowhood, or the faith pledged to her husband, which he himself has not kept in regard to his first marriage? Or what would be the difference between priest and people if they were bound by the same laws? The life of a priest ought to surpass others as its grace surpasses, and he who binds others by his precepts ought himself to keep the precepts of the law in himself.[130]

---

[129] This reference to the Council of Nicaea is probably based on an error, cf. PL 16², 1257f.

[130] *Epistulae* 63, 63f. (CSEL 82, 3, 268, 638–269, 664). [English translation by Sr. Mary Melchior Beyenka, O.P., *St. Ambrose, Letters* (New York: Fathers of the Church, 1954), 344–45.] Cochini, *Origins*, 234f. To explain the digamy prohibition in terms of the exemplary role of the priest is a rather meager argument; similarly Jerome, *Comm. in Tit.* 1:6 (PL 26, 598C); Ambrosiaster, *Comm. in* 1 *Tim.* 3:2 (CSEL 81, 3, 265, 3–7).

Remarkably, even Augustine, of all people, in his treatise "On the Good of Marriage" written in 401 against Jovinian, points out, in connection with the digamy prohibition, that marriage is not a sin and hence is not washed away by the water of baptism.[131] At around the same time Jerome writes to his Roman friend Pammachius, whom we have already mentioned, that he does not call into question the authoritative (papal) decision condemning the ordination of digamists. That he does not want to favor heretics in any way.[132] So he was making a retreat. Probably he had an eye to the celibacy decretals of Siricius, in which the author categorically rejects the ordination of digamists and, in doing so, obviously counts the marriages occurring before baptism. On this point as well, the papal instructions were already completed before Jovinian's appearance. Nevertheless, the dispute with him did lead to a clarification of the clerical discipline.

4. The Situation in Gaul under Pope Innocent

After North Africa, Spain, and Italy, we now come to the region known today as France, which even to this day is pleased to call itself the eldest daughter of Rome. The first reference we have worth mentioning is from Hilary, bishop of Poitiers in Aquitaine (d. 367). In his commentary on the Psalms, completed around 365, he concludes from 1 Corinthians 9:5 ("Have we not the right to take about with us a woman, a sister, as do the other apostles?" [Douay-Rheims]) that some of the apostles were married and that therefore Paul does praise celibacy but does not forbid marriage. It has been thought that, consequently, Hilary is speaking of the apostles' right to marry, even now that they are apostles. Such a possibility would naturally include the permission for clerics to marry, also. But that cannot be the point. The text does not admit such an interpretation.[133] Unfortunately we do not

---

[131] Augustine, *De bono coniugali* 18, 21 (CSEL 41, 214, 5–15).

[132] Jerome, *Apologia adversus libros Rufini* 1, 32 (PL 23², 444BC).

[133] Hilary, *Tractatus in Ps.* 118 *Nun* 14, 14 (SC 347, 142, 1–144, 10): "Habet hanc apostolus uoluntariae doctrinae, non et legitimae consuetudinem dicens: *De uirginibus autem praeceptum Domini non habeo, consilium autem do,* aut cum gloriam uiduitatis et continentiam laudat, non inhibita potestate nubendi, sed meritum caelibatus praedicat. Vltra legem instituit et ultra praeceptum adhortatur, uoluntaria legitimis anteponens. Et rursum ait: *Numquid non habemus potestatem manducandi et bibendi? Numquid non habemus potestatem mulieres circumducendi, sicut ceteri apostoli et fratres Domini et Cephas?*" Contrary to Vogels, *Priester*, 76.

have one single direct statement about clerical continence from Gaul during the first centuries. The situation here looks even less favorable than in Spain and North Africa.

a. Pope Innocent Writes to Rouen and Toulouse

We have to go on into the first years of the fifth century in order to find resources. Again our source of information is a papal document. That creates the impression that Rome was only now bringing the continence discipline to Gaul, after it had been exported to North Africa and Spain. This time we are dealing with Pope Innocent, the second successor of Siricius. In the year 402 he moved into the Lateran and remained there, like Siricius, for fifteen years. He studied well the records of his predecessor, whose essential arguments concerning the celibacy discipline appear again in his writings.

The decretal Etsi tibi. First of all, Innocent took action with respect to northern Gaul. There in Rouen, Victricius had served as metropolitan [arch]bishop since 386. We hear about him through the southern Italian priest Paulinus of Nola (d. 431), who wrote a letter to him around 397–398. In it he describes Rouen as the Gallic Jerusalem, full of churches and cloisters, monks, nuns, widows, and continent couples who devote themselves to unceasing prayer.[134] Naturally that is courtly rhetoric. Yet it does shed a certain light on the exemplary pastoral work of Victricius and, at the very least, mentions no abuses.

In the year 403 Victricius set out on the long journey to Rome in order to dispel slanderous rumors and declare his orthodoxy. On this occasion he asked the Pope, in all candor, to give him a conspectus of the essential points of discipline in the Roman Church. For Innocent that was a fascinating task, especially since Victricius was a very energetic missionary bishop who had already founded numerous churches in Flanders, northern France, and the regions of Hennegau and Brabant. In that way he could see to it that the complete Roman discipline was established everywhere. Accordingly, Innocent entered in his rulebook (*liber regularis*) everything that seemed important to him. This was in keeping with his ambition as a far-sighted churchman, who intervenes everywhere to put things in order and who has copies made

---

[134] *Epistulae* 18, 5 (CSEL 29, 132, 22–133, 5).

of all sorts of decrees.[135] On February 15, 404, he had the decretal *Etsi tibi* sent to Victricius.

> Moreover, the Church must by all means maintain what is worthy, chaste, and honest: that the priests and Levites [= deacons] have no intercourse with their wives, for the clergy are occupied with the daily duties of their ministries. For it is written, "Be holy, for I, the Lord your God, am holy" (Lev 11:44; 20:7). Indeed, if in former times the priests did not leave the temple of God during their year of service (Lev 21:12), as we read of Zechariah, and did not enter their houses at all—these men to whom it had been permitted to have relations with their wives so that they might have successors from among their offspring, since it had been decreed that none might enter the priesthood from any other tribe than from the seed of Aaron (Num 18:7)—how much more should those priests or Levites preserve chastity from the day of their ordination, to whom is given a priesthood or ministry that is not hereditary, when no day passes without the duty either of offering the divine sacrifice or of administering baptism? If Paul, writing to the Corinthians, says: "Abstain from one another so as to be free for prayer" (1 Cor 7:5) and thus instructs the lay people, how much more shall the priests, whose constant duty it is to pray and to offer sacrifice, be obliged to abstain from this sort of intercourse. If one is stained by carnal concupiscence, how can he presume to offer sacrifice in chastity? Or by what guarantee, by what merit does he believe that he will gain a hearing, when it is said, "To the pure all things are pure, but to the corrupt and unbelieving nothing is pure" (Tit 1:15)? But perhaps he believes this to be permissible because it is written: "the husband of one wife" (1 Tim 3:2). Yet [Paul] did not say this so that [a cleric] might persist in his desire to beget, but rather for the sake of future continence. Nor did he [Paul] refuse to admit even virginal candidates, for he said, "I wish that all were as I myself am" (1 Cor 7:7). And he stated his opinion even more clearly when he said: "Those who are in the flesh cannot please God. But you are not in the flesh, you are in the Spirit" (Rom 8:8–9).[136]

In his decrees about clerical continence, Innocent was to a great extent copying out the decretal *Cum in unum*, which Siricius composed about the decisions of the Roman synod. Because the documents are largely in agreement with each other, we can draw no inferences about the concrete situation in northern Gaul, not even with regard to the

---

[135] *Epistula* 2, 1 *ad Victricium* (PL 20, 469B–470A). Pietri, *Roma*, 2:978–91.

[136] *Epistula* 2, 9, 12 *ad Victricium* (PL 20, 475C–477A). [The English text has been translated from the Latin with reference to the German version.—TRANS.]

continence discipline. Innocent was concerned with preparing a conspectus of the essential points of discipline of the Roman Church, without being bound to a specific list of problems from Victricius' perspective. He was concerned about completeness, without asking whether this or that canon was now of current interest in Rouen. To be sure, Victricius was concerned also with having on hand a document with the highest authority, which would make it easier for him to remedy eventual abuses or rectify particular laws in his suffragan dioceses. But this does not justify the assumption that no continence discipline for higher clerics existed in Gaul until then.

The decretal Consulenti tibi. A year later Innocent was dealing with southern Gaul. Ministering there in Toulouse was Exsuperius, who had the reputation of being one of the exemplary bishops of Gaul.[137] That is also in keeping with the fact that he turned to the Pope because it was not clear to him how he should handle several rather difficult ecclesiastical matters. The Pope answered with the decretal *Consulenti tibi* of February 20, 405. Here Innocent was not at liberty to broach themes of his own choosing.

> You ask what is to be done about those who, while in the diaconal ministry or the priesthood, are proved to be or to have been incontinent, in that they have begotten children. About such clerics, the discipline of the divine laws is quite clear, and the plain admonitions of Bishop Siricius of blessed memory have been handed down, that incontinent men holding such offices must be deprived of all ecclesiastical dignity and must not be allowed to carry on a ministry that is fittingly performed only by those who practice continence.
>
> There is indeed the old authority of a very sacred law, which therefore has been kept from the beginning, that the priests are commanded to live in the temple during their year of service, so that the divine mysteries might claim pure ministers, cleansed of every stain, for the holy sacrifices. Nor was it lawful to admit to the sacrifices those who had sexual intercourse, even with their wife, for it is written, "Be holy, for I, the Lord your God, am holy" (Lev 11:44; 20:7). To these men it had been permitted, though, to have relations with their wives so that they might have successors from among their offspring, since it had been decreed that no one might enter the priesthood from any other tribe (Num 18:7)

---

[137] R. Nürnberg, *Askese als sozialer Impuls: Monastisch-asketische Spiritualität als Wurzel und Triebfeder sozialer Ideen und Aktivitäten der Kirche Südgalliens im 5. Jahrh.*, Hereditas 2 (Bonn, 1988), 246–51.

—how much more should those priests or Levites preserve chastity from the day of their ordination, to whom is given a priesthood or ministry that is not hereditary, when no day passes without the duty either of offering the divine sacrifice or of administering baptism! If Paul, writing to the Corinthians, says: "Abstain from one another so as to be free for prayer" (1 Cor 7:5) and thus instructs the lay people, how much more shall the priests, whose constant duty it is to pray and to offer sacrifice, be obliged to abstain from this sort of intercourse. If one is stained by carnal concupiscence, how can he presume to offer sacrifice in chastity? Or by what guarantee, by what merit does he believe that he will gain a hearing, when it is said, "To the pure all things are pure, but to the corrupt and unbelieving nothing is pure" (Tit 1:15)?

But perhaps he believes this to be permissible because it is written: "the husband of one wife" (1 Tim 3:2). Yet [Paul] did not say this so that [a cleric] might persist in his desire to beget, but rather for the sake of future continence. Nor did he [Paul] refuse to admit even virginal candidates, for he said, "I wish that all were as I myself am" (1 Cor 7:7). And he stated his opinion even more clearly when he said: "Those who are in the flesh cannot please God. But you are not in the flesh, you are in the Spirit" (Rom 8:8–9), and he said "having children" (1 Tim 3:4), not "begetting children".

But discern such matters thoroughly, and your judgment will be twofold. For if this norm of ecclesiastical life and ecclesiastical discipline, which was sent from Bishop Siricius to the provinces, cannot be proved to have reached some clerics, they should be dealt with leniently because of their ignorance, provided that henceforth they practice perfect continence. And so let them retain their present ranks, without allowing them to advance to higher ones. They ought to view it as a favor that they do not lose the position that they actually have. If it is discovered that any clerics knew about the manner of life prescribed by Siricius but did not immediately cast aside their libidinous desires, they are by all means to be removed from office, because after having heard the warning they decided that pleasure was preferable.[138]

Exsuperius was dealing with deacons and priests who, with their wives, were begetting children. He asked the Pope what should be done and how the punishment was to be determined. He did not call clerical continence itself into question. On the contrary, he was acquainted with it but did not know how he should act in individual

---

[138] *Epistula* 6, 1, 2–4 *ad Exsuperium* (PL 20, 496B–498A). [The English text has been translated from the Latin with reference to the German version.—Trans.]

cases. Uppermost in his mind, moreover, were neighboring dioceses where there were not a few bishops who were simply uninformed about the full ecclesiastical discipline, even though *Cum in unum* may well have been known already, at least in Arles.[139] In the dioceses of such bishops one could hardly speak of a consistent celibacy discipline. For Innocent, therefore, the inquiry of Exsuperius was a welcome opportunity to set up the regulations of Siricius as the definitive norm for southern Gaul as well.

Much the same was true in this instance as in the case of the letter to northern Gaul. Innocent again copied out *Cum in unum*, and hence we cannot infer from the formulas in the text anything about the concrete situation in Gaul. The Pope was not concerned with finding out where, in particular, the problems of Exsuperius might be. His concern was the overall strategy. And that demanded uniformity. The innovative feature of the decretal, therefore, is found not so much in celibacy practice as in celibacy law. It is a matter of gaining acceptance for a canonical rule and thus of achieving a certain legal stability. Lawlessness did not prevail, by any means, at the regional level, but Innocent was too skilled in ecclesiastical polity to want to keep grappling with peculiar local laws, when a decretal offered him the opportunity to construct an optimally broad basis for a universal law. Of course, one necessary consequence of this was the more severe and more consistent punishment of transgressions, because now a legal handle had been provided, which made Rome to an even greater extent the guardian of discipline.

b. Vigilantius Does Not Oppose Clerical Continence

The two decretals of Innocent were addressed to different regions of Gaul. It is not possible to establish a connection between them. The land was too extensive for that. At least for the south, though, there is still more information. The Toulouse of Exsuperius lay in the borderland of Aquitaine. At the beginning of the fifth century a priest named Vigilantius appeared in this area, who at first glance seemed to have problems with clerical continence. He carried out his pastoral ministry in Calagurris (today Cazères) in Aquitaine in southern Gaul,

---

[139] This is indicated by the Council of Arles a. 314, canon 29.

at the foot of the Pyrenees.[140] He maintained contacts with Sulpicius Severus (d. around 420) and Paulinus of Nola. One day he got into a vehement argument with Jerome, and it is to this circumstance that he owes his literary immortality.

It all happened as follows: Vigilantius traveled to the Holy Land around 395. In Bethlehem he became acquainted with Jerome, who was in charge of three convents and a monastery. Vigilantius gained an insight into the Latin monasticism of Palestine and its religious practices. Yet he does not seem to have been taken by it, particularly because of the theological squabbles about Origen. And so, after returning home to Gaul, to Jerome's great disappointment, he not only developed into his personal opponent, who painted him as an Origenist and a heretic, but he also turned out to be a vehement opponent of many forms of monastic piety.

Now one could say: Gaul is far away, after all. Then why should Jerome still be concerned about Vigilantius? Well, Gaul was by no means a *terra incognita* for Jerome. He had stayed there in his earlier years and had even traveled as far as Trier, and he continued to stay in contact with the monastic circles in Toulouse and Marseilles. There have been speculations as to whether Exsuperius was the diocesan bishop of Vigilantius.[141] That would be interesting, in that Jerome was in friendly contact with Exsuperius and personally thought very highly of him.[142] Exsuperius supported his monastery in Bethlehem financially, while this Vigilantius now was rejecting on principle the idea of supporting monks. Thus Jerome had contacts with Gaul in this regard as well. Calagurris, though, belonged to the neighboring diocese of Toulouse. Exsuperius, nevertheless, may well have been informed about what went on there, probably through the priest Riparius, a friend of Jerome. Of course it would be jumping to historical conclusions to assume that Vigilantius, through his criticism of celibacy, prompted the inquiry of Bishop Exsuperius to Innocent.[143] The facts of the matter were different.

---

[140] As to Vigilantius, see Grützmacher, *Hieronymus*, vol. 3 (Berlin, 1908), 154–63; M. Massie, "Vigilance de Calagurris face à la polémique hiéronymienne", BLE 81 (1980): 81–108.

[141] *Epistula* 123, 15, 4 *ad Geruchiam* (CSEL 56, 92, 15) and *Epistula* 125, 20, 3 *ad Rusticum* (CSEL 56, 141, 14f.): the holy Bishop Exsuperius; *Epistula* 109, 2, 1 *ad Riparium* (CSEL 55, 353, 8f.): the holy bishop.

[142] *Comm. in Zach.* prol. (PL 25, 1417A).

[143] Thus Massie, "Vigilance", 97.

First of all, Vigilantius' negative response was a bitter setback for Jerome in his efforts on behalf of the monastic movement—all the more so because the very same thing was now being played out in Gaul as had occurred previously in Rome, when Jovinian was making propaganda against him. Jerome learned about the machinations of Vigilantius in the year 404 through Riparius. The latter denounced Vigilantius as a dangerous heretic, because he attacked the veneration of relics and the celebration of vigil services, two forms of piety that had become dear especially to the ascetics. Naturally that was not reason enough to brand Vigilantius as a heretic, but people were very quick to take up such reproaches. In any case, at this point in time Jerome learned nothing further. Therefore he asked for the writings of Vigilantius, which did not arrive, however, until two years later. In the meantime both decretals of Innocent were issued.

In the year 406, one year after the two papal decretals, Jerome took up the pen with a holy zeal against Vigilantius after having received his writings.[144] In a single night he dashed off his treatise "Against Vigilantius" and thus made the Gallic priest famous in one stroke. To this day he is considered in most ecclesiastical histories an opponent of celibacy —whether correctly remains to be seen. We learn from Jerome what Vigilantius thought about clerical continence. He rediscovers in Vigilantius the doctrines of Jovinian:[145] Continence is a heresy, chastity is a nursery of desires (cf. 1 Cor 7:2), and he rejects virginity.[146] Jerome's portrayal of the situation implies that, as a result of such ideas, the bishops of Aquitaine no longer thought that celibacy was practicable and therefore, by ordaining married deacons exclusively, were establishing an altogether married clergy.

> How horrible! He [Vigilantius] is said to have bishops as accomplices in his wickedness, if the name bishop is still to be used for men who do not ordain deacons unless they have previously married. They do not believe in the chastity of any celibate and yet boast of what a holy life they lead—they, who suspect everyone of evil. And unless they see the wives of the clerics pregnant or hear children crying in the arms of their mothers, they will not administer the sacraments of Christ. What will the Churches of the East do? Or those of Egypt and the Apostolic

---

[144] *Epistula* 109, 4, 1 *ad Riparium* (CSEL 55, 355, 24–356, 1); *Adversus Vigilantium* 3 (PL 23², 356B).

[145] *Adversus Vigilantium* 1 (PL 23², 355A).

[146] Ibid., (PL 23², 355AB): "Continentiam haeresim, pudicitiam libidinis seminarium . . . impugnare virginitatem, odisse pudicitiam."

See, which only accept either virginal men as clerics or men who remain widowed [*continentes*], or else, if they have wives, those who refrain from marital relations? This is the doctrine of Dormitantius ["the Sleepy One" instead of "the Watchful One"—a taunt by Jerome], who gives full rein to lust and by his exhortations doubles the natural ardor of the flesh that usually glows in adolescence; rather, he extinguishes it by coition with women.[147]

At first glance one gets the impression that the situation in Gaul was chaotic. No trace of clerical continence, and valiant bishops leading the charge. Even publications favorably inclined toward celibacy find here a "different attitude of the bishops toward celibacy"[148] and suspect that there were priests in the south of France who disregarded celibacy.[149] That fits in then with the notion that the Roman celibacy discipline was accepted beyond Italy only with difficulty, only after repeated admonitions from the popes.

Of course, caution is required in regard to Jerome's statements. To be sure, his arguments were based on the writings of Vigilantius. But whether the latter really expressed therein his opinions about clerical continence is doubtful. Jerome, in any case, indicates that on this point he has the views of Vigilantius second-hand.[150] That is already reason enough not to take Jerome simply at his word. Above all one must realize: Jerome actually wanted to give precisely this (false) impression that hell had broken loose in Gaul. If historical criticism has any significance whatsoever, then it is to unmask such invective and not to take literally texts that are handed down without first scrutinizing the way in which they present themselves. One should never make the mistake of further embellishing the exaggerations of the Scripture scholar from Bethlehem with one's own imaginings, as, for instance, when Edward

---

[147] Ibid., 2 (PL 23², 355C–356A): "Proh nefas! episcopos sui sceleris dicitur habere consortes: si tamen episcopi nominandi sunt, qui non ordinant diaconos, nisi prius uxores duxerint: nulli caelibi credentes pudicitiam, imo ostendentes quam sancte vivant qui male de omnibus suspicantur: et nisi praegnantes uxores viderint clericorum, infantesque de ulnis matrum vagientes, Christi sacramenta non tribuant. Quid facient Orientis Ecclesiae? Quid Aegypti et Sedis apostolicae, quae aut virgines clericos accipiunt aut continentes: aut si uxores habuerint, mariti esse desistunt? Hoc docuit Dormitantius, libidini frena permittens, et naturalem carnis ardorem, qui in adolescentia plerumque fervescit, suis hortatibus duplicans; imo exstinguens coitu feminarum."

[148] Volume I of the *Generalregister* of the BKV, 2d ed. (Munich, 1931), 395.

[149] A. M. Stickler, *The Case for Clerical Celibacy: Its Historical Development and Theological Foundations*, trans. Brian Ferme (San Francisco, 1995), 60–61; Bickell, "Cölibat", 36.

[150] Jerome does not deal with the writings until *Adversus Vigilantium* 3 (PL 23², 356B), and there they are concerned only with the veneration of relics and the vigils.

Schillebeeckx deduces from the text that hundreds of bishops sympathized with Vigilantius' critique.[151] It would be very easy to mention
other cases from this period in which obvious untruths were circulated
about honorable bishops.[152]

Jerome's treatise was destined for the public as a calculated maneuver.
He wanted Vigilantius to be removed. And he seems to have succeeded;
in any case we never hear anything about him again. The strategy is
transparent: Jerome brands Vigilantius as a very dangerous and influential heretic, who is leading the entire region of Gaul astray; someone
must put a stop to him. Moreover he wants to mobilize, in the first
place, the Pope and harness him to the cart of his private feud.[153] The
polemical work aims from the outset at a Roman condemnation of
Vigilantius: Jerome presents him as *Jovinianus redivivus*, who in his day
was condemned by Rome as a heretic.[154] Therefore Rome ought to
intervene and condemn the new Jovinian as well. Jerome makes Vigilantius out to be an opponent of celibacy, probably in a way that hardly
does him justice. He knows that Pope Innocent is particularly sensitive
about clerical discipline. Therefore he suggests that Vigilantius is even
urging the bishops to admit to the priesthood incontinent men who
continue to beget children after their ordination.

But what is the real reason for these accusations? First of all, we
can assume that Vigilantius wanted to admit only married men to holy
orders. Only those candidates should be ordained who have married
before their diaconal ordination. On closer inspection one begins to
notice this important detail: Jerome is speaking only about the marriage
of men who are not yet deacons, who therefore still belong to the lower
clergy and are about to be "ordained to the diaconate" (*ordinant diaconos*). Lower clerics, though, were entirely free to marry and to beget
children, even according to Roman discipline.[155] Priests and bishops
are not mentioned by Jerome in this connection. Thus Vigilantius by

---

[151] *Amtszölibat*, 31. He conflates that with the digamous bishops, who were more numerous than the participants at the Synod of Rimini, mentioned in Jerome, *Epistula* 69, 2, 2 *ad
Oceanum*.

[152] For example, about the Gallic bishops Heros of Arles and Lazarus of Aix; A. Kun-
zelmann and A. Zumkeller, eds., *Aurelius Augustinus: Schriften gegen die Pelagianer*, vol. 2
(Würzburg, 1964), 37–41.

[153] Along the same lines, Jerome sees in the doctrine of Vigilantius an attack on the
Bishop of Rome, who venerates the relics of Peter and Paul; *Adversus Vigilantium* 8 (PL 23²,
361CD).

[154] Ibid., 1 (PL 23², 355AB).

[155] Gryson, *Origines*, 160.

no means wanted permission to marry for those who were already ordained deacons and for other higher clerics. Jerome says only: Under
the influence of Vigilantius, certain bishops want the lower clerics to
marry before their diaconal ordination.

Hence, if Vigilantius in no way intended to abolish the marriage
prohibition for higher clerics, it is not surprising that he did not intend to do away with the continence discipline for married clerics
and their wives, either. After all, Jovinian, too, accepted clerical continence. Jerome would certainly have taken up the debate energeti-
cally if Vigilantius had said that higher clerics were allowed to beget
children. If we hear nothing on this subject, then it is surely because
Vigilantius caused no difficulties on this point. That also explains why
he demanded marriage before diaconal ordination, but not afterward.
For a marriage contracted after ordination could not be consummated
on account of the continence requirement.

A marriage after ordination is not the point in the following sentence, either: "And unless they [that is, the bishops of Gaul] see the
wives of the clerics pregnant or hear children crying in the arms of their
mothers, they will not administer the sacraments of Christ." By clerics are probably meant the lower clerics, that is, lectors, acolytes, and
subdeacons, who still had their diaconal ordination ahead of them.[156]
Thus if Jerome is polemicizing against the clerics of Vigilantius with
their pregnant wives, then that refers to the same state of affairs as before: lower clerics were required to have married and to have begotten
children before their diaconal ordination.

That the argument concerned lower clerics and their ordination to
the diaconate becomes evident again from the concluding words of the
aforementioned book: ". . . I [that is, Jerome] shall watch for an entire
night and deal with him [that is, Vigilantius] and his companions, be
they pupils or teachers, who, unless they see wives heavy with child,
think that their husbands are unworthy of the ministry of Christ."[157]

---

[156] Grützmacher, *Hieronymus*, 3:162 translates "Christi sacramenta tribuant" correctly as
"administer the Sacrament of Holy Orders". The administration of Holy Eucharist would
not make sense. Augustine speaks of "sacramentum domini, sacramentum ordinationis" and
"sacramenta ordinationis"; *Contra epistulam Parmeniani* 2, 13, 28 (PL 43, 70f.); *De bono coniugali* 24, 32 (CSEL 41, 227, 9f.).

[157] *Adversus Vigilantium* 17 (PL 23², 368B): "Sed tota nocte vigilabo, et sociis illius, immo
discipulis vel magistris, qui nisi tumentes uteros viderint feminarum, maritos earum Christi
ministerio arbitrantur indignos."

Here again is a polemical use of the image of pregnant women whose husbands are just on the threshold of being ordained. Thus, if Jerome generalizes about clerics begetting children, he is deliberately leaving unclear the fact that he does not mean higher clerics at all, but lower clerics. If one were to fall for it and assume that deacons and priests, at the instigation of Vigilantius, were permitted to keep on begetting children, one would be doing him the greatest of favors.

When Jerome finally mentions the other Churches, "which only accept either virginal men as clerics or men who remain widowed, or else, if they have wives, those who refrain from marital relations", then it gives the impression that Vigilantius was in fact also opposing the continence discipline for married clerics and their wives.[158] But naturally, this too is precisely what Jerome wants to insinuate. In no way is it said that the bishops in Gaul wanted deacons, priests, and bishops who were begetting children. Jerome speaks only about "clerics" and by that doubtless means lower clerics again, who were still permitted to beget children.

As a preliminary conclusion we can state that Vigilantius, just like Jovinian, was attacking only celibacy or virginity. Naturally, that also had consequences for the clergy. But the continence of married clerics and their wives was not being called into question. There is no mention of permission for deacons, priests, and bishops to marry. The point is that unmarried lower clerics were supposed to marry before they were admitted to the higher clergy. As Jerome describes it, the decisive reason for this was the opinion that an unmarried man could not practice continence. But were they saying that in the future all deacons would in fact be married? In the long run that would have led to an exclusively married clergy. But we can hardly assume that the Gallic bishops were accepting married men exclusively to the higher ecclesiastical offices. Jerome has heard only vague rumors about that (*dicitur*). Besides, the bishops in question were not pursuing any dishonest objectives, for they themselves lived as celibates and were proud of it, as Jerome well knew. How could they have refused to ordain celibate candidates, then?

---

[158] Thus also Cochini, *Origins*, 299.

c. Do Young Monks Want to Marry and Join the Clergy?

What was it about Vigilantius and the Gallic bishops that infuriated Jerome so much, if they really had not done anything wrong? Let us return again to the comparison that Jerome makes between Vigilantius and Jovinian. The former was hardly dependent upon the latter, but it is clear why Jerome juxtaposes them: Vigilantius was, at least in Jerome's view of the matter, a troublesome opponent of monasticism, just like Jovinian. We must look to the monastic milieu for the reasons why Vigilantius was enrolled in the antagonists' club. Vigilantius worked not far from the diocese of Himerius of Tarragona. The North and South Pyrenean ecclesiastical regions at that time were closely connected with each other.[159] This justified a look at the letter of Siricius to that bishop from northeastern Spain.

We have heard of the abuses of many monks in northern Spain, who begot children in the shelter of their cloisters. There was reason, therefore, to doubt the continence of the monks.[160] Vigilantius was a realist and a skeptic. He probably did not believe that celibate men —especially when they were still young and the danger of inflamed passions was too great—were necessarily capable of continence, and he saw his opinion confirmed by the conduct of many monks.[161] Nor was Jerome, indeed, at all blind to such breaches of discipline, inasmuch as the comportment of many monks and clerics, one could say, had failed remarkably to comport with their promise of virginity.[162]

Now it was becoming increasingly more common for monks to be admitted to the clergy because of the need for candidates. At least Siricius expressed the wish that monks, too, might be admitted to the clergy if they had proved their virtue and had reached a minimum age of thirty years.[163] New ideas occurred to many of them as they did so. In fact at the time of Vigilantius there were monks who wanted to marry as they were being admitted to the clergy. We hear about that in

---

[159] Chadwick, Priscillian, 11f.

[160] On Spanish monasticism in the writings of Siricius, see Garcia Villoslada, Iglesia, 625–29; A. de Vogue, Histoire littéraire du mouvement monastique dans l'antiquité, vol. 1, Le Monachisme latin de la mort d'Antoine à la fin du séjour de Jérôme à Rome (356–385) (Paris, 1991), 206–10. Cf. Innocent, Epistula 2, 14, 16 ad Victricium (PL 20, 479f.).

[161] Cf. Adversus Vigilantium 12 (PL 23², 364C).

[162] Adversus Helvidium 21 (PL 23², 216A).

[163] Epistula 1, 13, 17 ad Himerium (PL 13, 1144A–1145A). Cf. Pietri, Roma, 1:690–96.

the decretal of Innocent to Victricius. Now one might object that that applies to northern Gaul and not to the south. But we have already said that *Etsi tibi* was not meant to deal with particular Gallic concerns but contained quite general regulations for clerics. Even though the decretal was addressed to northern Gaul, it still took into consideration canons that had arisen in particular Churches and had significance for other dioceses as well, especially since Victricius was very interested in founding monasteries in his episcopal see.[164] So in the discourse of Innocent we probably have in hand the key to understanding Vigilantius.

Innocent writes about monks who have lived for a long time in the monastery and then have been admitted to the clergy.[165] Perhaps a lack of clergy for pastoral work played a role in this. On this occasion some thought that they were allowed to marry. They seem to have given as their reason for this that they were now no longer monks but clerics who lived outside of the cloister. Other monks, who were widowed before being baptized, even thought that as clerics they were allowed to marry a second time. In any case by doing so they broke their vows. We recall that, as a result of Jovinian's appearance, many virgins renounced their vows in order to marry. Innocent refuses such an unreasonable demand, which appears here in this form for the first time.[166] Monks, even when they leave their cloister to enter the Church's ministry, are bound to their vows.

Obviously the development being discussed here had begun only in recent years and thus fell precisely in the period of Vigilantius. It could therefore be a description of events in southern Gaul pertaining to Vigilantius. That Innocent should mention them in his letter to Victricius was perhaps due to the fact that the latter, through his contact with

---

[164] P. Andrieu-Guitrancourt, "La Vie ascétique à Rouen au temps de saint Victrice", RSR 40 (1951/52): 90–106 at 93.

[165] *Epistula* 2, 10f, 13 *ad Victricium* (PL 20, 477A): "De monachis qui diu morantes in monasteriis, si postea ad clericatus ordinem pervenerint, non debere eos a priore proposito deviare. Aut enim sicut in monasterio fuit, et quod diu servavit, in meliori gradu positus amittere non debet: aut si corruptus (i.e., widowed) postea baptizatus, et in monasterio sedens, ad clericatus ordinem accedere voluerit, uxorem omnino habere non poterit; quia nec benedici cum sponsa potest jam corruptus. Quae forma servatur in clericis, maxime cum vetus regula hoc habeat, ut quisquis corruptus baptizatus, clericus esse voluisset, sponderet se uxorem omnino non ducere." Lafontaine, *Conditions*, 169–72.

[166] The East later had to contend with the same problems; Cochini, *Origins*, 357.

Martin of Tours, was interested in monasticism in Aquitaine.[167] So if we are, indeed, dealing with marrying monks in Aquitaine, then there could be a connection with Vigilantius. He might have prompted bishops to allow monks, especially very young ones who were not capable of maintaining virginity, to marry and to be admitted to the clergy. It is interesting, now, that Innocent speaks of the marriage of monks who are being admitted to orders. In the worst case, therefore, these monks were marrying as lower clerics. This does not mean marriage of deacons and priests. In this respect the passage confirms that Jerome, too, speaks only of the pregnant wives of clerics in minor orders.

Vigilantius and the bishops who had sided with him, then, merely wanted to allow younger monks to marry upon entering the secular clergy, that is, as lower clerics, and to beget children. It was not their intention that married candidates should be ordained exclusively. The Vigilantius affair was not based on a conflict between monasticism and the secular clergy, either.[168] At first glance one might well suspect that, since Vigilantius was a secular priest. But that certainly did not make him an opponent of clerical monasticism, any more than Siricius was (cf. *Directa*). On the contrary: he was courting the monks: Who else is supposed to carry out the Church's ministry, he asks. So he enticed the monks away from their ascetical endeavors, so that they would leave their cloisters to proclaim the gospel in the world, instead of retreating to the solitude of the cloister.[169] He advocated marrying as they did so, provided that they were only in minor orders. Maybe that was supposed to promote their integration into the secular clergy, which probably consisted largely of married men.

It is clear that Jerome saw in this an attack on everything that was sacred to him: an attempt to undermine the vows and the stability of the cloister. Bishops were letting monks marry. Well, presumably Innocent had already taken measures against the bishops. At least that can be inferred from the decretal. But for Jerome it was still a worthwhile opportunity, even in the aftermath, to put down Vigilantius (with whom he had a personal account to settle) as a dangerous heretic. Of course it was practically an honor to have Jerome contend with you; you be-

---

[167] R. Lorenz, "Die Anfänge des abendländischen Mönchtums im 4. Jahrhundert", ZKG 77 (1966): 1–61 at 16f. For what little is known about Spanish monasticism, see ibid., 18–23.

[168] Thus Brown, *Keuschheit*, 364f.

[169] *Adversus Vigilantium* 15f. (PL 23², 366C–368A).

came world famous in one stroke. In any case we can suppose that Jerome's treatise did not fail to achieve its purpose. Innocent esteemed him as an influential advocate of the papal prerogatives in the Orient and intervened for him in his dispute with Bishop John of Jerusalem.[170]

The decretal Dominus inter *addressed to the Gallic bishops.* The decretal *Dominus inter*, whose author has not been determined, could be ascribed to Siricius.[171] It is mentioned here by way of concluding this chapter, since it fits into the context of the Gallic decretals of Innocent. The author says that already, on more than one occasion, he has published the celibacy laws in the Churches. This could mean the decretals to Himerius and to the North African bishops. *Dominus inter* replies to explicit inquiries of the Gallic bishops. The decretal adds nothing new to our understanding of the concrete celibacy discipline. It does have significance, though, for the question of the apostolic origin and the universal ecclesiastical dimension of clerical continence. We will return to this subject farther on. For the sake of completeness the entire text pertaining to continence is quoted:

> 2. We know, dear brothers, that many bishops in various churches have hastily changed the tradition of the fathers, out of human presumption and to the detriment of their own good name, and that they have fallen thereby into the darkness of heresy. For they take delight in their reputation among men more than they have sought to obtain a reward from God. And so now, not for the sake of speculation, but in order to confirm the faith, Your Holiness has deigned to ask the authority of the Apostolic See about the state of the law and the traditions, wishing us to set forth frankly a reply to the proposed questions, which you sincerely and longingly seek. Hear, then! Insofar as divine favor grants it, I shall say, though with mediocre eloquence, yet with sure meaning, the things that are to be observed in order to remedy, indeed, all the deviations that have led to discord through downright arrogance, as Sacred Scripture says: "You leave the commandment of God and hold fast the tradition of men" (Mk 7:8). Therefore, if in the fullness of faith you want to know the true observances, graciously pay attention to the things that I say. In the first place the subject of modesty and chastity is presented to me. Then a great many questions are posed. And so we will apply the traditions to each particular subject in order. . . .

---

[170] Grützmacher, *Hieronymus*, 3:275.

[171] É. Demougeot, "Gallia I", in RAC 8 (1972), 822–927, at 905. See above, p. 225, n. 52 [of this chapter 6].

5. And we have already written often about such things to the various churches, especially about the priests, whose dignity requires that they be an example to the people by their good works. . . . As long as we keep repeating the same things that are thought to be neglected by some individuals, this is truly what was said to the adulterous generation: "Always learning and never arriving at a knowledge of the truth" (2 Tim 3:7). Indeed, when expedient warnings are not heeded, the apostolic commands are despised as though they were unknown. Nevertheless the judgment upon the things that they have committed cannot be changed. So much for the priests.

In the first place we should consider the bishops, priests, and deacons, who must participate in the divine sacrifices, by whose hands both the grace of baptism is conferred and the Body of Christ is confected. Not only we, but the Sacred Scriptures also compel them to be perfectly chaste, and the Fathers, too, commanded that they must observe bodily continence. Therefore let us not pass over this concern but rather address the issue. How can a bishop or a priest dare to preach virginity or continence to a widow or a virgin, or advise [spouses] to keep their marriage bed chaste, if he himself is more intent on begetting children for this world than for God? Adam, who did not obey the command, was cast out of Paradise and was deprived of the kingdom (Gen 3:23); and do you think that one who violates his duty can enter into the kingdom of heaven? Wherefore Paul says: "But you are not in the flesh, you are in the Spirit" (Rom 8:9), and again: "Let those who have wives live as though they had none" (1 Cor 7:29). Or would someone who thus exhorts the people, so flatter the Levites [= deacons] and priests as to give them permission to pursue the work of the flesh, when he himself says, "Make no provision for the flesh, to gratify its desires" (Rom 13:14), and elsewhere "I wish that all were as I myself am" (1 Cor 7:7)? How can someone serve Christ as a soldier or occupy the teacher's chair if he cannot keep the military discipline?

6. And so for these three degrees that we read about in the Scriptures, the precept of purity is to be kept by the ministers of God, for they must be ready at all times. For either baptism is to be administered, or else sacrifices are to be offered. Shall the impure man, then, dare to contaminate what is holy, when the holy things are holy for the holy ones? After all, those who used to offer sacrifices in the Temple, in order to be pure, would remain the entire year in the Temple for the sole reason of the discipline, without once setting foot in their houses. Even the idolators, in order to perform their impious rites and immolate to demons, make it their rule to abstain from women and even resolve to purge themselves of [certain] foods; and you ask me whether the priest of the True God, who has to offer spiritual sacrifices, must continually remain purified, or

whether, entirely in the flesh, he must attend to the cares of the flesh?! If commingling is a defilement, then the priest must be at all times prepared for the heavenly ministry so as to intercede for the sins of others; may he not be found unworthy himself! For if it is said to laymen, "Abstain from one another so as to be free for prayer" (1 Cor 7:5), and those clerics still serve the creature by begetting, then they may have the name of priests, but they cannot have the merit. If this is the case and the suspicion is confirmed, it behooves them to learn that the lives of bishops, priests, and deacons should not be associated with the lives of publicans. For which reason, beloved, prompted by nothing other than reverence for our religion, I warn you that it is not fitting for me to entrust the mystery of God to men who are so defiled and unfaithful, in whom the sanctity of the body is evidently polluted by filth and incontinence. Indeed, even right reason keeps them at a distance. Let them hear and mark well: "For flesh and blood cannot inherit the kingdom of God, nor does the perishable inherit the imperishable" (1 Cor 15:50). Does any priest or deacon still dare to subject himself to corruption after the manner of the animals? . . .

8. The Roman Church keeps this custom especially: that if a man who was baptized as a child has remained a virgin, he can be admitted to the clergy; or if a mature man is baptized and has remained chaste, the husband of one wife, he can become a cleric, provided that he is not fettered by the chains of any other crimes. Moreover, if a man has spoiled the sacrament of water by sins of the flesh, even if he marries after committing fornication, how could he carry out the ministry of forgiving sins when he has repeated (after baptism) the blindness of his former life? . . . Such men will be ministers or priests, not of Christ, but rather of the Antichrist! And where is that which the holy apostle Paul previously commanded, when he described what kind of a man is to be ordained a bishop, saying "above reproach, temperate, modest", and so on (1 Tim 3:2). In what sense is a man above reproach who has not been able to safeguard the grace [*sacramentum*] of baptism? What unheard-of audacity! To this man the priesthood is entrusted, who deserves penance alone so that he might purify by long reparation the benefits of forgiveness [that is, the baptismal grace] that he has defiled!

9. There must be one confession (of faith) among the Catholic bishops, according to the apostolic teaching. Hence, if there is one faith, there must continue to be one tradition as well. If there is one tradition, then one discipline must be observed in all the churches. In various regions churches have been founded, it is true, but throughout the whole world She is called one, on account of the unity of the catholic faith.[172]

---

[172] *Epistula* 10, 2–9 *ad Gall.* (PL 13, 1182A–1188A). [The English text has been translated from the Latin with reference to the German version.—TRANS.]

5. Summary

The western half of the empire in the fourth century offers an abundance of voluminous texts that, taken together, provide a clear picture of the situation in the clergy. In North Africa, after the references in Tertullian and Cyprian, we hear again in the year 390, on the occasion of a synod of bishops in Carthage, about an obligation of married clerics to practice perfect continence. Pope Siricius (384 to 399), the resourceful champion of clerical continence, probably collaborated in this decision. Nevertheless, it would be erroneous to assume that such a discipline was introduced for the first time in North Africa only under pressure from Rome. In reality the celibacy discipline, as it had been known since the days of Tertullian and Cyprian and from the Council of Elvira, took a beating as a result of the Donatist schism. Not until around 390 did the Catholic bishops succeed in extricating the Church gradually from her desolate condition through consistent organizational measures. On this occasion they also tackled the problem of clerical continence, with the help of Rome.

It can be proved that Pope Siricius then took action in Spain. His decretal *Directa* from the year 385 gave Bishop Himerius of Tarragona, in response to the latter's inquiry, instructions about the celibacy discipline: Higher clerics were not allowed to beget children. This was in principle nothing new for Spain: the Council of Elvira around the year 306 already knew of an obligation for married clerics to practice perpetual continence. The Church in Spain, meanwhile, was in the midst of a crisis; the reaction, under the spiritual leadership of Priscillian, led to an influential reform movement. This ascetical uprising was so rigorous, however, that its protagonists, among whom were found numerous bishops and clerics, were suspected of the Manichaean heresy. In the whirlpool of bitter disputations, the clerical and disciplinary reforms that had been kicked off by the reformers were in danger of being discredited also. Only the shrewd and decisive steps taken by Himerius and Siricius managed to prevent a breakdown of discipline: they made clerical continence their own concern, independent of Priscillian.

In Rome during the reign of Pope Damasus (366 to 384) continence celibacy was an established fact, as the writings of the anonymous Ambrosiaster show. Likewise, in northern Italy, Ambrose of Milan had no serious problems with his clergy, not even with the rural clerics (contrary to a common misunderstanding of one of his remarks). But in Italy there was concern about developments in Spain. There, probably in reaction to the reformers, there was talk about outspoken opponents of celibacy for the first time: married clerics who did not want to observe continence. Ambrose and Ambrosiaster took up the task of refuting their arguments. First the Spaniards pointed to a merely temporary continence of the Old Testament Levites, whom they wished to emulate. The two theologians from Italy did not allow that argument to stand: The frequency of the Divine Liturgy did not play a decisive role. This demonstrates that continence celibacy could not have been a late fourth-century invention of Rome on account of the daily celebration of the Eucharist; for neither in Rome nor in Spain was the Mass celebrated daily at that time. Furthermore, because of the connection with Priscillian, clerical continence was endangered by the suspicion of a Manichaean contempt for the body, even in regions beyond Spain. In response, Ambrosiaster defended the discipline and saw its justification rather in the appropriateness of this religious practice for the minister of God.

Clerical continence remained a topic of discussion under Pope Siricius. Uneasy about the events in Spain, he publicized the celibacy discipline for central and southern Italy at a Roman synod in the year 385 (decretal *Cum in unum*). We do not hear anything about an organized opposition, albeit there were violations of the continence requirement, which probably resulted from ignorance of the discipline. At that same time the monk Jovinian appeared in Rome. He put up a resistance to the ascetical propaganda of Jerome and the official line of the Church, which esteemed virginity more highly than marriage. His critique was aimed more at monasticism and less at the clergy. Jovinian accepted, in principle, the celibacy of many clerics and also the continence requirement for married ministers. His theological thinking may well have gone against the grain, but an opponent of celibacy he was not. He neither precipitated a celibacy crisis in Rome, nor did he cause the Church to react with a tightening of the discipline that would require married clerics and their wives, as well as celibate clerics, to practice continence from then on. The clergy had long been acquainted with the entire continence discipline, and Jovinian, too, accepted it.

In Gaul we first hear about a clerical continence discipline through two decretals of Pope Innocent (402–417). At the same time Jerome was railing at Vigilantius, a priest from southern Gaul, under whose influence clerics allegedly continued to beget children. This gives the impression that a celibacy discipline was first introduced in Gaul under Innocent. But the purpose of the decretals was merely to codify a clear and uniform discipline, especially with regard to consistent procedures for dealing with infractions, so as to establish reliable legislation in this territory. What the situation actually looked like in the particular regions of Gaul, we cannot really say.

Only for Aquitaine, where Vigilantius appeared, can more detailed information be given. Vigilantius was no more an opponent of clerical continence than Jovinian was. He did declare himself in favor of marriage for lower clerics before diaconal ordination. With this idea he found a hearing with his bishop. Young candidates, especially, were supposed to be able to marry. Of course, after their ordination to the diaconate, they would have to practice continence together with their wives. Presumably, though, there was a very concrete problem behind the initiative of Vigilantius. There must have been monks who left their cloister and were admitted to the pastoral clergy of their diocese, at first as lower clerics. Some of them believed that on this occasion they were allowed to marry and to beget children. Vigilantius supported this. However, he thereby made himself so unpopular with Jerome, the most influential promoter of monasticism, that the latter ostracized him as though he were the gravedigger of clerical continence, which he most certainly was not.

All in all: the West, during the fourth century, did not experience the birth pangs of an ascetical clerical discipline, but rather had to overcome great difficulties with continence celibacy, which had been for the most part the long-established practice.[173] The ongoing expansion of the Church brought about infractions and ignorance in many places. Through the initiative of the popes and the bishops the Church arrived at a universal and uniform set of regulations, which led to legal certainty and stability. There were abuses in the clergy, but that hardly amounted to a definite opposition to ecclesiastical policy. And there were assuredly not any serious theological critics. Popes, bishops, and theologians intensified their efforts on behalf of the theological cause of clerical continence, in order to set forth clearly its meaning and purpose. Such an undertaking had not been accomplished by anyone before that and was long overdue.

---

[173] Cochini, *Origins*, 250.

VII. The Common Heritage of Clerical Continence in the Subsequent History of the Church

In the second half of the fourth century, continence for higher clerics was a well-known and obligatory practice in wide sectors of the Church, and this was equally true in the East and in the West. At that time there was as yet no distinction between Roman Catholic and Orthodox. It was all the *Catholic* Church, in the fullest sense of the word, though in the East she was mainly Greek-speaking and in the West, Latin-speaking. More than a few theologians were competent in both languages, for instance a Tertullian or a Jerome. What a clerical discipline in common with the East was worth to Popes Siricius and Innocent, how this legacy was in danger of being lost in the fifth century, and how finally the common heritage was torn in two shall be our concern in the following discussion.

1. The Responsibility of the Popes for the Clerical Discipline of the Universal Church

The celibacy discipline of the early Church reached a high point of juridical definition and promulgation in the West under the two preeminent papal figures Siricius and Innocent. Just think of their decretals, which are important also in the history of canon law. Many see in them nothing less than the original sin of Roman centralism, which has had unforeseeable consequences to the present day.[1] In their view, the Church began at this point to be reorganized and transformed, starting from Rome. It is no accident that one encounters for the first time in these documents the clearly discernible claim of the popes to the primacy and, thus, to the administration of the entire Church.[2] The decretal *Directa* is famous not only for its treatment of clerical continence but also for its emphasis on the authority of the pope. The primacy

---

[1] H. Küng, *Das Christentum: Wesen und Geschichte* (Munich and Zürich, 1994), 369.

[2] Cf. K. Schatz, *Der päpstliche Primat: Seine Geschichte von den Ursprüngen bis zur Gegenwart* (Würzburg, 1990), 44–46.

and continence celibacy fall in the same time period. Someone who, as pope, makes the claim that he is the first in the universal Church must also have a view of the whole; he must be ecumenically oriented toward the Church throughout the world and include the entire East in his perspective. This opens up for us an important approach to the subject, which will enable us to reach a suitable judgment on the celibacy initiatives of the popes at the turn of the fifth century.

a. Do the Popes Promote the Continence Discipline of the East?

It is obvious that the clerical discipline of Popes Siricius and Innocent was in keeping with the practice of continence as we know it from the East. In this sense the popes were presenting nothing new but were rather promoting a continence celibacy discipline that was established in the East as well, in almost exactly the same form. That is not self-evident. The celibacy discipline, after all, is not a simple matter that can readily be summed up in one word; rather, it is composed of a whole bundle of regulations. Their formulation and biblical-theological foundation, as given by the popes, corresponded in large measure to the Eastern practice.

First of all, the celibacy regulations pertained only to higher clerics, but to them indiscriminately, from deacons to bishops. It is important to grasp this, inasmuch as later, in the East, there would be a differentiation between bishops, on the one hand, and deacons and priests, on the other. In contrast, in the first centuries the clerical regulations pertaining to continence applied indiscriminately to those in major orders in the East as well. It may happen that the sources make statements only for a particular rank of the clergy, but all in all the findings leave no doubt as to the above-mentioned uniformity.

Continence. The central consensus of the West with East lies in the fact that there were both married and unmarried higher clerics, who received equal recognition, yet complete sexual continence was demanded of all of them from the day of their ordination. No exceptions, no concessions were made. Clerical continence, therefore, was an essentially uniform discipline, which transcended the boundaries separating various manners of life. Those affected included both married and widowed as well as virginal clerics.[3] Their social relationships

---

[3] E.g., Ambrose, *De officiis ministrorum* 1, 50, 248 (PL 16², 104B); cf. *De viduis* 4, 23 (PL 16², 254D–255A).

and living arrangements, to be sure, took completely different forms. But the sole decisive factor was whether one could practice continence.

The marriage prohibition. In conformity with the East, the marriage prohibition was valid also in the West. It followed necessarily from the duty to observe continence.[4] Jerome knew of the prohibition.[5] It is true that it was not mentioned by Siricius, Ambrose, or Innocent.[6] But then again this is striking. Had there been no obligatory continence previously, one would certainly have had to rule out a marriage prohibition as well; it would have made no sense. Only obligatory continence for married clerics and their wives could provide a compelling reason for a marriage prohibition, too. If, however, continence celibacy had been an innovation of Siricius, one would have expected, for the sake of clarity, an explicit marriage prohibition. Because no such regulation was issued, we must assume that the marriage prohibition had long been undisputed in Spain and Italy. Actually, before Siricius we never hear of higher clerics who have married. In his time, moreover, something like that seems to have been completely unthinkable. Not even Jovinian came up with such an idea.

The digamy prohibition. In conformity with the East, the digamy prohibition was valid also in the West. Men who were already in a second marriage could not be admitted to the higher clergy. The fact that the precise explanation of this prohibition of the pastoral letters was disputed—inasmuch as many counted only those marriages entered into after baptism, while Siricius and Innocent as well as Ambrose and Augustine settled on a stricter interpretation[7]—only goes to show that,

---

[4] R. Gryson, *Les Origines du célibat ecclésiastique du premier au septième siècle*, RSSR.H 2 (Gembloux, 1970), 159f.; idem, *Le Prêtre selon saint Ambroise* (Louvain, 1968), 310.

[5] *Epistula ad Nepotianum* 52, 10, 3 (CSEL 54, 432, 12–16): "Ducant pontifices Christi uxores uirgines [cf. Lev. 21:13] . . . crescamus et multiplicemur et repleamus terram [cf. Gen. 1:28]." That refers to the Old Testament priesthood. For the priests of Christ, Jerome rules out marrying and begetting children entirely, as is clear from the context.

[6] Siricius, *Epistulae* 5, 2 (PL 13, 1159A), only appears to contradict a marriage prohibition (see above, p. 242, n. 82 [of chapter 6]). An apparent contradiction to a marriage prohibition is found also in Jerome, *Adversus Jovinianum* 1, 34 (PL 23², 268D): "Eligatur episcopus . . . , qui unam ducat uxorem." But that refers to candidates for orders. The quotation says the same thing as a passage farther above: "et episcopi et presbyteri et diaconi unius uxoris viri, et habentes filios, ab Apostolo constituuntur". A marriage prohibition follows from *Adversus Jovinianum* 1, 26 (PL 23², 256C). That a marriage prohibition existed in the West is shown also in Jerome's polemic against Vigilantius and, furthermore, in many statements about the possibility of a marriage by lower clerics.

[7] Innocent, *Epistula* 2, 5, 8–6, 9 *ad Victricium* (PL 20, 474A–475A); *Epistulae* 17, 3–6 (PL 20, 528B–530B). Siricius, *Epistula* 1, 8, 12 *ad Himerium* (PL 13, 1141A–1142A), vehe-

in the West, even before Siricius, there was an independent celibacy tradition, which deviated insignificantly from the understanding of it in the East. All in all, however, the two strands of tradition are strikingly similar. Jerome speaks of countless clerics of every rank "all over the world" who are living in a second marriage.[8] By that he expressly means those clerics whose first marriage took place during their pagan years. That is why he can speak, with not a word of explanation, about "a law valid for the priests: . . . a man who has been married twice is excluded from candidacy [for the priesthood]."[9] We are speaking then, at any rate, about the digamy prohibition that was valid in the East and the West, which is simply understood a bit differently in each case.

The unity despite this discrepancy is demonstrated above all in the justification of the digamy prohibition. In both instances its rationale was seen in the practice of continence after ordination. This was connected with the fact that, in the West, in keeping with the Greek theologians, digamists were considered incapable of continence and were therefore *propter suspicionem incontinentiae* excluded from ordination.[10] Someone who had remarried evidently could not practice continence. How in the world was a man supposed to be able to practice continence as a cleric with his wife, when he could not even do it without a wife? It made no difference whether the digamy prohibition was applied strictly or leniently: the cleric living in a first marriage (after baptism) had to practice continence. That is clear in the East, all the more so when such a connection between monogamy and continence was viewed very critically. At any rate, clerical continence regularly

---

mently opposes the ordination of digamists but really does not indicate whether this practice resulted from the discounting of pre-baptismal marriages. That is suggested, however, by the Council of Valence a. 374, canon 1 (CCL 48, 38, 20–24).

[8] *Epistula* 69, 2, 2 *ad Oceanum* (CSEL 54, 680, 11–15); cf. Siricius, *Epistula* 1, 10 *ad Himerium* (PL 13, 1142A). For a more moderate count of digamous clerics, see Jerome, *Apologia adversus libros Rufini* 1, 32 (PL 23², 444A).

[9] *Epistula* 123, 5, 9 *ad Geruchiam* (CSEL 56, 79, 5f.). The case, discussed by Jerome, of the Spanish Bishop Carterius was more of a singular instance, whereas in the Orient marriages usually were counted from baptism on; Gryson, *Origines*, 145.

[10] *Evangelium Bartholomaei* 5, 8; Clement of Alexandria, *Stromata* 3, 1, 4, 3 (GCS Clem. Alex. 2⁴, 197, 10–15); Augustine, *De bono coniugali* 18, 21 (CSEL 41, 214, 7f.) and *De bono viduitatis* 8, 11 (CSEL 41, 315, 25); Methodius, *Symposium* 3, 12 (GCS Method. 40, 1–41, 23); John Chrysostom, *Hom.* 2, 1 *in Tit.* 1:5f. (PG 62, 671); Jerome, *Comm. in Tit.* 1:6 (PL 26, 599B); *Epistula* 49, 8, 2, 17, 5 *ad Pammachium* (CSEL 54, 361, 20–363, 12, 380, 10–15); Zeno, *Tractatus* 2, 7, 9 (CCL 22, 173, 84–97); B. Kötting, "Digamus", RAC 3 (1957): 1020f.

came up for discussion whenever the topic of digamy was mentioned. In this respect, too, the West has an identical but thoroughly independent tradition. Siricius, Ambrose,[11] and Innocent saw in the digamy prohibition of the pastoral letters a decisive New Testament reference to obligatory continence for married clerics and their wives. The critique of the digamy prohibition, as it was formulated in the works of Theodore of Mopsuestia, met with no approval in the West.

Monogamy and continence belong together. We have to realize the preeminent importance of this point for the agreement between the Western and Eastern clerical discipline. Obligatory continence, after all, cannot be detected at first sight in the phrase "unius uxoris vir". How would an obligatory continence exegesis of the pastoral letters ever have occurred to anyone in the West unless a fully developed doctrinal tradition of the Church was behind it? We encounter here a connection that clearly points to the common beginning of the Latin and Greek practice of celibacy. Indeed, even the proponents of the various interpretations of digamy agree on this essential point: The rule that the bishop should be "the husband of one wife" was made for the sake of future continence.

Accompanying regulations. The continence discipline in the East was guaranteed by a whole system of regulations. They were not missing in the West either, which again clearly indicates that we are dealing with one and the same discipline. Roger Gryson sees the agreement quite well,[12] but the point escapes him that these regulations appeared both in the West and in the East precisely because they were only a legal framework for the common continence discipline in the first place. As in the East, the aforementioned digamy prohibition applied for clerics, but also the prohibition against being married to a woman who was living in a second marriage (see above, pp. 131–32).[13] In the West also, then, the digamy prohibition carried over to the wives, the reason being, again, for the sake of continence.[14] Furthermore no man who

---

[11] *De officiis ministrorum* I, 50, 248 (PL 16², 104A); *Epistulae* 63, 62 (CSEL 82, 3, 267, 630–37).

[12] Gryson, *Origines*, 197.

[13] Siricius, *Epistula* I, 12, 15 *ad Himerium* (PL 13, 1141B; 1143B–1144A); 5, 2 (PL 13, 1159A); Innocent, *Epistula* 2, 4, 7 *ad Victricium* (PL 20, 473A); *Epistulae* 17, 2 (PL 20, 527B–528A); *Epistulae* 37, 2, 4 (PL 20, 604A); cf. Jerome, *Epistula* 52, 10, 3 *ad Nepotianum* (CSEL 54, 432, 12f.). For the East, see R. Cholij, *Clerical Celibacy in East and West* (Herefordshire, 1989), 21–34.

[14] Jerome, *Epistula*, 64, 7, 2 *ad Fabiolam* (CSEL 54, 594, 15–595, 2): "Pontifex iste, quem

had been notoriously unchaste after his baptism could be admitted to the clergy, even if he had done penance for his sin (see above, pp. 126–28).[15]

Thus we have determined, as a first step, that the Western pattern of clerical continence was the same as that of the East. We are concerned about demonstrating that the popes, with their celibacy initiative, were not obsessed by an idea that they had thought up on their own. What they were doing was within the context of almost identical obligations on the part of the Greek clergy. Now one might deliberate as to whether the popes perhaps imported the clerical discipline of the East. Did they follow the motto, "The light comes from the East" and single-handedly impose the hitherto unknown practice of the Greeks upon the ecclesiastical regions within their sphere of influence? That would fit in with the commonly held notion of a centralist papacy. The question is, though, whether that image really does justice to the matter.

b. The Popes Speak of the Apostolic Origin of Clerical Continence

The agreement of the clerical discipline in the East and in the West is explained, rather, by a common development that took place from the very beginnings of the Church. Let us assume that a continence discipline for higher clerics was well known from apostolic times; the pastoral letters give evidence of that. Then in the course of the early Church's missionary activity it must have spread throughout the known world of that time. Accordingly, clerical continence in the West could trace a continuous history from the very beginning, just like the East. For this reason the celibacy discipline in the fourth century necessarily presented itself as a uniform phenomenon in every part of the empire.

The popes were not blind celibacy fanatics who just wanted to ram legislation through. They sought a consensus. In Siricius' opinion the celibacy regulations imposed no new requirements, but recalled the "guidelines of the ancients [*statuta majorum*]" (*Cum in unum*). This by no means refers merely to the previous decades, in which an obligatory continence discipline was familiar through the writings of Ambrosiaster. It means, rather, a continence discipline practiced in the Church

---

Mosaicus sermo describit, viduam . . . non ducet uxorem . . . ne pristinarum meminerit voluptatum."

[15] Siricius or Innocent, *Epistula* 10, 8 *ad Gall.* (PL 13, 1187AB): "Quomodo hic irreprehensibilis est [1 Tim 3:2], qui baptismi sacramentum non potuit custodire?" Innocent, *Epistulae* 39 (PL 20, 606B).

from the very beginning, as it was established by the apostles and the Fathers. In a similar manner Siricius speaks about the indissoluble law (*insolubilis lex*) of the apostolic decrees (*Directa*). Pope Innocent views it in exactly the same way (*Etsi tibi*). Naturally, one can consider all that as mere assertions and mendacious self-justification, as a frivolous appeal to the apostles in order to lend authoritative force to the papal demand for celibacy.

But did Siricius really get involved in such a nasty confidence game? His celibacy initiative, after all, was not an individual decision. *Directa* originated in a vote of the entire Roman presbyterium. *Cum in unum* records the results of a synod attended by eighty Italian bishops. Why did all of these bishops, priests, and deacons, a good number of them married, not refute the Pope and inform him of the fact that previously there had been no obligatory continence? In that way they could have kept him from introducing such a momentous innovation in North Africa and Spain on the basis of hollow arguments. And why did the North African bishops take up this alleged nonsense, inasmuch as they in turn maintained at their synod in Carthage that obligatory continence for higher clerics went back to the apostles? Evidently no one enunciated any criticism. Continence celibacy, therefore, seems to have been age-old and well known in the West, too. There was no reason to doubt Siricius on this point. Ambrose, also, was unaware of any sort of "old tradition" according to which clerics were allowed to beget children (see above, p. 232).

When the popes, together with the Italian and North African bishops, characterized continence celibacy as a norm going back to the apostles and Fathers that bound all higher clerics, then there was more behind this than we have intimated so far. Contrary to first impressions, it was not cheap, calculated propaganda. For behind the apostolicity there was at that time a lofty claim that still needed to be presented. Christian Cochini has referred to this point and to its significance for the early history of celibacy.[16] The term "apostolic" had always been a seal of approval in the Church. This title was not given out lightly. Irrevocable validity in the Church was by no means limited to things that could somehow be traced back to the apostles, that is, to the New Testament Scriptures. In that case one could have considered practically everything to be apostolic.

"Apostolic" at this time was, rather, a well-defined concept in the

---

[16] C. Cochini, *Apostolic Origins of Priestly Celibacy* (San Francisco, 1990), 47–64.

Church's dogmatic teaching. Only something that satisfied specific criteria could be termed apostolic. Apostolic continence celibacy meant, first of all: the apostles, whether they were married or not, practiced continence. Such a manner of life was thereby recommended and authorized. This was in fact the conviction held by all the leading theologians of the third and fourth centuries who addressed this subject.[17] Therefore Rome could depend on their unanimous opinion. "Apostolic" meant simultaneously, though, that this practice had been handed on from the apostles to their episcopal successors; and also, in the following centuries, (1) that the discipline had been observed everywhere and had been supported by all the leading bishops, (2) that no challenge in this matter had arisen from a contrary tradition, and (3) that clerical continence had not been subsequently introduced for the first time by a synod.

Thus, if the popes claimed apostolic status for continence celibacy, they were applying on behalf of their reform efforts the highest possible standard. Their initial reason for invoking the standard was not to gain an authoritative blessing upon the practice, but to raise questions and to examine the issue. Could the Church's celibacy discipline be justified in the first place on the basis of the original customs? For that to be true, it had to be, speaking concretely, a worldwide, constant practice. This constituted an appeal to the consensus of the universal Church through space and over time, that is, an appeal to the ecumenical dimension of clerical continence. The Pope bound himself to the collegial process that takes place in the general legislation of synods. Had it been announced at that time by a synod that it had introduced obligatory continence as a new discipline for the Church throughout the world, one would not have been able to speak any more of its apostolic origin. People were convinced that Elvira, too, had only renewed the injunction of an ancient practice.

Furthermore, the consensus of the universal Church comes about through the exchange among theologians. We have examined all of the pertinent texts of the Fathers of the West and of the East before the time of Siricius. Naturally, these texts were read at that time, also; their direct or indirect references to clerical continence were well known, even though the decretals only cite passages from Scripture and the Church's canon law, as was the custom then. There was a lively theological exchange between the East and the West. Despite the limita-

---

[17] Ibid., 79–83.

tions of our source material, we can say that the popes, in maintaining the validity of continence celibacy from the very beginning, were certainly able to rely on the consensus of the theologians. Eminent theologians and exegetes of the time, of the caliber of Epiphanius and Jerome, shared their view and likewise referred to the apostolic origin of clerical continence.[18]

Only the trial by fire of apostolicity authorized the popes to lend new force to the observance of the clerical discipline. Indeed, the critical events in North Africa, Spain, and Gaul were really only crises. The decretals of the popes did not construct continence celibacy out of thin air in those regions either, but rather set it upon old foundation walls that, of course, were partly dilapidated. Neither from Africa nor from Gaul do we hear of opposition. Only in Spain was there criticism. But even here this by no means implied that an innovation was being rejected; more likely, it signified that some wanted to relax the old discipline. As far as the bishops were concerned, there was much ignorance, but not one appears to have risen in protest against the Romans. Rather, the reception of the document *Cum in unum*, both in Africa (Acts of the Council of Telepte in the year 418) and in Gaul (the apocryphal canon 29 of Arles in the year 314) was such that it was transposed into canons of the regional Church, so that henceforth all clerics would have precise information about obligatory continence. It is only because this discipline was largely undisputed throughout the Church (though not always observed) that the popes could undertake comprehensive celibacy legislation and remedy abuses. To be sure, this also included authoritative revisions of the Eastern practice, for instance, the stricter interpretation of the digamy prohibition.

Probably, behind the opinion that a continence discipline was forced upon clerics only by the popes of the fourth and fifth centuries, there was an anachronistic notion of the options and intentions of the central administration in Rome. The canonical disciplinary options that Rome had during the post-Constantinian period were naturally fewer and far less rigorous than we might imagine on the basis of Vatican I and given our dependence on rapid means of worldwide communications. Rome was neither a paper tiger nor an omnicompetent big brother. It is somewhat misguided to think that Rome, faced with the count-

---

[18] Epiphanius, *Panarion lxxx haeresium* 48, 9, 5 (GCS Epiph. 2², 231, 15f.): Ὡς καὶ οἱ αὐτοῦ ἀπόστολοι τὸν ἐκκλησιαστικὸν κανόνα τῆς ἱερωσύνης εὐτάκτως καὶ ὁσίως διετάξαντο. On Jerome, see Gryson, *Origines*, 151–53.

less problems brought on by the expansion of the Church after Constantine, had nothing better to do than to establish a completely new clerical discipline. The popes, rather, took strong measures on behalf of clerical continence because they considered it an essential tradition with far-reaching consequences involving the sacramental ministry.

In doing so they were less intent on a disciplinary than on a spiritual authority and the strength of the arguments. They were concerned about the norm of the apostles and the Fathers.[19] One detects the same kind of fervor as arose in our time with the Second Vatican Council, which derived much of its prestige from the claim that it would revive and renew the venerable norm of the Church Fathers.[20] This approach brought about such a profound and fresh awareness of the nature of the Church; should it not have sparked a new enthusiasm for the cause of the Church in the fourth century as well? The popes did not think up the *norma patrum* argument on their own to use in ambitious power plays. It goes without saying that every reform means an increase of power for the central authority governing the reform. To take this secondary effect for the chief motive for a reform, though, is dishonest and misjudges the integrity of the persons who were acting then. Aside from this, the charge that celibacy was an institution of papal power and domination is debatable, if at all, only for celibacy in the strict sense.[21] A clergy composed exclusively of unmarried men places them very much at the disposal of the bishops. In the early Church, though, celibacy narrowly defined played a subordinate role.

---

[19] Siricius, *Epistula* 5, 1 (PL 13, 1156A): "Litteras tales dare placuit, non quae nova praecepta aliqua imperent, sed quibus ea, quae per ignaviam desidiamque aliquorum neglecta sunt, observari cupiamus, quae tamen apostolica et patrum constitutione sunt constituta"; *Epistulae* 6, 2 (PL 13, 1164B); *Epistula* 10, 2, 5 ad Gall. (PL 13, 1182A. 1184B): "Scimus, fratres charissimi, multos episcopos per diversas ecclesias ad famam pessimam nominis sui humana praesumptione patrum traditionem mutare properasse . . . quos non solum nos, sed et Scriptura divina compellit esse castissimos, et patres quoque jusserunt continentiam corporalem servare debere"; Innocent, *Epistula* 2, 2 ad Victricium (PL 20, 470B): "Non quo nova praecepta aliqua imperentur, sed ea, quae per desidiam aliquorum neglecta sunt, ab omnibus observari cupiamus, quae tamen apostolica et patrum traditione sunt constituta."

[20] *Sacrosanctum concilium*, no. 50. This was significant not only for the reform of the liturgy. Cf. *Dei Verbum*, no. 8.

[21] E. Schillebeeckx, *Christliche Identität und kirchliches Amt: Plädoyer für den Menschen in der Kirche* (Düsseldorf, 1985), 294: "Therefore it is historically inaccurate and sheer ideology to view the celibacy rule as a *means of acquiring ecclesiastical power*, at least in antiquity and in the Middle Ages." Cf. G. Denzler, *Die Geschichte des Zölibats* (Freiburg, 1993), 100f.

c. The Popes See in Clerical Continence an Ecumenical Concern

Siricius and Innocent, in writing about the apostolicity of clerical continence, were actually treating nothing short of its ecumenical, worldwide dimension as well. The legitimacy and endorsement of their reform efforts were entirely dependent upon the apostolicity and ecumenicity of celibacy. However important the popes may have considered their authority to be, the Italians, the Spaniards, and the Gallic Christians were quite self-assured. They did not belong to the Roman Catholic Church, which at that time did not yet exist as such. They were, instead, part of the one and only Catholic Church. If, contrary to the declaration of the popes, continence celibacy did not in fact belong to the common heritage of the entire Church, then the aforementioned ecclesiastical regions would have refused to honor this demand of the popes. They would not have stood for an innovation that was so radical and burdensome.

Churchmen in the West were very well informed about the customs of the Greeks.[22] If the Council of Nicaea had reached some decision against continence celibacy, as the Paphnutius legend maintains, then the plan of the popes most assuredly would have come to naught, because they appealed to the Church Fathers themselves as their authority, whose doctrine and disciplinary teaching never met with such undisputed approval as in that famous first ecumenical council. Furthermore, the decretals of Siricius (*Cum in unum*) and Innocent (*Etsi tibi*) explicitly refer to the canons of Nicaea, and the original records of that council were preserved in the Lateran archives.[23] It would be absurd if continence celibacy had been uncompromisingly championed in the decretals even though Nicaea had expressly declared against it.

The popes really had the entire world in view when they spoke about clerical discipline. A reading of the decretal *Dominus inter* makes clear the universal claim of the primacy. The author, whether it be Damasus, Siricius, or Innocent, feels that he is responsible for the *one* Church.

---

[22] A. M. Stickler, *The Case for Clerical Celibacy: Its Historical Development and Theological Foundations*, trans. Brian Ferme (San Francisco, 1995), 25. This is affirmed also by M. Meigne, "Concile ou collection d'Elvire", RHE 70 (1975): 361–87, whose late dating of Elvira is, of course, unacceptable.

[23] C. Pietri, *Roma Christiana: Recherches sur l'Église de Rome, son organisation, sa politique, son idéologie de Miltiade à Sixte III (311–440)* (Paris and Rome, 1976), 1:172–89, 672–74.

He sees his mission as being the first of all the Catholic bishops in the whole world. Among them there must be not only a common faith, but also a common apostolic tradition. The latter concerns all sorts of disciplinary questions, which the popes define in their decretals, of course with varying degrees of importance. Clerical continence has a prominent place among them; it is demanded on the highest authority. *Dominus inter* speaks so emphatically about the identical traditions of the Churches throughout the world, precisely because it sees in continence celibacy, not a particular practice of the West, but rather an apostolic legacy.

To do justice to the initiative of the popes on behalf of clerical continence, one must appreciate the fact that it was an eminently ecumenical concern. It was a matter of maintaining the selfsame practice in the East and the West.[24] Particularly in the fourth century, a heightened ecumenical awareness prevailed in Rome. There are reasons for that. For fifty years churchmen had supported the Council of Nicaea, although it was actually an almost entirely Eastern council. Yet Rome sided with it, because it was about the faith of the one Church. Then, when the Council was disputed more and more vehemently and the entire empire divided itself into adherents and opponents, Rome consistently took a stand against the Arians and in favor of the orthodox cause. Rome became the hinge upon which the conflicts turned, and under Pope Damasus it gained worldwide respect.[25] The common faith triumphed, the Council of Constantinople in the year 381 solemnly bore witness to it.

Only this overview of the entire Church makes the celibacy initiatives of the popes comprehensible. Never, not even once, was there a question of an innovation with respect to the Eastern practice. No pope in the entire world could have sold such an innovation as the common heritage of the apostolic tradition without ruining his credibility. The popes only wanted to teach again something that had led to a crisis in many of their ecclesiastical provinces, but which then, as before, had an uninterrupted validity in the East. It was a matter of not permitting a rift to develop between the Greek and the Latin Church. Considering the critical situation in North Africa and Spain,

---

[24] Siricius, *Epistula* 1, 2 *ad Himerium* (PL 13, 1134A), speaks, with reference to the baptism of heretics, of a discipline that is uniform through the Orient and Occident.

[25] Pietri, *Roma*, 1:791–853.

this may even have been the last chance. What would have happened if the popes had not intervened? Who else was supposed to take some action if not they? Here they were dealing with a matter for which a wider horizon was required than one might attain from the perspective of an ecclesiastical province.

In Rome there was an awareness that a divided discipline in the long run divided the Church (*Dominus inter*). Perhaps the Western view of conditions in the Eastern Church was a bit transfigured by optimism; but one does have the impression that clerical continence there was an honorable and highly respected institution. The West was in danger of being left behind in this respect. Jerome, who could not even breathe without an ascetical milieu and a campaign for continence, did not settle in the East by chance. He must have seen it as affirming his decision when he heard about how a crisis of clerical discipline was looming in North Africa and Spain. He was a lot safer in the Holy Land.

The legislators in Rome did not want to create something new. They wanted to dam up a flood that was threatening to carry off something that, in their eyes, was a hallowed tradition. Therefore they grappled theologically, too, with this discipline, with its principles and its origins. The determination and rigor with which the popes proceeded are in keeping with their conviction that they were the guardians of an inheritance that was as old as it was fragile. In a time of such unrest they would never have imposed the heavy burden of continence on the clerics had they not been convinced of the reliability of the apostolic tradition. Neither the objections of Jovinian nor all sorts of complications—not even a general laxity of morals—could have shaken their confidence in any way.[26]

For the West to fall behind the East would have been incompatible with the self-assurance of the Latins, as expressed in the idea of the primacy. The West, however, could lay claim to its preeminence only if it really was the guarantor of what was considered apostolic throughout the entire Church. And that included, for one thing, continence celibacy. Rome acted in this respect with an unflinching awareness of the rightness of its stand. Was all that a fiction, merely feigned confidence? Who could believe that? The decisive manner in which the subject was pursued in the West, the precision with which the legal

---

[26] Cochini, *Origins*, 250.

framework of the continence discipline was decreed, the organizational and disciplinary measures by which it was put into effect, all that, then, was of course something typically Western. To that extent one certainly can speak, in reference to the decretals, of legislative innovation by activist popes. But one must not forget that the East, too, would codify its celibacy law comprehensively, more than a hundred years later, to be sure. As for its content, there would be no essential difference.

One cannot accuse the popes of using strong-arm tactics on behalf of continence celibacy. They did so with a good, ecumenical intention. All in all, one must acknowledge that their initiative was successful. Within the parameters of their powers and their sphere of influence, which was largely limited to the West, Siricius, Innocent, and later Leo, too, consolidated clerical continence. They thereby made an important contribution to the universal Church, in that they maintained an equivalence between the Western clerical discipline and that of the East. They performed the service of unity, which is so important in the (self-)understanding of the ministry of Peter. The contribution of the East to this process probably did not lie so much in active support of these efforts; at least we do not know of any. Yet we may assume that an essential and indispensable contribution of the East consisted precisely in the firmness with which it adhered to the celibacy discipline. That made it easier for the popes to put out brush fires in the West.

2. The East Continues for a Long Time to Adhere Firmly to the Continence Discipline

We have considered the campaign of the popes on behalf of clerical continence in its ecumenical dimension. Christian Cochini rightly asks: Would not the same popes who wrote to North Africa, Spain, and Gaul have sent letters to the East as well, if they had heard of practices there that diverged from their norms?[27] The answer will probably have to be in the affirmative. To be sure, in the West no complaints were heard about a weakening of the Eastern clerical discipline. It seems that continence was still observed there absolutely. Only in the seventh cen-

---

[27] Ibid., 259.

tury does the East depart noticeably from the previous discipline. This occurred definitively at the Second Council of Trullo in the year 691 ["Quinisext"]. Since then nothing more has changed essentially for the Orthodox Churches. In the West, in contrast, the discipline remained largely unchanged from the fifth century until the Council of Trent. At most it was called to mind here and there. Only in the sixteenth century did the development lead to an exclusively unmarried clergy. In order to round off somewhat the picture of the celibacy discipline in the early Church, we must then forge ahead to the seventh century.

a. The Paphnutius Legend Champions the Interests of the Novatians

It has been thought that the practice of clerical continence was safeguarded in the West thanks to the juridical prerogatives of the popes, who reacted quickly to unavoidable infractions. In the East, in contrast, such an institution was lacking. For that reason, the theory goes, the continence discipline there—if it is assumed to have existed there at all during the first centuries—went to pieces during the course of the fifth century.[28] Such an account is questionable. Certainly, the papacy was a great support for the West. But in the East as well, traditions with that much mileage were not so easily thrown overboard. And that included clerical continence, too. As we have already seen, it is found around 400 in the writings of Theophilus and Synesius in Egypt; the Syrian tradition in Asia Minor, starting with John Chrysostom all the way up to Theodoret of Cyrrhus, knew of the continence discipline for higher clerics. With that we are already trolling the middle of the fifth century. No trace of a celibacy crisis is to be found.

Contradicting this impression, though, are the statements of the Constantinopolitan Church historian Socrates (d. after 439), whom we mentioned already at the outset in connection with the Paphnutius legend. Before we go into that again, let us turn to another passage in the ecclesiastical-historical work of Socrates. It plainly declares that there is no obligatory continence in the East:

> In the Church of Alexandria, lectors and cantors are appointed regardless of whether they are catechumens or baptized, while in the Churches everywhere else baptized men are proposed for these offices.

---

[28] Thus Stickler, Celibacy, 66–68.

In Thessalia I became acquainted with another practice regarding admission to the clergy of that place. If a man, after he is admitted to the clergy, sleeps together with his wife, whom he legitimately married before he became a cleric, he is deposed. In the East, on the other hand, all clerics abstain voluntarily; even bishops do so if they wish, not under constraint of law. Many of them, indeed, have begotten children of their lawful wedded wife during the time of their episcopacy. Heliodor, the bishop of Trikka, is said to have introduced this custom there in Thessalia. A love story is attributed to him, which he is said to have written as a young man and which is entitled "Ethiopian Tales". This same practice is found in, besides Thessalia, Macedonia, and Greece as well.[29]

Here Socrates is mixing truth together with fiction, experience with conjecture. Socrates speaks of those men who in Illyricum (Thessalia, Macedonia, and Greece)[30] have been *admitted* to the clergy and who then beget children. At first this applies only to the lower clerics, who are the subject of the preceding discussion also (lectors and cantors). If this is correct, then continence would have been expected of lower clerics and their wives since the time of Bishop Heliodor. In principle, that could very well be. At any rate one must draw the line at subdeacon. In the West, probably quite some time before the pontificate of Pope Leo (440 to 461), the discipline shifted so as to require continence of subdeacons as well.[31] Epiphanius too, who was favorably disposed toward Rome, knew of such an obligation. Therefore it can come as no surprise if subdeacons were practicing continence in Illyricum. In any case, Socrates could rightly view this as an innovation that became accepted as of the close of the fourth century and the turn of the fifth.

---

[29] *Historia ecclesiastica* 5, 22, 49–51 (GCS Socr. 301, 23–302, 8): Ἐν τῇ αὐτῇ δὲ Ἀλεξανδρείᾳ ἀναγνῶσται καὶ ὑποβολεῖς ἀδιάφορον εἴτε κατηχούμενοί εἰσιν εἴτε πιστοί, τῶν πανταχοῦ ἐκκλεσιῶν πιστοὺς εἰς τὸ τάγμα τοῦτο προβαλλομένων. Ἔγνων δὲ ἐγὼ καὶ ἕτερον ἔθος ἐν Θεσσαλίᾳ γενόμενον· κληρικὸς ἐκεῖ <τῇ ἰδίᾳ γυναικί, ἣν> ἦν νόμῳ γαμήσας, πρὶν κληρικὸς γένηται, συγκαθευδήσας ἀποκήρυκτος γίνεται, τῶν ἐν ἀνατολῇ πάντων <κληρικῶν> γνώμῃ ἀπεχομένων καὶ τῶν ἐπισκόπων, εἰ καὶ βούλοιντο, οὐ μὴν ἀνάγκῃ νόμου τοῦτο ποιούντων· πολλοὶ γὰρ αὐτῶν ἐν τῷ καιρῷ τῆς ἐπισκοπῆς καὶ παῖδας ἐκ τῆς νομίμης γαμετῆς πεποίηκασιν. Ἀλλὰ τοῦ μὲν ἐν Θεσσαλίᾳ ἔθους ἀρχηγὸς Ἡλιόδωρος, Τρίκκης τῆς ἐκεῖ γενόμενος <ἐπίσκοπος>, οὗ λέγεται πονήματα <εἶναι> ἐρωτικὰ βιβλία, ἃ νέος ὢν συνέταξεν καὶ Αἰθιοπικὰ προσηγόρευσεν. Φυλάσσεται δὲ τοῦτο τὸ ἔθος ἐν Θεσσαλονίκῃ καὶ αὐτῇ Μακεδονίᾳ καὶ <ὅλῃ τῇ> Ἑλλάδι.

[30] Pietri, *Roma*, 1:776–89.

[31] Cholij, *Celibacy*, 58f.; Cochini, *Origins*, 260; Leo, *Epistula* 14, 4 *ad Anastasios* (PL 54, 672B–673A), is perhaps reacting to the ecclesiastical history of Socrates, which had caused doubts to arise about the justification of obligatory continence for subdeacons.

It is possible that Socrates did not yet know of such a discipline in Constantinople.

The question now arises, though, whether Heliodor was also the first to introduce obligatory continence for higher clerics. Socrates seems to want to say that, but the statement is formulated more narrowly to begin with. Socrates says that in the East even married bishops are still allowed to beget children without being deposed; that throughout the Orient, unlike in the West, there is no obligation for bishops to observe continence, and certainly none for the lower clerics. Each cleric is said to have the option of practicing continence with his wife or not; and that, supposedly, has always been the case. Thus far Socrates. Thus only bishops are mentioned; possibly they are meant to stand by way of example for the entire clergy in major orders. According to this description, in the Eastern empire deacons and priests, but at least the bishops, were still allowed to beget children.

But that simply cannot be correct. This account is outnumbered by half a dozen testimonies that tell a different story.[32] These cannot simply be dismissed as nonbinding recommendations of celibacy, which then still leave everything open. At this point we must refer to everything that Chrysostom, Epiphanius, Jerome, Theodore, and Theodoret said about the continence discipline for higher clerics (Theodoret mentions Paphnutius in Nicaea, but not his intervention).[33] Socrates was a layman and evidently had not familiarized himself particularly well with the clerical discipline. True, during a stay in Thessalia he had become acquainted with the practice of continence for subdeacons, which for him was a novelty. But he combines this with information that he did not obtain in Thessalia, but rather took from the Paphnutius legend. To track down the truth, then, we must turn to that source.

Socrates was the first to include the Paphnutius legend in his ecclesiastical history (see above, pp. 15–18); it was then taken up by later historians, by Sozomenos (d. around 450) and Gelasius of Cyzicus (after 475).[34] Who started this story circulating? It was not Socrates, anyway. He did not invent his material, but rather researched and gathered historical information. In doing so he came upon the story. It was probably part of an oral tradition, like so many other items that

---

[32] Cochini, *Origins*, 321.

[33] *Historia ecclesiastica* 1, 6 (PG 82, 917B).

[34] Ibid., 2, 33, 1–4 (GCS Gelas. 118, 17–119, 6).

he was able to tell us about the Council of Nicaea. So we have to find the informant in order to understand the background of the story. We can assume that we are dealing with a legend of expediency, an anti-celibate-propaganda lie. It was not brought into currency by chance, but pursued a definite purpose. Who, then, had an interest in such a story?

The legend could have stemmed from the mainstream Christian camp. One could then suppose that there was an anti-Western thrust. The East drew a polemical line against the obligatory continence of the West. They wanted nothing to do with the initiatives of the popes. But doubts arise about this explanation. The legend gives no indication of a polemic against the West. Well, then, it began with an intra-Byzantine controversy. We are dealing with Eastern opponents of celibacy, who were taking action against the local discipline of obligatory continence for higher clerics. The legend itself speaks in favor of this view. For practically everyone present at the Council of Nicaea was a Greek bishop. And all of these bishops allegedly wanted clerical continence to be binding. Why does the legend not simply make a participant from the West the spokesman for the "innovators"? Given the way the legend presents itself, we must infer that a discipline of continence celibacy existed in the East. To do away with it was really the purpose of the legend. To accomplish that, though, the opinion of the overwhelming majority of the bishops had to be changed first.

Roger Gryson thinks that the aforementioned dispute about the celibacy discipline in Illyria gave rise to the legend.[35] The East wanted to prevent the Roman observance from prevailing in this border region. But here, too, second thoughts arise. Again we must point out the lack of any anti-Western polemic. The legend would have been formulated differently. Indeed, why do all the bishops in Nicaea want to introduce clerical continence, and not merely the Illyrian bishops? Besides, what Socrates says about Illyricum seems to have been influenced by the Paphnutius legend itself. Therefore he is not to be taken uncritically at his word. Finally, one wonders why the legend was thought up at all, if in fact the discipline was being disputed between East and West only in Illyricum, whereas throughout the East there was supposedly no talk of obligatory continence anyway. If, however, the discipline

---

[35] "Dix ans de recherches sur les origines du célibat ecclésiastique: Réflexion sur les publications des années 1970–1979", RTL 11 (1980): 165.

was valid in the East as well, as we must infer on the basis of a series of textual witnesses, then that is all the more reason that the legend must be regarded as a purely Eastern concern.

Here, consequently, we come upon a second possible way of attributing the legend to particular surroundings. It is striking that nowhere do bishops, theologians, or synods in the East cite it as their authority. This is all the more surprising since the legend must have been common knowledge thanks to the chronicles of the Church historians. Besides these references, however, the story left no traces, because its unanimous vote against continence simply does not correspond to the reality of celibacy in the Eastern Church. Therefore the only real possibility remaining is to attribute the legend to a separated Church in the East. The Paphnutius story is a typical justification legend of the sort that can only come from a schismatic or heretical church that opposes a tradition of the overwhelming majority of the bishops. Its purpose was not simply to report the reasons against obligatory continence that Paphnutius brought up at the Council, but rather to win the reader over to its cause by a great number of arguments. That is why the legend cannot simply be a story that was circulating among the people, which Socrates had picked up somewhere.[36] That could not explain why it was invented in the first place. There is some likelihood that the ones behind it were the Novatians, who were quite well regarded in Constantinople and who played a role in ecclesiastical life. As is true of other splinter groups, they found that, with the passage of time, peculiar customs were creeping in that deviated from those of the Catholic Church. For example, the Novatians in Phrygia celebrated Easter on the Jewish feast of Passover.[37] A similar separate development was the abandonment of clerical continence.

There have always been individual scholars who have seen the legendary character of the Paphnutius intervention and connected it with the Novatians. As early as the nineteenth century, the Orientalist Gustav Bickell started to reason along such lines[38] but was roundly criticized for it by the Tübingen Church historian Franz Xaver Funk. The latter

---

[36] Contrary to F. Winkelmann, "Paphnutius, der Bekenner und Bischof", in P. Nagel, ed., *Probleme der koptischen Literatur*, Wissenschaftliche Beiträge der Martin-Luther-Universität Halle-Wittenberg, 1968/1 (Halle, 1968), 150.

[37] H.J. Vogt, *Coetus sanctorum: Der Kirchenbegriff des Novatian und die Geschichte seiner Sonderkirche*, Theoph. 20 (Bonn, 1968), 239f. For liturgical deviations, see ibid., 277.

[38] "Der Cölibat eine apostolische Anordnung", ZKTh 2 (1878): 56–62.

absolutely insisted on maintaining the historicity of the intervention of Paphnutius.[39] Almost all subsequent scholarship relied on Funk's judgment and thus staked their research on the wrong theory.[40] Indeed, the most recent investigations show that Bickell was right. Friedhelm Winkelmann has proved the legendary character of the story. The editor of the ecclesiastical history of Socrates, the ancient philologist Günther Christian Hansen of Berlin, attributes it to the Novatians.[41] Socrates maintained benevolent contacts with this Christian sect.[42] The Paphnutius legend fits in extremely well with a whole spectrum of texts in his ecclesiastical history that tell about the Novatians. The legend itself stands right between two reports explicitly devoted to the Novatians.

Socrates' Novatian informant was the hoary priest Auxanon, who communicated to Socrates many details about the Council of Nicaea and its proceedings that are not confirmed in other sources. This Auxanon, as a young man, had accompanied the Novatian bishop Akesios to the Council of Nicaea. It is alleged that the emperor Constantine thought especially highly of him and invited him to the Council as the only Novatian bishop.[43] Now the Council Fathers did in fact deal also with the Novatian schism (canon 8). They were concerned about reinstating Novatian ministers into the Catholic clergy. The ministers were allowed to remain at their posts, provided that they submitted unconditionally to the Catholic Church, in regard to apostasy and digamy as well. Bishop Akesios, perhaps, gave his complete assent to the Fathers' profession of faith—without, of course, complying with the Catholic discipline. The faith of Nicaea had always been adhered to, though, by the Novatians.

Thus, with no further ado, we can ascribe the Paphnutius legend to Auxanon. For one thing, it is found immediately after the discourse

---

[39] "Cölibat und Priesterehe im christlichen Altertum", in *Kirchengeschichtliche Abhandlungen und Untersuchungen*, vol. 1 (Paderborn, 1897), 150–53. For a treatment of this absorbing controversy in the history of celibacy scholarship, see Cochini, *Origins* 32–36.

[40] In the French-speaking world, the encyclopedia article "Célibat ecclésiastique" by Vacandard became very influential.

[41] Sokrates, *Kirchengeschichte*, GCS N.F. 1 (Berlin, 1995), LIV. The same attribution was made previously by F. Geppert, *Die Quellen des Kirchenhistorikers Socrates Scholasticus*, SGTK 3, 4 (Leipzig, 1898), 115.

[42] A. Ferrarini, "Eresia e storia ecclesiastica: Contributi novaziani alla storiografia di Socrate (Scolastico)", in *Università degli studi—Padova—Annali della Facoltà di lettere e filosofia*, vol. 4 (Florence, 1979), 127–85.

[43] Socrates Scholasticus, *Historia ecclesiastica* 1, 10, 1 (GCS Socr. 41, 3–5).

on Akesios. Then too, the Novatians were particularly at home in an ascetical milieu. Many a monk-bishop emerged from their ranks.[44] Auxanon himself was introduced to the monastic life in Bithynia. He passed on to Socrates the legendary story about the monk Eutychianos, to whom the Emperor Constantine showed his favor.[45] Paphnutius was a monk and a bishop, famous for his continence and honored by Constantine. Furthermore he was a confessor of the faith. This is the strongest evidence for the Novatian provenance of Paphnutius. The Novatians, indeed, made it their hallmark to honor those who had not fallen away from the faith during the persecutions of the Christians. According to Socrates, Novatian himself died as a martyr.[46] So the legend builds Paphnutius up to be a Novatian, without explicitly designating him as one.[47]

According to this explanation, then, the Paphnutius legend championed the peculiar interests of the Novatians, as distinct from those of the Catholics. It marshaled a whole series of arguments against continence celibacy, among which was a conspicuous reference to the purity of marriage (Heb 13:4)—the Novatians were called "the pure ones" (Cathari).[48] "Paphnutius", therefore, was obviously under considerable pressure to justify a cause. Indeed, all the bishops present at the Council were in favor of continence. It is explicitly mentioned that Paphnutius himself was never married, but rather lived as an ascetic from childhood and proved himself as a confessor during the persecution. This probably betrays a situation in which the Novatian clerics themselves, these rigorous preachers of morality, were no longer observing continence.[49] That required, in fact, a very good excuse.

---

[44] Vogt, *Coetus*, 186, 239, 243, 262. For married Novatian clerics, see ibid., 279.

[45] Socrates Scholasticus, *Historia ecclesiastica* I, 13, 1–10 (GCS Socr. 44, 22–46, 4).

[46] Ibid., 4, 28, 15 (GCS Socr. 264, 29–31).

[47] On Novatians in Egypt, see Vogt, *Coetus*, 277.

[48] Ibid., 189.

[49] E. Vacandard, "Célibat ecclésiastique", in DThC 2, 2 (1932), 2078 for this very reason considers it impossible that the Novatians could have invented the legend. He fails to recognize that by no means all Novatians gave up celibacy. Furthermore, this was an innovation for them, too: originally, of course, celibacy had been required. And finally, the relaxation of celibacy is typical for separated Churches (cf. the fifth-century Persian Nestorians and sixth-century Western Gothic Arians). That it was difficult for "the pure ones" to justify the abandonment of celibacy, in contrast to the mainstream Church, again explains why Paphnutius is not explicitly designated a Novatian and why the legend veils its Novatian origin in the first place; in no way did they want the whole thing to be understood as a Novatian initiative.

And therefore this relaxation of clerical discipline was traced back to the irreproachable monk-confessor Paphnutius, who was widely noted for his strict asceticism and continence and who allegedly managed to convince all the bishops.[50]

So the Catholic Church did adhere to continence celibacy. Otherwise the legend would not have admitted that, as early as Nicaea, practically the entire hierarchy assembled at the Council propagated perfect continence and had to be brought around through the intervention of a single bishop. And in still another way the legend indirectly confirms the old discipline of universal continence, when it characterizes the marriage and digamy prohibitions as an ancient tradition of the Church: [Married] clerics had to be living in a first marriage and were not to marry again.[51] Both prohibitions, though, make sense only against the background of obligatory continence. Thus the legend itself presupposes what it is battling. It adheres to the traditional Novatian condemnation of remarriage and also to the marriage prohibition, but otherwise it slackens the discipline of the Catholic Church.

The Novatians of Constantinople, consequently, had abandoned clerical continence. Such a development was certainly within the Church's experience with schismatic groups. We ought to mention in this regard the Persian Nestorians, for example, who in the course of the fifth century went so far as to lift the ban on marriage. Much the same can be said then for the Spanish Arians of the sixth century. As soon as a schismatic group has been in existence over a long period and is scattered throughout the world besides, changes in faith and discipline creep in. Despite the lofty moral claims of the Novatians, the celibacy discipline could not be maintained in their ranks. And so after the fact they had to justify as an apostolic practice something that was really only a gradual drifting away from the former discipline they had brought with them from the Catholic Church.

Socrates had not detected the legend and had taken at face value everything that Auxanon served up for him. And so he spread the Novatian propaganda lie. That explains then his remarks about Illyria,

---

[50] Bishop Heliodor is just the opposite: he, of all people, allegedly the author of erotic literature ("Ethiopian Tales"), introduces obligatory continence for all clerics in Illyricum; Bickell, "Cölibat", 60, n. 1.

[51] Socrates Scholasticus, *Historia ecclesiastica* I, 11, 5 (GCS Socr. 42, 18–21): ἀχρεῖσθαί τε τὸν φθάσαντα κλήρου τυχεῖν μηκέτι ἐπὶ γάμον ἔρχεσθαι κατὰ τὴν τῆς ἐκκλησίας ἀρχαίαν παράδοσιν, μὴ μὴν ἀποζεύγνυσθαι ταύτης, ἣν ἅπαξ ἤδη πρότερον λαϊκὸς ὢν ἠγάγετο.

too. For in them he was merely following what the legend says. If Bishop Heliodor introduced continence for subdeacons, then he sees this through Novatian lenses as though continence were being introduced for the entire clergy for the first time. When he writes that even higher clerics in the East were still allowed to beget children, something that "many bishops" also proceeded to do, he actually has Novatian ministers in view. If those were Catholic clerics, that would violate the previous practice, which the legend presupposes and presents as still existing. One would expect to find some response to that by contemporary theologians. To be sure, Epiphanius knew of clerics who did not observe continence. But a massive departure of the East from the universal discipline is not corroborated in the writings from the fifth century.

b. Emperor Justinian Summarizes the Entire Clerical Discipline

The Code of Theodosius. The usual strong propensity for clerical continence in the East is evident in one regulation from the Theodosian Code that, in a law dated May 8, 420, addresses questionable living arrangements of clerics.

> One who occupies a position of importance in the world should not be discredited by the company of a so-called "sister". Therefore, all those who are vested with the priesthood, at any rank whatsoever [*cuiuscumque gradus sacerdotio*], or who are regarded as having the dignity of a cleric [*clericatus*], must know that common life with "outsider" women is forbidden to them. We concede only the option of sheltering their mothers, their daughters, and their sisters within their houses; for with these there is a natural bond that does not permit any evil suspicion.
>
> A chaste love further suggests that those women not be abandoned who, before the ordination [*sacerdotium*] of their husband, were worthy [of being united with him] by legitimate marriage; it is not without reason that they are associated with clerics [*clericis*], they who by their conduct rendered their husbands worthy of the priesthood [*sacerdotio*].[52]

---

[52] *Codex Theodosianus* 16, 2, 44 (851 Mommsen 1, 2): "Eum, qui probabilem saeculo disciplinam agit, decolorari consortio sororiae appellationis non decet. Quicumque igitur cuiuscumque gradus sacerdotio fulciuntur vel clericatus honore censentur, extranearum sibi mulierum interdicta consortia cognoscant, hac eis tantum facultate concessa, ut matres filias adque germanas intra domorum suarum saepta contineant: in his enim nihil scaevi criminis aestimari foedus naturale permittit. Illas etiam non relinqui castitatis hortatur adfectio, quae ante sacerdotium maritorum legitimum meruere coniugium. Neque enim clericis incom-

This regulation, on the one hand, was directed against clerical *syneisaktoi*, or at least against housekeepers of clerics, when they were not members of the immediate family. No cleric (whether in minor or major orders) was permitted to live together with a so-called "sister" in his household. The only female persons who were permitted to live in his house were his mother, daughters—in the event that he was married—or sisters, because in these instances there was no suspicion of unchastity. This already leads us to suspect a connection with obligatory continence for higher clerics. This becomes even clearer in the second section.

There the subject is a dubious form of radical asceticism. Many clerics sent their wives away. The law says, in contrast, that one can practice continence very well within marriage, too. One's duties toward a wife forbid separating from her. There is such a thing as a "chaste love". The decisive point, now, is that this section no longer speaks, as the preceding text did, about all clerics but only about those in major orders: after their ordination to the diaconate (also implied, most likely, in the term *sacerdotium*), these clerics were breaking off their marriage. Why did they leave their wives right after receiving major orders? Apparently there was the expectation that one practiced permanent continence with one's wife from the diaconate on. Many wanted to play it especially safe and separate from their wives. In contrast, the law defends the traditional form of continent married life.[53] We must assume that a discipline of obligatory continence existed, all the more so since the law was equally valid in the Latin West as well.

The Code of Justinian. What Siricius and Innocent were for celibacy legislation in the West, Emperor Justinian (527 to 565) was in the East a hundred years later; he was one of the most successful and glorious figures ever to rule the Byzantine Empire. It was as though he took over the function of the pope for the East. Thus he not only was responsible, as emperor, for the political concerns of his empire but also saw himself as the head of the Byzantine Church. In a word: he was a "Caesaropapist". Hence, in his monumental legal code, the *Corpus Juris Civilis* (this collection, also called the *Codex Justinianus*, includes

---

petenter adiunctae sunt, quae dignos sacerdotio viros sui conversatione fecerunt." [English translation of second paragraph based on Cholij, *Celibacy* 80.]

[53] E. Schillebeeckx, *Der Amtszölibat: Eine kritische Besinnung* (Düsseldorf, 1967), 27; Cochini, *Origins*, 318f.

laws from the years 529 to 565), he regulated the clerical discipline, too, so comprehensively, in fact, that his laws were in no respect inferior to the decretals of the popes. On the basis of this codification alone it would be erroneous to claim that the Greek-speaking East had no experience of celibacy legislation.

Let us recall that the Roman bishops' synod under Siricius thoroughly discussed the subject of "the chastity of the Church". The ecclesiastical legislation of Emperor Justinian is no less comprehensively concerned about the chastity of clerics: "The life of chastity is indeed for us a matter of concern over and above all others", "the origin and foundation of the divine canons". This makes clear that the multifarious individual laws were meant to ensure and protect the core of the Western clerical discipline, namely, continence.[54] What was meant by this, certainly, was not only that chastity and decency which is self-evident for every Christian, but rather permanent continence, for married clerics as well.

One section from the sixth Novel, dated March 16, 535, is particularly revealing with respect to the discipline for priests and deacons.

> Neither a man living in a second marriage nor one who has been married to two wives may be ordained a deacon or a priest, nor one who is living with a wife who has divorced and left her husband, nor one who has a concubine, either. Instead, only those men should be ordained who practice continence or who are not living together with a wife, or else who were once or still are the husband of one wife—and she should be continent and virginal prior to her marriage (ἐκ παρθενίας). For nothing is so much sought after with respect to holy orders as continence, the source and the foundation of the divine canons and of all other virtues. If it happens, though, that some priest, deacon, or subdeacon should take a wife or concubine, whether openly or in secret, let him be immediately removed from his sacred ministry and treated thereafter as a layman.
>
> If, however, a lector is said to have married a second time, possibly for one urgent reason or another, he must not advance to any higher rank nor enjoy any higher dignity in the hierarchy, but must remain thereafter at the same degree. A third marriage, though, is not permitted; the second is already enough. Yet if it should happen that after a second marriage he aspires to a higher rank, let him be deposed from that moment on and treated as a layman, removed from all sacred ministry. The life of chastity is indeed for us a matter of concern over and above all others.

---

[54] Comprehensively summarized Cochini, *Origins*, 352–70.

For when continent men aspire to a clerical office and are ordained, they can then readily advance to the episcopate, and in a large group of good men it will be easy to find such as are worthy of being promoted to the priesthood.[55]

Thus the marriage and digamy prohibitions applied for priests and deacons, whereby the wife, too, was not allowed to be living in a second marriage. From further regulations we learn that this applied equally to bishops as well. That points to a uniform discipline for the entire clergy in major orders. Bishops received special treatment inasmuch as they were not permitted to have children or to live together with a wife; at any rate they could be childless widowers (laws of March 1, 528, and July 29, 531; Novels 6, 1 of March 16, 535, and 123, 1 of May 1, 546). All in all the trend was toward a virginal, monastic hierarchy, for which the East had long been paving the way.[56] In this regard we need only think of the Ecclesiastical Canons of the Holy Apostles, which pleads for virginal or at least widowed bishops. In the treatment of the bishops there was a tightening of the discipline vis-à-vis that of the deacons and priests. Justinian wanted to prevent bishops from dissipating the (often extensive) property of the Church among their children and wives by inheritance.

It has been thought that this stricture was based solely on property law and had nothing to do with a universal celibacy discipline; that bishops previously had been perfectly free to beget children;[57] that priests

---

[55] Novel 6, 5 (42, 31–43, 23 R. Schoell and G. Kroll, *Corpus Iuris Civilis* 3): Μήτε δὲ τὸν δευτέρους ἔχοντα γάμους ἢ σχόντα χειροτονεῖσθαι διάκονον ἢ πρεσβύτερον, μήτε εἰ γυναικὶ συνοικοίη διεζευγμένῃ καὶ τὸν οἰκεῖον ἄνδρα καταλιπούσῃ, μήτε εἰ παλλακὴν ἔχοι· ἀλλὰ καὶ αὐτους ἢ μετὰ σωφροσύνης ζῶντας ἢ γαμεταῖς οὐ συνοικοῦντας, ἢ μιᾶς γαμετῆς ἄνδρα γενόμενον ἢ ὄντα, καὶ αὐτῆς σώφρονος καὶ ἐκ παρθενίας. Οὐδὲν γὰρ οὕτως ἐν ταῖς ἱεραῖς χειροτονίαις ὡς σωφροσύνην ἐπιλεκτέον, πρώτην ἀρχὴν καὶ θεμέλιον ἀκριβῆ κατὰ τοὺς θείους κανόνας καὶ τῆς λοιπῆς ἀρετῆς καθεστῶσαν. Εἰ δὲ καὶ τις πρεσβύτερος ἢ διάκονος ἢ ὑποδιάκονος ὢν εἶτα εἰσαγάγοι γαμετὴν ἢ παλλακήν, ἢ φανερῶς ἢ ἐσχηματισμένως, τῆς ἱερᾶς εὐθὺς ἐκπιπτέτω τάξεως, καὶ τὸ λοιπὸν ἰδιώτης ἔστω. Εἰ δὲ καὶ ἀναγνώστης δευτέραν εἰσαγάγοιτο γαμετὴν διά τινα καὶ τοῦτο ὡς εἰκὸς ἀπαραίτητον ἀνάγκην, μηκέτι προσωτέρω χωρείτω μηδὲ ἀπολαυέτω βαθμοῦ μείζονος ἐν ἱερατείᾳ, μενέτω δὲ ἐπὶ τοῦ αὐτοῦ βαθμοῦ διηνεκῶς. Μὴ μέντοιγε καὶ πρὸς τρίτους ἐρχέσθω γάμους· ἱκανὸν γὰρ δὴ καὶ τὸ δεύτερον. Εἰ δὲ γε τοιοῦτό τι πράξειε, καὶ πρὸς δευτέρους ἐλθὼν γάμους ἐπὶ μείζονα βαθμὸν σπεύσειεν, αὐτόθεν ἰδιώτης ἔσται καὶ λαϊκός, πάσης ἱερᾶς λειτουργίας ἐκπίπτων. Σώφρονος γὰρ ἡμῖν διὰ πάντων μέλει βίου. Εἰ γὰρ τοιοῦτοι καθεστῶτες οἱ εἰς κλῆρον ἀγόμενοι χειροτονηθεῖεν, εὔκολος αὐτοῖς ἡ πρὸς τὴν ἐπισκοπὴν ἄνοδος ἔσται, ἐκ πολλῶν ἀνδρῶν ἀγαθῶν ῥᾳδίως εὑρισκομένων τῶν ἀνάγεσθαι πρὸς ἱερωσύνην ἀξίων.

[56] Cholij, *Celibacy*, 108f.

[57] Gryson, *Origines*, 112.

and deacons now were still allowed to do so.[58] That can very reasonably be doubted. When Justinian made continence the supreme maxim for deacons and priests also, but bishops had to be without a wife, then the bishops' manner of life must be understood as a more stringent form of continence, which, in principle, applied to married deacons and priests, too. While deacons and priests were not allowed to beget children, the bishops were not allowed to have any at all. Especially desirable, in fact, judging by the last sentence, were the unmarried candidates for ordination ("continent men"), so that from this particular group[59] deacons and priests could be selected, and ultimately bishops as well.[60] The prospect of the *cursus honorum* [successive degrees of holy orders] makes it clear that perfect continence was expected of married clerics and their wives from the reception of major orders onward.[61] There is yet a further indication that the continence rule applied to priests also. For the law of March 1, 528, at least, excluded from priestly ordination those candidates who had children.[62] So a more stringent continence discipline seems to have been applied even for those who had advanced to the priesthood.

---

[58] Denzler, *Die Geschichte*, 32; Stickler, *Celibacy*, 50.

[59] Ἱερωσύνη, much like *sacerdotium* in the Codex Theodosianus, means the major orders; see Theodoret, *Interpretatio in epistulam ad Phil.* 1:1f. (PG 82, 560B); Epiphanius, *De fide* 21, 7 (GCS Epiph. 32, 522, 8); *Codex Justinianus* Nov. 22, 42 from March 18, 536.

[60] The last sentence, "For when continent men aspire to a clerical office and are ordained. . . ." could be misunderstood as though there had also been clerics who were not continent, who then could not become bishops. Nevertheless, by "continent men" are meant the unmarried, as is clear from the preceding formulations, e.g., "only those men should be ordained who practice continence or are not living together with a wife, or else who were once or still are the husband of one wife."

[61] Cochini, *Origins*, 359–61.

[62] *Codex Justinianus* 1, 3, 41 (42) (26 P. Krueger, *Corpus Iuris Civilis*, vol. 2, 12th ed. [Berlin, 1959]): Ὥστε προσήκει τοιούτους ἐπιλέγεσθαι καὶ χειροτονεῖσθαι ἱερέας, οἷς οὐκ ἔστιν οὔτε τέκνα οὔτε ἔγγονοι, ἐπειδὴ οὐχ οἷόν τέ ἐστι τὸν περὶ τὰς βιωτικὰς ἠσχολημένον φροντίδας, ἃς οἱ παῖδες μάλιστα τοῖς γονεῦσι παρέχουσι, τὴν πᾶσαν σπουδήν τε καὶ εὔνοιαν περὶ τὴν θείαν λειτουργίαν καὶ τὰ ἐκκλησιαστικὰ ἔχειν πράγματα. Τινῶν γὰρ διὰ τὴν εἰς θεὸν ἐλπίδα καὶ διὰ τὸ τὰς ἑαυτῶν περισῶσαι ψυχὰς προστρεχόντων ταῖς ἁγιωτάταις ἐκκλησίαις καὶ τὰ ὑπάρχοντα αὐτοῖς ταύταις προσφερόντων καὶ καταλιμπανόντων ἐπὶ τῷ εἰς πτωχοὺς καὶ πένητας καὶ ἑτέρας εὐσεβεῖς ταύτας δαπανᾶσθαι χρείας ἄτοπόν ἐστι τοὺς ἐπισκόπους εἰς οἰκεῖον ταῦτα ἀποφέρεσθαι κέρδος ἢ περὶ ἴδια τέκνα καὶ συγγενεῖς καταναλίσκειν. Χρὴ γὰρ καὶ τὸν ἐπίσκοπον μὴ ἐμποδιζόμενον προσπαθείᾳ σαρκικῶν τέκνων πάντων τῶν πιστῶν πνευματικὸν εἶναι πατέρα. Διὰ ταῦτα τοίνυν ἀπαγορεύομεν τὸν ἔχοντα τέκνα ἢ ἐγγόνους χειροτονεῖσθαι ἐπίσκοπον. S. N. Troianos, "Zölibat und Kirchenvermögen in der früh- und mittelbyzantinischen kanonischen Gesetzgebung", in D. Simon, ed., *Eherecht und Familiengut in Antike und Mittelalter* (Munich, 1992), 140f.

In any case, an explicit permission to beget children, as might be expected on the basis of the Paphnutius legend, was out of the question. Marriages contracted by priests, deacons, and subdeacons after ordination were illegitimate. Should such clerics beget children, even though "according to the priestly rule" they were not allowed to have relations with their wives, they had to resign from the ministry they exercised in major orders (law of October 18, 530).[63] This law seems to presuppose that even higher clerics who were lawfully wedded before their ordination were not allowed to beget children and that the "priestly rule" consisted precisely in that prohibition. However that may be: Justinian recommends continence as extraordinarily desirable, as the core of his entire celibacy legislation, and as the prerequisite for career advancement. All in all, his legislation assumes that the higher clergy practice continence.

That corresponds entirely with Western legislation and displays no antipathy whatsoever toward Rome. Justinian was driven by his ambitious desire for a reconciliation between Rome and Byzantium after long years of relations disrupted by the Acacian schism.[64] By long-drawn-out military campaigns he succeeded in restoring a Roman Empire extending over the entire Mediterranean basin. All of Justinian's initiatives in legislating religious polity are to be viewed from this perspective. So it will hardly be a coincidence that the same emperor who was extending his domain far into the West (Ravenna in northern Italy) was open to the Western continence discipline. Justinian did not innovate with respect to the Western points of this discipline, but cited again and again as his authority the existing holy, divine, and ecclesiastical canons, the canonical rules inaugurated by the apostles and the Fathers. He, too, like the popes, wanted to see the apostolic tradition

[63] *Codex Justinianus* 1, 3, 44 (45) (30 P. Krueger, *Corpus Iuris Civilis* vol. 2, 12th ed. [Berlin, 1959]): Ὁ αὐτὸς βασιλεὺς Ἰουλιανῷ ἐπάρχῳ πραιτωρίων. Τῶν ἱερῶν κανόνων μηδὲ τοῖς θεοφιλεστάτοις πρεσβυτέροις μηδὲ τοῖς εὐλαβεστάτοις διακόνοις ἢ ὑποδιακόνοις γαμεῖν μετὰ τὴν τοιαύτην χειροτονίαν ἐφιέντων, ἀλλὰ μόνοις τοῖς εὐλαβεστάτοις ψάλταις τε καὶ ἀναγνώσταις τοῦτο συγχωρούντων ὁρῶμεν τινας περιφρονοῦντας μὲν τῶν ἱερῶν κανόνων, παιδοποιουμένους δὲ ἔκ τινων γυναικῶν, αἷς ἁρμοσθῆναι κατὰ τὸν ἱερατικὸν θεσμὸν οὐ δύνανται. Ἐπειδὴ τοίνυν ἡ ποινὴ τοῦ πράγματος ἐν μόνῃ τῇ τῆς ἱερωσύνης ἦν ἐκπτώσει, τοὺς δὲ θείους κανόνας οὐκ ἔλαττον τῶν νόμων ἰσχύειν καὶ οἱ ἡμέτεροι βούλονται νόμοι, θεσπίζομεν κρατεῖν μὲν ἐπ' αὐτοῖς τὰ τοῖς ἱεροῖς δοκοῦντα κανόσιν, ὡς ἂν εἰ καὶ τοῖς πολιτικοῖς ἐνεγέγραπτο νόμοις, καὶ πάντας αὐτοὺς τῆς τε ἱερωσύνης τῆς τε θείας λειτουργίας τῆς τε ἀξίας αὐτῆς ἣν ἔχουσι γυμνοῦσθαι.

[64] F. Dvornik, *Byzanz und der römische Primat* (Stuttgart, 1966), 68–70.

ensured in its totality. If Justinian does not cite the Paphnutius legend, even though he occasionally quotes the third canon of Nicaea (Novels 123, 29 of May 1, 546, and 137, 1 of March 26, 565), that can only mean that his Code has nothing to do with this idiosyncratic discipline.

c. A Momentous Innovation at the Second Council of Trullo (691)

Around 150 years after the Code of Justinian it happened again that thoroughgoing celibacy legislation was established in the eastern half of the empire, this time at the initiative of Emperor Justinian III (685 to 711). The political and economic as well as cultural setbacks in the preceding decades had led to a breakdown of discipline in many places and made an all-embracing reform necessary. And so we have arrived at the Second Council of Trullo in the year 691 (also called the Quinisext), at which the emperor and the bishops settled the ecclesiastical discipline. In the domed hall of the imperial palace in Constantinople, the development in the East came to an end in a codification that has remained valid until today for the Churches of the Orthodox world. Trullo II published in seven canons (nos. 3, 6, 12, 13, 26, 30, and 48) the fundamental rules for clerical marriage and clerical continence.

The Council took up in its entirety the foregoing legislation, to which, for example, the canons concerning the digamy and marriage prohibitions belong (canons 3 and 6). This does not need to be treated in detail. Close attention should be paid to canon 13, however, since it blatantly falls outside the parameters of the rest. Roman Cholij, in his groundbreaking study, has proved that an innovation comes about here that cannot be connected with any earlier laws and that does not fit in with the overall concept of the Trullan legislation, either. The thirteenth canon in no uncertain terms rejects the practice of continence within marriage for married priests and deacons. Henceforth they— and only those clerics mentioned—should continue to have marital relations with their wives. They are expected to practice sexual abstinence only on liturgical days, that is, to observe the continence discipline that applies to lay people as well:

> About priests, deacons, and subdeacons, that they should keep their wives.
> As we have learned that in the Church of Rome the rule was established that candidates, before receiving ordination as deacon or priest, make a public promise not to have relations any more with their wives; we, conforming ourselves to the ancient rule of strict observation and

apostolic discipline, want the legitimate marriages of consecrated men to remain in effect even in the future, without dissolving the bond uniting these men to their wives, nor depriving them of mutual relations at the appropriate times. In such a way, if someone is deemed worthy to be ordained subdeacon, deacon, or priest, let him not be prevented from growing in this dignity because he has a legitimate wife, and neither should it be demanded that he promise, at the time of his ordination, to abstain from legitimate relations with his own wife; for otherwise we would insult marriage, which was instituted by God and blessed by his presence, while the voice of the Gospel calls to us: "What therefore God has joined together, let no man put asunder" (Mt 19:6), and the Apostle teaches: "Let marriage be held in honor among all and let the marriage bed be undefiled" (Heb 13:4); and again: "Are you bound to a wife? Do not seek to be free" (1 Cor 7:27).

On the other hand, we know that the Fathers gathered at Carthage, as a precautionary measure because of the seriousness of the morals of the ministers of the altar, decided that "the subdeacons, who touch the sacred mysteries, the deacons and the priests too, should abstain from their own wives during the periods that are specifically [assigned] to them, . . . thus we also will keep what was taught by the apostles and observed since antiquity, knowing that there is a time for everything, especially for fasting and prayer; it is indeed necessary that those who approach the altar, when they touch holy things, be continent in every respect so that they can obtain in all simplicity what they are asking from God." If, therefore, anyone, acting against the apostolic canons, dares deprive a cleric in sacred Orders—i.e., a priest, a deacon, or a subdeacon—from conjugal relations and the society of his wife, let him be deposed; in the same way, "if a priest or deacon sends away his wife with the excuse of piety, let him be excommunicated, and if he persists, deposed."[65]

---

[65] Council of Trullo a. 691, canon 13 (140, 2–143, 6 Joannou 1, 1): Ἐπειδὴ ἐν τῇ Ῥωμαίων ἐκκλησίᾳ ἐν τάξει κανόνος παραδεδόσθαι διέγνωμεν, τοὺς μέλλοντας διακόνου ἢ πρεσβυτέρου ἀξιοῦσθαι χειροτονίας καθομολογεῖν, ὡς οὐκέτι ταῖς ἑαυτῶν συνάπτονται γαμεταῖς, ἡμεῖς τῷ ἀρχαίῳ ἐξακολουθοῦντες κανόνι τῆς ἀποστολικῆς ἀκριβείας καὶ τάξεως, τὰ τῶν ἱερῶν ἀνδρῶν κατὰ νόμους συνοικέσια καὶ ἀπὸ τοῦ νῦν ἐρρῶσθαι βουλόμεθα, μηδαμῶς αὐτῶν τὴν πρὸς γαμετὰς συνάφειαν διαλύοντες, ἢ ἀποστεροῦντες αὐτοὺς τὴν πρὸς ἀλλήλους κατὰ καιρὸν τὸν προσήκοντα ὁμιλίας. Ὥστε, εἴ τις ἄξιος εὑρεθείη πρὸς χειροτονίαν ὑποδιακόνου ἢ διακόνου ἢ πρεσβυτέρου, οὗτος μηδαμῶς κωλυέσθω ἐπὶ τοιοῦτον βαθμὸν ἐμβιβάζεσθαι, γαμετῇ συνοικῶν νομίμῳ· μήτε μὴν ἐν τῷ τῆς χειροτονίας καιρῷ ἀπαιτείσθω ὁμολογεῖν, ὡς ἀποστήσεται τῆς νομίμου πρὸς τὴν οἰκείαν γαμετὴν ὁμιλίας, ἵνα μὴ ἐντεῦθεν τὸν ἐκ θεοῦ νομοθετηθέντα καὶ εὐλογηθέντα τῇ αὐτοῦ παρουσίᾳ γάμον καθυβρίζειν ἐκβιασθῶμεν, τῆς τοῦ εὐαγγελίου φωνῆς βοώσης· <Ἃ ὁ θεὸς ἔζευξεν, ἄνθρωπος μὴ χωριζέτω> καὶ τοῦ ἀποστόλου διδάσκοντος· <Τίμιον τὸν γάμον καὶ τὴν κοίτην ἀμίαντον,> καὶ· <Δέδεσαι γυναικί; μὴ ζήτει λύσιν.> Ἴσμεν δέ, ὥσπερ καὶ οἱ ἐν Καρθαγένῃ συνελθόντες, τῆς ἐν βίῳ σεμνότητος τῶν λειτουργῶν τιθέμενοι ἀπόνοιαν,

This permission for priests and deacons to beget children constituted, even for the East, a downright innovation that destroyed the intrinsic consistency of the other regulations. For, conversely, perfect continence was imposed upon the married bishops, inasmuch as they had to separate from their wives (not divorce them) (canons 12 and 48). The aspect of property law hardly played a role in this, for evidently it was quite permissible for bishops to have had children. The marital separation is explained on the traditional basis: to avoid giving scandal. But the question then arises, why did the rule for the bishops not apply equally to the deacons and priests as well, since they all shared a spiritual ministry in major orders?

The legislators cannot adduce any proof from tradition whatsoever for such an inconsistency. For this reason the canon falls back on texts that are, in part, only remotely pertinent, which in each instance are supposed to prove the apostolicity of its opinion. With this intent the canon first juxtaposes texts from two Carthaginian synods from the years 390 (canon 2) and 401 (canon 4). It abbreviates the texts and combines them in such a way that the result is exactly the opposite of what they originally asserted. The original canons speak about the perfect continence of married deacons, priests, and bishops. Trullo interprets them as though (only) deacons and priests, by virtue of apostolic teaching, had to practice continence only on days when the Divine Liturgy was celebrated. Thereby marital relations were indeed permitted but were then restricted again—a striking ambivalence. Striking also because bishops are no longer mentioned here, even though the original texts of Carthage listed them with deacons and priests.

Canon 13 then cites the fifth apostolic canon also, which forbids bishops, priests, and deacons to dismiss their wives (see above, pp. 181–83).

ἔφασαν, 'ὥστε τοὺς ὑποδιακόνους, τοὺς τὰ ἱερὰ μυστήρια ψηλαφῶντας, καὶ τοὺς διακόνους καὶ πρεσβυτέρους κατὰ τοὺς ἰδίους ὅρους καὶ ἐκ τῶν συμβίων ἐγκρατεύεσθαι,' 'ἵνα καὶ τὸ διὰ τῶν ἀποστόλων παραδοθὲν καὶ ἐξ αὐτῆς τῆς ἀρχαιότητος κρατηθέν, καὶ ἡμεῖς ὁμοίως φυλάξωμεν, καιρὸν ἐπὶ παντὸς ἐπιστάμενοι πράγματος καὶ μάλιστα νηστείας καὶ προσευχῆς· χρὴ γὰρ τοὺς τῷ θυσιαστηρίῳ προσεδρεύοντας ἐν τῷ καιρῷ τῆς τῶν ἁγίων μεταχειρήσεως ἐγκρατεῖς εἶναι ἐν πᾶσιν, ὅπως δυνηθῶσιν, ὃ παρὰ τοῦ θεοῦ ἁπλῶς αἰτοῦσιν, ἐπιτυχεῖν.' Εἴ τις οὖν τολμήσοι, παρὰ τοὺς ἀποστολικοὺς κανόνας κινούμενος, τινὰ τῶν ἱερωμένων, πρεσβυτέρων φαμέν, ἢ διακόνων ἢ ὑποδιακόνων, ἀποστερεῖν τῆς πρὸς τὴν νόμιμον γυναῖκα συναφείας τε καὶ κοινωνίας, καθαιρείσθω· ὡσαύτως καὶ εἴ τις πρεσβύτερος ἢ διάκονος, τὴν ἑαυτοῦ γυναῖκα προφάσει εὐλαβείας ἐκβάλλοι, ἀφοριζέσθω· ἐπιμένων δέ, καθαιρείσθω. [Scripture verses as in RSV; rest of English translation from Cochini, *Origins*, 405.] All of the celibacy canons from Trullo are reprinted according to Joannou in Greek and Latin in Cholij, *Celibacy*, 204–11.

Here, too, there is an inconsistency, in that bishops are swept under the rug. Hence we are dealing, so to speak, with a repeated contradiction that did not even creep into the Paphnutius legend. (According to that account, bishops, priests, and deacons were considered equally entitled to conjugal relations.) In this instance, too, the "ancient ecclesiastical tradition" has to bear the brunt of the argument. All this betrays the helplessness of the Trullan legislator in trying to find an authentic justification for the new practice. In reality he is making this point on his own authority, without any other support. This, however, does not answer the question of how he could have hit upon this change. Possibly the Paphnutius legend then served as godfather. That meant a late victory for the Novatians' version of history. Their notion of purity—"Marriage is honorable and the marriage bed is undefiled" (cf. Heb 13:4)—is enlisted again, anyway, in an attempt to deprive a strict clerical continence discipline of its theological legitimacy.

In all this it is difficult to miss the anti-Roman tongue-lashing.[66] Canon 13 explicitly rejects the practice of strict continence in the Roman Church and cites as it own "ancient rule" the Western Synod of Carthage. Is that sheer brazenness, or is there possibly some truth to it? Was it perhaps the original, apostolic practice to approve of conjugal relations for deacons and priests? Anyone pursuing such a line of inquiry ought to realize, at any rate, that the Trullan Council took place three hundred years after the time of Epiphanius, Siricius, and Innocent, who for their part, with the support of synods, considered perpetual continence for all higher clerics to be the apostolic tradition. That probably makes it clear who has more credibility in this regard. In any case, canon 13 displays little competence in making valid pronouncements about apostolic traditions. At the time it was promulgated, North Africa was already being toppled by Islam. Maybe this caused the legislators to forget that the Carthaginian celibacy discipline, which they call as their witness, had been absolutely identical with that of the Roman Church.

It would be erroneous, now, to understand the polemic against the West as a conscious repudiation of the entire Western clerical continence discipline. Had that been the intent, Trullo would have been

---

[66] By their very subject matter, canons 13 and 20 are certainly in opposition to the Western celibacy discipline, even if some of the particulars can be toned down by interpretation. H. Ohme, *Das Concilium Quinisextum und seine Bischofsliste: Studien zum Konstantinopeler Konzil von 692*, AKG 56 (Berlin and New York, 1990), 46, 49.

pulling the rug out from under its own feet. The critique of the West was focused solely on this one point concerning married priests and deacons. After all, with regard to bishops there was unanimity again; on this subject the West was even a little more lenient, since it did not require spouses to separate. At any rate, even there [that is, in the West] the separation of bishops from their wives was not unheard of.[67] The East advocated an all-embracing clerical discipline that coincided with that of the West in most of its elements and that Trullo, too, characterizes as an apostolic heritage. In both cases it was a matter of a precise mechanism for regulating clerical continence. Only in one, single, little point—which is nonetheless momentous—did Trullo deviate from the West: namely, that the continence of married priests and deacons was no longer propagated as an absolute, but rather as something temporary. Such periodic continence, though, could lead to complete abstinence as soon as the cleric had daily liturgical duties.[68]

3. Fundamental Considerations with Respect to the Consensus between the Eastern and Western Celibacy Disciplines

When we pass in review what has been said thus far, it presents us with a picture of the early Christian clerical discipline that, from today's perspective, can be exasperating. Thousands of married clerics in the East and the West renounced the normal course of their marriage at their ordination. They no longer had any sexual contact with their wives. Is that really imaginable? Could continence celibacy actually count on the approval of a broad majority of the Christian population and of the clerics? What was its status, then, and how widely was it endorsed?

a. Opponents of Clerical Continence Can Scarcely Be Detected

One might think that such a discipline owed its very existence to coercive measures. Nevertheless, continence celibacy is by no means found only in ecclesiastical laws and compulsory regulations, as though it had been forced upon an unwilling majority by the higher-ups in a disci-

---

[67] Cochini, *Origins*, 96f. on Severus of Ravenna. Ibid., 127–28 on two bishops from Clairmont and Autun.

[68] This is an important aspect for the celibacy discipline of the uniate churches of the East; Cholij, *Celibacy*, 161–94.

plinary clamp-down. Of course, there are the canonical celibacy regulations, too, but they do not stand alone—they are not even the earliest testimonies. Long before Elvira, the continence of clerics was judged to be suitable by various theologians, who actively took up the cause, as we have already seen. To the extent that the later writings of the fourth- and fifth-century theologians record a positive response, we will go into this subject again in more detail.

Furthermore, one essential insight that we have gained so far consists in the fact that continence celibacy in the first centuries of the common history of the Greek and Latin Church, aside from one exception, was never resisted and at worst was deliberately disregarded. The cloud of celibacy opponents that is sometimes discerned owes its existence to excessively vague interpretations of the texts or else to rank speculations with no claim to plausibility. Callistus in Rome was not an opponent of celibacy. Paphnutius in Nicaea was not one, either: he was a legend. Jovinian in Rome approved of clerical continence. Vigilantius in Gaul, to all appearances, merely wanted to allow young monks to marry while they were still in minor orders. Synesios in Cyrene would have given anything in the world to have obligatory continence maintained properly. The Paphnutius legend was a vehicle for the celibacy critique of the schismatic Novatians.

Many controversies in the North Africa of Donatism, in the Spain of Priscillian, in the Rome of Jovinian, in the Gaul of Vigilantius, and in the East of the great exegetes arose, not from a rejection of clerical continence, but rather from a difference of opinion as to how this rule, which was considered apostolic, could be preserved in changing times. Hence, in peripheral questions, divergent interpretations resulted, for instance with regard to the question of what significance baptism had for the digamy prohibition, or to what extent marriage could still be conceded to lower clerics (subdeacons). Yet from beginning to end, the real core of the celibacy discipline, the permanent continence of married higher clerics, remained undisputed.

What is left, then, in the way of historically demonstrable protest? Only the celibacy opponents in Spain at the end of the fourth century. That is the sole reliably attested case of outspoken resistance by married clerics to the discipline of permanent continence. Of course it came up simultaneously three times in the literature: in Siricius, Ambrose, and Ambrosiaster. But even in the case of the Spaniards, the principle of ritual purity in liturgical times was accepted. As a consequence of daily celebration of the Liturgy, then, permanent continence necessarily became acceptable here as well. In any case, that is how Pope Siricius caught these Spaniards, whose lot it was to enter history as the first known opponents of celibacy. Of course, they would remain for a long time yet without companions.

This is not to say that continence was observed with Stoic equanimity everywhere, down to the last man and his wife. Of course there were difficulties, too. This is amply demonstrated in the measures taken by the bishops and popes. Probably there were whole dioceses, also, that were unaffected by any formal obligation to practice continence. Indeed, many bishops blatantly ignored the universal discipline. But those were and remained exceptions. There will always be historians who take such exceptions for the rule. That, however, does not do justice to the entire historical context and the statements made by contemporary witnesses. Furthermore, it would be an absurd concept of Church to think that in the first centuries everything had to be undisputed and practiced by everyone in order to be of significance. That would be, after all, a remarkably archaic notion of an ideal primitive Church.

Once we accept this objective historical finding, the question becomes all the more urgent: How is the wide acceptance of a continence celibacy discipline to be explained? What social, intellectual, and spiritual motives were behind it? How is it that continence was felt to be appropriate for clerics? What is the basis for this Christian consensus, which also loomed large throughout society as a whole? In those days man was living in a different world and, accordingly, lived out his faith differently. This otherness of religious sentiment is now our theme. It can help us to understand why clerical continence was not perceived then as being all that rigid and coercive as people might think today; why it was seen, rather, as being religiously self-evident.

b. Is Marital Continence Imaginable in the First Place?

It must seem grotesque to demand that grown men and women renounce all sexual relations as of a given day. How was such an arrangement, which always involved two people, supposed to function?[69] Was

---

[69] Cf. H. Böhmer, "Die Entstehung des Zölibates", in *Geschichtliche Studien Albert Hauck zum 70. Geburtstag* (Leipzig, 1916), 8f. Some reflections on the human side of celibacy can be found in Gryson, "Ans", 176–79.

that not a recipe for psychological and familial catastrophes? Such objections are not new. The most prominent of all celibacy critics, the legendary Paphnutius, already opposed complete continence within marriage, claiming that it was too great a hardship to impose and that it would drive the weaker partner to immorality. Thus the difficulty of such a requirement was perceived quite clearly, and certainly there were shipwrecked attempts in evidence as well. The many regulations of the synods against *syneisaktoi*, that is, against "extraneous/extern" women in the houses of clerics, allow us to infer numerous abuses. Other witnesses to the dangerous shoals of marital continence include those ministers who separated from their wives so as to be able to practice continence more securely. How married clerics and their wives put obligatory continence into practice concretely in their married lives is, of course, something we do not learn from any written source.

Any historian who comes to the conclusion that a celibacy discipline existed from the very beginning, chiefly in the continence practiced by married clerics and their wives, must also be able to say whether that is at all plausible in daily life. First of all we must take seriously the *Zeitgeist* [spirit of the times] and the values of late antiquity. In today's world, life is planned on the basis of completely different premises from before: from the premises of one's own philosophy of life. Such an attitude is permeated with a strong awareness of being an individual. A decisive component of this is sexuality. The recognition that a human being always acts as a male- or female-gendered entity has as its consequence a subliminal or a manifest sexualization of each and every department of life. Sexual renunciation of any sort whatsoever must then be perceived as nothing less than a loss of personality development. If man *is* sexual, how is he then supposed to do without an expression of this, either temporarily or permanently?[70]

Christians accept the fundamentally ascetical view of man in late antiquity. Now this sensualization and sexualization is in fact a phenomenon of modern times. Sexuality and carnal desires are of course basic constants in human existence. But their concrete realization and social involvement, the priority given to them and the way in which they are

---

[70] For this entire complex of problems, see J. Arquer, " 'Zölibatär leben bringt doch überhaupt nichts!' Die charismatische Ehelosigkeit und ihre Bedeutung für die Gesamtkirche", in M. Müller, ed., *Kirche und Sex: Mein Körper gehört mir* (Aachen, 1994), 251–69, among the other essays in this volume.

translated into action, are by no means always the same. To this extent there is a "changing sexuality". The notions that early Christians had of sexual renunciation were based on an understanding of man and corporeality that is fundamentally different from that of today. Against this background clerical continence, too, was practiced and inculcated in a different way from what is lived today in the Orthodox and Catholic Churches.[71] We are worlds apart from the strict moral ideas of both pagan and Christian late antiquity, and it would be anachronistic to want to carry our highly sensitive feelings of justice and entitlement over to the time when the early Christians were eking out a meager living for themselves.

Their life was considerably more difficult, with less room for independent action, and more intensely focused on ensuring day-to-day existence than is the case now. One would have to depict a panorama of customs and mores even to begin to make this clear.[72] Life expectancy was lower, unequally so. Such things as the freedom to choose a career according to one's interests and inclinations, or long periods of time for education and thus for reflection, are a luxury of modern men. If we consider also the questions of sicknesses, physical and psychological burdens, life expectancy, social environments, education, opportunities for leisure and recreation, then we have an entire spectrum of deep-seated differences. If today sexuality is almost something of a cultural artifact, which deserves flattery on all sides and a place of honor in human thought and action, nevertheless in antiquity it was viewed much more soberly, and people did not even have the time to pursue everything to the extent they would have liked.

It is by no means a coincidence that in just such a society sexual continence was required of married clerics as of the day of their ordination. The Church lives with her times and, in doing so, adopts the serious discoveries of the natural sciences and the anthropological learning of the day. Medicine and philosophy existed in antiquity. Sexual abstinence and asceticism were important elements of a view of sexuality with a natural law orientation. The whole question of hygiene played a role in this, which, for lack of other means, necessarily

---

[71] Cf. P. Brown, *Die Keuschheit der Engel: Sexuelle Entsagung, Askese und Körperlichkeit am Anfang des Christentums* (Munich and Vienna, 1991), 9.

[72] A famous example is the four-volume work of L. Friedlaender, *Darstellungen aus der Sittengeschichte Roms in der Zeit von Augustus bis zum Ausgang der Antonine*, 10th ed. (Leipzig, 1921–1923).

consisted mainly of stable partnership and sexual restraint. It is clear that at that time sexual intercourse involved a certain health-related risk and therefore had consequences for the partnership. Hence, as early as the Old Testament, many regulations in the area of sexuality can be understood as sanitary precautions. Medicine, in turn, yielded essential information for anthropology and its overall ascetical image of man. The Christians, too, felt that they were bound by it.

Sexuality is submissive to the will. Not the Christian, but rather the pagan of late antiquity was the first to view sexual intercourse as a thing that he believed he had to restrain. He allowed himself to be led by an astonishing optimism concerning his ability to control sexual urges.[73] Antiquity, in essence, knew nothing yet about involuntary drives. Everything was subject to the will and could be decided this way or that. This is the doctrine of practically all of philosophy, from Stoicism to the Peripatetic school. The Christians saw no reason not to subscribe to this view. The Christian couple was free to act upon their sexual desires or to renounce them.[74] Jerome was confident that even the body could be influenced by means of dieting. Long fasting as well as care in avoiding wine and mixed company caused the sexual drive to slacken. This reflected the opinion of physicians of that time.[75]

In their battle with the sexual drives, Christians saw themselves as having an advantage over pagans: baptism put them in a better position. For it gave a new docility to the will, empowering it to choose a way of life pleasing to God. Paul saw disordered passions and desires as the root evil of the pagan way of life. In contrast, baptism gave to the will the strength to follow what it heard being preached. It enabled the Christian henceforth to resist disordered desires (Gal 5:16, 19, 24).[76] It provided the strength needed to withstand temptation[77] and freed the recipient from servitude to concupiscence,[78] not only in the sexual

---

[73] Brown, *Keuschheit*, 33.

[74] Augustine, *Contra Iulianum* 5, 5, 22 (PL 44, 797), Nemesius Emesenus, *De natura hominis* 17 (PG 40, 676B–677A); 25 (700A–704A). Brown, *Keuschheit*, 422, 428.

[75] *Comm. in Tit.* 1:7 (PL 26, 601C); *Epistula* 22, 11 *ad Eustochium* (CSEL 54, 158, 5–159, 6); *Epistula* 54, 9 *ad Furiam* (CSEL 54, 474, 17–176, 9); *Epistula* 79, 7, 7 *ad Salvinam* (CSEL 55, 96, 7–17). Brown, *Keuschheit*, 428.

[76] K. Niederwimmer, *Askese und Mysterium: Über Ehe, Ehescheidung und Eheverzicht in den Anfängen des christl. Glaubens*, FRLANT 113 (Göttingen, 1975), 67–69, 164f.

[77] *Acta Pauli* 25.

[78] Clement of Alexandria, *Stromata* 3, 5, 44, 4 (GCS Clem. Alex. 2⁴, 216, 24–27).

sense of the word, but completely.[79] Baptismal grace bestowed the possibility of freely deciding upon one's state in life, whether one chose marriage or continence.[80] It extinguished the fire of passion.[81] For Ambrose, furthermore, being baptized meant being clothed in the chaste body of Christ.[82] And that was not just a vague theory. He witnessed it himself in a man whom he baptized at the Easter Vigil in the year 387 in his cathedral in Milan and who was to become world famous: Aurelius Augustinus. From long years of dissolute living he converted to a continent way of life, received baptism, and lived thereafter untroubled by sexual drives.

But naturally, such glorious high points of early Christian experience were not the rule. And one wonders: was all that not an excessive enthusiasm for chastity and an all-too-euphoric evaluation of baptism? Was too much not being demanded here of a human being? There were in fact groups, especially in the first two centuries, that overestimated human capabilities. The Encratites demanded—in advance!—a celibate way of life of everyone who received baptism. Such radicalism was doomed to failure and was also rejected by the universal Church. The Catholic Church acted on the relatively moderate conviction that man cannot practice continence on his own, but the grace of baptism makes chastity possible. At the same time, this (periodic or complete) continence was, according to the philosophical teachings in antiquity, what was fitting for man, the most humane thing that one could think of. Christian ethics affirmed this image of man and adopted it, but considered it livable only now, in the era of grace.

Antiquity has a strict moral code. The culture of ancient Greece and Rome, then, left an imprint on all of social life, long before Christianity appeared and joined in. The scientific findings of the day gained immediate entry into the Christian milieu. Thus a strict moral code prevailed in families.[83] Under the influence of a markedly ascetical doctrine on baptism, the early Christian moral teaching on marriage

---

[79] Ibid., 3, 7, 59, 1 (GCS Clem. Alex. 2⁴, 223, 5–8).

[80] Ibid., 3, 9, 66, 3 (GCS Clem. Alex. 2⁴, 226, 16–19).

[81] Pseudo Clement, *Hom.* 11, 26, 4 (GCS PsClem. 1, 167, 10–130). Brown, *Keuschheit,* 111.

[82] Brown, *Keuschheit,* 357–60.

[83] Cf. E. Dassmann and G. Schöllgen, "Haus II (Hausgemeinschaft)", in RAC 13 (1986), 801–905; M. Gärtner, *Die Familienerziehung in der Alten Kirche,* KVRG 7 (Cologne and Vienna, 1985).

was far removed from the personalistic view of sexuality in our times, which a man of antiquity surely would perceive as being downright lascivious. Now the popular group of philosophers known as the Stoics placed man in the very center of their investigations and, through their humane maxims, made a name for themselves. According to them, though, sexual intercourse in marriage was said to have as its sole purpose the begetting of children.[84] Such an axiom was not just the melancholy view of fossilized ascetics but was completely in line with the contemporary modern medicine.[85] For marital life, then, that meant long periods of abstinence.

Particularly in the tenth chapter of his book on pedagogy, Clement of Alexandria gives us a good insight into this moral code. Marital relations had to be conducted morally, that is, without lustful concupiscence and with the exclusive aim of begetting children.[86] It was within the power of everyone to make the decision with regard to begetting children.[87] This meant that continence was in general an essential component of early Christian marital ethics. The practice of continence applied to all Christians in the sexual realm, indeed, within marriage as well.[88] Occasional marital continence "for the sake of prayer" was from the very beginning an undisputed practice in both the East and the West, based on the clear instruction of Paul (1 Cor 7:5).[89] This is not to be understood as a few days but rather in terms of weeks and months that accompanied prolonged fasting. To this sublimation of sexuality in marriage, which was typical of the new morality in the imperial age,[90]

---

[84] G. Delling, "Geschlechtsverkehr", in RAC 10 (1978), 812–29 at 817, 821, 823f.; H. Strathmann and P. Keseling, "Askese II (christlich)", in RAC 1 (1950), 758–95 at 771; A. Oepke, "Ehe I (Institution)", in RAC 4 (1959), 662; H. Chadwick, "Enkrateia", in RAC 5 (1962), 359; B. Lohse, *Askese und Mönchtum in der Antike und in der Alten Kirche*, RKAM 1 (Munich and Vienna, 1969), 165. On Philo, see Delling "Geschlechtsverkehr", 820. But see also *Testamentum XII Issachar 2, 3.*

[85] D. Wendebourg, "Die alttestamentlichen Reinheitsgesetze in der frühen Kirche", ZKG 95 (1984): 158.

[86] 1 Tim 2:15; Justin Martyr, 1 *Apologia* 15, 1–7; 2 *Apologia* 2, 4; Clement of Alexandria, *Stromata* 3, 7, 58, 2 (GCS Clem. Alex. 2⁴, 222, 30–223, 4); *Paedagogus* 2, 10, 83, 1 (GCS Clem. Alex. 1², 208, 2f.); 2, 10, 95, 3 (214, 26–215, 1); Cyril of Jerusalem, *Catecheses* 4, 25 (117 Reischl and Rupp 1). On Clement, see Brown, *Keuschheit*, 143–48.

[87] *Stromata* 3, 9, 67, 1 (GCS Clem. Alex. 2⁴, 226, 24f.).

[88] Ibid., 3, 6, 46, 4 (GCS Clem. Alex. 2⁴, 217, 20f.).

[89] Cholij, *Celibacy*, 144–47.

[90] Cf. P. Veyne, "La Famille et l'amour sous le Haut-Empire romain", *Annales* 33 (Paris, 1978): 35–63.

we can attribute also the low esteem in which digamy and multiple marriages were held.[91]

The age for ordination comes after the phase of actually raising a family. Also connected with the moral code was the age deemed suitable for marriage. Not by accident does Paul write that one should marry before giving in to lust and committing adultery (1 Cor 7:9). The First Letter to Timothy says explicitly that younger widows should marry for just this reason (1 Tim 5:14). Ultimately the parents were responsible for their children if the latter happened to become addicted to impurity because their parents did not marry them off at the opportune time. This was principally true of girls, whose virginity had been considered since time immemorial to require special protection. Thus, concern about the moral conduct of the children led as a rule to early marriages.[92] In that way, though, such spouses gained experience in marriage and family matters at a very early age. As a rule no man was ordained in the bloom of the youthful married years or in the midst of raising a family, for that would have deprived him of conjugal intercourse. Before ordination the candidate should already have lived married life to the fullest, which included bringing up children. Such men with the experience of a completed family were then ordained. The concept of the clerical state that the early Church had in mind for married clerics does not seem to have involved maintaining normal marital relations, anyway. As a consequence of the candidate's advanced age, ordination had, instead, the quality of an exclusive, complete dedication of self in total obedience. The married cleric had to devote himself entirely to ecclesiastical and liturgical concerns, just like his unmarried colleague. At any rate, his duty was no longer in the first place to govern the household.

This picture of clerical marriage finds its confirmation in the Church's regulations. The pastoral letters presuppose a certain maturity in the married candidates.[93] They were experienced men, *viri probati.* Their

---

[91] Kötting, "Digamus", 1018.

[92] Brown, *Keuschheit*, 163, 205f., 220; E. Pagels, *Adam, Eva und die Schlange: Die Theologie der Sünde* (Reinbek, 1991), 175, 188. The girls especially married early, between the ages of fifteen and twenty; C. Pietri, "Le mariage chrétien à Rome", in J. Delumeau, ed., *Histoire vécue du peuple chrétien*, vol. 1, *De la clandestinité à la chrétienté* (Toulouse, 1979), 105–31 at 125–30; B. D. Shaw, "The Age of Roman Girls at Marriage", JRS 77 (1987): pp. 30–46.

[93] H. Kruse, "Eheverzicht im Neuen Testament und in der Frühkirche", FKTh 1 (1985): 113, n. 63 sets the age for priestly ordination at sixty years. It is precisely the usual higher

active family life had to be over, practically speaking. The children were grown and were standing on their own two feet. The father now could attend wholeheartedly to the concerns of the Church. It was his chief vocation, just as it was for his unmarried colleagues. According to the Syrian *Didascalia* (first half of the third century) bishops had to be at least fifty years old; recourse was had to younger candidates only by way of exception. The Ecclesiastical Canons of the Holy Apostles (around 300) called for married priests only, who were already elderly.[94] The Council of Neocaesarea (around 314 to 325) required that no one be ordained a priest before his thirtieth year (canon 11). Pope Siricius (384 to 399) wanted the minimum age for married deacons to be thirty, for priests—thirty-five, and for bishops—forty-five.[95] That is quite an advanced age. This may have involved a precautionary measure, which promoted continence without drawing attention to itself. Very young aspirants to the clergy had to decide while still adolescents whether or not to marry.[96] Presumably, then, unmarried candidates were ordained at a much younger age than married ones.

Therefore we must not imagine obligatory continence for married clerics and their wives as a forced intrusion into private life. A man who was ordained started over again, in a certain way, with a second career. Many a woman, too, occasionally found that it was a gift from God to be free at last as a result of her husband's ordination, since he could no longer be occupied with her and the grown children.[97] Furthermore, the wives, it seems, not infrequently assumed the status of widows, so to speak, when the family situation permitted.[98] We have already seen the possibility that among the widows in the primitive Church (Acts

age of clerics that makes it necessary for the Church Fathers to explain why Timothy is so young (1 Tim 4:12; 2 Tim 2:22). Indeed, there were always exceptions to the general rule.

[94] *Constitutio ecclesiastica apostolorum* 18, 2 (26, 1 Schermann).

[95] *Epistula* 1, 9, 13 *ad Himerium* (PL 13, 1143A). *Codex Justinianus*, Novel 123, 13 of May 1, 546, expects that priests will be at least thirty-five years of age. On this whole subject, see E. Eyben, "Young Priests in Early Christianity", in M. Wacht, ed., *Panachaia, Festschrift K. Thraede*, JAC.E 22 (Münster, 1995), 102–20.

[96] Council of Carthage a. 397, canon 18 (CCL 149, 333, 133f.).

[97] Ambrose, *De exhortatione virginibus* 4, 24 (PL 16², 358C): "Experta sum, filii, labores copulae, conjugii indignitates, et sub bono conjuge, nec tamen sub bono marito libera fui: serviebam viro, et laborabam ut placerem. Miseratus est Dominus, et fecit altaris ministrum, continuoque et mihi et vobis raptus est: et fortasse, miserante Domino, ne diceretur maritus."

[98] Ibid.: "ne diceretur maritus". As to the wife of Severus of Ravenna, see Cochini, *Origins*, 96–97.

6:1) were to be found the separated wives of the apostles and of other ministers. With the passage of time, the order of widows took on a definite place and a wide range of duties within the Christian community. Besides this there was the community work of the deaconesses. It is also worth pondering whether the female order of deaconesses cannot in general be traced back to the service rendered by the wives of deacons (cf. 1 Tim 3:11).[99] If that is the case, then opportunities for advancement were available to the wives of clerics as well.

The topic "sex for seniors" has not yet been discovered in antiquity, or else it was viewed differently. The general idea was that sexual activity stopped at a certain age. Sexuality was considered volatile stuff, which quickly evaporated. The aging process, in which the body lost its youthful ardor, supported the will. It reduced the strength of sexual desires, while the Christian seasons of feasting and fasting trained couples to weather long periods of continence.[100] The opinion was that, after the change of life, the woman ceased to yearn for her husband.[101] Julian of Aeclanum, too, the spiritual head of Pelagianism, and the Pelagians in general viewed the sexual drive as mainly a phenomenon of youth, which faded away with increasing age.

More realistic, of course, was the view of Augustine, who was skeptical about mastering the sexual drive.[102] Maybe in Paradise sexuality was completely submissive to the will, but not after the Fall. This was in no way changed by redemption; in any case baptism does not eradicate sexual concupiscence. Augustine came to understand sexuality as a constant of human life throughout all its stages. The ardor of lust remained. Augustine heard about an eighty-three-year-old man, who for twenty-five years had lived continently with his wife on the basis of a pious vow and then for his amusement bought himself a slave-girl who played the lyre. The likelihood that it was a cleric is nil. But it does not take much imagination to realize that married clerics, too, were at risk in this respect. Augustine knew from his own experience: man is

---

[99] Canon 48 of Trullo in the year 691 provides that the wife of a bishop should enter either the convent or the order of deaconesses.

[100] Zeno, *Tractatus* I, I, 5 (CCL 22, 9, 40–47); Ambrosiaster, *Comm. in I Cor.* 7:5 (CSEL 81, 2, 72, 12–16). P. Veyne, ed., *Geschichte des privaten Lebens*, vol. I, *Vom Römischen Imperium zum Byzantinischen Reich* (Regensburg, 1989), 259.

[101] Jerome, *Adversus Helvidium* 20 (PL 23², 214C); John Chrysostom, *Adversus eos qui apud se habent virgines subintroductas* (PG 47, 495f.).

[102] Brown, *Keuschheit*, 420–29.

incapable of practicing marital continence—no matter how much he may exert his will, he cannot either request this of God or accept and safeguard it—unless he has divine assistance and support.

Of course we cannot conclude from this that Augustine considered such continence to be impossible. On the contrary, in baptism God does give that assistance to the will that makes continence possible. Augustine explicitly approved of married couples reaching an agreement at a certain time to give up conjugal relations for ever.[103] Such a decision was actually made by his friend Paulinus of Nola (d. 431). He was a descendent of an aristocratic, Christian family of senators and had been married since 385 to a Spanish Christian woman, Theresia, who gave birth to a son. After the early death of Celsus, he and his wife decided on a continent way of life (before 393). We should also mention Gregory of Nyssa (d. 394), the younger brother of Basil of Caesarea. They were both outstanding theologians working in Asia Minor. Gregory was married. But we do not know whether any offspring issued from his marriage with Theosebeia (d. 385), or whether the couple wanted children in the first place.[104] It is quite possible that even before his ordination in the year 372 they were living together in a spiritual marriage.[105]

Obligatory continence is socially acceptable. We know much about the opinions of bishops and theologians on continence celibacy. Unfortunately we know almost nothing about how the simple cleric and his wife coped with it. Nevertheless they probably undertook the practice of continence more easily than we can imagine today. The lofty prestige of the ministerial life was a contributing factor. Public opinion served as a support and a safeguard.[106] There was no doubt about the

---

[103] *De nuptiis et concupiscentia* 1, 11, 12–12, 13 (CSEL 42, 224, 3–226, 20); *De bono coniugali* 13, 15 (CSEL 41, 207, 5–24); 26, 34 (229, 13f.).

[104] *De virginitate* 3 (GNO 8, 1, 256, 1–257, 11); Brown, *Keuschheit*, 302f.

[105] In the year 371, while already married, Gregory became enthusiastic about the ascetical life (see his treatise *De virginitate*). Furthermore, the letter of condolence written by Gregory Nazianzen on the death of Theosebeia in the year 381 refers to a continent marriage (*Epistulae* 197, 2 [GCS Greg. 142, 22]: ἀδελφή; 197, 6 [143, 12]: ἱερὰν καὶ ἱερέως σύζυγον). J. Daniélou, "Le Mariage de Grégoire de Nysse et la chronologie de sa vie", REAug 2 (1956): 71–78, rules out a marital separation (or a continent way of life), probably because he still adheres to the views of Paphnutius (ibid., p. 72f.).

[106] We hear of lay people who complain about incontinent clerics: Isidore of Pelusium, *Epistulae* 3, 340 (PG 78, 1000AD); Innocent, *Epistulae* 38 (PL 20, 605BC). On the lofty prestige of clerics, see H. Achelis / J. Flemming, *Die ältesten Quellen des orientalischen Kirchenrechts*, vol. 2, *Die syrische Didaskalia*, TU 25, 2 (Leipzig, 1904), 266–74.

status of the cleric in Christian society. An impressive voice was that of Synesius of Cyrene. He was a truly happy father of a family and would have liked to remain so, but he fully accepted the suitability of the ecclesiastical norm, precisely because of his philosophical background and education. All in all we may say that married clerics and their wives did practice continence. That was not accomplished without sacrifices. It did not work, either, without mutual respect, whereby more was certainly demanded of the wife. She had to step back for the sake of her husband's vocation. He was now appointed to a sacred ministry, and, according to the convictions of the time, that raised him above his family, too. That was manifest even in the dark color of their clothing, by which the clerics could be recognized.[107] Presumably both single and married ministers wore it, as can be observed even today in the Orthodox Churches.

c. Can the Grace of Continence Be Made an Obligation?

The anthropological and societal parameters in late antiquity furnish many indications that make continence celibacy look not so strange after all. But another objection appears that casts doubt on a law of celibacy. Let us take as our point of departure the present celibacy discipline of the Latin Church. Priests are obliged to be unmarried [that is, celibate in the strict sense]. It is true that when the Church first began, priests were not bound to live as celibates; they could be married. Then it is concluded that the early Church did not know of obligatory celibacy. The candidate for ordination could choose freely between marriage and celibacy. In fact Ambrose says: Virginity stands above the law, it originates in a free decision.[108]

This, the argument goes, is in keeping with the Gospels, inasmuch as celibacy is a charism freely bestowed by God. Celibacy, according to the statements in the New Testament, is a gift and a grace and hence cannot be decreed by Church law. Celibacy, then, is a charism, a gift that one either has or has not, which in any case cannot be prescribed

---

[107] John Chrysostom, *De sacerdotio* 1, 4 (SC 272, 80, 40). As early as the Novatian Sisinnios, black clerical garb was criticized; Socrates Scholasticus, *Historia ecclesiastica* 6, 22, 3–7 (GCS Socr. 345, 15–29). On priestly garb, see A. Hermann and M. Cagiano di Azevedo, "Farbe", in RAC 7 (1969), 358–447, at 421–26.

[108] Ambrose, *Epistulae* 63, 35–38 (CSEL 82, 3, 253, 345–255, 388); Methodius, *Symposium* 3, 13 (GCS Method. 42, 12–17).

for all clerics. Heinz-Jürgen Vogels thinks that, according to the understanding of Jesus and Paul, the charism of celibacy is actually not
something one can ask for (Mt 19:11f.; 1 Cor 7:7). It is either given
to a man or not; at most one can pray for perseverance in this grace.[109]

And yet, at least in the first six centuries in both the East and the West,
anyone who became a deacon, priest, or bishop had to practice perfect
continence, regardless of whether he was single or already married. We
are dealing therefore with a discipline of obligatory continence. For a
candidate was allowed to be married, but once ordained he could no
longer marry. And a cleric who was already married could no longer
continue having marital relations as before. Turn it whatever way you
will: sexual renunciation was a duty and an obligation for every cleric
in major orders. Today the candidate for the priesthood is obliged to
live as a celibate; then he could choose between marriage and celibacy
but in either case was expected to practice continence after his ordination. Certain individuals have understood this very well and speak
polemically of a compulsion to practice continence instead of a duty
or an obligation, which is more appropriate.[110]

Criticism of obligatory celibacy is not new. "Paphnutius" brought
into circulation some arguments with regard to the demand for continence that still keep coming up today: human inadequacy—antipathy
to marriage—the danger of adultery—innovation (see above, p.17).
But one argument is missing from his appeal: the charismatic character of continence. Paul wants everyone to have the gift of chaste conduct, and then he distinguishes between the celibate and marital forms
thereof.[111] One can apply this directly to continence celibacy in the
early Church and say: Perfect continence in marriage, also, is a God-
given charism and is not within man's power or under his control. If
this is so, can a general obligation to practice continence ever have been
accepted in the first centuries? Given the doctrine about charisms, do

---

[109] H.-J. Vogels, *Priester dürfen heiraten: Biblische, geschichtliche und rechtliche Gründe gegen den
Pflichtzölibat* (Bonn, 1992), 23–36.

[110] Socrates Scholasticus, *Historia ecclesiastica* 5, 22, 50 (GCS Socr. 302, 2f.): Εἰ καὶ βούλοιντο, οὐ μὴν ἀνάγκῃ νόμου τοῦτο ποιούντων. Sozomenus, *Historia ecclesiastica* 1, 23, 5 (GCS
Sozom. 44, 22f.): Ἐπῄνεσε δὲ καὶ ἡ σύνοδος τὴν βουλὴν καὶ περὶ τούτου οὐδὲν ἐνομοθέτησεν,
ἀλλὰ τῇ ἑκάστου γνώμῃ τὸ πρᾶγμα, οὐκ ἐν ἀνάγκῃ ἔθετο.

[111] G. Sloyan, "Biblische und patristische Motive für den kirchlichen Amtszölibat", *Concilium* 8 (1972): 563–72, at 566.

we not have to assume that at the beginning continence was, instead, a voluntary practice of some clerics?

Continence is a charism for which one must ask. One would, in fact, have to assume that, if the theologians of the early Church were to interpret the New Testament exactly as Vogels does. But they understood it in a completely different way and therefore saw no contradiction between the Pauline doctrine about charisms and obligatory continence. It is by no means that obvious what Paul really meant. We need only to add Jesus' statement about those who "have made themselves eunuchs for the sake of the kingdom of heaven" (Mt 19:12). That does include an individual decision and a choice,[112] precisely on the part of those followers of Jesus who have left their families behind.

The early theologians, in any case, took the Pauline doctrine on charisms quite seriously and treated it often. They never disputed the gratuitous character of celibacy and perfect continence.[113] And nonetheless they saw very well the need to pray for this charism, to beg God for it. The charism in question was one of a free-will decision (regardless of the debate about the extent to which God moves the free will). Heinz Kruse has straightened out Heinz-Jürgen Vogels' crabbed interpretation of charisms.[114] Vogels sees the relation between man and God as being motionless and inflexible. For him, a charism is something like a natural phenomenon, which either strikes a man at birth or else does not.[115] In its unaccountability and relentlessness it almost loses the attractive charm of a gift. The early theologians saw it differently. Man stands in a relation of partnership to God. He can speak with God and express his wishes. And God accordingly and exquisitely selects the gifts that he gives.

---

[112] Kruse, "Eheverzicht", 104 is correct, contrary to Vogels, *Priester*, 23–34.

[113] Gregory of Nyssa, *De virginitate* 1; Eusebius Emesenus, *Sermo de martyribus* 6, 10. Chadwick, "Enkrateia", 364f.

[114] Kruse, "Eheverzicht", 104f. L. Hödl ("Die *Lex continentiae*: Eine problemgeschichtliche Studie über den Zölibat" ZKTh 83 [1961]: 325–32), too, is circumspect in his remarks about continence as a charism and a virtue.

[115] This view was flatly contradicted as early as Jerome: *Comm. 3 in Mt.* 19:11 (CCL 77, 168, 791–97): " 'Qui dixit: Non omnes capiunt uerbum istud sed quibus datum est'. Nemo putet sub hoc uerbo uel fatum uel fortunam introduci quod hi sint uirgines quibus a Deo datum sit aut quos quidam ad hoc casus adduxerit, sed his datum est qui petierunt, qui uoluerunt, qui ut acciperent laborauerunt. Omni enim petenti dabitur et quaerens inueniet et pulsanti aperietur."

Alexandrian theology is unanimous on this point. Clement sees continence as a gift of God, which simultaneously must correspond to a free personal decision: "He who has (publicly) declared by his celibacy resolution that he does not wish to marry, must remain unmarried",[116] and: "Continence can be obtained in no other way than by the grace of God. Therefore he [that is, Jesus] says, 'Ask and it will be given you' (Mt 7:7)."[117] Origen attached great importance to the necessity of prayer. But can someone then be sure of receiving the gift of continence from God? That is the decisive question. Origen thought that the charism of celibacy could be asked for while still remaining a gift of God.[118] This was particularly clear to the early Church. One who prayed for celibacy was indeed praying for something good and excellent (1 Cor 7). Why should God then withhold this gift? After all, he is just waiting to bestow his graces on those who long for them. And yet, for all that, celibacy remains a gift. Whoever asks for it always receives it from God alone and does not give it to himself. This consideration even led to a more rigorous set of demands (now and then with fatal results). For whatever God grants can be accomplished also, because God always gives his grace along with it.

When Origen emphasized that God grants continence for the sake of prayer, he meant to clarify a point of contention that even today has not lost its relevance. Many people thought that if a man who was unmarried for the sake of the kingdom of heaven subsequently failed to remain celibate, it was obviously because he had not received the gift of celibacy from God. Of course, anything at all can be excused in this way. To put a stop to such reasoning, Origen says: Once a man has undertaken celibacy, he has evidently prayed for this gift and desired it. And then God does grant what is requested, as it says in the Gospel: "For everyone who asks receives" (Mt 7:7f.).[119] Origen's position, then, was clearly that someone who has freely decided upon celibacy must stay with it; otherwise he calls God a liar. Naturally that applies by way of analogy for continence within marriage. With that

---

[116] *Stromata* 3, 15, 97, 4 (GCS Clem. Alex. 2⁴, 241, 4f.); cf. ibid., 3, 9, 66, 3 (226, 16–19). B. Kötting, "Gelübde", in RAC 9 (1976), 1055–99 at 1087.

[117] *Stromata* 3, 7, 57, 2 (GCS Clem. Alex. 2⁴, 223, 18f.); cf. ibid., 3, 18, 105, 1 (244, 21–28).

[118] H. Crouzel, *Virginité et mariage selon Origène* (Paris and Bruges, 1963), 105–17.

[119] *Comm.* 14, 25 *in Mt.* 19:3–12 (GCS Orig. 10, 345, 11–348, 9).

we have sketched in essence the understanding of both the Eastern and the Western Church.[120]

The candidate for holy orders and his wife must consent to the ordination. No one could be compelled to undertake continence. It always required the free consent of the candidate for holy orders. Before he was admitted to orders the candidate most likely was asked whether he agreed to this condition, or else it was simply assumed whenever a man offered himself as a candidate for ordination without demurring.[121] That was true particularly in a later period, when adolescent, as yet unmarried candidates for minor orders were admitted at the request of their parents; only when they were grown and capable of making a mature decision could they receive the major orders, which were bound up with obligatory celibacy. Whoever did not promise to practice continence, though, could not be ordained, even if he was unmarried. There is no conclusive evidence for any exception to this rule. At most the ordination was postponed (canon 10 of the Council of Ancyra).

If a candidate for holy orders was married, then his wife, too, had to be ready and willing to practice continence from then on. As Origen put it, this was because, in the case of spouses, the continence of the one put the chastity of the other at some risk. And therefore they were allowed to practice permanent continence only by mutual agreement.[122] This was in keeping with the pastoral rule that no ascetically minded lay person could force the spouse against his or her will to promise

---

[120] A more complete picture can be found in A. M. Ritter, *Charisma im Verständnis des Johannes Chrysostomos und seiner Zeit: Ein Beitrag zur Erforschung der griechisch-orientalischen Ekklesiologie in der Frühzeit der Reichskirche*, FKDG 25 (Göttingen, 1972), e.g., 187–89; A. Zumkeller, *Das Mönchtum des heiligen Augustinus*, 2d ed. Cassiciacum 11 (Würzburg, 1968), 307–11.

[121] To my knowledge there are no direct statements about such an inquiry as to whether continence is being undertaken freely. But in light of the comprehensive scrutinies concerning the suitability of candidates that have been carried out from the earliest times, and in which chastity, too, always played a role (P. H. Lafontaine, *Les Conditions positives de l'accession aux ordres dans la première legislation ecclésiastique (300–492)* [Ottawa, 1963], 103–20), there can be no doubt that the willingness to practice continence was either examined or at least tacitly assumed if someone did not refuse candidacy to begin with.

[122] Clement of Alexandria, *Stromata* 3, 12, 79, 1 (GCS Clem. Alex. 2⁴, 231, 16–21); Origen, *Comm.* 1, 1 *in Rom.* 1:1 (FC 2, 1, 78, 22–25, 80, 12f.); *Fragmenta 33 in epistulas ad 1 Cor.* 7:1–4 (501, 38f. Jenkins); Pseudo-Cyprian, *De singularitate clericorum* 31 (CSEL 3, 3, 207, 5); John Chrysostom, *De virginitate* 29, 2 (SC 125, 186, 24–188, 40); Augustine, *De bono coniugali* 13, 15 (CSEL 41, 207, 12–19); *De nuptiis et concupiscentia* 1, 11, 12–12, 13.

to renounce marital relations.[123] The grace of continence had to be something that the wife, too, prayed for. We must assume, therefore, either that the wife of the man aspiring to holy orders was required to make a formal promise also, or else at least that her husband had to have first obtained her consent.

To be sure, in the early Church things were occasionally not very romantic. This was related to the participation of the faithful in the selection and presentation of candidates for holy orders. Now and then this was accompanied by distressing demands upon many members of the community, including even physical and psychological coercion. For it was not uncommon that married men, too, were practically forced to receive holy orders. There was something of an overriding factor on the Church's side, that is to say: when the faithful selected someone as a future priest or bishop, then he and his wife had to comply, more or less. Countless men were ordained against their will or at least unexpectedly.[124] There was no point in being hypersensitive. Personal concerns had occasionally to be put aside. Of course, most of the surprise candidates were not married and were evidently capable of continence. But there were also married men who received holy orders rather hesitantly and reluctantly.

The aforementioned Paulinus of Nola had been practicing continence with his wife Theresia for quite some time when he was ordained a priest at the urging of the people of Barcelona. The election of Gregory of Nyssa (see above, p. 326) may well have been a similar case. Valerius Pinian was married to his cousin Melanie the Younger. After the early death of their two children they decide to live together as brother and sister. In the year 411 Pinian evaded ordination only by dint of his stubbornness. Synesius, on the other hand, was married and declared that he does not want to observe continence with his wife when he was urged to become a bishop. But he was willing to submit to the discipline, should the Church insist upon his ordination. And finally we have already heard from Augustine, who sheds an extremely positive light on the spirit of self-denial of those married men who,

---

[123] Augustine, *Epistulae* 262, 1–5 (CSEL 57, 621, 4–625, 16); John Chrysostom, *De virginitate* 32, 3 (SC 125, 196, 34–40).

[124] Lafontaine, *Conditions*, 71–100; Y. M.-J. Congar, "Ordinations *invitus, coactus* de l'Église antique au canon 214", RSPhTh 50 (1966): 169–97; Schillebeeckx, *Identität*, 293.

against their personal inclinations, allowed themselves to be recruited for the ministry and thereafter renounced conjugal relations.[125]

d. Continence Is an Expression of Religious Reverence from Time Immemorial

Continence celibacy is certainly one of the most astonishing phenomena in the ministry of the early Church. We have made clear that it has a certain plausibility, given the circumstances in which the people of antiquity lived, and that it was by all means practicable in the societal context of that time. But we have not yet understood what the intrinsic motives of such a discipline were. What kind of thinking and what mentality were behind it? What was it that convinced people that they were on the right path?

An important concept here is ritual purity. We mentioned in the introductory chapter that Roger Gryson, especially, points out how closely celibacy is bound up with notions of cultic purity and ritual competence. Even though Gryson dates the general validity of an obligatory continence discipline too late, nevertheless on this one point he has called attention to an essential aspect.[126] Today we have no idea how important and decisive questions of cult-related sexual asceticism were throughout all of antiquity. It was common currency, an entirely self-evident conviction that one must abstain sexually in order to participate in divine worship: "Cult trumps sex", was the taboo. This applies equally to Jewish, pagan, and Christian antiquity.[127] There is no doubt that ritual purity was one of the most basic components in the religious thought of Christendom as well, since we are dealing with a concept characteristic of antiquity in general, and no objection of any sort on the part of the Christians can be discerned.

How did it happen, then, that marriage was granted to the married cleric but was halfway taken back again, so to speak, once he was or-

---

[125] De coniugiis adulterinis 2, 20, 22 (CSEL 41, 409, 9-14).

[126] Since then this has been repeated often, e.g., E. Dassmann, Ämter und Dienste in den frühchristlichen Gemeinden, Hereditas 8 (Bonn, 1994), 164f.

[127] E. Fehrle, Die kultische Keuschheit im Altertum, RVV 6 (Giessen, 1910); H. Preisker, Christentum und Ehe in den ersten drei Jahrhunderten: Eine Studie zur Kulturgeschichte der Alten Welt, NSGTK 23 (Berlin, 1927); O. Böcher, Dämonenfurcht und Dämonenabwehr: Ein Beitrag zur Vorgeschichte der christlichen Taufe, BWANT 90 (Stuttgart, 1970); Wendebourg, "Reinheitsgesetze".

dained? The marriage bond remained, but the realm of sexuality was bracketed off, and that after so many years of wedded life. What other reason could there have been for it besides the view that sexual intercourse was something impure? Now one could object that such a continence discipline for married clerics and their wives was not ritually motivated but was merely ascetical, since married lay people, after all, were urged to practice continence for long periods, too. But the reasons given for this were cultic, inasmuch as the need for uninterrupted prayer was emphasized (Lk 18:1), which is possible for married couples only if they observe permanent continence. Paul himself knew of ritually motivated sexual asceticism for lay people and approved it (1 Cor 7:5).[128] The early theologians took very careful note of it.[129] The continence of married clerics, therefore, certainly had something to do with their occupational duties as sacred ministers.

Clerical continence is taken for granted from the very beginning. The principle of ritual purity is elemental, having been in force since time immemorial, and it did not have to be explained any further to a man of late antiquity, not even by the popes. It was taken for granted all the more so in the case of priests, whether they were Jewish, pagan, or Christian. Sexual continence on the occasion of cultic practices and divine worship was, for the priest, clearly the order of the day. A minimum of sexual self-control plainly belonged to his professional ethos, just as one expected the barber to have a steady hand. Ritual purity was taken for granted in Christian ministers, as well. Clement of Alexandria called those married couples perfect Christians and holy priests who decided together to practice continence henceforth. For Origen, perfect priests renounced all sexual intercourse. Not even the opponents of celibacy caused any problems in this respect. The difference of opinion only concerned the necessary degree of asceticism. One group of Spanish clerics wanted to limit it solely to liturgical days. The only way to explain the fact that Jovinian attacked celibacy but left continence celibacy alone is to conclude that ritual purity was indisputable for him, too. The kinds of celibacy laws that came afterward from councils and

---

[128] Chadwick, "Enkrateia", 362f.
[129] Clement of Alexandria, *Stromata* 3, 12, 81, 1–4 (GCS Clem. Alex. 2⁴, 232, 22–233, 5); Tertullian, *De exhortatione castitatis* 10, 2 (CCL 2, 1029, 13–1030, 18); Origen, *Hom.* 23, 3 *in Num.* (GCS Orig. 7, 215, 10–16); *Fragmenta* 34 *in epistulas* 1 *ad Cor.* 7:5 (501, 2–502, 33 Jenkins).

popes were only the legal codification of a self-evident duty, to which clerics were honor-bound and which had been observed long before without any sort of sanctions.

Therefore the fact that Christian priests practiced continence from the very beginning, at least in preparation for the Divine Liturgy, is so obvious that one has to marvel at the doubts of many scholars. It is said that a celibacy discipline arose from the fourth century on because, as a result of Constantine's Edict and the mass conversions to Christianity, pagan religious sentiments made their way into the Church and, with them, pagan notions of purity as well. The many new converts are said to have brought a wave of cultic anxiety into the Church, so that clerics started to abstain from sexual intercourse on liturgical days. Behind this there is the erroneous notion of a primitive Christian Church of the elite, a biosphere completely closed off from its environment, teeming exclusively with Christians unaffected by the Jewish thought of late antiquity, where only later on the decadence of the masses broke in. But why should the Church suddenly in the fourth century fall victim to unchristian insinuations, when from the very beginning she stood in the midst of the Greco-Roman culture?

Allegedly the idea of ritual purity really got started when the Christian Liturgy and official functions became sacralized from the third century on, which then coalesced in concepts like "cult", "priest" and "sacrifice".[130] Only when the Christian Liturgy came to be understood as a cultic sacrifice did sexual taboos then ensue. Massive quantities of sacral language are encountered for the first time in Tertullian, Cyprian, and Origen. These theologians are then supposed to be the ones who also favored a discipline of ritual continence. Nevertheless, the Christian ministry, even in its formative stages, was not simply anti-cultic. In the cultic terminology of the third century we find only the unfolding of views that had long been present and that can be traced back to the New Testament (for example, in the Letter to the Hebrews).[131] Christian worship from the very beginning was a cultic action. This sort of

---

[130] J. P. Audet, *Mariage et célibat dans le service pastorale de l'Église: Histoire et orientations* (Paris, 1967), 117–37; Schillebeeckx, *Amtszölibat*, 45f.; J. E. Lynch, "Marriage and Celibacy of the Clergy: The Discipline of the Western Church: An Historico-Canonical Synopsis", *The Jurist* 32 (1972): 14–38, 189–212 at 20–22.

[131] J. Colson, *Ministre de Jésus-Christ ou le sacerdoce de l'Évangile: Étude sur la condition sacerdotale des ministres chrétiens dans l'église primitive*, ThH 4 (Paris, 1966).

thing was not dependent on altar, candles, or incense. Even household worship services were not profane events, but indeed formed part of a cult as soon as they were understood to be public adoration of God by the community. How much more did the presiders over such worship have to be abstinent when even purely private prayer demanded sexual asceticism. That is how Paul saw it (1 Cor 7:5), and thus we have the idea of a cultic religion already within the corpus of New Testament literature.

We can trace it back even one step farther if we allow the assumption that clerical continence goes back to the apostles' way of life. Many apostles were married and practiced continence with their wives from the time of their calling (1 Cor 9:5). Their way of life was, in turn, the manner of life found in the original circle of Jesus' disciples, in which all practiced sexual continence as "eunuchs for the kingdom of heaven". At first glance sacerdotal and cultic considerations played no role in this. But is that any reason to conclude that Jesus rejected all notions of ritual purity?[132] His celibacy can certainly be viewed in a prophetic-cultic context.[133] It has by no means been determined that the cultic dimension of a continence celibacy discipline was added only in the postapostolic generation, as the ecclesiastical ministries were developing. It is conceivable that there was an interior priesthood and a spiritual cultic action of the original disciples, even though they were laymen, per se. The ritual sacrifice was surpassed by Jesus' self-offering. His offering can be understood as a sacrifice and an expiation, not in a technical, cultic sense, but certainly inasmuch as it was a martyrdom.[134] In that case, though, the continent life-style of the original disciples was an expression and an anticipation of the redemptive self-sacrifice of Jesus, the High Priest in the Paschal Mystery, into which the apostles were drawn in the upper room at the Last Supper.

If this view is correct, then the marital and virginal continence of clerics intrinsically pointed to and manifested the priesthood of Jesus, in which the apostles participated. Continence, then, was the suitable form for the kind of life that Jesus led and shared with the Twelve: priestly existence-for-others. In that case the cultic dimension of cler-

---

[132] Thus J. Blank, "Abbau kultischer Sexualtabus und überholter Machtstrukturen", *Diakonia* 2 (1971): 105–9. On Mk 7:15 see below, p. 345, n. 152.

[133] K. Berger, *Wer war Jesus wirklich?* (Stuttgart, 1995), 24–28.

[134] J. Ratzinger, "Ist die Eucharistie ein Opfer?", *Concilium* 3 (1967): 299–304.

ical continence must date back to its origins, in the apostolic way of life. Klaus Berger has pointed out that the old notions of taboo, which view divine worship and sexuality as being in competition with each other, are not simply unreasonable in themselves. Sexual asceticism has a sign value, adumbrating Israel's understanding of God. The God of Israel is, unlike the gods of the entire surrounding world, not married, which means that he is different from both idols and men. "For he is the one and only God, the mystery of the universe. Thus he is to be deemed 'higher' or 'deeper' than all sexuality, in exactly the same way that every human being has a personal core, which lies deeper than his sexuality, even though it does not exist independently of it."[135]

Ritual purity is an act of reverence for God. With the idea of ritual purity, the Christians were adhering to a pagan-Jewish model of conduct. This is not to say that we are dealing with a repaganization or a gradual backsliding into heathen ways of thought; rather, a religious idea was consciously being adopted here. Theology defined and discussed the theme of ritual purity; on Paul's authority it recognized and affirmed purity as an authentic expression of Christian worship. Theology saw it as appropriate conduct for the simple reason that ritual purity was considered in that era to be a profoundly religious (though not necessarily pious) act. And the Christians did want to be religious. Therefore they did not reject this practice, as they did many other heathen customs. Whether sexual asceticism was periodic or permanent, it served to bring one into contact with God: the purpose of cultic qualifications was competence in divinity. To this extent the strict ritual purity of Christian clerics is merely one aspect of the renewal of faith brought about in late antiquity by Christianity. Therefore we should not understand it so much as an ascetical item in the early Christian showcase or as the derangement of a popular contempt of the body, but rather as a genuinely religious (albeit not genuinely Christian) expression of reverence for God.

Continence made the cleric the vehicle for a transcendental world of meaning, the sign of man's surmounting of himself. The Christian saw in sexual asceticism an expression of his belief in the one God and a renunciation of the world of demons, which also seemed to be connected with sexuality.[136] In this respect liturgical asceticism always had

---

[135] Berger, *Wer war Jesus*, 28.
[136] 1 Cor 7:5; Justin Martyr, 2 *Apologia* 5, 4; Pseudo-Clement, *Hom.* 9, 10, 2; Irenaeus

to do with deliverance, with warding off the false gods of the heathens (1 Cor 10:20f.). Already in pagan and Jewish antiquity, continence was employed as a weapon against demonic action. The Christians were not about to set themselves apart from this consensus. If anything, they may have prescribed an even stricter form of continence: If even the heathen and Jewish priests kept demons away by means of periodic continence, how much more, then, should the servants of the one true God?[137]

We are dealing here with a deep-seated religious sentiment, about which it is not easy to form a judgment. Pagan society, too, was oriented toward divine law. There is something of a unanimity about transcendence in the ancient Greco-Roman world, evident also in the statements of leading thinkers, which is epitomized in early Neoplatonism. In those days it was entirely clear that there was a God who was the creator and to whom reverence was due. And this reverence demanded that one approach him with a pure heart. We find this formulated pellucidly by Ambrosiaster: It is befitting the dignity of God that his servants are more pure than all others (see above, p. 239 [in chapter 6]). Nothing more and nothing less than this was implied. Marriage and marital relations were good, but for someone in the service of the Church, continence was appropriate on account of his converse with God, and continence could in all fairness be expected. This is simply a different concept of reverence from that of today.[138] It was not considered fitting to bring sexuality and prayer together. The one excluded the other. The one was human service (*Menschendienst*); the other, divine service (*Gottesdienst* = Liturgy).

At the origin of clerical continence are at least two motives. The idea of ritual purity was certainly an essential force propelling early Christian continence celibacy. At the same time, one should not make this aspect into an absolute. Gryson has the celibacy law beginning only with the

---

(Satornil), *Adversus haereses* 1, 24, 2; Tertullian, *De exhortatione castitatis* 10, 2 (CCL 2, 1029, 12–14). Origen, *De principiis* 3, 2, 2 (GCS Orig. 5, 247, 7–28): the devil is not the author of the sexual drive.

[137] Tertullian, *De praescriptione haereticorum* 40 (CCL 1, 220, 1–221, 28); *De monogamia* 17, 2–5 (CCL 2, 1252, 5–1253, 24); *De exhortatione castitatis* 13, 1f. (CCL 2, 1033, 5–1034, 24); Clement of Alexandria, *Stromata* 3, 6, 48, 2f. (GCS Clem. Alex. 2⁴, 218, 14–18); Origen, *Contra Celsum* 7, 48 (GCS Orig. 2, 199, 12–25); *Fragmenta* 34 *in epistulas* 1 *ad Cor.* 7:5 (501, 2–502, 4 Jenkins).

[138] H. Doms, *Vom Sinn des Zölibats: Historische und systematische Erwägungen* (Münster, 1954), 15f.

papal decretals at the close of the fourth century, and so he is obliged to create the impression that ritual purity was the principal motive for it. But since the premise itself is false, in that a clerical continence discipline can be identified much earlier, his claim can have only relative validity. The farther it is traced back, the clearer it becomes that a derivation from a single cause is problematic.[139] Ritual purity, then, appears as only one aspect, besides which there was at least one other: the continent apostolic way of life for the sake of the kingdom of heaven. At the origin of obligatory continence, two motives meet, neither of which can be derived from the other: ritual purity and religious continence. There is no point in trying to force a decision here, after the fact, as to whether continence celibacy was determined solely by cultic considerations or whether it was only the expression of eschatological self-sacrifice. Radical sexual continence was an ancient and essential Christian phenomenon that was so thorough-going that it resists any attempt to resolve it toward one side or the other. Everything that the historian might say in favor of one direction would necessarily remain caught up in his own subjective impressions.

The equilibrium between ritual purity and eschatological continence can be clarified further by citing the ideal of *virginitas*. In the celibate clergy, notions of ritual purity overlap with the completely independent Christian ideal of virginity. The virginity ideal in the early Church was nourished by other considerations than that of ritual purity. The entire spirituality resulting from the complex scriptural image of the Bride of Christ (spiritual betrothal, and so on) played a part in this. We cannot elaborate on this any further because it is a distinct and, in the early Church, especially dominant theme. Let it simply be noted that celibacy for the sake of the kingdom of heaven was practiced by lay people (for instance, by widows who did not remarry) as well as by clerics.

---

[139] For arguments against an exclusively cultic derivation of early clerical celibacy, see H. Crouzel, "Le Célibat et la continence ecclésiastique dans l'Église primitive: Leurs motivations", in J. Coppens, ed., *Sacerdoce et célibat: Études historiques et théologiques* (Gembloux and Louvain, 1971), 333–71 (opposed in turn by R. Gryson, "Sacerdoce et célibat: À propos d'un ouvrage récent", RHE 67 [1972]: 75–78); H. Crouzel, "Les Origines du célibat ecclésiastique: À propos d'un Livre récent", NRTh 6 (1970): 649f.; P. Delhaye, "Les Origines de célibat ecclésiastique d'après un ouvrage récent", RTL 1 (1970): 320–33 at 328–32. Delhaye and Crouzel point out that even Gryson, *Origines*, plainly admits various other motives besides ritual purity and that it is only in his summary (*Origines*, 200, 203) that he claims to derive celibacy solely from the notion of purity.

This overlapping can be observed even among the married clerics. For their continent way of life, too, had something of that eschatological availability and discipleship about it that is usually associated only with celibates. This clarifies why married clerics practiced perfect continence, even though they may not have had daily liturgical duties. Evident here is an ordering of marital continence to virginity that was present from the beginning but that was articulated no later than the fourth century: Marital continence is required where the state of life actually desired, that is, celibacy, is not possible. To that extent the married clerics should imitate the virginity of their colleagues. This was the view of Jerome, for example.

Christian cultic asceticism is not the same as pagan sexual anxiety. Not only were other motives besides ritual purity present at the origins of clerical continence. We must also say: Ritual purity was not ritual purity. The term "ritual purity", when applied to both pagan and Christian practices, is completely equivocal. For all that was common to the asceticism of the ministers of Christian worship and their pagan priest-colleagues, there were nevertheless considerable discrepancies that resulted from their different views of God. Edward Schillebeeckx, therefore, in reference to the religious-cultic motivation of celibacy, speaks of a Christianization of existing pagan-religious notions.[140] Asceticism itself underwent a metamorphosis, and the importance of this must not be underestimated. For one thing, continence was no longer seen as the product of human effort. Rather, it was a charism, purely a gift from God (see above [in chapter 7], pp. 329–31).[141]

Another thing is that in the pagan world, ritual purity was not necessarily bound up with morality. One merely had to guarantee an external abstinence. Occasionally that was technically contrived, so to speak, as in the case of the Athenian hierophant, who smeared his genitals with a lust-inhibiting ointment—because otherwise he would not be considered capable of chastity, as Origen remarks. The Christians had in view also the Jewish priests who, during their time of service at the Temple, left their homes and families so as not to come together with their wives. Or one might think of the Jewish washings, for example, after a defilement. All of this was unknown to the Christian

---

[140] *Amtszölibat*, 39–43; E. Denzler, "Zur Geschichte des Zölibats: Ehe und Ehelosigkeit der Priester bis zur Einführung des Zölibatsgesetzes im Jahr 1139", StZ 183 (1969): 393f. A more detailed treatment is found in Crouzel, "Célibat", 345–52.

[141] Chadwick, "Enkrateia", 364. A particularly clear example is Clement of Alexandria, *Stromata* 3, 7, 57, 1f. (GCS Clem. Alex. 2⁴, 222, 14–19).

observance of ritual purity. The difference is evident: ritual purity was understood as a moral act of renunciation. Christian apologetics understood priestly chastity as a moral demand, as a non-burdensome, free, and generous gift of the cultic minister, which was not the object of suspicion. Precisely this quality of freedom and generosity of self-giving was demonstrated in the fact that many priests lived as celibates. The celibate clergy of the first centuries, in this respect, were evidence for a cultic continence discipline of married clerics and simultaneously for the spiritualization and moralization of their ascetical practices.

That casuistical sexual anxiety had been overcome is indicated by another observation: in the third century we do already have clear statements on the perfect continence of married clerics and their wives, but the daily celebration of the Liturgy is not yet mentioned (aside from Carthage at the time of Cyprian). Therefore we can hardly assume that the prescriptions concerning priestly purity were the consequence of more intensive liturgical customs. The very fact that absolute continence may well have been required from the beginning, regardless of the frequency of divine worship, contradicts a narrowly cultic explanation of the celibacy discipline. Here the intention was to overcome the pagan and Jewish cultic thinking that led to pettiness in counting days. Greeks and Jews were only marginally acquainted with a discipline of perfect continence. The usual practice among them was abstinence limited to those times when one was attending to the ritual services. The Christians, too—that is, the laity among them—were familiar with the very same practice. They restricted marital continence to the liturgical days and days of fasting.

It was different for Christian priests. If they had practiced continence only on liturgical days, then certain questions would necessarily have arisen. The more indispensable purity was for the priestly ministry, the more one would have to worry about the extent to which marriage had to be restricted, how far one could go, and so on. Scrupulous individuals, at least, would then have asked how long they could keep sleeping with their wives, how many hours before the Liturgy they had to abstain, what would happen if they suddenly had to administer baptism. In short: the higher the ideal of purity, the more one could expect a continence-casuistry. The fact that nothing of the sort can be found demonstrates also how little Christian continence had to do with a formalistic preoccupation with sex. There was never any thought of a limited period of time centered on the cultic services. Complete continence was required for the sake of the perfect priesthood of the New

Covenant. Involved in the permanent continence of married clerics, to be sure, was also the thought of a purity superior to that of the laity: one could say the idea of ritual purity in the superlative (based on a fortiori reasoning).[142] But even so there was still something else at stake, above and beyond anxieties and taboos.

Sexual renunciation makes Christian worship a spiritual sacrifice. Ritual purity does not exhaust the ideal of the Christian priesthood. Christian worship is, in fact, a sacrificial offering, the presentation of the eucharistic gifts. But unlike the pagan practices, that must not remain an external action but should be accompanied by an interior attitude of self-offering on the part of the faithful. Origen formulates it this way: "If I mortify my members and rid them of all carnal concupiscence, if the world is crucified to me and I to the world, then I have presented a burnt offering at the altar of God and have become the priest of my own sacrificial gift."[143] Priesthood is victimhood, and that must not remain a thing of the spirit but must be made good existentially. The priest cannot merely lay a sacrificial offering upon the altar; he must offer himself as victim. This personal sacrificial offering of all those who serve at the altar can only be understood as a sacrifice of the body, as the renunciation of any sort of sexual activity. The spiritual sacrifice (*sacrificium rationabile*, later termed "the unbloody sacrifice") of the altar demands a spiritual (noncorporeal) sacrifice of the minister.[144] Such an ascetical practice is a spiritual sacrifice in two respects. The body is set aside in a certain way, and this occurs through a spiritual act of the will.

That is really a spiritualization, because no ritual purification is required here after an act of sexual intercourse, as was the case in Greco-Roman antiquity and Judaism.[145] Distancing oneself from an external

---

[142] Epiphanius, *Panarion lxxx haeresium* 59, 4, 5–7 (GCS Epiph. 2², 368, 3–12); Siricius, *Epistulae* 5, 3 (PL 13, 1160A); Jerome, *Comm. in Tit.* 1:8f. (PL 26, 603B); Ambrosiaster, *Comm. in* 1 *Tim.* 3:12f. (CSEL 81, 3, 269, 24–270, 1).

[143] *Hom.* 9, 9 *in Lev.* (GCS Orig. 6, 436, 22–24): "Si >membra< mea ab omni concupiscentia carnis >mortificavero<, si >mundus mihi crucifixus sit et ego mundo<, holocaustum obtuli ad altare Dei et ipse meae hostiae sacerdos efficior." Cf. ibid., 9, 1 (418, 29–419, 3); Gregory of Nyssa, *De virginitate* 23 (GNO 8, 1, 341, 18–343, 16); Ambrose, *De virginibus* 1, 11, 65 (PL 16², 218A).

[144] Origen, *Hom.* 1, 5 *in Lev.* (GCS Orig. 6, 287, 25–28): "Vult ergo sermo divinus, ut rationabili sensu carnem tuam in castitate offeras Deo, secundum quod Apostolus dicit: >hostiam vivam, sanctam, placentem Deo, rationabile obsequium vestrum<." For a discussion of purity and holiness in the worship of the New Covenant, see L. Legrand, *Jungfräulichkeit nach der Heiligen Schrift* (Mainz, 1966), 79–88.

[145] Justin Martyr, 1 *Apologia* 10.

action (sexual intercourse) is interiorized, because it has to be accomplished spiritually. And on these terms sexual purity is never a merely external purity. Antiquity could establish a direct relationship between conduct and prayer. Chastity was a guaranteed way to God, not only because it created the necessary purity, but also because a spiritual act was involved in it, a spiritual sacrifice and thus a gesture of humility. Such thinking included the whole man, not only the head. I do not just talk; it costs me something. And this price was paid also by the married clerics and their wives. For such a spiritual act of renunciation was just as possible for them as it was for celibate ministers. Their sacrifice made an even greater demand on them, for in their case they renounced something that they knew and loved.

Surely other existential acts of renunciation would also have been conceivable as the clerical expression of a spirit of self-sacrifice, for example, a life of poverty, which became important for the monastic movement from the fourth century on.[146] But the fact remains that sexual abstinence was considered to be the authentic sacrifice of the priest. Since it was a prerequisite for ordination, it became a *specificum sacerdotale*. In this respect, not even the celebration of the Eucharist was all that important; the decisive factor, rather, was the all-embracing religious service rendered by the deacon, priest, and bishop. In other words, the ministerial duty of prayer made continence appropriate. The connection with the ministry was clearly evident in the fact that continence was an obligation from the day of ordination onward. The historical record shows that this was true even for the beginnings of the ministry, but it was clearly stated toward the end of the fourth century: "By reason of ordination" higher clerics were bound to practice continence.[147]

---

[146] A Faivre, "Clergé et propriété dans l'église ancienne: Statut des biens, hiérarchie, célibat", *Lumière et Vie* 129/130 (1976): 51–64.

[147] Council of Carthage a. 390, canon 3 (112 Jonkers): "Gradus isti tres, qui constrictione quadam castitati per consecrationes annexi sunt, episcopus, presbyter et diaconus"; Siricius, *Epistula* 1, 10 *ad Himerium* (PL 13, 1139A): "Omnes sacerdotes atque levitae insolubili lege constringimur, ut a die ordinationis nostrae, sobrietati ac pudicitiae et corda nostra mancipemus et corpora"; Innocent, *Epistula* 2, 9, 12 *ad Victricium* (PL 20, 476A): "Quanto magis hi sacerdotes vel levitae pudicitiam ex die ordinationis suae servare debebunt"; Jerome, *Epistula* 49, 21, 3 *ad Pammachium* (CSEL 54, 387, 1–3): "Episcopi, presbyteri, diaconi aut uirgines eliguntur aut uidui aut certe post sacerdotium in aeternum pudici." Council of Elvira, canon 33 (13 Jonkers): "Omnibus clericis positis in ministerio abstinere se a coniugibus suis."

Ritual purity can veer off into sexual anxiety and contempt for the body. Of course there were dark, even anxious moments, too, in early Christian liturgical asceticism, for instance when the assurance of continence was seen as a guarantee that priestly prayers would be heard; when it was thought that God refused to accept a sacrifice from "unclean hands". Such notions could then be used to impose an over-fastidious adherence to the continence rule.[148] Herein lay a danger of coercive restrictions. But this potential danger is involved in every religious concept. It cannot outweigh the real concern: the religious, "vertical" dimension of Christian worship of God and the consequent demands on the ministers of God.

Another complex of attitudes was occasionally combined in a disastrous way with ritual purity: the unhealthy or even drastic denigration of everything sexual, which raises the hackles of people today. Nevertheless, for all the righteous indignation, the case should not be overstated. For instance, again and again you hear the opinion that Pope Siricius was disparaging marital obligations. In reality the only thing he was opposing was illicit sexual intercourse. In this regard he was not designating legitimate marital relations as *turpis coitus*; rather, that was the name he used for adultery, to which even married clerics were certainly not immune.[149] One must guard against reading into the decretals of the popes things that the text, despite all claims to the contrary, does not contain; Daniel Callam has pointed this out in an impressive way.[150]

By all means, though, let us take those sometimes crude-sounding faux pas of many theologians literally. They must seem all the more odd, because antipathy to sex does not necessarily have anything to do with the origin of ritual purity. Otherwise ritual purity would not have been advocated by those who held the body in contempt and likewise by moderate thinkers. Contempt for the body and its opposite often have something to do with a personal attitude that is then carried over into religious ideas. In its origins, ritual purity had little in common

---

[148] Siricius, *Epistulae* 5, 3 (PL 13, 1161A); *Epistula* 10, 6 *ad Gall.* (PL 13, 1186A).

[149] Kruse, "Eheverzicht", 109, n. 54 is correct, as opposed to Vogels, *Priester*, 41; cf. Denzler, *Die Geschichte*, 26. Siricius, *Epistula* 1, 9 *ad Himerium* (PL 13, 1138B): "Sacerdotes Christi atque levitas . . . tam de conjugibus propriis quam etiam de turpi coitu sobolem didicimus procreasse."

[150] In his article, "Clerical Continence in the Fourth Century: Three Papal Decretals", TS 41 (1980): 3–50.

with contempt for the body, but very much in common with medical and hygienic considerations.[151] According to the Jewish and pagan understanding, in fact, it had to do with the bodily secretions. In principle all excretions of the body, above all blood and sperm, were evidently secretions expelled from the body and, as was therefore suspected, incompatible with it, since demons clung to them. What is harmful and demonic, however, may not come into contact with God. Jesus himself may have shared this understanding.[152]

Therefore if someone had become unclean and had thus been rendered incapable of worship, that meant first of all an external defilement, but that was a far cry from sin. Origen subscribed to this view in the dialogue with the pagans.[153] The papal decretals still had this objective understanding, in principle, when for instance *Dominus inter* states, "If commingling is (an external) defilement, then the priest must be at all times prepared for the heavenly ministry so as to intercede for the sins of others; may he not be found unworthy himself!"[154] Taken in this way, it was a strictly religious matter, which could get along quite well without any moral evaluation of uncleanness. Such evaluations, of course, were not always absent, as soon as concupiscence and sexual inclinations were considered egotistical and bad in and of themselves.[155] This happened, to be sure, as a result of good intentions. The point was precisely not to leave things at a merely external purity. The purpose of the admonitions was an interiorization and a moralization of the entire liturgical activity of Christians. But

---

[151] Gryson, "Ans", 181f.

[152] It is still frequently maintained that Jesus completely abolishes the ritual notion of purity by means of the logion: "There is nothing outside a man which by going into him can defile him; but the things which come out of a man are what defile him" (Mk 7:15). J. Blank, "Prophetische Ehelosigkeit und kultisches Sexualtabu", *Diakonia* 1 (1970): 373–82 at 377: "This saying of Jesus signifies a fundamental stance toward the entire cultic-magical complex of ideas about purity, which, no doubt, is to be viewed thereafter as finished." But exactly the opposite could be the case. Jesus builds upon the cultic idea of purity: What comes out from inside (that is, bodily secretions) makes one unclean (Mk 7:19f.). However—and here is the point—not only the secretions but also the thoughts that come from within make a person unclean (Mk 7:21f.).

[153] Gryson, *Origines*, 17.

[154] Siricius, *Epistula* 10, 6 *ad Gall.* (PL 13, 1186A): "Si commixtio pollutio est." Cf. Jerome, *Adversus Jovinianum* I, 20 (PL 23², 249B): "omnis coitus immundus".

[155] Siricius, *Epistulae* 5, 3 (PL 13, 1160f.): "contaminatus fuerit carnali concupiscentia." This idea is already suggested in Origen; see Crouzel, *Virginité*, 60–66.

this sometimes backfired. For he who pointed a finger was very soon in danger of demonizing sexual matters in general.

Certainly the idea of ritual purity is especially susceptible to tendencies that are hostile to sexuality. It can be otherwise, though; examples for this can be provided. In the writings of Clement of Alexandria the ritual purity he advocates as something self-evident was accompanied by a decidedly positive evaluation of the sexual act: For baptized couples, sexual intercourse is not something impure; even semen is sacred.[156] The Syrian *Didascalia*, while referring to the cleansing power of baptism, vehemently objects to Jewish purification rituals, which were still being observed by Jewish converts; in doing so, however, it hardly meant to do away with Christian ritual purity altogether.[157] For in Antioch Chrysostom, too, says that relations with a woman do not render a man unclean,[158] yet at the same time he firmly adheres to the practice of religious abstinence during times of prayer. Ambrosiaster, who laid such emphasis on the appropriateness of clerical continence, in one passage examines Paul's advice to married couples to abstain from sexual intercourse so as to pray (1 Cor 7:5). On this subject he explicitly opposes Manichaean notions by saying, "Although conjugal intercourse is pure, one should nevertheless abstain from legitimate relations, so that prayer may more easily attain its goal. . . . For if someone refrains even from things that are allowed, he shows that he wants to obtain what he is praying for."[159]

It would be a mistake to think that a celibacy law could have been forced upon the men of those times by the sheer madness of eccentric bishops and popes. The Church certainly did not drive credulous men into an act of renunciation that only went against the grain in every case. Clerical continence sprang, rather, from a religious need. What began with the Council of Elvira was merely the process of legally codifying what was being practiced universally for reasons of religious

---

[156] *Stromata* 3, 6, 46, 5 (GCS Clem. Alex. 2⁴, 217, 23–25): Μιαρὰν δὲ εἶναι τὴν συνουσίαν λέγοντες οὗτοι οἱ τὴν σύστασιν καὶ αὐτοὶ ἐκ συνουσίας εἰληφότες πῶς οὐκ ἂν εἶεν μιαροί; τῶν δὲ ἁγιασθέντων ἅγιον οἶμαι καὶ τὸ σπέρμα. Ibid., 3, 12, 82, 6 (234, 3–8).

[157] *Didascalia apostolorum* 26 (CSCO.S 180, 223–48). Paul, too, rejects the Levitical prescriptions concerning cleanliness, but not ritual purity per se (1 Cor 7:5).

[158] *De virginitate* 30, 2 (SC 125, 192, 39–41); *Fragmenta in epistula* 1 *ad Cor.* 7:5 (CGPNT 5, 125).

[159] *Comm. in* 1 *Cor.* 7:5 (CSEL 81, 2, 71, 19–72, 3): "Quamvis munda sint coniugia, tamen etiam a licitis abstinendum est, ut facilius ad effectum deducatur oratio . . . cum enim quis etiam concessa non contingit, ostendit se velle quod precatur accipere."

reverence. The Church's teaching and practice with regard to clerical continence possessed a high degree of plausibility and coherence. For all its peculiarity, it had a persuasive power that was due in some measure to its proximity to generally accepted religious ideas. Without this immersion in the culture of late antiquity, the religious claims of Christian worship and priestly ministry could scarcely have been communicated to the surrounding pagan world.

4. Summary

The frequently voiced opinion that clerical continence was first introduced in the Latin West under Popes Siricius and Innocent is untenable. For one thing, various documentary sources attest to the existence of a continence discipline already in the first four centuries in the Greek-speaking East. Moreover there is a striking unanimity between the comprehensive celibacy legislation of the papal decretals and the celibacy rules of the East. This is true of the continence practiced by all clerics in major orders, whether they were married or not, of the marriage prohibition, and of the digamy prohibition, which also included the wives of clerics. Therefore the most one could say is that the popes, in their various regulations for the West, had adopted a clerical continence discipline already practiced in the East. But contradicting this theory, on the other hand, is the Spanish Council of Elvira, which was acquainted with continence celibacy already at the beginning of the fourth century.

The agreement between the celibacy regulations of the West and the East can most readily be explained on the basis of a continuous history of the undivided Eastern and Western Church. In the course of the missionary expansion of the Church, the clerical continence discipline, which went back to the very beginnings, made its way into all the territories then belonging to the empire. The statements of the papal decretals characterizing clerical continence as an ancient and apostolic arrangement are to be understood along these lines. This can scarcely be a mendacious claim. For it was made by a Roman clergy synod, by a synod of Italian bishops, and by a synod of North African bishops.

The reasons for the legitimacy of the papal celibacy initiatives and for their positive reception lie in the universally acknowledged apostolicity and ecumenicity of clerical continence. It was by no means a monopoly of the West but was also the common practice in the East, and therefore the popes were successful. It is no coincidence that in those very same celibacy decretals of Siricius and Innocent, their understanding of their primacy is noticeable as well. The claim of the popes to preeminence over the entire Church included their pastoral concern for the Church throughout the world. For the sake of unity in the universal Church they strived to maintain in the West the same celibacy discipline that was taken for granted in the East also.

In the fifth century continence celibacy in no way underwent a crisis in the East, as one might suspect on the basis of statements by the church historian Socrates. His remarks about Illyricum (Thessalia, Macedonia, Greece) must be understood to mean that, as of recently, married subdeacons there had to practice continence also. What he says besides this about bishops begetting children probably reflects the views of the Novatians. The Paphnutius legend might very well be attributed to them. This propaganda lie was supposed to justify the Novatians' failure to require continence any more of their married clerics. Hence if there were opponents of celibacy and clerics begetting children in Constantinople at the beginning of the fifth century, then we have to look for them among the Novatian schismatics.

The Paphnutius legend itself presupposed that clerical continence was required and honored in the Byzantine Church. The Theodosian Code (in the year 420) allows us to infer the practice of continence by higher clerics. Emperor Justinian (527–565), whose political influence extended well into the domain of the Latin Church, restored the entire celibacy discipline as it was known also in the West, the essential purpose of which was to guarantee that clerics in major orders practice continence. Bishops had to live without wife and children; married deacons and priests, after all was said and done, had to practice permanent continence.

The Second Council of Trullo in the year 691 (Quinisext) adopted the previous celibacy legislation almost in its entirety, but with canon 13 it introduced a momentous innovation, which veered off from the whole tradition of continence celibacy: married deacons and priests could and had to abstain from relations with their wives only at times when the liturgy was celebrated. Permanent continence was strictly forbidden them, whereas bishops had either to be celibate or at least separate from their wives. In taking this inconsistent line, the canon was explicitly aimed at Rome, whose strict continence discipline it rejected for the East.

Notwithstanding this later development, a deeply rooted consensus existed from the beginning between the Eastern and Western clerical discipline. The continent way of life had, for married men and women in the world of that era, a high degree of practicality and plausibility. It fit in with the picture of man determined by science and medicine and with the sense of life that resulted from them. It was characterized by a basically ascetical attitude. It was thought that sexuality could be controlled more or less at will. Christians viewed baptism as placing them in an even better position to keep such urges in check. The early age for marrying, together with the late age for ordaining married clerics, meant that for them the phase of actively raising a family reached its conclusion in a certain sense at ordination, because the children, too, were already grown. Continence celibacy, by reason of the high prestige of the cleric, was generally accepted and integrated into society.

The theologians of the first centuries on many occasions described celibacy and permanent continence as a grace, as God's free gift. One may ask how it was possible for such a charism of continence to be imposed upon clerics as an obligation. After all, the candidate for holy orders could be married; in any case, however, he had to practice continence from the day of his ordination. Of course theologians see charisms as being something other than a natural phenomenon; they can, indeed must, be obtained through prayer. Therefore it made sense and it was necessary to examine candidates for ordination, to ascertain whether they were ready and willing to keep the continence rule. If a candidate had promised continence, he evidently possessed the requested charism. If he was married, the agreement of his wife had to be present, too, since she likewise had to practice continence.

The rule of continence was connected with the practice of cultic continence, which was taken for granted in Judaism and the pagan world. It was for the entire Greco-Roman culture of antiquity an eminent expression of religious reverence for God. In this respect Christians could —indeed, they had to—adopt it and even intensify the discipline. It was authorized by the New Testament (1 Cor 7:5). Sexual continence simply belonged to the vocational ethos of the priest in antiquity. It was seen as being that much more of a requirement for Christian priests. With certainty we can say, therefore, that ritual continence of Christian priests existed from the very beginning, in a periodic form at least, but most likely as a permanent practice.

The cultic asceticism of Christian priests had simultaneously undergone a transformation. In the first place it had to do with a spirit of self-sacrifice, with a willingness to be subsumed in Christ's priestly sacrifice of himself. Renouncing the expression of one's sexuality was understood to be such a spiritual act. Besides this, Christian continence involved at the same time a moral claim. Complete abstinence, moreover, prevented the priests from slipping into petty purification rituals. In this way the cultic motive was to a great extent protected from the danger of a scrupulous purism. Even the antipathy toward sexuality that was sometimes connected with the continence of priests was by no means a genuine or unavoidable heritage of a cultic understanding of purity. Ritual purity in its origins had little to do with moral value judgments. Many testimonies by early Christian theologians, in disputing with the Manichaeans, explicitly shunned the notion of contempt for the body in their interpretation of cultic purity.

Table of Patristic Sources

ActaSS   *Acta Sanctorum.*

CCL   *Corpus Christianorum, Series Latina.*

CGPNT   J. A. Cramer. *Catenae Graecorum Patrum in Novum Testamentum* 5. Hildesheim, 1967.

Courtonne   Y. Courtonne. *Saint Basile, Lettres* 1–3. Paris, 1956–1966.

CSCO.S   *Corpus Scriptorum Christianorum Orientalium, Scriptores Syri.*

CSEL   *Corpus Scriptorum Ecclesiasticorum Latinorum.*

Devreesse   R. Devreesse. *Le Commentaire de Théodore de Mopsueste sur les Psaumes* (I–LXXX). Città del Vaticano, 1939 (= StT 93).

FC   *Fontes Christiani.*

Funk and Diekamp   F. X. Funk and F. Diekamp. *Patres Apostolici* 2. 3d ed. Tübingen, 1913.

GCS   *Die griechischen christlichen Schriftsteller.*

GNO   W. Jaeger. *Gregorii Nysseni Opera.*

Jenkins   C. Jenkins. "Origen on 1 Corinthians". JThS 9 (1908): 231–47, 353–72, 500–514.

Joannou   P.-P. Joannou. *Discipline générale antique (IIe–IXe s.)* 1, 1. *Les Canons des Conciles Oecuméniques.* Rome, 1962; *Discipline générale antique (IVe–IXe s.)* 1, 2. *Les Canons des Synodes Particuliers.* Rome, 1962; *Discipline générale antique (IVe–IXe s.)* 2. *Les Canons des Pères Grecs.* Rome, 1963.

Jonkers   E. J. Jonkers. *Acta et Symbola Conciliorum quae saeculo quarto habita sunt.* Leiden, 1954 (= Textus minores 19).

Lipsius and Bonnet   R. A. Lipsius and M. Bonnet. *Acta Apostolorum Apoc-rypha* 2, 2. Darmstadt, 1959.

Mommsen   T. Mommsen and P. M. Meyer. *Theodosiani libri XVI* 1–2. 3d ed. Berlin, 1962.

PG   *Patrologia Graeca* (Migne).

PL   *Patrologia Latina* (Migne).

PO   *Patrologia Orientalis.*

Reischl and Rupp   W. C. Reischl and J. Rupp. *Cyrilli Hierosolymarum Archiepiscopi Opera quae supersunt omnia* 1–2. Hildes-heim, 1967.

SC   *Sources Chrétiennes.*

Schermann   T. Schermann. *Die allgemeine Kirchenordnung, früh-christliche Liturgien und kirchliche*: Uberlieferung 1. *Die allgemeine Kirchenordnung des zweiten Jahrhunderts*. Pa-derborn, 1914 (= SGKA.E 3,1).

Swete   H. B. Swete. *Theodori Episcopi Mopsuesteni in Episto-las B. Pauli Commentarii*. The Latin Version with the Greek Fragments 2. Cambridge, 1882.

Vives   J. Vives. *Concilios Visitóticos e hispano-romanos*. Barce-lona and Madrid, 1963 (= España Cristiana, Tex-tos 1).

Bibliography

Audet, J. P. *Mariage et célibat dans le service pastorale de l'Église: Histoire et orientations.* Paris, 1967.

Auf der Maur, I. *Mönchtum und Glaubensverkündigung in den Schriften des hl. Johannes Chrysostomus.* Par. 14. Fribourg, 1959.

Bardenhewer, O. *Geschichte der altkirchlichen Literatur.* Vol. 2, 2d ed. Freiburg, 1914. Vol. 3. 1912.

Bickell, G. "Der Cölibat eine apostolische Anordnung". ZKTh 2 (1878): 26–64.

Böhmer, H. "Die Entstehung des Zölibates". In *Geschichtliche Studien Albert Hauck zum 70. Geburtstag,* 6–24. Leipzig, 1916.

Boelens, M. *Die Klerikerehe in der Gesetzgebung der Kirche unter besonderer Berücksichtigung der Strafe: Eine rechtsgeschichtliche Untersuchung von den Anfängen der Kirche bis zum Jahre 1139.* Paderborn, 1968.

Brown, P. *The Body and Society: Men, Women, and Sexual Renunciation in Early Christianity.* New York: Columbia University Press, 1988. German trans.: *Die Keuschheit der Engel: Sexuelle Entsagung, Askese und Körperlichkeit am Anfang des Christentums.* München and Vienna, 1991.

Callam, D. "Clerical Continence in the Fourth Century: Three Papal Decretals". TS 41 (1980): 3–50.

———. "The Frequency of Mass in the Latin Church ca. 400". TS 45 (1984): 613–50.

Chadwick, H. "Enkrateia". In RAC 5 (1962), 343–65.

———. *Priscillian of Avila: The Occult and the Charismatic in the Early Church.* Oxford, 1976.

Cholij, R. *Clerical Celibacy in East and West.* Herefordshire, 1989.

Cochini, C. *Apostolic Origins of Priestly Celibacy.* San Francisco, 1990.

Crespin, R. *Ministère et sainteté: Pastorale du clergé et solution de la crise Donatiste dans la vie et la doctrine de saint Augustin.* Paris, 1965.

Crouzel, H. "Le Célibat et la continence ecclésiastique dans l'Église primitive: Leurs motivations". In J. Coppens, ed., *Sacerdoce et célibat: Études historiques et théologiques*, 333–71. Gembloux and Louvain, 1971.

―――. "Les Origines du célibat ecclésiastique: À propos d'un livre recent". NRTh 6 (1970): 649–53.

―――. *Virginité et mariage selon Origène*. Paris and Bruges, 1963.

Dassmann, E. *Ämter und Dienste in den frühchristlichen Gemeinden*. Hereditas 8. Bonn, 1994.

Denzler, G. *Die Geschichte des Zölibats*. Freiburg, 1993.

―――. "Zur Geschichte des Zölibats: Ehe und Ehelosigkeit der Priester bis zur Einführung des Zölibatsgesetzes im Jahr 1139". StZ 183 (1969): 383–401.

―――. *Das Papsttum und der Amtszölibat*. Vol. 1, *Die Zeit bis zur Reformation*. PuP 5,1. Stuttgart, 1973.

Funk, F. X. "Cölibat und Priesterehe im christlichen Altertum". In *Kirchengeschichtliche Abhandlungen und Untersuchungen*, 1: 121–155. Paderborn, 1897.

Garcia Villoslada, R. *Historia de la Iglesia en España*. Vol. 1, *La Iglesia en la España romana y visigoda (siglos I–VIII)*. Madrid, 1979.

Gnilka, J. *Jesus von Nazaret: Botschaft und Geschichte*. HThK.S 3. Freiburg, 1990.

Grützmacher, G. *Hieronymus: Eine biographische Studie zur Alten Kirchengeschichte*. Vol. 1, Leipzig, 1901. Vol. 2, Berlin, 1906. Vol. 3, Berlin, 1908.

Gryson, R., "Dix ans de recherches sur les origines du célibat ecclésiastique: Réflexion sur les publications des années 1970–1979". RTL 11 (1980): 157–85.

―――. *Les Origines du célibat ecclésiastique du premier au septième siècle*. RSSR.H 2. Gembloux, 1970.

―――. *Le Prêtre selon saint Ambroise*. Louvain, 1968.

―――. "Sacerdoce et célibat: À propos d'un ouvrage récent". RHE 67 (1972): 67–80.

Haller, W. *Iovinianus: Die Fragmente seiner Schriften, die Quellen zu seiner Geschichte, sein Leben und seine Lehre*. TU 17, 2. Leipzig, 1897.

Harnack, A. von, *Der kirchengeschichtliche Ertrag der exegetischen Arbeiten des Origenes*. TU 42, 3. Vol. 1. Leipzig, 1918. TU 42, 4. Vol. 2. Leipzig, 1919.

Heid, S., "Grundlagen des Zölibats in der frühen Kirche". In K. M. Becker and J. Eberle, eds. *Der Zölibat des Priesters*, 45–71. Sinn und Sendung 9. St. Ottilien, 1995.

Hödl, L. "Die *lex continentiae*: Eine problemgeschichtliche Studie über den Zölibat". ZKTh 83 (1961): 325–44.

Hunter, D. G. "Resistance to the virginal Ideal in Late-Fourth-Century Rome: The Case of Jovinian". TS 48 (1987): 45–64.

Koch, H. "Tertullian und der Cölibat". ThQ 88 (1906): 406–11.

Kötting, B. *Die Beurteilung der zweiten Ehe im heidnischen und christlichen Altertum*. Diss., Bonn, 1942.

———. "Digamus". In RAC 3 (1957), 1016–24.

———. *Der Zölibat in der Alten Kirche*. Schriften der Gesellschaft zur Förderung der Westfälischen Wilhelms-Universität zu Münster 61. Münster, 1970.

Kottje, R. "Das Aufkommen der täglichen Eucharistiefeier in der West-kirche und die Zölibatsforderung". ZKG 82 (1971): 218–28.

Kruse, H. "Eheverzicht im Neuen Testament und in der Frühkirche". FKTh 1 (1985): 94–116.

Lafontaine, P.-H. *Les Conditions positives de l'accession aux ordres dans la première legislation ecclésiastique (300–492)*. Ottawa, 1963.

Laub, F. "Sozialgeschichtlicher Hintergrund und ekklesiologische Rele-vanz der neutestamentlich-frühchristlichen Haus- und Gemeinde- Tafel-paränese: Ein Beitrag zur Soziologie des Frühchristentums". MThZ 37 (1986): 249–71.

Legrand, L. "Saint Paul et le célibat". In J. Coppens, ed. *Sacerdoce et célibat: Études historiques et théologiques*, 315–31. Gembloux and Louvain, 1971.

Lochbrunner, M. *Über das Priestertum: Historische und systematische Untersuchung zum Priesterbild des Johannes Chrysostomus*. Hereditas 5. Bonn, 1993.

Lohse, B. *Askese und Mönchtum in der Antike und in der Alten Kirche*. RKAM 1. Munich and Vienna, 1969.

Meigne, M. "Concile ou collection d'Elvire". RHE 70 (1975): 361–87.

Niederwimmer, K. *Askese und Mysterium: Über Ehe, Ehescheidung und Eheverzicht in den Anfängen des christl. Glaubens.* FRLANT 113. Göttingen, 1975.

Oberlinner, L. *Die Pastoralbriefe.* HThK 11, 2, 1. Freiburg, 1994.

Oepke, A. "Ehe I (Institution)". In RAC 4 (1959), 650–66.

Pagels, E, *Adam, Eva und die Schlange: Die Theologie der Sünde.* Reinbek, 1991.

Pietri, C. *Roma Christiana: Recherches sur l'Église de Rome, son organisation, sa politique, son idéologie de Miltiade à Sixte III (311–440).* Paris and Rome, 1976.

Potterie, I. de la. " 'Mari d'une seule femme'. Le Sens théologique d'une formule Paulinienne". In L. de Lorenzi, ed. *Paul de Tarse: Apôtre de notre Temps,* 619–38. SMBen.P 1. Rome, 1979.

Preisker, H. *Christentum und Ehe in den ersten drei Jahrhunderten: Eine Studie zur Kulturgeschichte der Alten Welt.* NSGTK 23. Berlin, 1927.

Reichert, E. *Die Canones der Synode von Elvira: Einleitung und Kommentar.* Diss., Hamburg, 1990.

Richert, C. *Die Anfänge der Irregularitäten bis zum ersten Allgemeinen Konzil von Nicäa.* StrThS 4, 3. Freiburg, 1901.

Ritter, A. M. *Charisma im Verständnis des Joannes Chrysostomos und seiner Zeit: Ein Beitrag zur Erforschung der griechisch-orientalischen Ekklesiologie in der Frühzeit der Reichskirche.* FKDG 25. Göttingen, 1972.

Schillebeeckx, E. *Der Amtszölibat: Eine kritische Besinnung.* Düsseldorf, 1967.

———. *Christliche Identität und kirchliches Amt: Plädoyer für den Menschen in der Kirche.* Düsseldorf, 1985.

Schöllgen, G. "Hausgemeinden, οἶκος-Ekklesiologie und monarchischer Episkopat". JAC 31 (1988): 74–90.

Stickler, A. M. *The Case for Clerical Celibacy: Its Historical Development and Theological Foundations.* Translated by Brian Ferme. San Francisco, 1995.

Troianos, S. N. "Zölibat und Kirchenvermögen in der früh- und mittelbyzantinischen kanonischen Gesetzgebung". In D. Simon, ed. *Eherecht und Familiengut in Antike und Mittelalter,* 133–46. Munich, 1992.

Trummer, P. "Einehe nach den Pastoralbriefen: Zum Verständnis der Termini μᾶς γυναικὸς ἀνήρ und ἑνὸς ἀνδρὸς γυνή". *Biblica* 51 (1970): 471–84.

Vacandard, E. "Célibat ecclésiastique". In DThC 2, 2 (1932), 2068–88.

Vogels, H.-J. *Priester dürfen heiraten: Biblische, geschichtliche und rechtliche Gründe gegen den Pflichtzölibat.* Bonn, 1992.

Vogt, H. J. *Coetus Sanctorum: Der Kirchenbegriff des Novatian und die Geschichte seiner Sonderkirche.* Theoph. 20. Bonn, 1968.

Wendebourg, D. "Die alttestamentlichen Reinheitsgesetze in der frühen Kirche". ZKG 95 (1984): 149–70.

Winkelmann, F. "Paphnutios, der Bekenner und Bischof". In P. Nagel, ed. *Probleme der koptischen Literatur,* 145–53. *Wissenschaftliche Beiträge der Martin-Luther-Universität Halle-Wittenberg 1968/1.* Halle, 1968.

Abbreviations

AHC   *Annuarium Historiae Conciliorum*

AKG   Arbeiten zur Kirchengeschichte

AuC   *Antike und Christentum*

BBB   Bonner Biblische Beiträge

BGrL   Bibliothek der griechischen Literatur

BHTh   Beiträge zur historischen Theologie

BKV   Bibliothek der Kirchenväter

BLE   *Bulletin de littérature ecclésiastique*

BoBKG   Bonner Beiträge zur Kirchengeschichte

BWANT   Beiträge zur Wissenschaft vom Alten und Neuen Testament

DP   *Dizionario Patristico e di Antichità Cristiane*

DThC   *Dictionnaire de théologie catholique*

EKK   Evangelisch-katholischer Kommentar zum Neuen Testament

FKDG   Forschungen zur Kirchen- und Dogmengeschichte

FKTh   *Forum für katholische Theologie*

FRLANT   Forschungen zur Religion und Literatur des Alten und Neuen Testaments

FzB   Forschung zur Bibel

GCS N.F.   Die Griechischen christlichen Schriftsteller der ersten Jahrhunderte. Neue Folge.

GNT   Grundrisse zum Neuen Testament

GuL *Geist und Leben*

HKG Handbuch der Kirchengeschichte

HThK.S Herders Theologischer Kommentar zum Neuen Testament (Supplementband)

JAC.E Jahrbuch für Antike und Christentum (Ergänzungsband)

JRS *Journal of Roman Studies*

JThS *The Journal of Theological Studies*

KLK Katholisches Leben und Kirchenreform im Zeitalter der Glaubensspaltung

KVRG Kölner Veröffentlichungen zur Religionsgeschichte

LMA *Lexikon des Mittelalters*

LThK *Lexikon für Theologie und Kirche*

MThZ *Münchener Theologische Zeitschrift*

NRTh *Nouvelle revue théologique*

NSGTK Neue Studien zur Geschichte der Theologie und der Kirche

Par. Paradosis

PTS Patristische Texte und Studien

PuP Päpste und Papsttum

QD Quaestiones Disputatae

RAC.S *Reallexikon für Antike und Christentum (Supplementband)*

RBen *Revue bénédictine*

REAug *Revue des Études Augustiniennes*

RfR *Review for Religious*

RHE *Revue d'histoire ecclésiastique*

RKAM Religion und Kultur der Alten Mittelmeerwelt in Parallelforschungen

RNT Regensburger Neues Testament

RSPhTh *Revue des Sciences Philosophiques et Théologiques*

RSR *Recherches de Science Religieuse*

RSSR.H Recherches et synthèses de sciences religieuses, section d'histoire

RSTh Regensburger Studien zur Theologie

RTL *Revue théologique de Louvain*

RVV Religionsgeschichtliche Versuche und Vorarbeiten

SacDo *Sacra Doctrina*

SGKA.E Studien zur Geschichte und Kultur des Altertums (Ergänzungsband)

SGTK Studien zur Geschichte der Theologie und der Kirche

SMBen.P Série monographique de "Benedictina", section Paulinienne

StrThS Strassburger Theologische Studien

StT Studi e Testi

StZ *Stimmen der Zeit*

SUC Schriften des Urchristentums

ThA Theologische Arbeiten

Theoph. Theophaneia

ThF Theologische Forschung

ThH Théologie Historique

ThQ *Theologische Quartalschrift*

ThWNT *Theologisches Wörterbuch zum Neuen Testament*

TRE *Theologische Realenzyklopädie*

TS   *Theological Studies*

TU   Texte und Untersuchungen

WdF   Wege der Forschung

ZKG   *Zeitschrift für Kirchengeschichte*

ZKTh *Zeitschrift für katholische Theologie*

General Index

abortion, 139–41
Abraham, 116, 257
abstinence on days Eucharist celebrated. *See* periodic continence
Acacian schism, 310
Adulterinis coniugiis (Augustine), 214–15
adultery
 of a cleric, 106, 111n58, 138
 defined, 138n125, 196n344
 among wives of clerics, 129–31, 143
 See also infractions of obligatory continence
ages of candidates
 for bishop, 93–95, 108–9, 324–25
 for priest, 46, 93, 107–9, 213–14, 274–75, 323–24, 331–32, 349
Akesios (Novatian bishop), 302
Ambrose of Milan
 on baptism, 260–61
 cathedral chapters, 201
 De exhortatione virginibus, 324n97
 De officiis ministrorum, 229–32, 245
 opposing digamy, 245, 254
Ambrosiaster, 224–28, 234, 236–40, 246n159, 247n94, 346n159
Ancyra, Council of (314), 122–26, 142, 331
Andrew (apostle), 32
Annuarium Historiae Conciliorum (journal), 19
Antioch, Council of (268), 133
Antoninos of Ephesus, 106, 197
Apology (Justin Martyr), 59
apostles
 as continent, 27–33, 56–57, 277–79, 288–92
 marriage and, 56–57, 76, 170, 239–40
 wives of, 26–27, 29–32, 67–69
 women with, 30–33, 56, 87–88
 See also names of individual apostles

Apostolic Constitutions/Canons
 age of clerics, 108n50, 109
 celibate clergy trend, 170–71, 173n53, 176, 181n74
 digamy, 82, 131n108, 164, 164n38
 lewd conduct, 137, 138n124
 marital separation, 106, 181–83
 marriage permitted to lower clerics, 125–26, 170
Apostolic Origins of Priestly Celibacy, The (Cochini), 20
Arian schism, 216, 294, 303n49, 304
Arles, Council of (314), 112n64, 241, 291
asceticism
 biblical authority argument, 33–41, 53–54, 334
 celibacy distinguished from, 38–39, 110–11
 Encratism, 38, 61–65, 147, 179, 222, 239, 258, 323
 Eustathians, 154, 172, 180–83, 199–200
 popularity of, 177–79, 318–22, 326–27
 sacralization and, 335, 342–43, 345
ataraxia (freedom from passion), 39
Athanasius of Alexandria, 191–93
Augustine, 126, 204, 214–15, 248n95, 260n126, 262, 325–26, 332
Aurelius Augustinus. *See* Augustine
Auxanon (priest), 302–4

baptism
 celibacy and, 147, 179, 222, 239, 258, 323
 continence and, 63–64, 84–85, 286–88, 320–21, 349
 digamy and, 82–85, 158–59, 164, 198, 223, 246, 259–62, 286–88
 of heretics, 212, 285–86
 lewd conduct and, 126–28, 288n15

Scripture Index